The Stirring Giant

THE STIRRING GIANT

RENEWAL FORCES AT WORK IN THE MODERN CHURCH

EDITED BY

BOB E. PATTERSON

WORD BOOKS
Waco, Texas
London, England

Dedicated to my parents
Mr. and Mrs. Dewitt Patterson
and the members of the
First Baptist Church of
Kings Mountain, North Carolina

Special acknowledgment is made to the following who have granted permission for the reprinting of copyrighted material from the books and periodicals listed below:

ABINGDON PRESS

The Church Creative edited by Malcomson, Molton, and Clark. Copyright © 1967 by Abingdon Press.

A Hard Rain and a Cross by Harold DeWolf. Copyright © 1966 by Abingdon Press.

From Tradition to Mission by Wallace E. Fisher. Copyright © 1965 by Abingdon Press.

Preaching and Parish Renewal by Wallace E. Fisher. Abingdon Press.

Preface to Parish Renewal by Wallace E. Fisher. Copyright © 1968 by Abingdon Press.

The Rebirth of the Laity by Howard Grimes. Copyright © 1962 by Abingdon Press.

Tomorrow's Church: A Cosmopolitan Community by William A. Holmes. Copyright © 1968 by Abingdon Press.

The Renewal of the Ministry by Thomas J. Mullen. Copyright © 1963 by Abingdon Press.

Planning for Protestantism in Urban America by Lyle E. Schaller. Copyright © 1965 by Abingdon Press.

Protestantism in Suburban Life by Frederick A. Shippey. Abingdon Press.

The Congregation in Mission by George W. Webber. Copyright © 1964 by Abingdon Press.

God's Colony in Man's World by George W. Webber. Copyright © 1960 by Abingdon Press.

ASSOCIATION PRESS

The Creative Role of Interpersonal Groups in the Church Today, by John L. Casteel. Copyright © 1968.

Spiritual Renewal Through Personal Groups, by John L. Casteel. Copyright © 1957.

Life Is Commitment, by J. H. Oldham. Copyright © 1959.

The Free Church Today: New Life for the Whole Church, by Arthur A. Rouner, Jr. Copyright © 1968.

The Freedom Revolution and the Churches, by Robert W. Spike. Copyright © 1965.

In But Not Of The World, by Robert W. Spike. Copyright © 1957.

THE BETHANY PRESS

Horizons of Christian Community, by Paul S. Minear, © 1959.

BROADMAN PRESS

Findley B. Edge, *A Quest for Vitality in Religion* (Nashville: Broadman Press 1963) pp. 203, 204, 205-212, 121-122, 38, and 23. Used by permission.

E. Glenn Hinson, *The Church: Design for Survival* (Nashville: Broadman

SOUTHWESTERN JOURNAL OF THEOLOGY
"Seeking a Regenerate Church Membership," by James Leo Garrett. Vol. III, No. 2 (April, 1961), pp. 35-36.

UNION SEMINARY QUARTERLY REVIEW
"The Search for New 'Wine Skins'" by Harold R. Fray, Jr., Vol. 16, no. 3, 3 paragraphs from pages 318-319.
"Requirements for Renewal" by John W. Meister, Vol. 16, no. 3, 6 paragraphs from pages 259-261.
"Small Groups Are Here to Stay" by Clyde H. Reid, Vol. 18, no. 4, 4 paragraphs from pages 395-396.

Julia A. Lacy: "The Lay Renaissance," by Julia A. Lacy, *Religion in Life*, Vol. 31 (Winter 1961-Fall 1962). Used by permission of the author.

PRINCETON SEMINARY BULLETIN
"Church versus Non-Church," by Ray Billington. Vol. 60 (Oct. 1966-June 1967).

NEW CHRISTIAN
"Church versus Non-Church," by Ray Billington. Used by permission.

CONTENTS

PREFACE

Compiling and editing this book has been lots of fun. But originally it grew out of a sense of frustration. As the leader of a fellowship-Bible study group of young married couples meeting in my home I tried to provide the members with a wide selection of the best books on "church renewal." In my eagerness to expose these bright couples to the ferment going on in the church I encouraged them to read, read, read. I recommended books, reviewed books, quizzed them about the books after they had read them, and quickly pressed two more into their hands for every one they returned. I was guilty of badgering them with my own interest "for their own good." I was reminded again of something that I already knew but find hard to accept—that laymen, even when they have the interest, do not always have time to read. And even when they have both interest and time, they do not always have a solid enough concept of the church to read with discrimination. Finally, in self-defense, my fellowship-study group asked me, "Is there *one* book on church renewal that will give us everything?" I had to answer, "No." But in my frustration I rushed on to recommend half-a-dozen which, if they would only read, would surely bring them up to date in at least one area.

My second line of frustration came from my formal lecture course in Christian theology given to university junior, senior, and graduate students. Many of these students, "turned off" by unhappy experiences in their home churches and cynical about the relevance to society's needs of the "over thirty" church hierarchy, "tune out" when I lecture on the doctrine of the church. These students, genuinely concerned about the Christian faith, will sometimes say to me, "Why don't we skip the lectures on the 'church' and get to something exciting like 'eschatology'?" In my attempts to infect them with my own excitement about what God is doing to renew the contemporary church, I recommend books. These "paperback" people are rapid and avid readers, reading anything in print even under the most adverse conditions. But with their heavy course loads they can allot only a limited time for reading in any one area. Thus I have been faced again with the problem of *one* book on church renewal that covers the field in a general and introductory way.

My third line of frustration originated with my pastor friends, who were frustrated. As a frequent speaker in churches and to church groups I am in conversation with pastors who are experimenting with new structures and

11

ideas. Some of these pastors are discouraged—they have tried something from the "church renewal bag" and it has exploded in their faces. They feel alone and defeated, unaware that scores of churches and pastors are engaged in the same struggle and have shared their testimony of success and failure in printed form. Others, having successfully explored some form of church renewal, are beginning to look for other forms to apply to their congregation's needs. These pastors are exceptionally busy men and they do not have the time nor energy nor money to buy and read all of the church renewal books that are flooding the market. They have caught a vision of what a renewed church can mean, and they are looking for something to guide them through the resource material now on hand. *The Stirring Giant*, then, is an attempt to fill a need of my own and to give guidance to my friends.

When I began to compile this material I hoped to be comprehensive and representative, but as I continued to read my ambition was whittled down. I have limited the selections to ones that deal primarily with the American Protestant churches during the past decade. For every selection that I have included I have easily omitted a dozen that could have served equally well. Furthermore, I have not pulled material from all the books even in this restricted area, and I have hardly touched the gold mine to be found in the religious journals. The whole field of renewal in the Roman Catholic church in America has scarcely been mentioned, and the church in Europe (both Roman Catholic and Protestant) is virtually passed over.

As I read the church renewal books I hoped that a structure would emerge from them, but it did not. George Webber's books and Colin Williams' book, *The Church*, came very near what I was looking for. Finally I constructed a framework which pretends to cover most of the field. Being a theologian by profession I naturally cast it in a systematic mold, moving the material from a diagnosis of the church's ills to a definition of the church to the theological basis for renewal. Then I turned the structure to a positive prescription for the internal renewal of the church and concluded with the church's outer mission to the world. I have included a sprinkling of creative experiments that should appeal to both small and large churches, to the suburbanites and the downtowners, to the individual in search of personal renewal and to the social reconstructionist looking for new tools to carry out his vision.

Besides the general framework which indicates the nature of the material included, I have written a heading over each quote which points to the specific content of every piece selected. This should enable the reader to thumb through the book at his leisure, reading what appeals to him at first sight. Or again, he can read the book at one sitting as a theological primer in church renewal. Or thirdly, the reader can concentrate in one area (e.g., *koinonia* groups), and then turn from this book to the original sources for a much more extensive treatment. If I have wronged an author by mislabeling his material, I will appreciate being informed of my unintentional error and proper corrections will be made in future editions.

I love to read, and I love to share my reading with my friends. I know that you will enjoy some of this book, and I feel that parts of it will stimulate you to experiment with your own renewal projects.

I am grateful to Baylor University for providing me with a research grant to complete this work. I thank my two graduate assistants, Mr. Charlie Coffee and Mr. Michael Habermehl, for the research they have done on this project. I express my appreciation to my secretaries, Mrs. Ronald Scott and Miss Carolyn Hudson, for the long hours they spent at the typewriters. My thanks are also due to Dr. Ray Summers, my departmental chairman at Baylor University, who encouraged me in this effort.

Bob E. Patterson

I

Which Way to the Revolution?

An Introduction

A. A Revolution Is Taking Place in the Church

God's Spirit is at work in a special way in our time.

George MacLeod, founder of the Iona community, utilizing a formula prevalent in the circles of religious enthusiasm, has divided the history of the church into three periods. The first three centuries are said to be the age of the Father and the fourth century to modern times the age of the Son. According to MacLeod we are now beginning to live in the age of the Spirit in which the old forms and traditions will be superseded by new and more dynamic patterns of Christian life. This interpretation can be questioned, but it cannot be denied that the Spirit is at work in a special way at the present time. MacLeod is on firm ground in his view that the church is entering a new and promising period.

—Donald G. Bloesch, *Centers of Christian Renewal*, pp. 11–12.

The first signs of a new Reformation.

If today voices are beginning to speak of a new Reformation it is because, perhaps, we can sense that moment and movement again. We cannot be sure: there was many a false dawn before, and I suspect the night must get much darker yet. But the speed of change is so much swifter today that we cannot afford to neglect even the first signs of it—lest we be overtaken by it.

—John A. T. Robinson, *The New Reformation*, p. 16.

The Church is at a turning point in history—much promise and danger.

A new society is taking shape before our eyes. This is a society full of promise; it signifies the possibility of life and education on a truly democratic basis. At the same time, the hope of this new society is clouded by the threat of worldwide holocaust, and the promise of its productive power is darkened by alienation between social classes and racial groups. We are experiencing the hope and anxiety that characterize great turning points in history. Only the first few centuries of Christian history, the twelfth century in Western Europe, and perhaps the era of the Reformation can be compared with our own time for critical possibilities. Such periods offer unusual opportunities for Christian proclamation; by the same token, their potential destructiveness exceeds imagination.

—Gibson Winter, *The New Creation As Metropolis*, pp. 1–2.

Nothing can prevent the birth of church renewal.

The renewal movement stirring within the Church today may be as radical in some ways as any reformation the Church has ever known. This movement is a natural extension of the reformation of the sixteenth century—especially such basic doctrines as the priesthood of all believers. The shape of the movement is more like the Wesleyan Revival of the eighteenth century. It is of God. Nothing can prevent its birth.

—Russell Bow, *The Integrity of Church Membership*, p. 11.

The Church is experiencing a new Exodus.

As Robert Spike has commented, ours is an "exodus" time, in which we remember where we have been but are not quite sure where we are going. We are on the way in the wilderness and it is a way of venture, risk, and anticipation. The whole church is in a time of uneasy travail, which we may hope is the anguish implicit in creation.

—Robert A. Raines, *Reshaping the Christian Life*, p. ix.

God is killing the Church in order to bring it new life.

Who's killing the Church? An explanation of our title is in order. In recent years, observers in and out of the churches have spoken of a general decline in religious interest. Man, they say, has become secularized. He no longer needs the props of faith and he is losing interest in the institutional expression of religion, the Church. In Europe the churches are practically empty and in the United States there is a gradual decline in membership, particularly in large metropolitan areas. From this perspective, the Church is dying because modern man is either too apathetic or too self-sufficient to involve himself in the life of the religious establishment. Who's killing the Church? Modern man who, contrary to the late Professor Jung, is no longer in search of a soul. His accomplices are the depersonalized modern metropolis, the sweep of contemporary technology, and the general lack of concern for one's fellow man that these forces seem to produce.

There are some, however, who feel this analysis is too simple. It does not take sufficient notice of the Church's own shortcomings. Who's killing the Church? Don't blame the world, says this second group, because the real crime against the Church is being committed from within. The Church is being killed by her own failure to take the shape that the world needs. If the Church were being murdered by villains from the outside, if it were facing persecution for its witness in the world, there might be hope. But the world doesn't persecute a Church that seems to stand for nothing. So the verdict is more serious: suicide, a slow death resulting from what Arnold Toynbee has called a "failure of nerve."

There is a third interpretation which grows out of the second. It recognizes that the Church today is in ferment. Some are feverishly trying to maintain the status quo—the emphasis on expensive buildings, on wishy-washy moralizing that masquerades as preaching, on studious efforts to involve laymen in trivial tasks rather than honest confrontation with the demands of the Gospel. But others are sensing a new spirit in the wind, a spirit which is calling the Church to lay down its life for the world. The spirit has moved Christians into the heart of the fight for justice in our society; it has begun to replace inconsequential church work with a renewed wrestling with the deep implications of Christian faith. It blows through traditional parishes and gives birth to experimental ministries, whether in the bars of Chicago, the slums of New York, or the leisure spots of Las Vegas. There are some who feel that this is the spirit of God—whether expressed in the vision of a Pope John XXIII or in the martyrdom of ministers and laymen in the deep South—and that this spirit is calling for the death of the Church as we know it. Who's killing the Church? God Himself. The Church is called to lose her life in order to find new life.

—Stephen C. Rose, *Who's Killing the Church?*, pp. 4–5.

Four different prescriptions for a sick parish.

A typical meeting of these students or critics of the churches will soon fall into one of two or three patterns. At the base of each pattern, one can predict, there will be a nearly unanimous agreement by all present that the parish as we have inherited it is not doing the task and cannot do the task to which Christ has committed His church in the world. In other words the parish is sick—deathly sick. The participants in the meeting will gather around their subject, the parish, just as surgeons in a medical school gather around a patient on the operating table. These participants will then discuss what to do about the sick patient, the local congregation. Some will suggest a prescription. Give it a few pills and pep it up, and it will live for a while and somehow get to be "up and around." A second group will advocate surgery: Cut deep and far; do some grafting and transplanting; sew with care and heal with concern. Out of such radical surgery may come health. A third group may say, in effect: The patient is too far gone. If we devote our attention to him, we may be diverted from some that we could save. We will be busy devoting ourselves to a hopeless case and letting others become hopeless cases. Let this one alone and let us be about our real work. A fourth group is more hasty. It seems to be saying: This patient is taking up time and space which should be given to another. Administer euthanasia; kill him off. Get him out of the way so that we can be about our business.

—Martin E. Marty, ed., *Death and Birth of the Parish*, p. 4.

Constructive proposals replace sad conclusions.

Not many years ago, the great Christian thinker Reinhold Niebuhr summed up his attitude toward American Protestantism in one devastating word. The Church, he said, has become "trivial." He uttered that judgment despite the fact that, in the decade from 1950 to 1960, the American religious establishment was widely held to be in the midst of an unprecedented postwar revival.

During the first half of the 1960s, Niebuhr's verdict was repeated so often as to become almost trivial itself. A new rash of books hit the market, calling in quasi-prophetic tones for the renewal of the Church. We were inundated with visions of solemn assemblies, suburban captivity, comfortable pews, and ecumenical scandals on main street. Unrest *within* the Church became far greater than the outsider's concern *about* the Church. Scarcely a religious gathering was held without the presence of an iconoclastic jet-age circuit rider who, for an honorarium, flagellated the audience with visions of Christian irrelevance in our time. Others simply left the Church, convinced that bureaucracy and institutionalism had snuffed out all hope of renewal. The conclusion of both those who leave and those who remain to inveigh against the status quo is that the "structures" of the Church have become utterly irrelevant: the local congregation is obsolete; the denominations are hopelessly anachronistic; the minister's role is impossible, etc. But virtually no one has gone beyond these sad conclusions to suggest a comprehensive new structure for Protestantism. We are left with diagnoses aplenty, but scarcely a single prescription.

Now it is time for constructive proposals.

—Stephen C. Rose, *The Grass Roots Church*, pp. xv–xvi.

It's time for the Church to retool.

I conclude this chapter with the personal acknowledgment that—like many other churchmen—I am a sentimentalist at heart. In any group I am usually the first to become nostalgic about the "good old days" when the church was more vigorous and relevant than it seems to be today. I am nostalgic about the early church waiting in the catacombs for the end of time, the monastic church with its corporate life of discipline and prayer, the medieval church embracing culture and the civilizing process, and the Reformation church with its vitality and rediscoveries. More recently, of course, I am nostalgic about the church as village center, and I realize that there are still some rural pockets in America where this image continues to prevail and meet a need. I have the deepest respect for the image of the church as missionary to the heathen and am not implying that we should withdraw our personnel and missionary efforts in other countries. Finally, the definition of the church as social servant through church-related institutions is perhaps the most difficult of all the images for me to question and rethink. I am certainly not suggesting that we now close down the host of outstanding hospitals, orphanages, schools, and humanitarian programs sponsored by the church. What I am calling for is an awareness that our nostalgia and emotional attachments to these images are not enough to warrant their priority as *primary* working models of the church's mission in the closing decades of this century.

I am nostalgic about the village blacksmith, too. His was a time in history for shoeing horses, and the village smithy was a master of his craft. But you and I know full well that any character who opened a blacksmith shop today on any street or highway in the nation would be judged by all of us to be a foolish and irrelevant old man.

If we really believe that the images of village center, missionary to the heathen, or social servant through church-related institutions present *primary* options for the church's ministry today, then let us proceed with haste to recover and recapture these old concepts of our mission to the world. But I would risk the affirmation that our day of metamorphosis is here again, and that we are at a point and place in history when we must dare to ask—as did our fathers—"What does it mean for *us* to be the church?" It is time for blacksmiths to retool!

—W. A. Holmes, *Tomorrow's Church: A Cosmopolitan Community,* pp. 32–33.

Let's take a look at the sick patient.

Some church leaders are still so impressed by the apparent success of the church at a superficial level that they are not yet aware of the need for renewal. Others know something is wrong, but do not want to admit it for fear we will give comfort to our enemies. If we who love the church and are dedicated to its ministry are not aware of its weakness, we are the only ones who are so poorly informed. Ask the man on the street if you want to know what is wrong with the church! The trouble is that the man outside the church is doing nothing to make the church better. The only critics who can improve the situation are the critics within. We must not become spiritual hypochondriacs, but it is just as dangerous to ignore the symptoms of sickness, hoping they will go away. If a patient has cancer, he had better listen to the doctor. Too many spiritual doctors have warned us of the sickness of the church for us to ignore the symptoms. The symptoms of sickness in the church today will not go away if we simply look in the other direction. We cannot right the wrongs by sweeping the dirt under the rug. So with due caution for the dangers involved, let us proceed with the diagnosis.

—Russell Bow, *The Integrity of Church Membership*, pp. 26–27.

B. What Is Wrong with the Church?

During a revolution, the church cannot find the battle.

In the first volume (entitled *Russia Leaves the War*) of Ambassador George Kennan's study of Soviet-American relations, he tells of a series of strange events that took place on November 7, 1917. The scene was Petrograd, the seat of Kerensky's provisional government. On the previous night, the Bolsheviks, seizing power, had sabotaged the official government cars. Kerensky determined to leave the capital and seek troops loyal to him in order to suppress the Bolshevik thrust for control. He sent out an ensign to commandeer a motor vehicle with which he might search for loyal troops. In a scene full of chaos and confusion, the ensign finally located two automobiles in which Kerensky and his aide fled the city. At first the aide's car led the way, but no one in it knew where to go. Later the Pierce-Arrow carrying Kerensky jockeyed into first place and sped from the city at tremendous speed. A short distance outside of Petrograd, the car in which the aide was riding "ran into a rock" and was abandoned; the aide went to a railroad station, where he took a train. Kerensky, meanwhile, searched the countryside for troops and for the revolution that was occurring all around him.

This incident suggests the situation in which the Church finds itself in the era of metropolis. A revolution is occurring in our world. The Church and its leaders have shown a desire to be part of it. But at times the Church cannot seem to find the troops with which to do battle, and cannot even find the proper battles to fight.

—Richard E. Moore and Duane L. Day, *Urban Church Breakthrough*, pp. ix–x.

1. Inner Failure—Membership

a. The pastor and the sermon

Good men vs. the ministry.

Our problem is this: *We have enough good men who are fit for the ministry, but we do not have a ministry that is fit for our best men.*
—Thomas J. Mullen, *The Renewal of the Ministry*, p. 35.

Pastors are forced into the role of the Pharisee.

Surely what the work of the ministry should be patterned after would be more like the figure of Christ washing his disciples' feet than the Pharisee praying in the temple. Yet, in actual practice the roles which Protestant pastors are expected to play and usually do play are frequently patterned more nearly after the Pharisee than the servant. The crucial difference in the two kinds of ministry is this: One is a ministry built upon status; the other is concerned with function.
—Thomas J. Mullen, *The Renewal of the Ministry*, p. 40.

We stifle our creative young pastors.

Dr. C. R. Feilding, a former Dean of Trinity College, University of Toronto, who has been completing a thorough study of theological schools in North America, believes the system feeds upon itself. It is his impression, based on various psychological tests of Roman Catholic, Protestant, and Jewish divinity students, that the modal (or average) personality of these students is what is known in the jargon as "passive-dependent." It has been discovered that theological students of a markedly aggressive type are unlikely to succeed. Dr. Feilding believes there are three reasons for this.

First, the whole process by which theological students become what they are tends to select those who have been kept apart from the real world. "They're always at the clerical end of the church and not at the lay end. It starts, really, with the parental remark: 'Wouldn't he make a lovely priest?' And it proceeds from acolyte to choir and so on. He's always 'up front' in the church."

Second, there are the theological schools themselves, whose system of teaching by lecture appeals to the passive-dependent personality. "The professor answers all the questions. If there's open and free discussion, the student gets upset. Once he gets out of the seminary, having been trained in the passive-dependent style of life, he fits in admirably. If he's a young clergyman in the Anglican Church and becomes a curate, he'll succeed as a passive-dependent man. There are too many sad stories about curates with bright ideas who got into trouble with the rector. The curate is expected to do the rector's leg work; the system doesn't operate to produce aggressive clergy."

Third, the system is such that the minister's life is composed entirely of response. "The job is such that the passive-dependent type of personality is needed. The local minister is required to respond instantly to phone calls and other requests, dropping everything if necessary. If he doesn't, he's in trouble with the laymen who run the church. The lay people want a 'dependent' minister. The man who proposes to run his own life will probably clash with this kind of set-up."

—Pierre Berton, *The Comfortable Pew*, pp. 62–63.

There are not enough pastors to fill the pulpits.

The Protestant ministry is sick. There is not likely to be a real renewal of the Christian Church without a vital ministry, but the trouble is that the ministry, which should be a cure for the lethargy and confusion which plagues the church, itself resembles the disease.

A primary symptom of the sickness is the fact that young men and women in the 1960's are not entering the pastoral ministry in anything like sufficient numbers. In nearly every Protestant denomination the current complaint is the same: there aren't enough pastors to fill pulpits. There aren't even enough men to meet high priority needs, much less enough men to satisfy the needs of new churches and the expanding ministry of large churches which are growing larger. Even a cursory glance at available statistics clearly demonstrates this fact.

—Thomas J. Mullen, *The Renewal of the Ministry*, p. 17.

The pastor's image is fuzzy.

The essence of the problem is the meaning of the pastoral ministry. The ministry itself is not hale and hearty, and until this fact is taken seriously, a vital and dynamic ministry will not appear to stimulate the Christian cause which now lies dormant. To many, what it means to be a local pastor is badly confused. The mental picture of what Protestant pastors do between sermons is vague and unclear. It is true that some few Americans now think that the pastor does nothing but preach, marry, bury, and baptize. Others know that he is "busy," but they are not really sure what he is busy doing or what his business is. The image of the physician or the lawyer or the teacher or the research chemist is sharp and clear. The image of a Protestant pastor between Monday and Saturday is fuzzy and confused.

—Thomas J. Mullen, *The Renewal of the Ministry,* pp. 19–20.

The pastor runs an ambulance service.

The pastor runs an ambulance service, so to speak—an important and indispensable aspect of the Church's ministry; but his services in this respect are performed without ever contacting the powers that shape the destiny of the metropolis and the world. Religion is now relegated to the sphere of personal emotional adjustment. The metropolis perishes from the void in its public sphere; yet the pastors who sense this crisis are daily pressed more deeply into a private sphere of life, and end up tending the machinery of the organization and bandaging the bloodied heads. The crisis in the Christian ministry which is so often discussed stems largely from the dissipation of the ministerial vocation in private emotionality.

—Gibson Winter, *The Suburban Captivity of the Churches*, pp. 165–66.

We can't go any faster than our laymen.

The church is constantly seeking to save herself, to build herself up in terms of worldly status and power. The church is afraid of her mission, and well she might be. Her mission is to lose her life in the world, that her life and the world's life may be saved. . . . We have declined the cross which beckons us into a world of suffering, evil, and injustice. We have turned away from reconciling the world, thinking it enough to be reconciled ourselves. In a recent conference on human relations, a church leader was asked what the church ought to do in the problem of race relations. The reply was: "Well, we can't go any faster than our laymen." This appears harmless. But, in fact, it is a way of saying: "If the will of our people and the will of God are in conflict, we shall do the will of the people."

—Robert A. Raines, *New Life in the Church*, pp. 16–17.

Preaching is powerless.

If the congregation is made restless or sleepy by the modern sermon, it is not only because the message is obscured through the use of an archaic terminology, or because clergymen preach by rote—"like actors who have learned their lines," in Mumford's phrase. It is also because the message itself, apart from its language and its method of delivery, is irrelevant and weak. It is a saying among ecclesiastics that most ministers preach to the right of theology, that they are more conservative in the pulpit than they are in the parlour. Many a man known to be liberal in his own philosophic approach to Christianity may sound like a mossback when he preaches; often enough, because church elders are elderly in attitude as well as age, he will purposely clothe his ideas in an ancient terminology. In doing so he waters down and obscures a message that, delivered honestly, forthrightly, and in simple language, could electrify his congregation. The fact is that most ministers do not want to electrify or disturb anybody, and that is why so many preachers have lost their power.

—Pierre Berton, *The Comfortable Pew*, p. 97.

b. The congregation.

A contemporary Christian gathering—the same old record.

How far we have departed from the New Testament practice may be shown by describing a contemporary Christian gathering, the example being taken almost at random. The gathering was organized to strengthen the Protestant forces of the city, a speaker being brought from a distance. The entire affair was conducted by the local ministerial association, one pastor giving the invocation, one reading the Scripture, another praying before the offering, a fourth introducing the speaker and a fifth giving the benediction. The whole service was practically identical with that which most of the attenders had experienced earlier the same day, except that the professional participants were now more numerous. There was no surprise, no novelty, no real beauty or dignity, and consequently very little attention. It was as though an old record, worn by much use, were being run again and no one seemed to have any clear reason for running it. The hymns were sung, not because some great testimony was being jointly made, but because hymn singing was the conventional thing to do, and the prayers were given, not because of inner compulsion, but because praying was expected.

—Elton Trueblood, *Your Other Vocation*, pp. 30–31.

The Church's conspiracy of silence about Christianity.

It sounds strange to suggest that religious organizations and religious leaders reject spiritually sensitive persons! It does not sound nearly so strange when we recall the reception given to persons like Luther, Savonarola, Joan of Arc, or St. Francis by the religious organizations of their day. Nor is it so difficult to understand when we recall the treatment accorded Jesus of Nazareth by the religious leaders of his time. The sad but inescapable truth is that we in the modern churches would crucify him as readily if he came today —in truth, we do it daily. We crucify him daily when he comes to us in the guise of the laboring man, or the slum-dweller, or the ex-convict, or a strangely dressed woman to whom we refuse the communion of our supper table.

The other side of this same coin is the appalling spiritual poverty in our church fellowships. Speak to the average church officer today and you will discover that he has little awareness of his denomination's history or beliefs, little religious conviction, often doubts the existence of God. And sadly, he has had to carry on a smiling deception in regard to his doubts, for his church has never allowed him an opportunity to admit them honestly and work them through. Or speak to a group of church people about the power of silent prayer and observe their discomfort. Observe a deacons' meeting in some church and note the perfunctory opening prayer, simply a curtsy in the direction of God, bereft of relevance or power for those listening. The truth of the matter is that the spiritual life of the laity is almost nonexistent in many churches and that of the clergy not much better!

The adult members of churches today rarely raise serious religious questions for fear of revealing their doubts or being thought of as strange. There is an implicit *conspiracy of silence* on religious matters in the churches. This conspiracy covers up the fact that the churches do not change lives or influence conduct to any appreciable degree.

—Clyde Reid, *The God–Evaders*, p. 19.

Let the Church be converted.

What we need now is a true conversion, not merely of individuals, but of the Church itself. They are wholly mistaken who suppose that this means the rejection of our basic theology. What is needed, instead, is an understanding of how the Church may become the vehicle for the expression of the basic theology already known. Indeed, one of our important steps is to begin to realize how exceedingly revolutionary the primary Christian convictions really are. If God *is*, if He is like Christ, and if each human being is made in His image, we have a world view more revolutionary than Marxism or any other system which claims to be able to change the world. The trouble lies not in the theology, but in our failure to comprehend its dynamic qualities.

—Elton Trueblood, *The Incendiary Fellowship*, p. 30.

Worship is a spectator sport.

How can the conventional congregation in our time become a family of Christ? Sunday worship alone is inadequate. It is clear that those who do not even know one another's names among the scores of hundreds of worshipers on a Sunday morning can scarcely belong to each other in any personal sense. No matter how inspirational a service of worship may be, it simply is not in itself the context in which people can become related to one another as brothers and sisters in Christ. For many, worship is largely a spectator experience that is almost anonymously carried on for years without significant personal involvement in life together with other Christians.

Preaching alone is inadequate. However powerful and brilliant preaching may be, it cannot bring persons into the family relationship. Preaching can inspire some people to *go* to church, but it cannot enable them to *be* the church. We cannot preach people into loving one another.

Pastoral counseling alone is inadequate, if, when a man who comes to us cracking with fear at a crisis in his life and begs us "Teach me to pray!" we give him merely a book on prayer, talk to him about a life of prayer, and assure him that we will pray for him. All these things we may do, but they are not enough. For such a man needs to know that he is undergirded by a brotherhood of persons aware of his need and praying for him. He will learn to pray as a Christian by sharing in the fellowship of a praying people.

What do we do with a woman who has been a member of the Christian church for thirty years and says to us, "I want to surrender my life to Christ. I have never fully committed myself to Him. What do I do?" Do we give her a book on commitment, talk to her about it, assure her that she has already been following Christ in some measure? Perhaps, but it is not enough. She needs to be led into a company of pilgrims who are learning to surrender to Christ by walking in mutual surrender to one another.

—Robert A. Raines, *Reshaping the Christian Life*, pp. 22–23.

The delegation of personal involvement.

Here is the major problem. Our conventional structure is not geared to enable people to come into deep personal relationship. Social clubs and groups in the church are at best only a vestibule to the family and may be false substitutes for real belonging together in Christ. The committee structure of churches does not necessitate or even encourage the personal sharing of life which is the heart of the family. In pursuing many useful things, we have neglected the one thing needful. What can we do? How can the conventional church become a family of Christ?

The conventional church will become a family of Christ only for those who find a way of belonging together in a small group of growing, serving Christians. We are not called to walk alone; we are called to share the pilgrimage of a people. We cannot delegate our personal involvement to somebody else. Sending our money will not achieve this involvement; neither will merely sending our children or a husband or wife. Serving on most committees cannot achieve it. Nor will sitting in a pew on Sunday morning by itself. The only way to penetrate the trappings of the life of the modern congregation and to discover the risen Christ is to become personally involved with a few persons in whom He lives and works.

—Robert A. Raines, *Reshaping the Christian Life*, pp. 23–24.

Brethren, remove your masks.

First, I think we are unreal about ourselves, even as Christians, because we are afraid that if people find out what we are actually like inside, behind the mask, find out that we really don't honestly want to be with them socially as much as we imply, they will not accept us and therefore we won't be able to fulfill our self-centered needs through our associations with them. You think this is too strong an indictment to level at us churchmen? Think it over.

—Keith Miller, *The Taste of New Wine*, p. 25.

Osmosis Christianity.

But liberal Protestantism has left the field of conversion to the Fundamentalists. We have neglected the central mission of the church, which is to go and make disciples, in favor of the easier and more congenial task of nurturing church members. We have not expected lives radically to be changed; we have been content with ourselves as we are and others as they are; we have tried to live by allegiance to the Father and respect for Jesus, but without the Holy Spirit. We have taken refuge in the staid, comfortable, totally unbiblical notion of what may be called *osmosis Christianity*. This is the optimistic assumption that people soak up Christian faith by being reared in a Christian home or by spending enough hours in the atmosphere of the church—the idea that we get onto the heaven-bound escalator in the cradle room, and more or less inevitably are landed on the top floor of the building, which is heaven. This is something like the process of enrolling a newborn child in a fashionable preparatory school, guaranteeing his entrance there years hence.

So it is that our churches are crowded with honest, genial folk who stopped going to Sunday School when they were ten years of age, and thus have a foggy, halo-ridden picture of a Jesus preoccupied with lambs: folk who were swept into church membership around the age of twelve because it was the thing all the other children were doing, folk who perhaps never once have been challenged to make an adult commitment of life to Christ, with all its implications.

—Robert A. Raines, *New Life in the Church*, p. 23.

Will you still respect me?

What is the result of this easy membership? For one thing, fewer people respect the church. Almost every other institution has standards or requires disciplines. The church requires less of its members than is expected by a good luncheon club. When a patient goes to the hospital, he gets into bed and submits to some rather unpleasant hospital routine. But one can join the church by simply having his name on the roll, and can remain a member for years without attending, paying, or submitting to any disciplines except those of his own choosing.

—Russell Bow, *The Integrity of Church Membership*, p. 34.

Paper membership.

You may get a visual picture of what has happened to church membership in America if you will draw three concentric circles. The outer circle represents all non-members who have any relationship to the church. The middle circle represents the nominal members—those whose names are on the roll. The inner circle represents the real church—the committed Christians who are in fellowship with God and one another. During the past two hundred years we have made great gains in "paper" membership. We have meticulously added names to the roll so that the middle circle has grown out of all proportion to the inner circle. There have been many genuine conversions, but much of our apparent success has come about because we have lowered membership requirements. It is easy to be a "paper" member, without vital commitment to Jesus Christ.

—Russell Bow, *The Integrity of Church Membership*, pp. 27–28.

The non-biblical character of attendance records.

The point is that attendance records are a non-biblical and essentially non-Christian standard of success. Yet they represent the accepted mark of religious achievement—along with huge budgets—of the contemporary church *and its pastor.*

—Thomas J. Mullen, *The Renewal of the Ministry*, p. 23.

Straight ahead into the past.

If the church were to stop trying to be what it thinks it used to be but never was, it could begin to be what it might be in this changing world. But it clings to notions of infallibility which it locates now in its scriptures, now in its own constitution. They belong to the past, and the only certain thing about them is that the man of today can no more entertain them than he can entertain the idea of a geocentric universe. He rejects these ideas and also the church which cannot do without them, even if this means that he is branded as irreligious.

—A. Q. Morton and James McLeman, *Christianity in the Computer Age*, p. 57.

Church attendance is equated with the Christian life.

The paradox of the apparent victory, yet real defeat, of the contemporary Church is nowhere more vividly demonstrated than in the present concentration upon *attendance.* Great billboard advertisements appear by the hundreds with a single message, "Worship Together This Week." The fact that the donors of the advertisements are undoubtedly motivated by goodwill toward the life of religion, as they understand it, does not obscure the fundamental ineptitude of their effort. Obviously, the sponsors of the advertisements look upon attendance at a religious assembly as the major religious act or the major evidence of church membership. It is no wonder that they think this, if they observe the frantic and sometimes ingenious efforts of pastors, week by week, to surpass all previous records of attendance. The promotional purpose of local church newsletters is transparent.

The tragedy of the billboards lies less in what they say than in their revelation of a suppressed premise concerning the central nature of Christ's cause. Many betray the same unargued assumption when they describe themselves by announcing which church they go to. The trouble with this response is that a church, in its very nature, is not really something to which men and women can *go.* Rather, it is something which they may be *in.* The difference is fundamental and far-reaching. We can go to a railroad station or to a motion picture theater or to a ball game; but a church is something which demands a wholly different human relationship, the relationship of belonging. If a man is really in—really belongs to—a church, he is just as much a member of it when he sits at his desk in his business house as when he sits in a pew at his meetinghouse. The point is that the relationship, if real, is continuous, regardless of time and place and performance. Christians made a great step forward in human history when they took from Stoicism the germ of the membership idea and developed it.

The radical difference between the Church and most human organizations is so important that unless it is truly understood our chance for renewal of vitality is slight indeed. Though it is sad that people fail to respond to public worship with the enthusiasm and devotion which they evince at basketball games, the greater sadness lies in the fact that supposed Church members do not even understand the difference between the two kinds of relationship. If Christianity is primarily a matter of attendance at a performance, it is not different in kind from a host of other experiences. Though membership may *include* attendance at performances of a certain character, such attendance is not the primary meaning of the Christian effort at all. The fact that this is not generally understood is one of the chief evidences of the spiritual erosion which distresses us.

—Elton Trueblood, *The Company of the Committted*, pp. 18–20.

The great god is Activity.

This essentially pragmatic test of the authenticity of any group calling itself a church in terms of faithfulness to the Word of God is the strongest safeguard against the church falling victim to metaphysical pragmatism. That is, there is strong pressure in the American scene to exalt activity and interest itself as the sufficient test of the worthwhileness of any enterprise. If people are attending meetings, volunteering their time, enjoying their participation, then this often seems to justify the organization. Such a philosophy of busyness is widespread in the life of the church, and there are few people who are completely immune from its cogent persuasion. Thus, any kind of heresy can be preached or paraded in the church, if people like it.

The two kinds of churches which most easily seem to fall victim to the idea that "anything goes, as long as there is a crowd" are the old established city churches losing their congregations and bright new churches in the suburbs. Old churches can often find a new following if a persuasive spellbinder offers attractive homilies directed toward the assuaging of bodily and mental ills. The cities are filled with lonely people who find comfort or excitement in such a display, albeit not necessarily the glad good news of Christ.

New suburban churches are often put in the embarrassing position of not being able to cope with the great number of people who want to join them. Organizing meetings are held, ministers settled, new buildings erected, and a Sunday School and congregation of several hundred gathered, often without any large number of those who participate knowing any more about the Christian church than what they had gleaned from *Life* magazine and *Reader's Digest*. Governing boards of new churches sometimes consist of people who have had a great deal more experience with the Boy Scouts, the U.S. Army, and college fraternities than with the Christian church.

—Robert W. Spike, *In But Not Of The World*, pp. 48–50.

Depart, ye poor and needy!

In the Gospel according to Mark, Jesus is reported to have said, "Those who are well have no need of a physician, but those who are sick; I came not to call the righteous, but sinners" (Mark 2:17). The Gospel according to Luke reports it this way: "The Son of Man came to seek and to save the lost" (Luke 19:10).

Strangely, those persons who most dramatically fit the category of modern sinners are precisely those who feel least welcome in the churches, and with whom church people are most ill at ease. (This is not to deny that church people are sinners!)

Consider the alcoholic, the person caught in the compulsive need to drink. Partly because of his own feelings of guilt, but also because of the moralistic attitude of so many churches, the alcoholic usually turns away from the church rather than toward it. His behavior is regarded as weak and immoral, and he finds help through his doctor, a hospital, or a group like Alcoholics Anonymous—if he finds help at all.

In a similar way, the person who has been convicted of a crime rarely finds a warm welcome in the fellowship of those who follow him who came to "seek and to save the lost." The adulterer is often cut off from the fellowship of his church, the "loose woman" is regarded as a social outcast, the juvenile delinquent stops coming, and the unwed mother no longer feels accepted. While the churches claim to be fellowships of forgiven sinners, they rarely reach out to these persons who stand in obvious need of support and guidance to straighten out the "sinful" part of their emotionally or morally confused lives. Again the contradiction between words and actions becomes an embarrassment to the church.

—Clyde Reid, *The God–Evaders*, p. 20.

A gathering of vague acquaintances in Christ.

These facts indicate why it is hard to have *koinonia* in the local church today. Many sociological forces are working against it. Yet, *koinonia* is the missing element in most churches. How many of our main-line Protestant congregations could be said to be like a family today? Most could be said to be more like gatherings of acquaintances who may vaguely recognize one another when sighted across the room at worship on certain Sunday mornings.

—Thomas J. Mullen, *The Renewal of the Ministry*, p. 54.

The Church is a field white unto harvest.

The fact that the church so often fails when it could be exceedingly power-ful rather than merely respectable defines, in large measure, our problem. This problem is the conversion of the church. Since most Americans at least *claim* to be affiliated with some church or synagogue, it is obvious that the major field of evangelism must be within the alleged membership. If anyone can show how new life in the existing church is possible, that is great good news.

—Wallace E. Fisher, *From Tradition to Mission*, pp. 7–8.

c. The structure

A few bright spots are not enough.

The local church today is at a dead end, not because it is totally irrelevant, but because it is cynical to assume that a few bright spots will compensate for the structural weakness of the whole.

—Stephen C. Rose, *The Grass Roots Church*, p. 95.

Shields against the best.

The present structure of Protestantism effectively shields most laymen, not to mention outsiders, from the best the Church has to offer.

—Stephen C. Rose, *The Grass Roots Church*, p. 32.

Institutional pressures—succeed or else.

By their very nature our modern institutions are called to succeed. They cannot afford to fail, and institutional self-interest quickly becomes the sole criteria.

The churches of our time have got caught up in this world of institutions that have lost the power of effective self-criticism and achieved a considerable institutional inertia. The integrity of the church is related to its missionary purpose given by the Lord. To fulfill its function institutional patterns are necessary and right, but integrity requires that these patterns serve the purpose of the church and never become ends in themselves. At last the churches are beginning to recognize that they have become so entangled in structure that they have forgotten what their structures are for, and instead of enabling communities of witness and service to arise and function, they have sought only to become successful in an inverted, institutionalized life. Neither the failure of these patterns in the inner city nor their great success in suburbia reflects faithfulness to the gospel.

—George W. Webber, *The Congregation in Mission*, p. 40.

Denominations are doubting Thomases.

The Protestant version of Dostoevsky's Legend might be set in a denominational conference room. Christ would not be imprisoned, as in the Legend, but merely doubted. The Protestant counterpart of the Inquisitor would say: "Your notion, if you really *are* Christ, of human freedom may be followed by some in our Churches, but what of the rest—those who have never seen the vision or heard the Word? There will always be a remnant perhaps, but we must concern ourselves with the others, with those who need the activities, the services, yes, the comfort, that we provide. So leave us. We have budgets to plan, annual reports to write, statistics to gather. With luck, if there's not too much rocking the boat, we shall survive."

—Stephen C. Rose, *The Grass Roots Church*, p. 61.

Faith is secondary, institutional loyalty first.

Secularism in religion is the substitution of religious structures and authorities for the Gospel. Secularism in the churches is the attempt to preserve a fragment of absolute authority for the churches in a secularized world, denying man's responsibility for his future and making faith secondary to institutional loyalty. If the religious institution can maintain even a partial monopoly on faith and truth, it can preserve its own autonomy against history, fashioning its future and the future of the world on the basis of some unchanging form or truth which it possesses. The churches, in this state of secularism, call men away from historical responsibility to an ahistorical, unchanging truth.

—Gibson Winter, *The New Creation As Metropolis*, pp. 43–44.

The test of success is a balanced budget.

The world outside has long been radically critical of the churches. There is nothing written today more radically critical of the churches as they are than that which is written by ecumenical Christians from inside them, with the single exception of those who don't believe in God, or in any religion. This criticism of the churches from within is based essentially on two charges: institutionalism and provincialism. Ecumenists generally agree that the churches, as organized, too often allow their organizations to stand in the way of the purpose of the organization. The balanced budget too easily becomes the crucial test of the church's "success." The number of members seems to become more important than what happens to the members. Personal power within the organization and the power of the organization in the world become more important to the churches' leaders than obedience to Jesus Christ. Churches become ends in themselves, representing the morality of their members, instead of being agents of God representing God's morality to the members.

—Eugene Carson Blake, *The Church in the Next Decade*, pp. 102–3.

Layman, sit down and shut up!

Even if Church conventions were more representative, it is questionable whether the laity could inaugurate serious reforms. The sad reality is that laymen are rarely given an opportunity to vote on substantive issues of Church policy and programming. This is because these issues are rarely raised in specific form. Questions of membership standards, major changes in financial policy, or alteration of forms of Church government are seldom brought up, much less brought to a vote. The layman's role in denominational decision-making is most often limited to the ratification of matters that have already been predetermined by the Church bureaucracy. Even if a layman takes a progressive stand within a particular denominational board, his decisions can be offset by another countervailing wing of the denominational establishment.

—Stephen C. Rose, *The Grass Roots Church*, p. 47.

Mission and drastic structural implications.

The nature of the emerging theological consensus implies that much of importance in present congregational life is either irrelevant or detrimental to the missionary purpose of God's people.

—George W. Webber, *The Congregation in Mission*, p. 13.

Wedded to the inappropriate.

When we consider the time and place of the Churches' activities in Metropolis, we are more inclined to give the advocates of new structures and forms of ministry an attentive ear. For it is remarkable that Churches hold on with such tenacity and uncritical allegiance to long-established church ways when it is obvious that they no longer meet a real need, or that they have become inappropriate because of changing circumstances.

—Jesse McNeil, *Mission in Metropolis*, p. 52.

Morphological fundamentalism.

Structural rigidity and inertia, that is "morphological fundamentalism," is an overwhelming obstacle to renewal. In a world of tremendous change it is demanded of the church that it, too, do more than increase the efficiency of its present ecclesiastical machinery.

—George W. Webber, *The Congregation in Mission*, pp. 46–47.

The Church is the most complacent institution of the Western world.

Anyone who stands back and looks at the situation of the church within the context of the twentieth century must be pardoned if he finds this upsurge of euphoria a little mystifying. The church is being left high and dry to cherish whatever illusions it may choose while the stream of life is changing course. That churchmen can be quite happy in a world of their own, however congenial, is set down to the account of taking religion too seriously. Either that or not taking life seriously enough.

For the church is probably the most complacent institution in the western world. Its psychological attitude towards itself and its surroundings is moribund. In nineteen centuries of history it has stored up vast reserves of confidence in its own indestructibility. Its survival in the twentieth century depends on writing off those reserves quickly and without regret, yet there is no indication that it is ready to take a comprehending look at itself in relation to the world as it really is.

Deep below the surface appearances of hectic reorganisation and readjustment, the church is untroubled by the fact that it has entered on an unprecedented era of change without any new ideas about its place and function in such an age.

Worse still, it appears to be unaware that this kind of new thinking is in any way necessary. It has every confidence that it alone can face the future with the ideas and ideals of the past—as it has done these many generations. It still thinks of itself in terms that were once more or less appropriate but are so no longer. Its attempts to break into the life of the twentieth century are vitiated by its refusal to let the past bury the past. The church, in short, is suffering from a hangover of its own history, a surfeit of smugness.

Few churchmen seem to realise that what they have been traditionally taught to think about the church may be quite unrelated to its real situation at the present time. Any suggestion that this is so is immediately countered by an apologetic, designed for other ages, which cuts no ice today and which is based on the proposition that the church has always survived because it is not like other organisations.

—A. Q. Morton and James McLeman, *Christianity in the Computer Age*, pp. 67–68.

A sacred island in a secular world.

The signs are out that we are reaching what can only be called "the crisis of the local congregations." At the seminary of a major denomination over 40% of first year students report that they do not desire to become ministers of a local congregation. It is reported further that there is a decline in students offering themselves for the ministry, and that many who could be expected to offer refuse to do so because they believe that to become the minister of a congregation does not place them at the point where the true frontier of the Christian mission is to be found. That frontier is in the world; but the local congregation is now so structured that it is a sacred island in the secular world, pulling individuals out of the world and causing them to act as commuters shuttling back and forth—leaving the world to enter Church, and leaving the Church to go back to the world, with no real relation between the two parts of their life.

Many pastors of local congregations seem to agree that there is something drastically wrong with this basic unit of present church structure. They feel that the way the congregation is organized prevents them from fulfilling their primary roles as ministers of the gospel; that in the congregation their life is institutionalized in such a way that they are not free to be servants of the Church's true mission. They are busy—but not with the one thing needful.

—Colin W. Williams, *Where in the World?*, pp. 1–2.

2. Outer Failure—Mission

The virtue of criticism.

In examining again the failure of the church to meet the challenge of urban life we lay the ground work for testing the validity of the emerging structures that are being called forth by the needs of congregations that do commit themselves again to a serious missionary vocation.

—George W. Webber, *The Congregation in Mission*, p. 34.

Face forward, toward the world.

The church cannot hope to be an important and inspiring agency in the modern world unless it is prepared to face the world, to look outward at things as they are, without benefit of delusions of grandeur derived from its actual or imagined past.

This means that it must be less egocentric and more anxious to serve the needs of this generation. It cannot continue to think of itself as a supernatural agency not answerable to the conscience of mankind. It has been in danger of extinction in the past at precisely those times when it refused to move forward in thought and deed as the conscience of mankind advanced. It has survived because it finally consented to serve and was not resigned to be outdistanced by the pace of life, intellectually, morally and materially. If it had been ultimately reconciled to being the church of a particular age it would have died when that age died.

—A. Q. Morton and James McLeman, *Christianity in the Computer Age*,
pp. 70–71.

Rejoin the human race!

The reaction of institutions, as of most persons, under attack is to become defensive. Social forces have been at work cutting the many strands that joined the Church of a century and more ago to the life of the community. It used to be an institution in society to which every other institution was in some way related. It is now one institution among many. The Church has, to a large extent unconsciously, retreated within its own borders: *it has become itself a world*. How to break out again from isolation into communication with the world is becoming an urgent concern for many in the churches.

—Kathleen Bliss, *We the People*, p. 17.

The sanctuary of mumbled promises.

Christianity is statistically the largest religious community on earth, known in some measure within every country, and widely accepted as a fact of life both east and west. No longer the creator of culture, or the judge of men, or the inspirer of national policy, the Christian church (and this most especially in the Protestant genre) simply waits to enfold those who would seek sanctuary within its mumbled promises.

—Wesley C. Baker, *The Split-Level Fellowship*, p. 23.

See how the irreligious love the Church.

A more generalized feature of our society which obscures the relative failure of the Church is its public acceptance. We cannot normally have a public occasion, however secular, without religious representation. Thus, at President Kennedy's inauguration the committee in charge felt that it was wise or necessary to give public recognition, through vocal prayer, to four communions: Roman Catholic, Orthodox, Protestant, and Jewish. Furthermore, all four prayers were printed in *The New York Times*. This national recognition is only a consummation of what occurs at countless lower levels. In most communities leading clergymen are automatically invited to membership in the best luncheon clubs; ministers of all faiths are given reduced rates on the majority of railroads; and every church has the immense advantage of nontaxation of its physical property.

Before we take too much satisfaction from popular acceptance it may help our sense of historical balance to remember that the popular religion of ancient Greece succeeded in maintaining its shrines after the real vitality had departed. Representatives of Greek religion provided "services" long after what went on at the shrines had ceased to have any relevance in the life of business or education or government. It was to existent yet really obsolete shrines that the Apostle Paul referred when he began his famous address at Athens by saying, "Men of Athens, I perceive that in every way you are very religious" (Acts 17:22). They *were* religious; and their religion had some good features, as scholars like Gilbert Murray and Edith Hamilton have shown; but their religion died in spite of its assets. It died because it could not meet the tests of intellectual validity and social relevance; it could not match the new vitality of the fellowship which stemmed from the life and teaching and death and resurrection of Christ.

—Elton Trueblood, *The Company of the Committed*, pp. 4–5.

Here am I, Lord. Send him.

The church too has lost her sense of mission. The church has accommodated herself to the cultural climate. The church is no longer changing culture, but is being changed by culture. The church is not enabling her people to live with purpose in a world without purpose. The average church member has little sense of individual mission in the world. If one were to ask him if he were a member of a "chosen race, a royal priesthood, a holy nation," he would surely reply, "Why no. I'm a member of Main Street Methodist Church"; or worse, "Why no, I'm a member of Sam Smith's Church." He wouldn't understand that *to be* a Christian means precisely that one *is* a member of a chosen race, a royal priesthood, a holy nation. The people believe in God and support the institution of the church and enter into its activities, but they do not believe they are chosen to be salt, light, and leaven in the world. They do not believe they are chosen to be Christ's witnesses in the world. They shrink from the very idea of personal witness. Their typical response to Christ's summons, "You did not choose me, but I chose you and appointed you that you should go and bear fruit . . ." (John 15:16), is: "Here am I, Lord. Send *him.*" They accept the conditions of life in the world with little thought that these conditions ought to be changed, and no idea that they as Christians are called to be the agents of God's reconciling changes.

The loss of mission appears in the local church, which is usually content to grow in physical stature and in favor with its immediate environment. The whole idea of outreach is delegated to a "Committee On Missions," which concerns itself largely with the financial support the church gives to foreign and home agencies of the denomination. This "segregation of concern" neatly exempts ninety-nine of one hundred people in a church from a sense of personal responsibility. Thus we lose our individual concern in corporate irresponsibility.

—Robert A. Raines, New Life in the Church, pp. 14–15.

Out of sight is out of mind.

To my mind more important and more telling criticism than that which comes from sociologists and theologians comes from missionary thinkers and strategists. Indeed in public they are often quite amiable. They must be content to go along with "the best we now have," the existing forms of congregational life. They have to be content to pick up the financial crumbs and to work on the basis of the leftover imagination and energy of people in the parish. But when they are given the opportunity, almost all of them are more searching. Picture yourself in the situation of a man charged with bringing the message of Jesus Christ to people around the world in the name of, say, a 2.5 million-member denomination made up of perhaps 5,000 parishes. You travel and see a world of desolation and despair, a world—as you see it—in need of Christ and of bread. Then you come home and tour

the denomination. You see people investing luxuriously in church parlors and
cushioned pews and each year tossing a tip (say, for example, $3.00) for the
whole worldwide work of the church. Would it not occur to you that every
brick placed in the wall of such a parish church is a brick placed over against
a world of need? What is worse, you enter these walls and find that they not
only commit a congregation financially but they obscure the vision of the real
world from people. That is, people lose their imagination for the remote.
They live in the illusion that everyone could have their standards and way of
life. They lose sympathy for the people who are screened off from their view.

—Martin E. Marty, ed., *Death and Birth of the Parish*, pp. 13–14.

Private values, yes. Society, no.

The residential community is preoccupied with the maintenance of emotional stability and the nurture of children. These are its principal interests;
significant aspects of life, indeed, but they do not exhaust the values of
personality and society.

—Gibson Winter, *The New Creation As Metropolis*, p. 12.

Sanctuaries are built by the respectable for the respectable.

In the decisive moment the city has been forsaken by the church. Let us not
turn that around and act as if the city dwellers have left the church. This is
repeatedly suggested, for instance, in our evangelistic hymns ("O Straying
Sheep, Return"), but also—more generally—in the whole manner in which
the church called the city toward it. This call did not sound very convincing
anyhow. As soon as—in the nineteenth century—one began to check with
one's eyes what one heard with one's own ears, it became quite noticeable
that a return was not counted on.

Just look. In the sanctuaries, built by the respectables for the respectables,
there was no room. Take, for instance, Sheffield in 1820: four thousand seats
for the more than sixty-five thousand inhabitants. Of these, three hundred
places were free (in the aisle and up in the gallery). And the poor had to be
dependent on those, for who could afford every year a sum for seat rental,
which was the equivalent of about one or two weeks' wages? "Your houses
belie your words."

—J. C. Hoekendijk, *The Church Inside Out*, p. 114.

We are weakest at the point of greatest human need.

In a time of so-called revival of religion the failure of Protestantism in the
inner city points to a tragic failure at the very center of our culture. Here
at the point of greatest human need and most human problems we are at our
weakest. The religious situation in the inner city is clearly a missionary
challenge in which less than 20 per cent of the residents maintain an active

affiliation in any church. American Negro families, traditionally strongly Protestant, and Puerto Ricans, supposedly Roman Catholic, seemed neither to maintain their religious heritage nor to develop any new religious affiliation amid the pressures of urban life.

—George W. Webber, *God's Colony in Man's World*, pp. 36–37.

The introverted Church is an apostate Church.

The introverted church is one which puts its own survival before its mission, its own identity above its task, its internal concerns before its apostolate, its rituals before its ministry. These contrasts distinguish the Church as a structure and the Church as a living power—its static and dynamic aspects. Historical embodiments of the Church tend to stress one of these aspects at the expense of the other; in recent times the introverted church stresses the Church as structure at the expense of the mission and task of the Church. The middle-class search for social identity has led to emphasis on the collective form of the Church; consequently, the Protestant congregation, one of the most dynamic forms in the history of the Church, has become a static, organizational entity. Undue emphasis on the static structure of the Church has led to the disappearance of a significant lay ministry in denominational Protestantism. Loss of dynamic form and surrender of mission undercut the lay ministry, for it is the Church as mission which rests its case upon the laity and their outreach to the world. The more introverted the Church, the more it becomes subject to priestcraft and routinized activities. The introverted church substituted celebrations of its own unity for witness in the metropolis. An introverted church is an apostate body, for it denies the essential quality of Church—the testimony of reconciliation in the world.

The denominations refuse to take the introversion of the churches seriously. They believe it is accidental and will be overcome by building enough churches in the suburbs. They will not face the fact that they are doing the same thing today which they did at the turn of the century, and will shackle the churches even more firmly to the treadmill of the introverted congregation.

—Gibson Winter, *The Suburban Captivity of the Churches*, pp. 103–4.

Silence thunders on the great issues.

In the great issues of our time, the voice of the Church, when it has been heard at all, has been weak, tardy, equivocal, and irrelevant. In those basic conflicts that ought to be tormenting every Christian conscience—questions of war and peace, of racial brotherhood, of justice versus revenge, to name three—the Church has trailed far behind the atheists, the agnostics, the free thinkers, the journalists, the scientists, the social workers, and even, on occasion, the politicians. In other areas, the Church has simply stood aloof. It has, for instance, virtually ignored the whole contemporary question of business morals, the tensions within industry and labour, the sexual revolution that has changed the attitudes of the Western world.

In this abdication of leadership, this aloofness from the world, this apathy
that breeds apathy, the Church, as Canon Collins stated, has turned its back
on its own first principles. No wonder, then, there is indifference.

—Pierre Berton, *The Comfortable Pew*, p. 16.

A revolutionary fellowship? You must be joking.

The renewal of the Church in the contemporary metropolis cannot be
resolved by naïve optimism or grand-sounding phrases. One of the writers
was in Detroit several years ago listening to a denominational leader speak
to a group of city planners and ministers concerning spiritual renewal in the
city. The dynamic young church leader gripped the table and leaned forward
for emphasis. "The Church," he said "is a revolutionary cell in American
society." When the speaker concluded, the moderator of the meeting asked
for questions. A layman standing in the wings spoke out. He said, "I've heard
that claim more than once, and I've been looking a long time for this revolutionary fellowship. I do have a question. Where is it?"

The question "Where is it?" articulates a growing frustration within the
institutional Church, which seems in many ways unrelated to the world
around it. The Church appears to function in our society as a preserver of
the best values of the past and as the promoter of a way of life set apart from
the world. The prophets bring in minority reports, and official Church groups
occasionally formulate visionary pronouncements, but the emphasis is on
conservation rather than creation, disengagement rather than involvement,
ritual rather than prophecy.

—Richard E. Moore and Duane L. Day, *Urban Church Breakthrough*, p. 3.

Denominational piety vs. the servant Church.

The institutional crisis of Christianity arises, thus, from the preoccupation
of the religious community with private concerns while the forces that are
shaping human destiny dominate the public realm. Pastors feel this estrangement in their own isolation from the processes of the society—their sense of
working in a hothouse atmosphere of women's emotional difficulties and
children's programs. Laity experience this crisis in a search for a significant
ministry in place of the organizational activities to which the churches usually
consign their efforts. Religious leaders sense the depth of this crisis at the
very moment when they press for organizational expansion, since the proliferation of residential churches seems to have so little impact on the increasing chaos of the metropolitan areas. The institutional crisis of contemporary
Christianity is manifest in the simultaneous appearance of spiritual emptiness
and intense religious activity. The crisis is generated by a situation calling for
a servant Church over against a denominational commitment to pietism.

—Gibson Winter, *The New Creation As Metropolis*, p. 30.

Let the church staff take care of it.

There is a general weakness which may be termed *segregation*, especially segregation from common life. Whether our religion is segregated from common life by being limited *geographically* (i.e., to a religious building), or *temporally* (by undue emphasis on one hour a week, which is usually on Sunday morning), or limited in *personnel* (by the assumption that religion is the responsibility of a special professional class called clergy), the damaging effect is the same.

When we think that religion is what goes on in a building of recognizable ecclesiastical architecture, the damage comes in the perfectly natural human tendency to minimize religion in *other* places. When we think of religion as what transpires on Sunday morning, the harm lies in the tendency to suppose that what goes on at other times, in factories and offices, is not equally religious. When we think of religion as the professional responsibility of priests, clergymen, and rabbis, the major harm lies in the consequent minimizing of the religious responsibility of *other* men and women. The harm of too much localizing of religious responsibility in a few—however dedicated they may be—is that it gives the rank and file a freedom from responsibility which they ought not to be able to enjoy.

—Elton Trueblood, *The Company of the Committed*, p. 9.

3. Potpourri—A Catalog of Ills

Ignore it. It's only theology.

My plea is that theologians should take stock of where they stand in relation to the "creative centre" of the age into which we are moving and of the "coming great Church" which one trusts will be there to baptize it. There are plentiful signs that theology need not be a dead discipline: in fact, it is probably more "on the map" in Britain today than it has been for a hundred years. And yet it remains true that for the ordinary person—and indeed for most practical purposes for the ordinary parson— theology as it is generally understood and purveyed is miles away (and probably getting further) from the creative centres of our new society. Indeed, Mr. Harold Wilson, who would doubtless like to see himself as the embodiment of that new society, accurately reflected the current "image" of theology, when, in his dispute with Hugh Gaitskell over the famous Clause Four of the Labour Party constitution (on nationalization), he sought to dismiss the whole thing as "theology"—theoretical discussion bearing no vital relation to the real concerns that made the Party "tick." Increasingly, to men of the second industrial revolution, theology seems to belong, if not to the "grouse moors," at any rate to the small shopkeepers, of the spiritual world. And both its retailers and wholesalers have sheltered for too long behind a Retail Price Maintenance which is fast breaking down.

—John A. T. Robinson, *The New Reformation*, p. 76.

The racial crisis spotlights the Church.

The basic problem has nothing to do with race, but with the fundamental essence of man in relationship to God. And this we all share regardless of color. The racial crisis has simply spotlighted the deeper problem of the churches—their lack of genuine integration of religious beliefs in the lives of their members—in a vivid and inescapable way.

—Clyde Reid, *The God-Evaders*, p. 38.

Guess who we have chained in the church basement?

One of the aberrations of propositional theology has been biblical literalism. This is perhaps the worst form of the chaining of Christ in which the church has engaged. It begins with a very important concept: namely, that the Scriptures are the most continuously reliable source of knowing Christ and Christian teaching. But when you affix to this a wooden insistence that the poetry, parables, history, aphorism, teaching, hymnody, dramas of the Bible, all be read as if the Bible were a scientific catalogue, then you are in bad trouble.

What you get is the exact opposite of accurate and deep understanding of Christian faith. You can read any previous emotional commitment into bits and pieces of the Scripture. Thus, the curse of Ham is extended (by what authority, no one seems to explain) to apply to all people of dark skin. Thus, the explanation that God has "set the bounds of the habitation of men" (simply a statement to explain the appearance of different nations in different parts of the world) becomes a defense of segregation. A much more apt conclusion to be drawn from this literal rendering of Scripture, would be a condemnation of white slave traders who seized black men from the bounds of their habitation in Africa.

The horror of the proof-texting segregationists is that they can escape the powerful punch of the parable of the Good Samaritan, while righteously distorting a verse to condone social sin. Governor Ross Barnett was for many years the teacher of a large Sunday school class in Jackson, Mississippi, propounding this kind of propositional theology in defense of the closed society.

—Robert W. Spike, *The Freedom Revolution and the Churches*, pp. 77–78.

Welcome, paleface.

The most damning critique of our failure resides in the very existence of separate Negro denominations in this country. That it was not the gospel which was at fault is apparent in the decision of various Baptist, Methodist, and Christian groups to form their own fellowships. The Negro heard and responded to the glorious good news of Christ, but quickly experienced the fact that the new life in Christ, to be lived out in the church, could not be done in white churches. White church members often interpret the existence of the Negro church as being prima-facie evidence that Negroes really "prefer" to be with their own kind. This softened interpretation of the situation that produced the Negro church is a part of the blindness of the white majority. They do not comprehend the depth of the rejection that made it necessary for Negroes to organize their own churches if they were to worship in freedom and joy—two fundamental pre-requisites of Christian worship. Indeed, perhaps they took most of both commodities with them when they left. Is this one reason why white establishment church worship is often so cold and sterile—the erecting of the forgotten wall within which white worship takes place?

—Robert W. Spike, *The Freedom Revolution and the Churches*, pp. 71–72.

We make small what ought to be large.

The major danger of our contemporary religion, then, is that it makes small what ought to be large. By segregating religion in place or time or personnel, we make religion relatively trivial, concerned with only a part of experience when it ought to be concerned with the *whole* of life. Whenever the Church means merely a building on the corner, or a special kind of service, or a man with a round collar, the salt has already lost much of its savor. But there can be no serious doubt that for millions the Church *does* mean precisely that. It seems successful, but it is fundamentally unimportant because it is deemed to be marginal in its relevance. In so far as this is true, it is not only Church *members* but the *Church itself* which requires a radical conversion. Few phrases deserve currency in our time more than the phrase "The Conversion of the Church."

—Elton Trueblood, *The Company of the Committed*, p. 10.

The organization Church is filled with white collars.

The activity of the congregations of the major denominations and their appalling superficiality have often been noted by foreign observers; these visitors from afar look wistfully at church activities and budgets but stand aghast before the spiritual emptiness of these associations. This strange combination of vitality and emptiness can be understood in the light of the peculiar coalition between the major denominations and the emerging middle class. A wholly new style of religious life emerged in this coalition; in fact, the constellation of forces at work in the metropolis gave birth to the organization church. The bond between the organization church and the particular interests and needs of the white-collar ranks can be discerned, but the real problem remains as to whether this fabricated community can serve as a platform for a mission to the metropolis or must be abandoned for a renewed church.

—Gibson Winter, *The Suburban Captivity of the Churches*, p. 35.

Living, but exhausted by the effort.

It would be false to imply that the church has been utterly complacent about its failure in the twentieth century. It has become fashionable for churchmen to declare that the church must modernise itself. The Bible has been translated into more modern speech. Clergy are urged to use "the language of the people." Chaplains have been appointed to institutions and industries. Finances have been overhauled, church architecture reviewed, forms, orders and times of services altered. But the general picture is unchanged. The church appears to be exhausting itself merely to keep alive.

—A. Q. Morton and James McLeman, *Christianity in the Computer Age*, p. 47.

The illusion is "business as usual."

The churches, despite the institutional crisis, believe that they only have to do business as usual. This illusion is perpetuated principally by the insulated character of their residential base. They search frantically for techniques to improve their activities, and yet each renewal movement leads to further isolation from the metropolitan struggle. However, the servant Church takes the secularized world seriously; it acknowledges the limited role of residential congregations.

—Gibson Winter, *The New Creation As Metropolis*, pp. 57–58.

The pagan as a prospective customer.

The stranger who is visited by a representative of the Church frequently gets the impression that he is being viewed as a prospective customer, a potential addition to the numbers or the income, rather than a person who is approached for his own sake. Part of the shame of the contemporary Church is that it seems to be motivated by self-interest. We need to be reminded that the Church exists for men and not men for the Church.

—Elton Trueblood, *The Incendiary Fellowship*, p. 28.

The church building, the body of Christ.

Often people's loyalty is merely to the church building. Membership in rural areas is often not based on residence but on kinship. When people move to another area they tend to retain their membership in the former parish—often resisting transfer even though they have moved far from the effective parish area. Activity in the parish is certainly related to how close people live to the church building; a radius of 10–15 miles may be the outside limit for effective communication and participation. Further, many who are dechurched used to belong to parishes that have since disbanded. When the familiar ties to family unit, custom, or to a church building have been severed, the vacuum that is left has not been filled by loyalty to Christ. Rural people tend to identify the body of Christ with the familiar church in which they grew up.

—Paul R. Biegner, "In Town and Country," *Death and Birth of the Parish*, ed. Martin E. Marty, pp. 65–66.

Needed on every committee: one insane member.

One pastor, upon emerging from a boring and uninspiring session of his board, commented that if "our church is ever going to get anywhere, we should have at least one person on the board who is totally insane." We can see his point if we realize that radical Christianity in the local church is necessary, and the body which should produce it is that church's most responsible group. Hopefully, radical ideas will be wisely tempered, but our problem today is not that we have too much radical thinking. Our problem is that there is not enough.

—Thomas J. Mullen, *The Renewal of the Ministry*, p. 78.

We are caught in a demonic cultural trap.

And so we Protestant churchmen work hard, but we are on a treadmill. We are sincere, sacrificing, generous with time and money, loyal to our weary and harassed pastors, attentive to sermons, church bulletins, and denominational literature, but, sadly enough, without really understanding what is going on—what is happening to the church or to ourselves. We are, in fact, caught in a cultural trap which, in terms of its tyranny over our essential humanity, its defection from the deepest sources of the Judaeo-Christian heritage, its almost irresistible determination of our thoughts and actions, has all the characteristics of that which the New Testament knows as the demonic. There is nothing left for us but to fight our way out.

—Gayraud S. Wilmore, *The Secular Relevance of the Church*, p. 16.

The conventional church is neither being nor doing.

Recently I found myself one member of a panel of three persons discussing the nature and mission of the church. It happened that I sat in the middle, between a representative of the Church of the Saviour in Washington, D.C., and the minister of Judson Memorial Church of Greenwich Village, New York. The Church of the Saviour is a community of Christians who have grown through commitment, discipline, and mission into an extraordinarily deep fellowship. They are impressive chiefly because of what they *are*—their quality of being. The Judson Church is a community of Christians who have gone redemptively into the nightclubs, apartments, and cultural world of their neighborhood to be salt, light, and leaven. They are impressive because of what they *do*—their quality of doing. As the conversation proceeded, it struck me how strangely appropriate it was that I, a representative of the "conventional" parish church today, should be seated between representatives of two such unconventional Christian congregations. I felt both personally and representatively judged by the quality of *being* embodied in the Church of the Saviour and the quality of *doing* embodied in the Judson Church. In the light of their witness, the darkness of the being and the doing—the life together and the mission—of the conventional church became painfully clear.

—Robert A. Raines, *Reshaping the Christian Life*, pp. 1–2.

Give me anything but change.

The major progress that the Protestant churches will make depends on a slow change of emphasis rather than on the swift implementation of some new program. Someday it will become apparent that the churches are not social clubs or real-estate operations. Someday the prodding of a God who acts and judges will force current unsolved problems into the open: automation, true integration, population, a creative approach to the relationship of government to the individual, equal education—a host of others. One can cajole, ridicule, warn—and still we shall remain lukewarm. It is easier for us to erect monuments and rename expressways and light eternal flames (in order to avoid commitment ourselves) than it is for us to change. And it is naive to expect the churches to accept even the changes that are obviously designed to increase effectiveness. There are big if's ahead for Protestantism. They are related to the question of whether basic, entrenched attitudes can be changed. There will always be small pockets of obedience within society; often the legitimate mission of the churches has been taken over by persons who have left the church in rebellion because of the church's slowness and insensitivity. Thus one need not rest all of his hope upon the chance that major reforms will take place on the congregational and denominational level. Chances are they may not. The point is that it would be nice if they did.

—Stephen C. Rose, *Who's Killing the Church?*, p. 141.

Don't stand there talking, do something.

One of the best ways to avoid living by the gospel is to spend time discussing the doctrine of the church. A whole shelf of books has been written on this subject in recent years. In theological schools it is the center of a great deal of debate and concern. Christians are called by God to be and to act, not endlessly to discuss.

—George W. Webber, *God's Colony in Man's World*, p. 42.

The Church is caught in the sociological trap.

Religion in America is caught in a sociological trap. One jaw represents the fixed expectations of the parishioners who want a solid church organization with all the trimmings, church-as-usual on Sundays, the same old rules by which they've always lived. "I've had ten children," an angry woman told her priest. "If they change the rules on birth control I'm quitting the church." The other jaw is the pressure of a society whose slackening interest in religion brings great pressure on the churches to modernize, to arouse public interest, to get "where the action is," to be vital, to prove that they do have a useful and honest social function. To change in this direction risks alienating the great bulk of church members, while not to change risks becoming ever more isolated from the secular society. Leadership and laity, then, have different ideas about church. The leaders want a platform, a place from which to be heard on social issues. It may well be that the churchly stress on the woes of secular society betrays an inability to talk to their own members in terms meaningful to them. For the laity does not appear to be deeply involved in the pronouncements and judgments the leadership makes to the world. Church members in America look to religion for guidance, support, direction, and help in personal problems, but to individuals churches have less and less to say.

—Arthur Herzog, The Church Trap, p. 9.

Church-a-go-go.

It's not at all surprising, in view of the circumstances in which organized religion finds itself, that the churches should long to attract new people, to appeal to the urbanites and the young, to reclaim their centrality and importance. So we find, presided over by slightly anxious but always smiling "get-with-it" ministers (crammed with Harvey Cox's guidebook to religious urbanity, *The Secular City*), the jazz vespers and beat services, the guitars, the lonely-hearts socials and showings of what looks to the more straitlaced like prurient art—to bring the customers. But religion's modernity smacks of borrowed gear, as though change does not spring from genuine inner impulse but is imposed from the outside, by external necessity. Walter Kaufmann speaks of the churches' attempts "to balance the imposing archaism of most of their thought with some of the latest jargon," and indeed the churches want so hard to swing. They would like to be "relevant," "where the action is," "at the cutting edge," to "come alive in a church of dialogue" in the "inner city." The goal for themselves and for others is to become "truly human," to all but religious ears a tautology. Repeated endlessly by writer after writer in religious journals, catchwords like these reveal religion's inability to come up with fresh ideas of its own.

—Arthur Herzog, The Church Trap, p. 19.

A successful religion but a timid Church.

Religion is enormously successful. We build hundreds of millions of dollars worth of new church buildings a year. Ministers are respected and, in some cases, are national folk heroes. More significant than that, however, many

Americans are again interested in religious problems with great seriousness. And yet in our church life there is a hesitancy of purpose, a suspicion that the religious renewal in America is superficial.

                                        —Robert W. Spike, *Safe in Bondage*, p. 4.

The false dichotomy of the sacred and the secular.

The false dichotomy of the *sacred* and the *secular* is a devastating hindrance to Christian influence, and we must abandon the spurious notion that the business of the Church is sacred, while the business downtown or in the marketplace is secular; that teaching the Bible is sacred, while work is secular. For at least half of Jesus' lifetime He worked as a carpenter, and His public ministry lasted only about three years. Was He involved in *sacred* activities only during that three year period? The answer is painfully obvious! Everything He did was sacred. Even at a very young age He made it clear that He must be "about His Father's business." It is also clear that the Apostle Paul felt strongly about this when he said, "Whatever you do, whether ye eat or drink, do all to the glory of God."

                                        —Richard C. Halverson, *Relevance*, p. 77.

C. Concept of Renewal

The gathering of the weak.

The renewal of the Church will be in progress when it is seen as a fellowship of consciously inadequate persons who gather because they are weak, and scatter to serve because their unity with one another and with Christ has made them bold. This is the only kind of Christianity that can stand up to the challenge of the militant paganism and the fanaticism of the New Left. It will win, in the long run, because it is more revolutionary than they are.

                                        —Elton Trueblood, *The Incendiary Fellowship*, p. 31.

Renewal is recovery, reformation, relevance.

First, though, a paragraph or two for definition and focus are in order. The very word 'renewal' has the seeds of arrogance whenever it is allowed to suggest our human making-new of what has already been given by God. By 'renewal' I would want to suggest that process (which is always going on) by which the Church is enabled to discover the forms of Christian nurture and mission which are as faithful to the Gospel as they are appropriate to the times. With regard to this Gospel, renewal essentially means recovery; with regard to the structures, reformation; and with regard to the world, relevance. To the extent that renewal involves these elements, it has its vital and authentic origins in repentance, that 'godly grief' over our aimlessness and sin, that turning back to the sovereign God who makes all things new.

Most of us would be quick to acknowledge that renewal is as much a gift as the original Gift which inspires it, but we turn right back to the moving about of our structural furniture or vigorous efforts to "create *koinonia*." Indeed, in our haste to replace the old structures we often end up making golden calves of our new (or wish dreamed) ones. Renewal therefore seems to me to be more properly a matter of sainthood than of strategy. "The increase among men of the love of God and neighbor" remains a better criterion of church effectiveness and renewal than our questions about structure.

Further, the sociologists have made us aware, if Church history hadn't already, that institutions, like the poor, we shall always have with us. Indeed, it seems we shall always have poor institutions with us, since it is quite clear that "Institutions can never conserve without betraying the movements from which they proceed." So in all our talk of 'structures' and 'institutions' we shall need to be more concerned for their *flexibility* and *integrity* than for their replacement or abandonment. With the Bishop of Woolwich we acknowledge that the reformers and the reactionaries, the renewers and the conservers each exist by the grace of the other.

Even with these qualifications the question remains: "Can the old wineskins hold new wine?" I am tempted to answer, "Of course they can . . . if you have a thousand loyal and creative members, a budget in the hundred-thousand-dollar range, four reasonably effective ministers, and—perhaps most essential—a changing neighborhood!"

—Jared J. Rardin, "Sainthood Before Strategy," *Who's Killing the Church?*, ed. Stephen C. Rose, pp. 70–71.

Renewal is response to need and return to the faith.

But there is a quickening in the life of the Church today, visible over wide areas. It contains two elements—a response to the needs of men, and a return to search out the roots of the faith and lay hold afresh on it as a living reality. Whatever the critic may say in judgement of the darker pages of church history, he cannot deny that the Church has something of inestimable worth—a central point of recall. Christians have in certain circumstances been as rapacious, persecuting, indifferent and arrogant as other men, but always in denial of the central theme of Christianity—an act of condescending love by God to men, shown in all his dealings, and supremely in a human life given up wholly for men. Men turn back to this central theme of Christianity, usually under the stimulus of some outward pressure, some demand made by others which they cannot meet in their own strength.

—Katheen Bliss, *We the People*, pp. 19–20.

What is the only institution that does not exist for itself?

First, who are the people for whom we seek Church reform? We can give two answers to this question. Either we can say, we want more people to be with us in Church, in which case, we are the centre, and it is ourselves in whom we are interested, or, we can say, we want the Church to be with those who do not come to Church, in which case we will reform the Church for mission. We will endeavour to make it more able to go to the people and to be with them. Secondly, what are we after? Again, two answers can be given. Either we are after the preservation of our own church to continue its heritage, in which case, the centre of gravity is ultimately ourselves again, or else, we can be after the good of others. Is not this really what the Church exists for? Just as William Temple used to say that the Church is the only institution which does not exist for the benefit of its own members, and as Bonhoeffer described Jesus as "the man for others," so now the aim of reform, to which we are called by the pressures which are upon us, is to make the Church more fitted to exist for others.

—B. N. Y. Vaughan, *Structures for Renewal*, pp. 67–68.

How is the Church "born again"?

But the church is born again only as specific congregations are born again.

—Wallace E. Fisher, *From Tradition to Mission*, p. 17.

To find and follow God's will.

What happens to a man or woman in modern American church life who suddenly finds a completely new orientation by making a serious beginning commitment to find and follow God's will? Paradoxically many of us have found this sense of newness and deep engagement with life contrary to all our honest expectations as conscientious church attenders.

—Keith Miller, *The Taste of New Wine*, p. 105.

Church renewal—some conclusions are now possible.

My chief reason for writing the present book is that I believe the discussion of Church Renewal has now progressed sufficiently to make something of a conclusion possible. In recent years I have sought to read all that has been written on this important subject and to learn from all. Though all people ought to learn from one another, Christians should be particularly careful in this regard. Our model is that of the Apostle Paul, who, in writing to his fellow Christians in Rome, corrected himself to say that his purpose was to encourage the faith, not merely of the recipients of his letter, but of both parties in the correspondence (Rom. 1:12).

—Elton Trueblood, *The Incendiary Fellowship*, p. 9.

D. Theology of Renewal

Rumors about my death are greatly exaggerated.

The truth that the unconverted church can perish as a finite center in a perishing finite culture is inescapably clear, but the judgment that its demise has taken place is premature.

—Wallace E. Fisher, *From Tradition to Mission*, p. 20.

1. God's Initiative

Only God can convert people.

How wrong I have been so many times in these past few years in trying to change people instead of loving them. I believe we delude ourselves in thinking we can change people anyway. I am convinced that only God can convert anyone.

—Keith Miller, *The Taste of New Wine*, p. 51.

God has invaded our planet.

Renewal will begin when denominational decision-makers set priorities, allocate funds, procure and place staff, and judge general effectiveness by an adequate understanding of the human and divine shape of the Church of Jesus Christ, an understanding fortified by the conviction that God is at work in the city where the Church is to witness. The recognition of the activity of God in present-day political as well as personal history is not a matter to be affirmed piously and then forgotten as the Church returns to business as usual. An awareness of the involvement of God must increasingly influence and determine the way denominations spend their money in the city. This awareness must affect the kind of Church-school curriculum our denominations write, the classes and varieties of people to whom they minister, the very nature of the ministry in which they engage, the types and goals of specialized and experimental ministries they develop, the criteria they use to choose their executive leadership, the theological training they give their ministers, and the standards by which they judge the over-all success or failure of their missionary endeavor.

—Richard E. Moore and Duane L. Day, *Urban Church Breakthrough*, p. 21.

How does God make the dry bones live?

The starting point is that the renewal of the Church is the work of God and not of man by himself. That is not meant as a pious reminder that we need the help of God in all that we undertake. It is meant in a much more radical sense. All that we have found in the Old and New Testament confirms that the renewal of the Church means first of all the creative work of God among his people, the victories won by the new age over the old age. The Church does not renew itself: it is the object of God's work of renewal. 'Be ye renewed' does not mean: 'Get busy and find some different and better method of Christian action.' It means: 'Expose yourself to the life-giving work of God. Pray that he may make the dry bones come to life. Expect great things from him. And get ready to do what he commands.'

This is a very practical truth. For it implies that the renewal of the Church does not begin with more or less solemn decisions of synods, conferences or committees, but with an encounter between God and men, in which God takes hold of the situation and empowers them to serve as his instruments of renewal. . . .

But how and where do we discover what renewal according to God's will means? Every true renewal of the Church is based on the hearing anew of the Word of God as it comes to us in the Bible. This seems at first sight impossible. How can the new result from a return to the old? There have therefore been many who have sought the renewal of the Church by breaking away from the Bible or by adding to and improving upon the Bible. But we must maintain this simple truth that outside the Word of God there is in this world no true source of renewal. Why is that so? Because the Bible is the authentic record of the only radically new event that has ever taken place in the world. All other newness is either borrowed from that event or it is only newness in appearance. If the Church which seeks to renew itself takes its lead from some new religious or cultural development or some new technique, it remains in fact within the closed circle of the old world. If it turns for inspiration to some period of its own past it is not directly in touch with the source. It can only break out of the old world and enter into living touch with the new world by submitting itself to the judgment and inspiration of God's revelation itself and that revelation is given to us through the Holy Scriptures. Here alone a true dialogue can take place between the Church and its Lord. Here the Church discovers that it needs renewal and what renewal means. This 'orientation to the centre' (Cullmann) has been and is the great life-giving force in the Church and this is the true return to the source. In saying this we do not forget the work of the Holy Spirit. As we have seen, the New Testament teaches with the greatest clarity that there is no renewal except through the Holy Spirit. The Bible is a dead letter if the Spirit does not make it the living Word of God for us. But it is wholly unbiblical to oppose the spirit and the Word of God or to separate them from each other. The Spirit does not speak 'on its own authority' but speaks 'whatever he hears'. He 'takes what is mine', says Jesus (John 16.13-14). And all appeals to the Spirit which seek to by-pass the historical record of the actual work of the Lord are therefore appeals to the spirit of man rather than to the Holy Spirit.

—W. A. Visser't Hooft, *The Renewal of the Church*, pp. 90–93.

The heart of renewal is renewal of the heart.

I am convinced that the "easy Christianity" that characterizes so much of the life of the church today is totally inadequate for the kind of world we are facing. "Cheap grace" is not God's grace. It is being weighed in the balance and found wanting. The best hope for the Christian movement is fellowship at a deeper level. This fellowship does not depend so much upon new structures as upon new life within the structures we already have. New wineskins without the vital new wine of the Spirit will be just as useless as the old. The present denominations can, if they will, provide the new wineskins that are needed. The church in its present condition has many faults, but it still offers our best hope of salvation in a broken world. The greatest need, whatever the shape of the church, is for members who know "the washing of regeneration and renewal in the Holy Spirit" (Titus 3:5, RSV). Bishop Roy H. Short is right when he says "the heart of renewal is the renewal of the heart." The renewal of the church can begin with me when I pray with the Psalmist: "Create in me a clean heart, O God; and renew a right spirit within me" (Psalm 51:10, KJV).

—Russell Bow, *The Integrity of Church Membership*, p. 8.

Possessed by God's Word and proper understanding.

Disheartening personal failures and a congregation-wide fiasco in evangelistic work convinced the clergy and lay leaders that unless the Word possesses the evangelist, there is no witness to Christ; and equally, unless the evangelist understands his cultural situation, his witness will be blunted or aborted.

—Wallace E. Fisher, *From Tradition to Mission*, p. 102.

Only God can work wonders through the Church.

When the Word is heard in the congregation in real repentance and in faith—when the sacraments become the medium of the presence of that Word of Christ to each of us in his own immediate situation—then the church can be the new People of God, related to Him in confession and trust, and so related to one another and to their social environment in love and service. Only thus, through the presence of the transcendent, holy God in His congregation and not through any efforts of our own to enlarge our plants, attract more members, or gain more influence, can the church perform its task. For only God is holy, and only He can work wonders through His instrument, the church.

—Langdon Gilkey, *How the Church Can Minister to the World Without Losing Itself*, pp. 126–27.

New life comes from the Lord of life.

Reformation and renewal do not just happen by themselves, however. Nor can they be effected solely by hierarchical decrees or by stepped-up programmes of denominational advance. New life for the Church can come only from the Lord and giver of life, the Holy Spirit. And He works according to His own divine wisdom and power, which is a way of saying that He brings renewal through the continuous effect of the Word of God, incarnate in Jesus Christ, perceived and witnessed to by the apostles, and appropriated by the Church. When we deal with the idea of the Church in terms of Jesus Christ and the apostolic witness, however, we do not limit ourselves to a static situation in ancient times when Jesus of Nazareth and later some men called apostles did and said certain things. We are dealing also with the health, reformation and renewal of the Christian Church in the present day.

—J. R. Nelson, *Criterion for the Church*, p. 18.

Congregations are always reformable by the Holy Spirit.

It is extremely optimistic to hold that the pattern of the New Testament Church can be exactly reproduced today. It is excessively pessimistic to consider the present-day churches as totally beyond the possibility of expressing the genius of the Church's community in their normal life. The evidence is unconvincing that either of these extreme views need be held. Rather, we can surely hold the median position that the Church and its constituent congregations are always reformable by the effective power of the Holy Spirit. The acknowledged and deplored deficiencies of communal life and faith can be corrected by the same Spirit and according to the same criterion of the Church that was known and exemplified in the apostolic fellowship.

—J. R. Nelson, *Criterion for the Church*, pp. 29–30.

Proposition: God in Christ brings hope to the world.

What is required if both clergy and laity are to be the Body of Christ in the world is a renewed and deepened personal and corporate commitment to the gospel, and this means essentially an active, informed dedication to the proposition that God in Christ brings meaning and hope to a distraught and divided world.

—Howard Grimes, *The Rebirth of the Laity*, p. 159.

Reconciliation is the prelude to commitment.

If commitment is a necessity for the renewal of the Church, reconciliation is the reality which can make commitment possible. As adequate a summary of the gospel as John 3:16 is II Cor. 5:19: "God was in Christ reconciling the world to himself." Reconciliation is essentially the bringing of man to the place where he is himself and where he is in right relationship with God and neighbor. It is the healing of broken relationships and the restoration of the image of God in man.

—Howard Grimes, *The Rebirth of the Laity*, p. 163.

The Church as God's "happening."

The report demonstrates that, while the impasse between theology and activism in the parish can be broken, the vital congregation does not exist simply by sound theology or by the formal possession of the gospel. It testifies that the church exists by the power of the Holy Spirit through the Word in preaching, teaching, the sacraments, and man's response in commitment to this recurring Event. It views the church as "happening."

—Wallace E. Fisher, *From Tradition to Mission*, p. 19.

Renewal is men and women abandoned to God.

The church-in-the-house is a first-century church structure which can have meaning in the twentieth century, but there is no house congregation unless there are persons infused by the Holy Spirit to go out under its guidance. We can discover the twentieth-century structures, learn modern techniques, and originate challenging programs, but these in themselves are not enough. They may win people to our organizations, but not to the living Christ. For this we need men and women abandoned to God, contagiously radiant because in their inner lives a conversation goes on with Him who is Lord. They are the people who fill one's soul with a free, spontaneous worship. Thoughts begin to hurdle the usual boundaries, and you wonder why you ever doubted. In their presence your spirit has wings; you sense the very presence of God.

—Elizabeth O'Connor, *Call to Commitment*, p. 85.

Remove the cotton from your ears and listen to the Spirit.

So the question is really *how* the Church is to be in the world. How is the Church—2000 years after the Christ event—to organize itself? The Bible provides ample cause for discouragement in the face of this question. At one level, the Scriptures can be seen as the story of man's abortive attempts to capture God, to freeze Him into an inflexible and easily handled mold. Man continually attempts to perform surgery on God—usually of the heart or brain—in order to avoid the passion of His restless activity in all the world and to escape the endless depths of His mysterious presence. But the Bible is also the story of God's response. He demonstrates the folly of these attempted operations in a supreme act of self-revelation culminating in the crucifixion of the God-man who consorted with prostitutes, cast out money-changers, and suggested the possibility of resurrection. He unleashes His Spirit in the world, and when man is seized by this Spirit he can no longer remain content with his little efforts to confine God, to remove all the elements of risk and joy and suffering that the Spirit opens up. Finally, one must affirm that the Church that is deaf to the Spirit is not the Church. And with that affirmation, one rests the case for renewal, not on human plans and notions but upon the biblical call for continued openness to the Will of God. If our only achievement is to remove the cotton from the ears of the Church, that Christians might stand ready to obey, that is satisfaction enough.

—Stephen C. Rose, *The Grass Roots Church*, pp. 65–66.

2. Man's Responsiveness

And now, folks, it's time to repent.

Neither modernisation nor introspection can help the church in its present plight. Neither goes deep enough. Both have taken place without the church coming face to face with the real situation. For the church still believes that the crisis of the twentieth century is like all the others in its long history. It will pass and the church will go on. It does not see that it is fighting for its life. It is blinded by its traditional belief in its own permanence. The new thinking is of old thoughts.

For this reason the church's programme of modernisation has been limited to methods. It has not extended to aims. For this reason its self-examination has been directed to psychological reassurance, not to repentance.

For all its desire to meet the twentieth century on real speaking terms, the church is not prepared to ask radical questions about itself and its job in the twentieth century. It does not realise that new methods of doing the same thing are sometimes useless because it is not the same thing that requires to be done. It is unaware of the danger of self-assurance based on propositions it has refused to question. In the language of the church itself, the need is for repentance. And repentance is a change of heart, not a change of method or of self-esteem. To admit one's failures when they are patent to all the world is not repentance. Repentance means saying not only, "I agree that some actions have been inadequate, mistaken, wrong"; it means saying, "I have been wrong" or even "I am wrong." It is this that has not happened.

—A. Q. Morton and James McLeman, *Christianity in the Computer Age*,
pp. 48–49.

In renewal, the Church is its own worst enemy.

We need not continue the story. For these illustrations suffice to make it abundantly clear that in this task of renewal the Church is its own worst enemy. Like other institutions it seeks the security of the status quo. And almost imperceptibly it slides back from the open, dynamic life into which the

Holy Spirit pours his gifts, to the closed, introverted life of self-perpetuation. But we have also seen that this need not be its final fate. For if it allows the Word of God to do its creative work, there is always hope for its renewal.

—W. A. Visser't Hooft, *The Renewal of the Church*, p. 84.

Change is a test of the Church's faith.

Conviction that the world has not changed in any significant way usually lies back of this hope that the churches may continue in the old paths. But the Church has never continued in an old path when she has been about her true work. To be sure, the Church is the Church only as she lives out of her saving history rather than out of her own instincts or the standards of the world. However, the Church is only the Church as she mediates that saving history in the actual world where she is called to minister. That actual world has never been static and never will be until the end of time. The Church has continually altered her forms of proclamation and ministry as she has borne her witness in the changing situation in the world. Now she is being summoned to radical changes in her forms of apostolate and ministry. Her response to this summons in our time will be the test of her faith and the measure of her apostolicity as the Church.

—Gibson Winter, *The New Creation As Metropolis*, pp. v–vi.

We are called to act responsibly as God's agents.

Only God can in the final analysis reform the Church. But we are called to act responsibly even in the face of difficulties. Whatever else the clergy must do in our time, they must call the laity to responsible action as Christian disciples both in the Church and in the world.

We cannot predict how fully God will be able to work among us his work of grace. It is our responsibility only to plant and water, to be faithful in our response to the demands of the gospel. God must give the growth, but "we are fellow workers in God's service." In this service we—both clergy and laity, but especially the laity—are sent into the world God loves to be his agents of reconciliation.

—Howard Grimes, *The Rebirth of the Laity*, p. 170.

Needed: men who trust and obey God.

The church is full of men and women who are pious, religious, busy, learned, courteous, attractive. The world is full of exactly the same kind of people. The church talks a great deal about God, but the world cannot see that he makes any difference. The church has exhausted the possibilities of propaganda. In the process, it has cheapened such words as preaching, mission, and gospel to the point where they are almost meaningless. If you doubt this, spend a Sunday listening to "religious broadcasts" sponsored both by the established denominations and by fringe sects. If you don't find yourself screaming: "Words, words, words. I'm so sick of words. . . . Show me!"— well, you can listen again the following Sunday and have your reward.

What both the church and the world need—and at the moment the church needs it more than the world—is to be shown. God needs men who have heard the call, who are aware that they are free, who accept their freedom and the other riches God has bestowed, who recognize that God has sent them to the place where they are and to the people around them. God needs men who trust and obey, who believe and respond. The Bible is the record of what God has done, of the lengths to which he has gone, of the price he has paid, that there may be such men in the world.

—Francis O. Ayres, *The Ministry of the Laity*, pp. 134–35.

Good news is worth getting excited about.

And so it is perfectly natural that we should rationalize our weakness and impotence by putting a brand on the words "decision for Christ." We relegate the words and the experience to the sawdust trail or the aisle of an arena crusade, while thinking to ourselves: "This business of 'decision for Christ' is for people who like their religion hot and heavy, chiefly those who generally get overly excited about it all; but not for me; not for reasonable, dignified, well-bred me; I like my religion quiet and always in good taste."

We forget that the New Testament is not good taste but good news! And if news is really good—like the end of a long war, or the discovery of a man thought dead, or the healing of a loved one feared dying, or the coming of Almighty God to earth in person—then this news is worth getting excited about; it's worth all we are and have!

—Robert A. Raines, *New Life in the Church*, pp. 40–41.

Is there a half-way house in commitment?

A pastor, or a lay leader, who issues a serious challenge for reality of membership may shock many indifferent members. If he makes much progress, he may make some angry. When a church begins to proclaim the kind of discipleship to which we are called by Christ in the Gospels, the opposition does not come from totally inactive members. It comes from those who have some shallow commitment to the church, and may even be quite active in the program, but who do not want to be called to a deeper commitment. There is always resistance to anything more demanding than nominal membership. On the other hand, in almost every congregation there is a readiness on the part of some for a serious call to discipleship. Many more, though not ready to pay a price for genuine renewal, at least are willing to discuss it.

—Russell Bow, *The Integrity of Church Membership*, p. 7.

There is a new willingness to move out of past security.

We see the new mood also in the steady emergence of lay training centres, industrial missions, groups seeking to bring the centres of decision-making in the public world into dialogue with the gospel, and the imaginative and moving ministries which reveal an increasing sensitivity to the structured forms of need as they are produced by the relentless pressures of our urbanized technological society—ministries to drug addicts, to excluded minority groups, to demon-tossed teenagers, to school drop-outs, to the dispossessed.

As one receives from across the world the evidence of a mounting feeling that the church must now be released from its self-concern and find its life by becoming the servant body of Christ in the world, there arises the feeling that we are on the verge of the long awaited new Reformation. We have been in the midst of a renewal of Biblical theology for some time; but the renewal of theology did not lead (as many expected) to renewal of church life. But now there seem to be increasing signs of a renewal of obedience—of commitment—and a willingness to move out from the security of past forms to the shapes of contemporary need. The theological renewal which marked the movement back to the rediscovery of the roots of our faith is now being marked by the movement forward to the discovery of the 'signs of the times' from which Christ is calling us to present obedience in the world.

—Colin W. Williams, *What in the World?* pp. xiv-xv.

Breaking with the established order takes courage.

About A.D. 1206 a young Italian known to us as Francis of Assisi undertook literally to fulfill Christ's command to follow him in pouring out life in service. Embracing "Lady Poverty." as his bride, he proceeded to sever all ties with his family and to subsist by begging. He plunged himself into the labor of restoring the churches of Assisi which had fallen into disrepair. He spent much time in prayer and meditation and in doing deeds of love for those in need.

Soon, others, inspired by Francis' zealous devotion, joined him in his poverty and labor. By 1209 he had eleven followers, who counting himself, composed a latter-day version of the twelve. Together they made a profound impact on those around them.

In our day, of course, what Francis and his little band attempted for the renewal or revival of the church would not work. He lived in a society where poverty was rife and begging common; we live in a society which knows poverty only as the exception and affluence as the norm. Yet one idea in Francis' simple plan merits our consideration and perhaps emulation, his willingness to initiate something radically different in order to discharge Christ's command. It was this courage to break with the established order and to try something new that earned for him such a distinguished niche in Christian history. Our day calls for the same courage.

—E. Glenn Hinson, *The Church: Design for Survival*, p. 101.

Resources and the wise use thereof.

We can build a lot of buildings or no buildings. We can shape them like fish or like factories. We can make them round or square, or we can pitch a tent in the field. We can set up shop in a coffee house, an abandoned store, a tavern, or a county jailhouse—it does not make any difference where. The point is that unless those who are *of* the church are clearly and demonstrably different from those who are *not*—forget it. We have people, buildings, and money. Use these resources properly, and they will be added to, in great abundance.

—Perry L. Norton, *Church and Metropolis*, p. 95.

E. Search for Renewal—The Need for New Wineskins

Needed: a plunge into the concrete.

Out of the resulting frustration has come a feeling that the church is too "philosophical" in its orientation and that the philosophic mind easily forgets its base in the actualities of a man's life. It can get lost in abstractions.

—Keith Miller, *The Taste of New Wine*, p. 16.

A parable of pure prophecy for Church renewal.

In one of O. Henry's stories two parties to a feud find themselves the sole survivors when the smoke clears away. Bereft of relatives, Cal Harkness disappears from the Cumberland Mountains and gets a job driving an express wagon in New York City. A year later Sam Folwell, discovering his new place of residence, follows him to cancel out the Harkness clan once and for all.

Sam starts out on the New York sidewalks looking for Cal, his pistol strapped to his side and feud hate red in his eyes. He walks the busy streets all morning, darting nervous glances over his shoulder, fearful that Cal may be waiting in ambush behind a door or window to shoot him first. At noon Sam stands at the corner of a giant intersection. People rush at him from four directions. No faces turn toward him and no voices confirm his presence. Suddenly the foolish fear that he is dead and disembodied seizes Sam.

"Nobody can see me," he cries, as the city smites him with loneliness. There is no response.

"The Rankin's hog weighed more 'n ours," he shouts at a plump passerby. The fat man hurries on and buys a bag of roasted chestnuts to mask his alarm.

A club tickles Sam in the ribs. "Move along," says the cop. "You've been loafing here long enough." As Sam retreats across the street an automobile grazes his knee. A cab bumps him with its hubcap. The cabby purples the air with threats and profanity. A streetcar motorman clangs his bell and a newsboy joins the fray by pelting him with banana peels.

About this time Cal Harkness, whose work is over for the day, turns the corner. There, three yards away, he faces his blood enemy, the last Folwell, who has come to obliterate the last Harkness. Unarmed and unprepared, Cal wavers, but Sam's sharp eyes pick him out of the crowd. Sam rushes toward him and reaches—but not for his gun. He reaches for Cal's hand. "Howdy, Cal, I'm darned glad to see you." At the corner of Broadway and Fifth Avenue the Cumberland enemies shake hands.

Here is a parable of our life and time, a suggestive parable for the renewal of the Church in the metropolis. Written in the first decade of our century, the story is pure prophecy and basic myth. Here is the awareness that we are an urban culture in which rural values and methods of solving problems are no longer relevant. Here in the shorthand of storytelling are the migrations from farm to city and the problems of urban adjustment. Here is dramatized the opportunity to build new community in the all-pervasive environment of the metropolis.

—Richard E. Moore and Duane L. Day, *Urban Church Breakthrough*, pp. 5–6.

Five basic guidelines for renewal.

1. There must be increased participation by trained Christians in the fight to obtain social justice not only in the United States but throughout the world. . . .

2. There must be equal emphasis placed on the necessity of a renewal of the traditional functions of the Church—the nurturing of community, the teaching of the faith, and the pastoral and preaching ministries. . . .

3. An effective renewal movement will be radically ecumenical. Members of such a movement must be willing to forsake loyalty to their denominations when the denominational structures impede the development of united, ecumenical mission, particularly at the local level. . . .

4. The renewal movement must emphasize the need for a new theology which can be developed within the context of the Church as it is, rather than in the isolated corridors of the seminaries and the technical pages of scholarly journals. . . .

5. The renewal movement will accept three general principles which will form the basis for the development of a constructive strategy:

a) the priority of local ecumenicity; b) the necessity of combining existing forms of Church government to allow for decentralization, increased participation at the local level, and the development of a streamlined structure at regional and national levels; c) the need for a redefinition of Church membership in terms of "basic membership" (through baptism, confirmation, etc.) and "functional membership" (through voluntary participation in specific areas of Christian witness).

—Stephen C. Rose, *The Grass Roots Church*, pp. 4–6.

Deep thought, good tools, and an open mind.

In this time of ours three things are needed in the Church.

First, deeper theological thought about the nature of the Church as "the divine community." This theological thinking is going on actively today because churches have been coming out of their geographical, cultural and confessional isolation into living contact with one another through the ecumenical movement. Their confrontal has compelled them to ask "What is the Church?" with new insistency and openness to one another and to the Holy Spirit.

Second, a more thorough use of the tools of sociology, social history and psychology, so that we see the institutions of the Church factually and not romantically (i.e. too rosily or too blackly!).

Third, a knowledge of, and response to, some of the new ideas emerging in the life of some churches or in their common action and thought. By ideas I do not mean bright ideas. I hesitate to call them "movements of the Spirit" because that prejudges them before examination. Ideas have a history and cannot be understood apart from it. But I do not apologize because they are ideas. There is a general impatience in many circles with ideas, as an egghead's way of holding up action. However, the shape of our modern world has been very largely determined by what Karl Marx wrote in the reading-room of the British Museum. The ideas which I have in mind are ideas which seek to embody the spiritual purposes of the "divine community" of the Church in forms of social life which are more appropriate to our time.

—Kathleen Bliss, *We the People*, pp. 11–12.

What's happening in the laboratory?

What is now needed? Thought and experimentation seem to be proceeding in two directions:

First, there is the development of "small group" life (often called *koinonia groups*)—places where opportunity is given for the discovery of self-identity in the free and open meeting of persons. Here again, we may see two bases for small-group life: (i) around the Word and in seeking immediate awareness of God's will in prayer and mutual care; (ii) around a shared concern in the world—a neighbourhood, a common task, a particular problem. These are by no means exclusive bases. In fact, there is evidence that it is when these two centers coalesce—the "vertical" gathering around the Word and the "horizontal" gathering around a worldly concern—that there is a vital rediscovery of mission.

Second, there is a reaching out toward *a more inclusive strategy of mission.* There is a feeling that small group life is essential to a penetration of the broken fragments of our culture in order that the lost may be found at the scene of their lostness and there find meaning through the personal approach of Christ through the neighbour. Nevertheless the Christian mission requires more. It demands that persons be brought out of the isolation of the separated pieces of culture into the fuller unity of life in the Church. There is then the second major task. How can people be brought to a life of new unity across the separations of culture, class, race, language?

—Colin Williams, *Where in the World?* pp. 13–14.

Conservatism, hypocrisy, and cynicism—three enemies to defeat.

What then must we attack? I mention three enemies that we must defeat:

1. The too-prevalent conservative attitude that innovation is wrong per se. You will remember that I listed the new facts that we face in a changing and revolutionary world. To try to be conservative by ignoring the new conditions in which all men find themselves today and to resist for this reason the efforts to change anything is the new way to lose the battle. It is because we are conservative in the right sense that there must be innovations and risks undertaken. . . .

These are the reasons it is good to be alive in the Christian movement today and I feel sorry for all those who, through fear or misunderstanding, have not become a part of it. It is new patterns of life conserving the values of the past that are the hope of the future.

2. Again we must attack hypocrisy, which is today, as it was two thousand years ago, the chief sin of religious people. I do not believe we ought to be easily charging all who disagree with us with hypocrisy. But I do suggest that we must attack root and branch those who profess Americanism and Christianity to cover up their major concern of holding on to special privilege. We will never successfully resist atheistic communism unless we stop using God to defend pocketbooks and privilege. . . .

3. Finally, I suggest that we must attack that blighting cynicism which takes the heart out of the troops. This is where the Church has a very specific contribution to make in the course of this battle. To believe in God is to have courage in the face of defeat. To follow Jesus Christ is not to be a romantic idealist but to believe despite the sin of man, realistically observed, that men may be converted by the power of God. To be a Christian is to believe that with God the battle may be won in this world now and in eternity.

—Eugene Carson Blake, *The Church in the Next Decade,* pp. 26–28.

1. Structural Reforms

Give me room to experiment.

The salvation of a church that has almost lost its Lord lies not in forgetting Him, but finding Him again in its life. If that is to be possible, however, we must be free to experiment, not only with our theological language and our forms of mission and service, but even more with the structures of church life and organization which we have inherited from an age whose customs and spiritual forms were vastly different from our own.

—Langdon Gilkey, *How the Church Can Minister to the World Without Losing Itself*, p. 146.

What do we do with the structure?

1. The first possibility is simply to abandon the churches altogether. This is an attractive option for many people. It saves time, energy, and money. It frees us from many of the unpleasant features of church life today. The difficulty is that no matter how corrupt our church institutions may be, God is still real, and we need some structure, some fellowship through which to share and test our relationship to God. The lone individual cannot relate to God creatively without some kind of group sharing and support over the long haul. Attractive though it may be, the person who is not evading God entirely will not find this answer satisfying.

2. The second possibility is to maintain our church institutions as before. This means you must dismiss the "prophets of doom" like myself as cranks and justify what the churches are currently doing by citing all their good works. It too has many advantages. It is usually easier to maintain the status quo than to try to change it. The mass of public opinion supports the existing situation, even though most people have some deeply ambivalent feelings about it. You can maintain this stand and be recognized as a defender of right, justice, and virtue. The disadvantage is that time is running out, and the world is increasingly impatient with these self-centered and self-satisfied institutions, and it is now clear that they are not really forwarding the religious aims they claim.

3. The third possibility is to continue basically the same structures we now have but with a new vision and awareness of the Church's task to be the Church in the world. This means *adding to* the traditional worship services and church school program some renewal groups or Bible study groups, engaging in some civil rights activities, and generally coming alive to the twentieth century. This will often mean functioning as a small church within a larger church, a corps of true believers within the larger uncommitted congregation. This may be excellent as far as it goes, but it does not go far enough. It leaves the congregation with the burden of carrying the whole weight of the uncommitted fellowship. The larger group will often call the

shots and blunt the witness of the smaller group. Much of the energy and time of the committed group is necessarily spent on housekeeping details to support the religious evasion of the others. It has the advantage that it can be carried forward rather quietly without offending too many in the congregation. It adds a new dimension of depth to the life of the congregation, which appeals to some. Hopeful and encouraging as it is when this begins to happen, it is not enough.

4. The fourth possibility is being tried by groups here and there. It is to withdraw from the existing institutional structures for the purpose of becoming free to create a new and more flexible structure for a particular mission in the world. The Church of the Saviour in Washington, D.C., is one prime example of this style, and is an exciting illustration of a church that is more geared to service than to evasion. When I have spoken of the tremendous importance of this group's pioneering efforts, I have heard Christian leaders who know little about the Church of the Saviour dismiss it by saying, "Yes, but that's a special situation" or "I know, but the Church of the Saviour couldn't exist without Gordon Cosby's leadership." In spite of these neat intellectual evasions, it is increasingly difficult to dismiss the Church of the Saviour as a prototype of what a church can be. I do not mean to suggest that we try to copy what the Church of the Saviour is in its present form, for that form is constantly changing. Rather, I am suggesting it as a prototype in its capacity for continual change to meet different circumstances, its radical openness to the leading of the Spirit. It is a church on mission. Other smaller groups have followed this alternative of withdrawing from the institutional structures, but few have done it with the faithfulness of the Church of the Saviour, whose story is so well described in Elizabeth O'Connor's book *Call to Commitment*. This approach has disadvantages, too. It has the implicit danger of cutting the group off to some extent from the ongoing life of other Christians. There is the danger that the separated group may emphasize one narrow aspect of the faith and fail to see the larger whole. In spite of these dangers, it is clear that some will continue to be called to experimental structures, and some of these will surely speak a needed and welcome word of judgment or of light.

5. The fifth live option open to sincere Christians today is to work for the renewal or re-formation of the existing church organizations, so that the entire fellowship can become the Church on mission. The basic question before the churches today is whether or not such renewal is possible. It is a question to which we do not know the answer. . . . Our church structures *are* clearly rigid and resistant to change. However, appealing as his solution may be in some ways, we cannot yet surrender the possibility that the old structures may be reformed. I am not optimistic that this may be done, but I am hopeful. And I would like to be specific about the source of my hopefulness.

—Clyde Reid, The God-Evaders, pp. 99–102.

Do you think St. Paul's missionary method will work today?

The proposed structure which I shall elaborate takes into account the fundamental wisdom (and unquestionable effectiveness) of St. Paul's missionary methods: the direct training of the Church membership to assume specific tasks; the necessity of an organizational pattern that is simple, direct, and unencumbered by inflexible habits and procedures; the need for a financial policy which enables the indigenous Church to act freely and for which the local membership assumes maximum responsibility; and, above all, a sense of mutual responsibility that is truly ecumenical in scope.

—Stephen C. Rose, *The Grass Roots Church*, p. 14.

That terrible word again—"pluriformity."

In our day this can only mean that the structure of the church will be characterized by "pluriformity." This is not new. When we enter the world of the Bible we can soon see that God's presence was discerned in multiform ways. Confessions and theological expressions are expressed in a variety of the thought forms Israel encountered. But today's world is increasingly multiform. We live in an amazing variety of interdependent worlds—family, vocation, education, leisure, politics, sports, etc.—and use a wide variety of ways of thinking, feeling, and acting; consequently, there is a need for a variety of forms of Christian presence.

—Colin W. Williams, *The Church*, p. 153.

That blessed event—the local church.

To come alive at the local level, at the grass roots, can mean nothing but a re-emphasis upon the local church, and a recognition that if the church is to live anywhere it must live here, and be vital here, and powerful here, and affect human lives here. The wave of the future, in the progress of Christian unity, I am sure will be a re-emphasis upon and a new appreciation of the local church.

—Arthur A. Rouner, Jr., *The Free Church Today: New Life for the Whole Church*, p. 153.

When the chips are down, life begins to emerge.

The organization church is introverted, activistic, often superficial, and too insulated from the public concerns of life, but, when the chips are down on personal and even some communal issues, a deeply religious quality begins to emerge. This quality needs cultivation, if the organization church is to break out of its vicious circle of introverted activities. Discussion of a sector ministry and a training academy is merely indicative of possibilities for such a breakthrough; even the hope of transforming the organization church into a missionary platform assumes that the members of the churches are searching for an opportunity to share in the life of the Church—a life which is essentially mission and ministry.

—Gibson Winter, *The Suburban Captivity of the Churches*, p. 158.

Prime qualities are flexibility and specific functions.

One is forced to the conclusion that renewal is most possible when the institutional life of the congregation is most flexible. Also, one can conclude that renewed local congregations that have started from scratch have tended to concentrate on specific mission functions, rather than on attempts to give equal emphasis to every function of the Church.

—Stephen C. Rose, *The Grass Roots Church*, pp. 70–71.

Necessary structures must change and be born again.

Whether present church structures are impervious to renewal or not, there does seem often to be an unfortunate perversity about contemporary discussion of the issue. The "old structure" party is defensive; the "new structure" party is offensive. We must not let the heat of the dialogue divert us from the light of truth emerging from it. The threefold truth is that some structure is *necessary*, that structures must *change*, and that new structures are *begotten*, not made.

Structure—institutional form—is necessary for communication. Jesus was "revealed in human shape" (Phil. 2:8, NEB), the Word became flesh, and the treasure was lodged in earthen vessels. Human shape, flesh, and earthen vessel are neither expendable nor harmful; they are vehicles for the incarnation of the presence of God among us. Therefore, we will always need some structures to express and embody our life and work as the church of Jesus Christ. We cannot get away from structure, nor do we will to. Structure comes to us by the grace of creation.

But structures need constantly to be changing. . . .

So the church must always live in the tension of the old order yielding place to the new, holding fast to that which is good and reaching out to that which is better.

New structures are begotten, not made. We do not achieve new forms, we receive them. God gives both the new wine and the new wineskins, in His own time and way. It is not by our ingenuity that the reformation comes but by our obedient perception and reception of the new shapes God is preparing. There is, then, a paradoxical urgency and nonchalance about our waiting upon the Lord. We know *Who* is coming, but we do not know *what* is coming. And the question is, will we recognize Him when we see Him revealed in human shape?

—Robert A. Raines, *Reshaping the Christian Life*, pp. 7–8.

2. Relevance to the World

Shape up to the shape of reality.

Dialogue and exposure and worship and mutual acceptance are important. They are no substitutes for coming to grips with the issues in the society, that create or corrupt. Neither the minister-program-building shape nor the cross-city shape is an adequate structure for the Church in mission. There is another shape, dimly seen, tentatively identified, and partially embodied in some residential congregations, which approaches adequacy. The hope of the local congregation lies in recovering the shape of reality, of human reality in all its richness and fullness.

—Richard E. Moore and Duane L. Day, *Urban Church Breakthrough*, p. 30.

Life is a project, full of change and fury.

What is at stake in this transition? Perhaps two illustrations will indicate something of its significance.

1. Cultural analysts such as Walter Ong are speaking of the underlying change as a move from a society of *order* to a society of *movement* or constant change. It is a move from the relatively static culture of classical and medieval life where man's self-awareness was expressed in spatial, visual symbols (space being the great symbol of order) to the open, dynamic culture of contemporary life where man's self-awareness is increasingly temporal. Man no longer sees life within a fixed framework; he is aware of life as a "project" which is being realized in an emerging future.

Now if (as Ong and many other theologians are saying) this change to the open, future-regarding view is inseparably related to the Hebrew-Christian understanding of history, it follows that the dissolution of the old ecclesiologies, in favor of event or happening views is a development to be expected and welcomed. It reflects the growing victory of the historical view of existence that characterizes the Biblical understanding of God's relation to the world. But more important still, the event ecclesiology will serve to free the Christian community from overconcern with its own order and life to more active participation in the struggles of the world as the servant of Christ's historical purpose.

2. From another angle, the change has been described in terms of the collapse of a sacral framework which men previously felt essential to life's meaning. Men assumed that there was a sacral order surrounding the temporal order from which authoritative truths and sacred influences were introduced into life through divinely-given religious channels. But now this old sacral framework has collapsed, delivering life into historical categories, and delivering man into a freer way of thinking and acting. Under the sacral order attitude, society is looked upon in basically conservative terms. It is assumed that society must have structures that reflect the eternal order and that it is

held from falling into chaos only when that authoritative order is respected. The church tends to be conceived as the guardian of the sacral order. The collapse of the sacral world involves a movement from this basically conservative view of life to a future-oriented, change-expecting view of existence. When ecclesiology is changed accordingly, then the church is freed from its conservative role and freed for its task amid the radical changes of our times.

—Colin W. Williams, *The Church*, pp. 38–39.

The gospel is for the simple heart.

It is astonishing how primitive the enlightened man of the modern age has again become and how elementary his reactions are. If the church wants to win his heart, it must first find this simple heart.

—Eberhard Stammler, *Churchless Protestants*, p. 164.

Called to a full-time life in the world.

The real crisis in the life of the Church today is surely our discovery, under the guidance of the Word of God, and under the disciplines of worldly movements around us, that God is not calling us to be 'more religious' but to a persistent caring for His world and His children. We need to discover and confess that we had ceased to care about the life of the world. In the words of the Japan consultation, 'The church must not only share the burden of man's sufferings but must determine what God wills His people to do at this very moment. It must also rear the kind of men who will stand up and fight to improve the structure of our society.'

It is obvious that if we are to regard Christian service in this light, if we are to bring the dynamic faith right into the life of our congregations, it will bring about a radical alteration to the familiar structures of our congregational life, and a new mutual dependence between the minister and his people. The minister will truly become the servant of his people for Christ's sake (and not their master as chief organizer or agent in all the work of the Church). The calling of the layman will not be conceived as his 'spare-time' devotion to the needs of the Church, but as his full-time life in the world. And the worship life of the congregation will become the inspiration and power house of its whole life, for the relevance of the Gospel that is powerful, because of the fellowship of His people in worship, will become clear to them.

What is implied is a revolutionary change of direction, of understanding the structures of Christian service, one of the main characteristics of which will be that every Christian will be aware that he stands as a minister of Christ's redemption in the life of a world which, whatever its appearance and present reality, is being redeemed.

—Alan A. Brash, "The Church's Diakonia in the Modern World," *Service in Christ*, eds. James I. McCord and T. H. L. Parker, p. 205.

You are saints. Show this to society.

But two strong convictions undergird the pastors' convictions about the church's mission. First of all, they believe *individual church members need to relate what they believe to the tasks to which God has already called them.* "Some of our people are in strategic positions of leadership already," Lloyd observes, "in social organizations, in institutions working with the troubled and the indigent, in groups working toward racial integration, in educational agencies, in the power structures of industry and civic government. Our people have infiltrated every corner of the community. Our task is to equip them to communicate the love and forgiveness and lordship of Jesus Christ to the world of business and society. I still think the way the world will be changed is through changed people who take seriously their witness in the community and become involved in changing the laws, regulations, housing conditions, or whatever binds or debilitates human beings in discovering their full heritage as children of God. In a time like this a Christian must spend time in prayer and study to know the mind of Christ. He must also be in fellowship with others for encouragement and correction, and he must discern what Christ is doing in the world. In other words, we are not to work to win the world for Christ; it already belongs to Him. We are to allow Him to work in us and through us.

"When you're in a town like this with a large major industry," he goes on, "it's wrong to spend your energy complaining about its influence in the church. Our men are steel men and God loves steel men. I think it's my responsibility to be with these men in the stream of life as well as in the church—at their jobs, at breakfast and lunch, asking them the question, 'What does your faith mean to you here, in the responsibilities and ambiguities and conflicts of this kind of life?' "

A second conviction underlies the mission of First Presbyterian Church, Bethlehem, in the world: *no social action can be authentic unless it has a solid base in redeemed individuals.*

"I envision the layman," Lloyd Ogilvie says, "out in the stream of life, in the situations and crises of our community, equipped with a personal relationship to Christ, empowered by His Spirit, knowledgeable with the plumb line of His will, in fellowship with other Christians so as to withstand the pressures and ambiguities of life. In the church, I ask what we must do to provide all the resources to train and equip that person. I see everything in that light—worship, fellowship, study—and it provides the basis to judge what should have priority and what should be eliminated as irrelevant."

—Walden Howard, *Nine Roads to Renewal*, pp. 120–22.

Denominational showdown in the city.

Should the mood of the Church as it confronts the ever growing, often engulfing development of urban life be one of profound despair, anxious alarm, measured optimism, or euphoric rejoicing? Perhaps it should be a mixture of all these to do justice to the complex situation in which the Church in the city finds itself as the world moves toward the end of the twentieth century. To the degree that denominations are turning to the city with rekindled zeal to develop a relevant and revolutionary ministry, renewal is taking place. To the degree that they drag their ecclesiastical feet, renewal is only a fond hope for the future.

—Richard E. Moore and Duane L. Day, *Urban Church Breakthrough*, p. x.

The retreat to "fortress suburb" is slowing down.

The city is the place from which main-line Protestantism retreated—physically, mentally, and morally—during the twenties and thirties of the present century. As newcomers arrived at the center of the city, the older inhabitants, many of whom had a traditional Protestant background, spilled over into the suburbs. They packed up their churches and took them along. In the cities where these churches once ministered, there are as many people as there ever were. But now the ghost of a demolished church hovers over a parking lot; or the church building, still standing, bears the sign of some exotic sect on its door.

This retreat has not consisted simply of a withdrawal of residential congregation from the inner city. It has been marked by an increasing preoccupation with self-serving institutional programs, a separation of religion from the structures of reality, and a shrinking from encounter with the public and vocational world where the metropolis shapes its future. If the Church is the outpost of the Kingdom of God on the frontier of human need, thrust into urban life to witness and to serve, then Christians have much to account for. While the angel of the Lord has blown the trumpet for the charge against forces that confuse and depersonalize those who throng the city streets, the faithful have stumbled over each other in their retreat to a fortress farther out.

There are clear signs that this retreat has been or is being reversed—in the fifties, with the development of the Protestant Parish movement; in the sixties, with the employment of urban specialists, the assumption of responsibility by denominations for inner-city churches, the experiments in new forms of encounter with the "worlds" of the metropolis, and the general ferment for renewal that pervades all these activities and others unnamed in these pages.

—Richard E. Moore and Duane L. Day, *Urban Church Breakthrough*, pp. x–xi.

3. A New Quality of Life—Recovering the Gospel

The Church is both obstetrician and pediatrician.

The church must prepare her people for a lifetime of growth. With one hand the church reaches out to awaken persons to decision for Christ; with the other hand the church guides persons to grow up in every way into Christ. The church is both evangelist and educator, both obstetrician and pediatrician, helping deliver those newly born in Christ and nurturing them from infancy to maturity in Christ. The pastor corrects the evangelist by preparing his people for the struggle for growth.

—Robert A. Raines, *New Life in the Church*, p. 48.

Want to see the Church explode?

The Church cannot fulfill its sacred vocation unless it is a penetrating force, as salt is, and the penetration cannot even begin unless the fellowship which is the Church has something of the character of an explosion. Little can be done with a smoldering fire; somehow there must be a blaze. But how is this to be achieved? We do not know all of the answers to this practical question, but we know something. Since the starter of the fire is Christ Himself, our initial means of achieving a real blaze is that of confronting Him as steadily and as directly as is humanly possible. When the closeness to Christ is lost, the fire either goes out or it merely smolders, like the fires in the great swamps which are hidden from the sun. A Christianity which ceases to be Christ-centered may have some other valuable features, but it is usually lacking in power.

To confront Christ is really to allow Him to confront us, both as a group and singly, for we are changed by direct acquaintance. Fortunately, this is made possible, in part, by the incredibly valuable accounts preserved in the Gospels. These we can study scientifically, as well as devotionally, and the reader is almost sure to be deeply moved by both approaches. If any sincere seeker will try the experiment of reading the Gospels for a year, slowly and consecutively, but, above all, prayerfully and also with an open mind, it is practically certain that something of importance will occur in his life. If he stays close enough, for a sufficiently long period, to the central fire, he is likely to be ignited himself. But, since Christ is alive, we need not be limited to the written word. He is really as close to any humble searcher now as He was to Andrew and Simon by the Sea of Galilee. The history of the Church, in all of its most vital periods, has been a continual verification of the prediction that, if anyone hears His voice and opens the door, He will come in (Rev. 3:20).

—Elton Trueblood, *The Incendiary Fellowship*, pp. 115–16.

There is a little Church within the Church.

The idea of *ecclesiola in ecclesia* (the little church within the church) is a useful one for our time. . . .

In churches and schools I have found many people who say they wish someone would start a group for serious religious study, prayer, and action. Anyone who holds such a desire should himself begin.

Let him first of all seek, by meditation and prayer, to purify and sharpen his own Christian concern for the venture.

Then, if a layman in a local church, he will usually do well to approach the pastor and ask for his leadership or at least cooperation. Such a request would be most heartily welcomed by innumerable pastors and would bring a whole new life to the ministry of many.

In some situations the person to be approached for leadership should be the teacher of a church school class, an officer in a women's society, a deacon, or lay leader. Sometimes the person with the concern should simply take the initiative by inviting some others, by personal call or a general announcement, to meet together for serious consideration of means for deepening spiritual life and making more effective Christian witness.

Whoever makes such a call must be ready for surprises. Perhaps no one will respond. In that event, the person who is concerned must simply work harder at his own life of prayer, study, and concerned action, and try to win some other person or persons to similar involvement. On the other hand, the number and kind of people responding may be startling.

—L. Harold Dewolf, *A Hard Rain and a Cross*, pp. 208, 210–11.

How the apostles did it—preach and teach.

Preaching, teaching, the administration of the sacraments, counseling, visitation, pastoral conversation, "encounter" groups, Bible study groups, youth meetings, catechetical classes are some of the human activities which were employed at Trinity. To assign priority to any one of them would be to report inaccurately. The key to parish renewal does not lie in any single function of ministry. The apostles did not cease to *preach and teach* Christ daily in many ways, in many places. We took this to be the tactics for parish renewal. Certainly we did not assume that preaching, independent of other functions of ministry, could motivate and equip members to witness and render priestly service. But reminding ourselves daily that "Jesus came preaching," we did discover that it is not the ineffectual activity which some contemporary critics consider it to be. However, the critics were right in this: parishes which are mired in religiosity and preoccupied with their institutional life are heavily insulated against the demands and promises of God.

—Wallace E. Fisher, *From Tradition to Mission*, p. 50.

If the pastor is on fire, people will come to watch him burn.

Who is responsible for the situation we are in? As a clergyman, I must accept my part of the blame. Very little renewal will take place without the renewal of the ministry. Any pastor who is willing to pay the price can start where he is with the renewal of his own ministry. If he allows the Holy Spirit to set him on fire, people will gather around to see him burn! At least some members of the congregation will catch on fire. The church is so ripe for renewal today that a few more fires here and there may be enough to start a reformation.

—Russell Bow, *The Integrity of Church Membership*, p. 29.

Communicating living Christianity is a way of life, not a program.

As I began to read the New Testament accounts I saw that Christ almost never "went out of His way" to help anyone. He seems to have walked along and helped the people in His path. He was totally focused on doing God's will and going where God led Him. *But* he never failed to help the people He met along the way while going where God directed Him. This made for an amazing steadiness and spiritual economy in His direction and ministry. This one change in my perspective made witnessing not a program but a *way of life*.

The second thing I realized was that we Christians have so cheapened the Christian message that most thinking people don't want any part of it. Our attitude betrays our lack of real faith. We act as if we were selling tickets to something, or memberships, instead of introducing people to Almighty God in an eternal and conscious relationship. When a person buys a theater ticket he doesn't even have to think about it, it is such a casual thing; and his attitude and verbal exchange with the ticket girl reflects this. But when you walk into a room in which two large corporations are about to consummate a merger, there is an air of gravity. Even a casual observer can tell that something important is taking place—because of the attitudes of the participants as they go about their business.

—Keith Miller, *The Taste of New Wine*, pp. 91–94.

Developing a well-grounded set of convictions.

What the church of Christ and the leaders of the church of Christ must understand is that the world—seeking masses and church members alike—is looking for a quality and not a quantity in the church's worship. It is looking for something intangible, undefined, but nevertheless very real. It is looking for something in the very heart and life of both the preacher and the people who represent the church to them.

There is a great deal of talk these days about "communicating the gospel" as if what is needed is not only new means and media, but also a new language, a new idiom. Unquestionably new words must be found and new meaning put into old words if the eternal Word is to get through to modern men. But what the avant-garde leaders of the church today do not yet understand is that the world is looking to the church not nearly so much for new words and a new idiom as it is looking for new men and a new people. For two thousand years it has been the changed life, the new creature, the new man, the man with a faith, the man with the Spirit who has been really convincing, who has really "communicated," who has really convinced and changed other men.

It is this quality of "spirit" with which the world unconsciously, I think, is testing the church today. It is out of patience with the staid forms, the stuffy customs, and the shallow people it has too often found. It wants an end to insincerity and preachy tones and unreal piety.

This is why the great interest in new forms of worship and church life: the small groups, the idea of retreat, store-front churches, worker-priests as in France, coffee shops manned by Christians as in Burlington, Vermont, and Washington, D.C., the Jazz Mass, and the whole relation between religion and drama, religion and painting, religion and poetry.

They are hungry for the Spirit—and they really want to find it in people.
—Arthur A. Rouner, Jr., *The Free Church Today: New Life for the Whole Church*, pp. 85–86.

What the world wants is quality, not quantity.

Unless we have a better study of theology in the Church there will be a disastrous falling away. Many members admit, when pressed, that they think that much of what the leaders of the Church are saying is not true and is said only as a kind of ritual. Thousands, who try to be good Christians, are deeply worried about the contrast between science and religion, convinced that scientific truths are verified, while religious truths are only affirmed. Nearly all of this problem could be solved by a better understanding of the impossibility of absolute proof, in science or anywhere else, and by a deeper conception of what the evidence for the basic Christian affirmation really is. Almost any thoughtful student can come to see that the alleged contrast between scientific certainty and religious wish-thinking is not what it is popularly supposed to be.

The best insurance against falling away is the development of a profound and well-grounded set of convictions. The good teacher can deal with the powerful cumulative evidence for the being of God; he can deal realistically with the difficulties of belief, such as those involved in the problem of evil; and he can show that survival after bodily death is more than a mere hope. Millions who are now church members have never engaged in any such study in all their lives. This is why they are such easy targets for the passing intellectual fads and also why they finally lose interest in the life of the Church. Ushering on Sundays and singing in the choir will not, in the long run, be substitutes for genuine conviction.

—Elton Trueblood, *The Incendiary Fellowship*, p. 46.

II

The Crisis

of the

Institutional Church

The imperative for our time is conversion within the church.
—Robert A. Raines, *New Life in the Church*, p. 77.

A. THE EDIFICE COMPLEX—EXPOSING THE PROBLEM

An institutional crisis is upon us.

Metropolitan and urban conflict press the churches toward a reconsideration of their nature and task; in fact, we are experiencing an institutional crisis in American Christianity. This crisis appears in almost every aspect of the life of the churches. Pastors, for example, are raising more and more questions about the pastorate—wondering if the proliferation of organizational activity is really an expression of their vocation. Furthermore, an institutional crisis undermines the office of leadership; there is considerable evidence that pastors feel the instability of their position—often manifesting this instability in emotional disturbance. The literature on the inadequacies of organizational Christianity gives further testimony to this crisis, even as recent attempts to renew the congregation indicate an awareness that the

76

successful church may be spiritually empty. The major impact of the metropolitan struggle, however, is to disclose to the churches their isolation from the moving forces of the society, to convince them that they have lost touch with the central dynamic of the society.

—Gibson Winter, *The New Creation As Metropolis*, pp. 6–7.

Metropolis has forced the crisis.

The churches are becoming aware of their isolation in an interesting way; their awakening represents the final stage in a long process during which Christianity lost touch with the mainstream of American life. *The emergence of the laity* as the ministering center of Christianity is the creative response of Christianity to this social and cultural estrangement. The institutional crisis may be the moment of birth for a new form of Western Christianity— a new image of the Church—the servanthood of the laity. This new form of the Church can be understood only in the light of the metropolitan struggle and the institutional crisis which it has precipitated.

—Gibson Winter, *The New Creation As Metropolis*, pp. 6–7.

The stage is set for debate.

The stage for debate is set: In an era of change, what kind of Church? In a world of personal and social disease, what character of ministry? In a period when diffused energies only perpetuate and deepen confusion and decay, what are the vital thrusts, the positive programs, the crucial understandings?

The emerging debate centers on the nature of the Church, and of the individual congregation within the Church. The reason for debate is that the working out of a positive Church program in this decade will threaten the existence of established structures. What emerges should thus be the product of a willingness of all concerned to openly and honestly evaluate every aspect of church life, looking toward renewal.

Surely the first mark of renewal must be the recovery of a sense of authenticity that can be communicated both in public worship and in the activity of the laity both in and beyond the church building. Such renewal can occur only with a different concept of the ministry and of church organization.

—Stephen C. Rose, *Who's Killing the Church?* p. 126.

The organization Church is an arrested form of the true Church.

The organization church is an arrested form of development of the Church. Many forms of embodiment of the Church have emerged in the process of history—the New Testament household, the community of saints in Jerusalem, the medieval parish, the monastic communities, the mendicant orders, the

Protestant congregation, the lay academies. Each of these forms provided a mode of communion for Word and people and a vehicle of proclamation to the world. *A true form of the Church always appears as a mode of communion between God and man and a vehicle of mission to the world, for the ministering fellowship is simultaneously the receiving community.* The organization church is arrested at the stage of creating a viable mode of communion —a stable form for receiving community in the changing metropolis. The introversion of the organization church is symptomatic of its struggle to survive as a receiving community; yet, this very introversion corrupts its nature and transforms it into a collective. The elaboration of this organizational form—staking out its area of responsible ministry across the lines which divided the metropolis—can renew the receiving community as a ministering fellowship. This is the crucial step in the evolution of the organization church as a true expression of the Church. When the receiving community becomes the giving community, its form will be true to the Church. For this reason, the organization church, despite its activity, is not really organized enough; it is an arrested form of the co-ordination of ministries in the missionary task.

The organization church can only evolve toward a true form of the Church if its formation is guided by the missionary task. Our common calling—the missionary task—presses us toward the proper form of our life, and is precisely the point in question today. Beyond their own survival, the churches evince little sense of their task in the metropolis; yet, this task alone can light the way to the true form of the Church in the metropolis.

—Gibson Winter, *The Suburban Captivity of the Churches*, pp. 158–59.

From experiential religion to a secondhand faith.

While the beginnings of three major religious movements were characterized by a vital and experiential type of religion, yet each, unaware of what was happening, went through the usual stages into institutionalized forms. The first movement was Judaism from Ezra and the return of the Jews from Exile to the Pharisaism denounced during the earthly ministry of Jesus. The second movement was Christianity from the time of Jesus to the matured Roman Catholicism of the Middle Ages. The third covers the period from the Reformation under Martin Luther to the state churches in England and on the Continent.

—Findley B. Edge, *A Quest for Vitality in Religion*, p. 38.

Institutionalism—from womb to tomb.

Another evidence of the world in the church is the frenzied institutionalism which marks the Christian movement on many fronts. This institutionalism may well be prompted by the fear that the church's power and glory are slipping and that we must build boxes in which to keep these qualities lest we lose them entirely. The time was when the verbalized motto of most foreign mission societies was, "Institutionalize or Die." The policy still generally prevails. So while Communists are sending one man or a half dozen operatives into key spots like a national university to touch the lives of literally hundreds of tomorrow's key leaders, the churches have pursued a policy of building huge brick buildings to house institutional programs even if this approach clearly and abysmally fails to produce spiritually acceptable results.

Our institutionalism is to be seen not only in our local churches and in our foreign mission programs but also in our colleges, our children's homes, our homes for the aging, our bent to building, our edifices and "sanctuaries," our boards, bureaus, committees, and our parochial schools.

—Foy Valentine, *The Cross in the Marketplace*, pp. 46–47.

Institutionalism—a good instrument but an inadequate God.

What can the free churches do with their institutionalism? They can give up their radical freedom or they can give up their institutionalism. They cannot have both. No consequential organized group in history, however, has ever voluntarily given up its institutions and its institutional programs. None probably could have done so and lived. It is clear that the radical freedom which many American churches have wistfully clung to is going. Perhaps it has, in fact, already gone. One of the most important questions facing Christians today is the evolving of a satisfactory integration of Christian freedom on the one hand and Christian institutionalism on the other. Institutionalism is an impressive instrument but a grossly inadequate god.

—Foy Valentine, *The Cross in the Marketplace*, p. 48.

The "live ones" and the defensive institution.

This new order of "live ones" has realized that the universality of Christ's message is only intelligible as it is focused in *specific* lives and *specific* vocational situations which demand specific decisions for or against Christ's will as it can be perceived in the struggles for power, for prestige, and for material goods.

This new fellowship was brought into existence when some deeply concerned laymen found the institutional church defensive concerning the structured programs and in many cases unprepared to face the problems confronting this new body of missionaries—to the specialized vocational life of our generation. Some Baptist, Methodist, Episcopal, and Presbyterian laymen who were trying to commit *their whole* lives to Christ found that they had more in common with each other than with some of the pillars of their own denominations.

These men and women were not the "Junior-Preachers" of a day gone by. They were not like clerical assistants wanting only more academic knowledge than their fellows about the theology and worship of the church—though they wanted this too—; instead they constitute a new body of disciples concerned about the *love* of God.

—Keith Miller, *The Taste of New Wine*, pp. 16–17.

The way of the dinosaur.

The real trouble is not in fact that the Church is too rich but that it has become heavily institutionalized, with a crushing investment in maintenance. It has the characteristics of the dinosaur and the battleship. It is saddled with a plant and a programme beyond its means, so that it is absorbed in problems of supply and preoccupied with survival. The inertia of the machine is such that the financial allocations, the legalities, the channels of organization, the attitudes of mind, are all set in the direction of continuing and enhancing the *status quo*. If one wants to pursue a course which cuts across these channels, then most of one's energies are exhausted before one ever reaches the enemy lines.

—John A. T. Robinson, *The New Reformation*, p. 26.

Oh where, oh where has the charisma gone?

A second social fact revealed by a close scrutiny of the tension between the elect and the elected is the decline in charismatic authority as the charisma (gift of grace), which originally was doubtless personal, becomes institutionally structured. The effectiveness of a free and institutionally unrestricted charismatic individual leader seems to deteriorate as the charismatic authority attaches more to an office. Put another way, the personal charismatic is free to be emotional and to exercise authority without regard to the structures and imperatives of an organization. The institutional charismatic, the office-holder in an organization, whose authority inheres in his office, is obliged to be more rational, performing as a member of a team according to what the team or staff expects of him. Moreover "institutional charisma" tends to become differentiated and standardized. In large-scale ecclesiastical bodies it becomes an elaborate system of ranks and functions with corresponding degrees of authority, privilege, and honor.

As increasing emphasis is placed upon preparation, training, and professional qualifications, the tendency is to find persons who measure up to the external specifications of a given office. The office-holder who is personally endowed with great spiritual and intellectual and moral gifts (personal charismatic authority) is under a great tension to keep his gifts exercised within bounds and institutionally channeled, lest he interfere with the orderly and efficient administration of the work of the Church.

Because the official or institutional charismatic church leader must be preoccupied with the needs of the organization he serves; because he must preoccupy himself with the correctness of institutional form and procedure and demonstrate a continuing concern for the public image of his Church, he tends to neglect those other gifts (charismata) which keep him and his Church vital, efficacious, and creative. Charismatic authority in Churches, therefore, is inevitably dissipated by such things as an overemphasis upon the rationalization of church offices and the Churches' concern with correct belief more than a qualitative Christian experience of their members. Yet we cannot deny the relation of sound doctrine and faith to the qualitative Christian experience. Also, this charismatic authority is dissipated by an insistence upon the exercise of law to the neglect of a balanced emphasis upon the Spirit.

—Jesse McNeil, *Mission in Metropolis*, pp. 48–49.

If it's good enough for the institution, it's good enough for Christ.

Local churches, and denominations, tend to become institutionalized, and as this happens they become subject to the effects of institutional blight.

One of the tragic failures of churchmen today is to recognize that by its nature the local Protestant church is both a part of the body of Christ and a secular organization; the church is both a called-out community in which the Word is preached and the sacraments are duly administered and a highly institutionalized human organization.

Every church member who is involved in helping his local church plan for its future should be aware of this factor of institutionalization and of the blighting effects it may have on the congregation. Without an appreciation of this factor it will be difficult to understand the perspective of many members of the congregation. It may even be impossible to communicate with them.

Institutional blight is an affliction which plagues many organizations, not just churches, and is a growing problem in our society, in which formal organizations play such an important part in the private lives of most individuals. This malady takes many forms, and only a few are peculiar to Protestant churches.

Perhaps the most common form of institutional blight is that the instinct for self-preservation becomes the dominant motive in decision making. In the church this will mean that alternative courses of action are selected, not on the basis of service in the name of Christ, but on the basis of increasing the institutional strength of the church. "What is good for this church is good for Christ" might be the appropriate motto in these circumstances.

—Lyle E. Schaller, *Planning for Protestantism in Urban America*, pp. 137–38.

Institutional churchmanship cannot express the new life.

In their examination of the Scriptures as converted Christians, men and women are discovering that institutional churchmanship, as it is commonly known in the United States, simply does not express for them the wholeness of the new life they are experiencing. Christ is tearing out the partitions in men's souls between vocation, church, and home and making a one room dwelling place for Himself in their whole lives.

—Keith Miller, *The Taste of New Wine*, pp. 17–18.

Martin Luther, do you recognize your children?

It is ironical that Protestantism, after rebelling against the institutional character of Roman Catholicism, should emerge in the 1960s with a membership predominantly oriented to organizational activities and concentrated in the middle years—families with growing children, high earning power, and more than average energy. In other words, Protestantism today represents the dominant group in America's productive process.

—Gibson Winter, *The Suburban Captivity of the Churches*, p. 100.

We are stranded on the shores of the stream of change.

If we continue to live in the received institutions, we are in danger of being stranded on the shores of the stream of change. So our question is, How can a church that still lives in many of the institutional forms it created in the lost religious age—the age of Christendom—reshape its life so that it is freed for a real encounter with the present secular age?

—Colin W. Williams, *The Church*, p. 30.

This is the end of the road.

We find ourselves in a situation that is strangely paralleled by the beginnings of Christianity. There are many similarities between that era and ours. To discern them calls for considerable care and concentrated attention. We are beginning to discover a connection between the launching of the Church nineteen hundred years ago and the end of a road that we now seem to have reached. The validity of historic ecclesiastical structures (and all that goes with them) is now open to question. That validity seems certain to vanish. The Church, as we know it, was always subject to rapid changes and divisions, yet it has nevertheless, at any rate over the last fifteen hundred years, had a discernible inner and outer unitary structure. The question as to whether this Church can survive into the future has only now become a radical reality.

—Hans Jurgen Schultz, *Conversion to the World*, pp. 54–55.

The bureaucratic mind-set of denominational executives.

And though these denominations seem stronger than ever, though their official positions in favor of racial justice and social concern and mission to the secular city would seem to put them in the vanguard of the great movements of our time, there is noticeable already the beginning of impatience with the denominational stance, the heavy machinery of denominational apparatus, the slow-moving process of denominational decision, and even the bureaucratic mind-set of denominational executives. Men in the field, men out in the church where the fight is on daily to win the minds of modern men, are not likely to have patience long with the back-stage struggles and the open floor fights of the power struggles of denominations. Whether it be Peter Berger raising the cry in his *The Noise of Solemn Assemblies,* or Stephen Rose making pointed jibes in his *Who's Killing the Church?,* criticism of the tendency of large structures of the church's life to heavy-footedness is growing.

—Arthur A. Rouner, Jr., *The Free Church Today: New Life for the Whole Church,* p. 49.

Institutions are flexible; institutionalism is not.

The basic obstacle facing the renewal movement is the tendency to confuse *institutions* and *institutionalism.* The Church is necessarily an institution. The question is one of how the institution is organized, of whether it is flexible enough to adapt to new situations. The institution that takes renewal seriously makes continual provision for its own transformation from one form into another. Institutionalism, on the other hand, is the loss of flexibility, the tendency to cling to old patterns, the stubborn refusal to change. The distinction should be clear enough, but there are those within Protestantism whose discouragement with present structures is so great that they have made institutions rather than institutionalism the archenemy. This has enabled preservers of the status quo to make the common charge that many critics of the Church want to throw out the baby with the bath water. The anti-institutional approach enables persons who defend the *institution* to avoid the more relevant charge that the Church has become mired in the mud of *institutionalism.*

—Stephen C. Rose, *The Grass Roots Church,* pp. 17–18.

An experiment in freedom, always on the move.

The only principle that can maintain the Church is its renewal.

The Church is in no position to base itself on the Incarnation if at the same time it attempts to justify the immobility and untouchability of its institutions. My criticism is not an attack on institution that becomes an end in itself, that goes on functioning when it has become irrelevant, that has no historical perspective and that in the last resort is a perversion of true spirituality. The relative is treated as though it were absolute. And at the same time, it is not understood that absolute values can only be recognized in the context of the relativities of ordinary life. Christianity cannot be institutionalized independently of the processes of history. The Church is an experiment in freedom always on the move. It must always be contemporary. An antiquated Church is not merely a tragedy but an impossibility; it is no Church at all. Those therefore who want the Church to remain as it is are hardly likely to be its friends.

If the Church has the will to start serving those from whom it has hitherto stood aloof it will need to stop defending its present structure and begin to reshape and diversify itself imaginatively and generously. Failing that, it will never be all it should be to all men and will continue to be of no more than little use to a few men. As it is, the Church is reduced to a middle class institution, narrow-minded and stuffy. And so a totally misleading image is created. We label as faith what is a mere expression of opinion. To many people this bourgeois code, this stuffy atmosphere, the blinkered outlook is unbearable. In consequence their relationship to the Gospel remains an open question. Their queries, expectations and hopes never come near to being taken seriously.

—Hans Jurgen Schultz, *Conversion to the World*, pp. 112–13.

The official credentials of the transformed.

There is no organization; there are no dues, no memberships—in fact there is only one reason they can be called a "band." They have in common only the Lordship of Jesus Christ and a deep conviction that His call is to the *whole man*—vocation and all. When investigated, the only credentials this group can present to their sometimes skeptical denominations are the hundreds of transformed and growing lives in the wake of their witness. They are often disturbing. For these modern disciples are not satisfied with abstract statements of doctrine—however accurate. They feel a strange dichotomy between the church's doctrinal statements and the problems of the market place as they *actually are*.

—Keith Miller, *The Taste of New Wine*, p. 16.

Be prepared. God may destroy the present form to create a new one.

The Church is a historically evolved form, a vessel of the *Ecclesia;* not to it, but to the *Ecclesia* alone, was given the promise of invincibility and eternal durability. Since Christianity for the first time in the Reformatoin era grasped the fact that the essence of the *Ecclesia* was in principle distinguishable from, and in part opposed to, the vessel of the church which contained it, ever new attempts have been made to give the Christian community the external form which best fits it. One of the most important results of the ecumenical movement has been to make Christianity aware of the multiplicity of these outward forms, and the necessity of their manifold variety. We have become painfully aware that the multiplicity of the churches calls in question the fundamental oneness of the *Ecclesia:* but whether this fundamental unity of the Christ-community requires unified expression in one church is extremely doubtful.

Through ecumenical conversations we have learnt to realize the relative justification of all these various forms and the specific service which each of them in virtue of its special characteristics renders towards the maintenance, the purification, the strengthening and the propagation of the *Ecclesia*. In most recent times we have been compelled to recognize that the same *providentia Dei* which permitted the growth of the Church or churches, has brought into being totally new forms of Christian communion wherein any hint at the classic traditional ecclesiastical form has been consciously avoided. We must therefore be prepared for the possibility that it might be the will of God eventually to destroy the ancient churchly framework of the *Ecclesia* or at least—as is now already happening—to complete it by structures of a very different order. One of the chief practical concerns of this book has been to try to ensure that we do not oppose the divine intention by any self-willed *a priori* ecclesiasticism.

The second is this. During the whole course of its history, by reason of the fact that it was essentially a collective rather than a fellowship, the Church has not only neglected to create a true brotherhood in Christ, but in many ways has positively hindered such a development. Yet just here lies the essence of the New Testament *Ecclesia*—the oneness of communion with Christ by faith and brotherhood in love. Therefore efforts to create new forms of Christian communion at the present time are directed to this end and will be so much more in the future. It is because the Church has neglected in almost all ages to create a true fellowship in Christ that we are confronted by the phenomenon of modern communism which has grown like a wasting disease. With or without the churches, if necessary even in opposition to them, God will cause the *Ecclesia* to become a real community of brothers. Whether the churches yield to this recognition or on the contrary blind themselves to it will determine the question whether or not they have a future.

—Emil Brunner, *The Misunderstanding of the Church*, pp. 117–18.

B. Debate—Can the Present Scaffolding Bear the Stress?

The old structures can't be renewed.

I want to clarify several things. The Holy Spirit is still at work in the old structures. People still get converted in them, and personal growth takes place in them. One reason it has been so difficult for me to come to the conclusion stated above is that I, myself, came to know Jesus Christ through the old structures. This reproach has been thrown at me time and again, and it is true. So it is with great reluctance that I have to say that I do not believe

that the old structures can be renewed. This is not the way it seems to me
God will work in our time.

—Gordon Cosby, "Not Renewal, But Reformation," *Who's Killing the Church?*
ed. Stephen C. Rose, p. 54.

Present structures need not be abandoned for renewal.

This much is clear: the reformation of tomorrow's church is not dependent
on our abandonment of today's institutional structures.

—William A. Holmes, *Tomorrow's Church: A Cosmopolitan Community*, p. 55.

Bend, but don't abandon.

The time is here to test the resiliency of structures, stretching and straining
them with bold new images and working models for radical renewal. If the
skin gives way and tears, God, as always, will create new wineskins and
earthen vessels.

—W. A. Holmes, *Tomorrow's Church: A Cosmopolitan Community*, p. 67.

The "splitting-off" strategy vs. transforming structures.

I believe there are two main forces for renewal within Protestantism. The
first is that represented by Cosby, the approach that rejects present institutions and moves forward in fragmented fashion into the promise and pain
of the world. In various ways, the Cosby approach toward renewal is becoming a pattern at certain points in the Church. In some cases congregations
have split on various theological and social issues, and the result has been
the formation of new congregations (often without buildings) which seek to
mirror more fully the relevance of the biblical faith. I have little doubt that
if this continued splitting off of the "dedicated minority" from the status quo
church as the *only* strategy of renewal is encouraged, it will occur increasingly
throughout the Church as a whole. If I read the writings of an influential
theological thinker like Johannes Hoekendijk correctly, this splitting-off
strategy is seen as both valid and salutary. Certainly the idea of a dedicated
minority is not new and, in the past, it has functioned well as an approach
to change. It is at present the most likely pattern for a renewal movement
among the American Protestant churches.

The second approach to renewal is the one that is partially outlined in this
book. It assumes that the era of sectarianism within Protestantism is over
and that ecumenicity is a more constructive path than fragmentation. It
assumes that sects in our increasingly pluralistic society are likely to resort
to self-righteousness and subtle but real forms of otherworldliness in order
to gain a certain self-definition. It also assumes that it is highly improbable
that a disorganized sectarian proliferation of self-proclaimed "creative minorities" can be the chrysalis of the renewal of the whole Church. The idea of

giving up on the institutional Church is most tempting to me and to many others. I say that precisely this giving up *may* have to happen eventually. But I say with equal intensity that to adopt this giving up as the basic approach *now* is to eliminate a crucial step in the process of change, namely, the step of proposing a concrete alternative to the status quo. It gives up on the institution without trying to change it. It proclaims the revolution before there are more than a handful of revolutionaries. It tends to blur the issues at stake, since most Church splits today are based more on *sub rosa* issues than on the honest definition of theological and social disagreements. I agree entirely with the anti-institutional renewalists that there is no point in trying to resuscitate the denominations in their present form. But I ask them in all honesty whether they are willing to invest at least some of their energies in a truly ecumenical renewal movement that seeks not to siphon off an "elite" from existing congregations, but to transform the structures and lives of these congregations. If they are willing to do this and find it of no avail, then they can move on to fight the institution, and they will have more allies than they can now claim.

—Stephen C. Rose, The Grass Roots Church, pp. 23–24.

Outside the structure?

This conviction has come to me gradually—I have worked with it consciously for the past 15 years and have been disturbed about it for the past three. Just recently I crossed a line in my thinking. Now I am convinced that the institutional structures that we know are not renewable. Even when there is renewal (and this goes on in many congregations), the stance of the church almost always remains the same—a stance which is contrary to the very nature of a church committed to mission.

The church, properly, does not engage in mission or merely send missionaries—the church *is* mission and the congregation should express its life in the world. Its very structure must be changed to allow it to be itself.

Of course, there will be a coming, and a gathering, and the koinonia. But the church, if it is to "go into all nations," must exist within the secular structures of mankind.

When the structures get as rigid and as resistant to change as they are now, perhaps the wisest strategy is not to try to renew them. It may be wiser strategy to bypass them and let God do with them what he will. The new structures which will appear may be so drastically different from the old as to constitute reform rather than renewal.

I would suggest that those of us who are called by the living God to belong to him will be on mission to his world and we will take the shape appropriate to our calling. These new shapes will throw light upon the path of those Christians who are still active in the old structures.

I want to clarify several things. The Holy Spirit is still at work in the old structures. People still get converted in them, and personal growth takes place in them. One reason it has been so difficult for me to come to the conclusion stated above is that I myself came to know Jesus Christ through the old structures. This reproach has been thrown at me time and again, and it is true. So it is with great reluctance that I have to say that I do not believe the old structures can be renewed. This is not the way it seems to me God will work in our time.

I am not in any glib way writing off the whole church. But I am saying that as I now see it and as I now understand the nature of the world, the structures in which the church is contained are irrelevant and simply do not allow the church to be on mission. They hinder the proclamation of the Gospel rather than further it.

—N. Gordon Cosby, "Outside the Structure? Church Renewal: Outside . . . Or Inside?" *The Christian Advocate*, 12 September 1963, p. 7.

Time has run out for the denominations.

If we are to be truly conscious of what time it is, one of the chief facts we must know is that, so far as the Christian religion is concerned, we are in the post-denominational age. The person who spends his effort attacking denominationalism is fighting a battle of another period. Denominations, as we know them, are not evil; they simply are not very important! There is no harm in their continued existence, and they may do some good that would not be done otherwise. But they are no longer in the central Christian stream; they occupy the side channels. It is as inept to condemn the side channel as it is to spend one's life limited to it. Strong denominational loyalty and bitter attacks on denominationalism are equally out of date.

It is important to remember that denominations as we know them are only about 400 years old at most. The period of denominational usefulness and manifest strength is only a fraction of Christian history—a fraction that has already come to an end. . . .

A Christian who tries to know the time of day will usually retain his denominational affiliation while at the same time he puts his major effort into the new movements that are really on the Christian frontier in this last third of the twentieth century. I myself am a Quaker both by heritage and by conviction. My family has been Quaker, without a lapse, for more than three hundred years. . . .

What I want to make clear is that my heritage is one for which I shall always be grateful and to which I shall always adhere. But I cannot be loyal to it if I am loyal to it alone! Although I take my Quaker membership seriously, my purpose is to mingle constantly with Christians of all denominations or of none, in the effort to put my energies where the real battles of our time are found. The membership is necessarily of the *part*, but the concern is for the *whole*.

Most of the Christians whom I most respect today recognize clearly that it is the total cause of Christ to which they are loyal. They do not know how big

the Church of Christ is, but they at least know that it is bigger than their particular church. They are not, for the most part, arguing for one great monolithic ecclesiastical structure, but they are humble enough to try to learn from one another. They realize that no group has a monopoly of truth. They are perfectly willing to allow their denominational affiliation to stand, but they know it is out of date to get excited about it. A man who is visibly enthusiastic about his denomination is now obsolete, so far as the main thrust of Christianity is concerned.

As we move further into a time in which the denomination is neither an idol nor a target of attack, our major effort should be to envisage the new forms the Christian movement ought to take. Some of these we dimly see. For example, the Christian task force may come to be a standard unit in our operation. The basic Christian fellowship may be that in which the members see themselves as missionaries rather than those who merely *support* missionaries. The promotion of the general lay ministry is more important than the promotion of any particular denominational viewpoint and, fortunately, is consistent with any. The new evangelical theological stance, which is marked by a union of mind and heart, transcends all sectarian lines and is far more important than those lines.

—D. Elton Trueblood, "Post-Denominational Christianity," *Christianity Today*, 24 November 1967, pp. 171–72.

C. The Necessity of Institutions

Institutions belong to the Church's well-being, not its being.

We have already made the point that the church must have institutions but that it does not have to have *particular* institutions. Certain institutions even characterize the church but the church would not cease to exist if those institutions ceased to exist. In a word, institutions belong to the church's well-being and not to its being.

How, then, are they to be understood? Primarily as tools designed and cast by the church under Christ's leading for discharging its tasks. Since some of the tasks remain the same, the church may continue to use some of the same institutions. However, in that many of its tasks are subject to frequent change, it must design and cast new ones or redesign and recast old ones. Here, of course, we confront perplexing problems of deciding which institutions to retain, which to supplant with others, and which to dispense with entirely.

—E. Glenn Hinson, *The Church: Design for Survival*, p. 58.

Structures are a tool for mission.

Structures cannot guarantee the renewing power of the Holy Spirit or the ability to be sensitive to the world around. They can, however, provide an openness and new possibility of hearing and service, of responsiveness and compassion, that do not presently exist.

—George W. Webber, *The Congregation in Mission*, p. 14.

There are no Lone Ranger Christians.

But the point that we must be perfectly clear about is whether the organization of the Church is right or wrong, whether it is worth struggling with or not, whether we would be better Christians if we sought God as individuals and separately tried to do his bidding in the spirit of Christ.

The answer of the Catholic part of the Church is abundantly clear on this. Salvation is in the Church alone. By the sacraments properly administered, by the historic Church through its appointed ministers alone does God give salvation to men. Their answer then to the question of organization is clear and unanswerable. There must be such organization to administer the sacraments.

But we Protestants do not believe that God is so limited in His power and sovereignty that He cannot save except through an official priest. "The spirit of God works when and where and how he pleases." Then why the organization of the Church? Because essentially you cannot be a Christian alone. It is where two or three at least are gathered in the name of Christ that He promises to be present in their midst. As Dr. Ganse Little has said: "Herein lies the only saving power the church possesses—the saving power of Christian fellowship"—not by magic sacraments, not by legalistic moralities, not by intellectual creedal isms, but by the fellowship of a dedicated and worshiping community.

If it is true that we need each other, in communities, intimate and loyal, to teach and to learn of God, to work at the tasks of the Kingdom, to share one another's burdens and joys, to reach out into the community and the world for Christ, then we must have organization to do it. If the Church is an amorphous mass, with no long arms to reach out and embrace the lonely and the lost, if it has no legs and feet to march forward, to capture new areas of life and territory for Christ, if it has no vertebrate structure to resist evil (organized well, it is), then today, as in the first century, we may be sure that the cause of Christ will stumble, fall, and die.

—Eugene Carson Blake, *The Church in the Next Decade*, p. 18.

The hidden life becomes visible through forms.

We are in something like a new exile situation. Our churches have been taken out of the securities of the Christendom situation. We have been forced to leave many of the institutional forms that were characteristic of the period of the Christian West. As the pilgrim people moving through the previous thousand years, our fathers used the social institutions, the thought forms, the cultural patterns of their day as the vehicles for their missionary witness, and the rich and complex life of that "Christian civilization" were the result. Now that we are leaving behind these forms—as pilgrim people we use them without obligation, and fold up our tents and move on when God shifts the scene of action—we have the problem of deciding what is the continuing institutional life that we need. The event character of our life has priority; the Abraham covenant precedes the covenant with Moses. And so we can speak of the church, to quote from the report of the study on "The Missionary Structure of the Congregation," as a "happening 'on the road' from one event to the next." The church has to be free in this way because it is in the service of the One who is the hidden center of history's moving action. Nevertheless, the church must have institutional forms; it is called to bring the hidden meaning of life to visibility, and its Lord equips it with continuing forms which express both his care for it and his purpose for it.

—Colin W. Williams, *The Church*, pp. 28–29.

Get together, get organized, get going.

The Church exists as a functioning institution as well as a spiritual fellowship. As a spiritual fellowship *(koinonia)* it is organic; as a functioning institution it is organizational. The institution is always grounded in its spiritual relationships. The church as living organism becomes the militant institution. Bishop Gore declared that Christianity would never have done what it has done in the world if it had been a mere body of abstract truth, like a philosophy, to be apprehended by this and that individual.

Christianity must be organized if it is to fulfil its mission.

—Franklin M. Segler, *A Theology of Church and Ministry*, p. 11.

Structures multiply opportunities for involvement.

The truth of the matter is that the institutional life of the church is a necessary part of its existence. No social organism can come into being without taking some form as an institution in society. The task of the Christian fellowship is not to deny its institutional nature but to see that this, like the life of the Christian, is used to bear witness to God's rule and judgment and loving grace. Like its members, the institution itself must live its life in the world as a service to its Lord.

In a suburban community the metropolitan area community drive asks that representatives of the churches sit on its board; the church as an institution needs to be represented. In a depressed neighborhood the improvement council asks that a local congregation become a member; the church as an institution needs to participate. In the city the mayor calls for a council of churches to name people for his committee on youth conservation; the church

as an institution needs to show that this is part of its concern. The leaders
of the metropolis are often ignorant of the church's concern for its life because
they fail to see the church as an institution moving out of its own walls and
getting involved in the issues that most deeply trouble the citizens. Every
way that the churches find to bring their institutional life into the arena of
civic life may open the way for criticism and opposition to their viewpoint,
but it will also multiply their opportunities to be involved in the work that
God is already doing in the city.

—George D. Younger, *Church and Urban Power Structure*, pp. 79–80.

The Underground Church bag is connected with the Establishment.

The whole Underground Church bag is different from the sectarianism of
the radical Reformation and the American frontier in one critical respect:
there is no intention whatever of forming a new Church. The token of this
is that there is never any question of informal ordination of ministers. The
clergy in the movement are children each of their own Churches; it is
through those Churches that we first learned Christ. There is an exact parallel
here to the Peace movement generally, which operates by coalition among
representatives of various groups, with the universal presumption that
proselytism is ruled out of the question. In fact, as I say, there is a sense
in which the renewed Church and the Peace movement are the same thing. To
the extent that we have formulated our aim, we intend to surface as a
nucleus of Church union and renewal, in hope that what we represent will
melt the denominations from the bottom up. If we meet an Establishment
ecumenism painfully trying to push its way down, so much the better; but
if we want something to boil, it's always the bottom of the kettle to which
we apply heat. If we like, we could say that for its ministry the Underground
Church exists parasitically on the Establishment. But I can point out that
theological seminaries overseas rely parasitically for their faculties on Western graduate seminaries—and that still the overseas Churches have moved
ahead of us.

—John Pairman Brown, "Toward a United Peace and a Freedom Church," *The
Underground Church*, ed. Malcolm Boyd, pp. 42–43.

Institutions are both necessary and desirable.

It is no broadside condemnation of institutions and organizations *per se.*
They are both necessary and desirable instruments for the orderly and
adequate propagation of the faith. They provide an effective means by which
converts to the movement are made. They provide the structure in which
and through which guidance is given to the adherents through teaching and
study. They provide an effective means of cooperation by which the adherents
as a group can accomplish tasks which are too large and complicated for
individuals to do alone. Thus, it would be utterly impossible for any move-

ment to survive without institutions and organizational structure. Certainly it would be impossible for any adequate propagation of the values of the movement to be made without such institutions. Institutions are not inherently evil. Rather they are a valid and valuable part of any significant movement.
—Findley B. Edge, *A Quest for Vitality in Religion*, p. 23.

D. What Are We To Do?

Don't jettison the machinery. First try to make it work.

The denominations of the Church, while diminishing in strength and influence, are still formidable. They command great financial resources, including almost unbelievable investments in corporations and real estate. It is highly unrealistic to assume that the power inherent in the current denominational enterprise will not be used in some way, and it is highly irresponsible to forfeit at least the possibility of some influence on how this power is used. Actually, if Church power were used responsibly, the result would be a far greater social relevance (Cosby's goal) than now exists. If church homes for the aged were truly integrated, if church housing were truly innovative, if church schools were truly imaginative, if church funds were wisely invested, in short if the great institutional machinery of Protestantism were deployed with a certain flair for strategy and service, we should accomplish many aims that we often conceive to be beyond the institutional capacity of the Church. In the best of all possible worlds, the Church might not have as much real estate as it now owns, but it owns this property, and we have a responsibility to do something about it, even if what we finally do is to sell or give it away. The Church invests in corporations, and it is our responsibility to question these investments and to develop a voice within the power structures of the Church's financial units. We could go on. But suffice to say that we owe the Church the obligation of trying to develop institutional relevance before summarily jettisoning the institution. We must, at least for now, place renewal and restructuring ahead of total rejection of the institution.
—Stephen C. Rose, *The Grass Roots Church*, pp. 25–26.

The antidote for institutional blight.

The antidote for institutional blight is a rather simple prescription and is widely available. It can be found in the New Testament definition of the church as a community of persons called by God and filled with the Holy Spirit (Acts 20:28; II Cor. 1:1; Acts 2:1). The Christian congregation must remember and act on the biblical premise that it is dependent on the triune God and that each member is dependent upon all other members, past,

present, and future. When it forgets this and regards itself as an independent
and autonomous organization it becomes highly vulnerable to the ravages of
institutional blight.

—Lyle E. Schaller, *Planning for Protestantism in Urban America*, pp. 139–40.

Challenge the dragon and see what happens.

I suggest the answer does not lie in sweeping away every vestige of the
present structure. We have yet to challenge the present institution with the
specifics of renewal. Let us do so, and let us see what happens.

—Stephen C. Rose, *The Grass Roots Church*, p. 28.

The time has come. Let us move on.

We have passed through a decade of false religious revival. We have
passed through five subsequent years of carping and backbiting and discouragement with Church structure, five years in which the most vital expression of the Gospel was in the worship of men of many persuasions in the
prison cells of the South. Now it is time to start walking toward the new
structure; it is time to move on; it is time to become the Church we claim
to be; it is time that Jesus Christ be mocked for the right reasons; it is time
to teach once more, to preach once more, and to walk the Jericho Road once
more. It would be pleasant to forget all of the structural problems involved in
a responsible approach to Church renewal, to venture each in our own way
into the wilderness where, at least, we would hear no more vapid sermons,
no more comforting charades. But that may be the all-too-easy road today.
And if, in the coming years, we could truly revolutionize the structures of the
Church, we would find the wilderness soon enough, for the Church would no
longer be safe from the Gospel it so haltingly proclaims today.

—Stephen C. Rose, *The Grass Roots Church*, p. 161.

Some remedies only aggravate the sickness.

The institutional crisis in Christianity is erroneously attributed simply to
institutionalism. The pietistic tradition of the United States penetrates deeply
into the American religious consciousness and fosters the notion that pure
religion is formless and spiritual, implying that religion is corrupted by
formal ministries, rites and organization. Hence, the institutional crisis is
often attributed to the growth of denominational bureaucracies and religious
organizations. Two remedies are suggested for this excessive institutionalism:
on the one hand, spiritual inspiration of the kind that Billy Graham represents
is recommended to enliven the dry bones; on the other hand, mobilizing lay
manpower to take a more active part in things is suggested as a way of adding
vitality to the machinery. Clearly, the inspirational approach of the Graham
variety only deepens the institutional crisis, since it widens the chasm between

metropolitan problems and religious preoccupation with the nurture of personal needs. Tapping the great resource of lay manpower has proved again
and again since World War II to be a way of siphoning off the servanthood
of the laity into irrelevant activities around the religious establishment. In
both cases, the institutional crisis is misunderstood and the remedy only
aggravates the sickness.

—Gibson Winter, *The New Creation As Metropolis*, pp. 30–31.

Suggestions—what to do?

Rather than attacking and defending present church structures let the
denominations take some of the most talented young rebels and explore today's
world. The young men who are so critical of present institutions must produce
some models of ministry that focus on God's missionary activity in the
world. Similarly, pastors in residential congregations must seek to define and
strengthen their ministry to the residential community and see to it that
people at this level are likewise called into participation in God's activity
rather than into a Cult of Remembrance. Perhaps most important of all is that
the dialogue between residential and paraparochial situations must continue
as we move into the new world where we shall face our God in stark reality.

—Don Benedict, "Structures for the New Era," *Who's Killing the Church?*,
ed. Stephen C. Rose, p. 48.

The Church is experimenting with new structures and must live with anxiety.

There are, indeed, exciting signs and fragile shapes which are appearing:
coffee houses, inner city missions, apartment ministries, house churches, half-
way houses, and many other promising explorations in the church's com-
mendable new posture of missional involvement. But as yet, few of us are
bold enough or wise enough to say, "At last the blueprint!" and settle down
with one or even several shapes as the unrefuted harbingers of an adequate
new structure. Whether the present institutional structure can be radically
recast or must simply be replaced by altogether new equipment is a question
yet to be worked out.

The anxiety resulting from such uncertainty about the future of the institutional church is sufficient to tempt many of us to jump to premature conclusions and either abandon the present structure or settle down uncritically
within it. But it is *in* the anxiety and uncertainty themselves that we are
called to live right now.

—W. A. Holmes, *Tomorrow's Church: A Cosmopolitan Community*, p. 152.

How to prepare for the Judgment.

How may we prepare for judgment that we may be ready for renewal?
The first thing to reaffirm is that we must stick with the church. As some-

one has remarked: "The church is like Noah's Ark; if it weren't for the storm outside, you couldn't stand the smell inside." There is a storm outside, and the church, pervaded as it is with the smell of genial paganism, is still the ark of salvation, and there is no other.

The second thing to reaffirm is that by ourselves we cannot do anything about it. We as men are powerless to start revivals. We cannot schedule or blueprint or conjure into being the reviving Spirit of God. The Holy Spirit, like the wind, comes when and where He wills. So, with men, it is impossible.

The third thing to reaffirm is that with God all things are possible. And in fact, the most exciting truth of our generation is that God has already started something! This is the tremendous experience we are having in our different churches, and in different ways. The Holy Spirit is loose again in the world; lives are changing; the church is being reborn and renewed in place after place; a new Pentecost as of the days of the early church is at hand. So our privilege and obligation are not to start a revival; rather, to watch for the tide rolling in, to catch it, to seek to ride with it, and to make new channels for these rivers of grace. We are to be instruments for the Holy Spirit who is awakening us and breathing His power into our sleeping churches. Quite specifically, it is the job of Christian laymen and ministers to create the conditions for conversion within the life of the local church. It is God who converts lives; it is we who are called to create the conditions of conversion.

—Robert A. Raines, *New Life in the Church*, pp. 76–77.

Three ways to move beyond the institution to meet the needs of society.

The response of the Church to the pressing problems of general society must not be primarily institutional. Rather,

1. The corporate Church must promote justice in and through the general community. Our future will be determined by the kinds of decisions which are made for or against humanity in the complex structures of modern urban life. What counts is consistent and intelligent participation in, and pressure on, the structures of power where decisions are daily made. This means supporting those federal, state, and city programs which deal with the causes and not the symptoms of human misery: medical care for the aged, adequate unemployment compensation, adequate education, social security, job retraining, community organization, and community action programs which seek to change the structures of discrimination and poverty.

2. As long as the poor, needy, and sick are with us, the corporate Church must support those state- and community-sponsored agencies which deal directly with human suffering. Although social welfare is not the same as social action, it will be needed until social action is successful. And even in that far-off and blessed day, mental and physical sickness will still be with us. Modern welfare and health programs call for professional skills which the Church, as such, does not possess, and resources of which the Church has

only a fraction. Piety, good will, and a proper theological perspective are not substitutes for professional competence in operating health and welfare agencies.

3. For purposes of research to determine proper action—for purposes of informing the Church community concerning the extent of specific social problems—and for purposes of dramatizing a need and its viable solution or amelioration—the Church has a limited role in direct health, welfare, and educational services. When the Church sponsors an institutional program for the avowed purpose of raising standards and demonstrating excellence, it must be certain that the excellence can be recognized by others than the promoters of the program. Staff must be employed on the basis of their qualifications rather than because they are ministers. Most important: when any program of a health, welfare, or educational nature becomes a substitute for action rather than a spur, it should be discontinued.

—Richard E. Moore and Duane L. Day, *Urban Church Breakthrough*, pp. 152–53.

Hold fast to the local congregation.

The first fallacy of the young leaders who call for an end to the residential congregation as a means of mission and a restructuring of the entire church is their failure to be very much concerned, either about the faith itself, or the nurturing and developing in the lives of people a faith that could change the world.

The second fallacy in such thinking is the failure to recognize the historic effectiveness of the residential congregation not only as an instrument for teaching of the faith and for nurturing it through worship and fellowship in the life of the congregation, but also as an instrument for mission and renewal itself.

As such a weapon in the battle for a new life in the church the local congregation has already been discounted as of little value by many of the most radical and most adventurous innovators.

Surely any pastor who has loved and cared for a congregation of God's people, and any layman who has been one of those people, knows full well the sins of the church: knows very well that the residential congregation, like the residential family, is not perfect and is full of sin. But he also knows that the church at that level, just like the family at that level, offers something to the whole church and the whole world that no other institution can.

—Arthur A. Rouner, Jr., *The Free Church Today: New Life for the Whole Church*, pp. 110–11.

I dare you. Send out small groups.

The church must take the risk of sending out small groups. This may mean that instead of giving less attention to the historical/institutional dimension of its life, we may need to give more, lest these groups become separated from the whole and engage in the idolatry of the particular. The church may need to change its institutional forms, but it will always need them for its missions and the nurturing of people in their belonging both to the whole and to the particular.

—Elizabeth O'Connor, *Journey Inward, Journey Outward*, p. 92.

The secularized Church is the Church on mission.

The religious institutions face a choice in the contemporary world: (1) they can strengthen their confessional assemblies in the residential enclaves and provide a religious refuge, leaving the world to seek its own peace; or (2) they can relinquish the comforts of these enclaves and become involved with the organizational structures that shape our emerging society. The former possibility, the organization church, is most attractive to religious professionals because it guarantees affluence to the churches, albeit at the cost of more ulcers and nervous breakdowns for the religious leaders, not to mention an impoverished proclamation. The second possibility, secularization of the churches, poses serious threats to institutional stability but opens the way to direct engagement with the principalities and powers that dominate our lives. The organization church is the affluent church; it is the Church of the middle class. The secularized Church is mission in an organizational society; it is the servant Church in history. Many religious leaders would like to combine these approaches, but they soon discover that the residential enclaves swallow up the religious enterprise in private interests.

—Gibson Winter, *The New Creation As Metropolis*, pp. 67–68.

What can the denominations do?

To this end, there are a number of things which the denominations can do.

(a) For one thing, the barrage of denominational pronouncements on public issues can be kept up. A survey by Glock and Ringer has shown that while such pronouncements do not materially affect the laity, they do significantly encourage and support the clergy.

(b) Second, denominations must learn to select and treat public issues on the basis of objective concern for the whole body politic, with the least possible admixture of churchly self-interest.

In order to counteract this legacy of self-interest and the skepticism which it has bred, we would propose that the denominations take two steps, one of a short-range, the other of a long-range nature.

We would propose a network television series, sponsored by the National Council of Churches, showing facets of the checkered record of the slavery issue; the original hostility of the churches to organized labor and their gradual, belated endorsement of the labor movement; the largely uncritical— though increasingly critical—endorsement by the churches of all the wars our nation has fought thus far. There must be no breastbeating, nor any pretence that all is well now since we are confessing our past sins. This should be an historically honest, artistically persuasive, and theologically solid documentary series!

We would propose, further, that the denominations begin to take steps toward ending the tax-exempt status of the church. If this step proved too drastic, somewhat the same effect could be obtained by a voluntary levy of "taxes" on church property—in the form of donations to at least the local governing body. Such action would speak to the world about the meaning of the Incarnation as a ton of sermons could not.

(c) Third, the denominations can greatly strengthen the position of the local ministerial organization or ecclesiastical judicatory.

This vesting of effective power close to the point where power must be exercised is something for Protestants to ponder. Local area organizations should have more power and exercise it more frequently. They should also have their boundaries redrawn so as to correspond as far as possible to political communities. Thus revitalized, they would be more effective in assisting pastors in prophetic witness.

(d) Finally, since economic pressure on the pastor is probably the greatest deterrent to his exercising prophetic leadership, the denominations can initiate changes to mitigate the pastor's economic dependence on his congregation. To this end we would propose that all contributions by members be given to the local area organization (e.g. the presbytery, the district, the classis) and that the budget of each local church be determined, upon proper consultation and concerted planning, by this organization. This is not as un-Protestant as it may seem; the Swiss Reformed Church, for instance, operates on this basis.
—John R. Bodo, "The Pastor and Social Conflict," *Religion and Social Conflict*,
eds. Robert Lee and Martin E. Marty, pp. 166–68.

How can the denominations retool for renewal?

We believe that denominationalism is obsolete, both theologically and in terms of the capacity of denominations to organize the Church in the most effective and obedient manner. We believe that participants in a renewal movement must openly express their willingness to forsake denominational loyalty at every point that such loyalty impedes the ecumenical witness of the Church, particularly at the local and metropolitan level. . . . Thus we have little hope in renewal movements aimed at restoring the life of individual denominations. Such movements are too easily domesticated. We advocate, as an alternative, the formation of a pandenominational grass roots organization of all persons, clergy and lay. who wish to fight for the Church structure which we shall propose. . . .

Denominations would be called to restructure in the following manner: The bulk of current denominational expenditures are used for servicing the needs of local denominational congregations. This includes funding new church development projects, producing curriculum at the national level, and the support of local congregations that are unable to support themselves. We believe that all of these functions should be turned over, as much as possible, to the metropolitan and regional structures of the several denominations. This would include the transfer of church extension funds, funds for educational programs, and all other funds now used for the maintenance of local denominational programs. The denominations should, before turning these funds over, elicit an agreement that the local denominational units will use these funds on an ecumenical basis with other local denominational units. The basic principle informing the use of these transferred funds should be the priority of the cooperative ministry concept. We are calling here for the decentralization of approximately ninety per cent of current national programs conducted by denominations. We recommend that the national denominations see themselves in the future as research and development agencies serving the whole ecumenical Church. In particular we urge that endowments and other funds that could not legally be removed from the jurisdiction of national denominations be seen in the future as seed money for creative experimentation in areas that are beyond the purview of the proposed cooperative ministries. Denominations, shorn of many current institutional functions, would be free to concentrate on pilot projects, *ad hoc* experimentation, and on creative ecumenical projects that would still be needed on the national and international level.

The original purpose of denominations was to do what no single congregation could do for itself. Our proposal assumes that functions once carried out by denominations can most fruitfully be returned to the local level. We feel that the future of the denominations lies in experimentation, research, and development, and in serving the needs of a Church that would be truly ecumenical at its base.

We feel, in addition, that the distinctive theological contributions of individual denominations will be enhanced, rather than eliminated, in our proposed cooperative ministry structure. The worship of the cooperative ministry, in particular, would provide room for all legitimate traditions, because it would bring all the current resources of the denominations into a central worship facility serving the local neighborhood. We feel strongly that genuine dialogue at the local level is preferable to the creation of a routinized "ecumenical" theology forced upon the local churches from the upper echelons of Protestantism.

Thus our impatience with denominationalism is impatience with its present form and structure. We wish to free denominations for service, not to eliminate them.

—Stephen C. Rose, *The Grass Roots Church*, pp. 167–68, 171–73.

III

The Theological Basis

for Renewal

A. WHAT IS THE CHURCH?

Hard and clear theological thinking is crucial.

Christians, if renewal of the Church is to come, must engage in hard and clear thinking. In short, one of the most important steps in readiness is *theological*. Perhaps we are already past the time when "theology" was a bad word, even in the Church. We hope so! We dare not neglect theological thinking for the clear reason that theology cannot be avoided. Since there is no such thing as "no theology," the only alternative to a valid theology is a poor or confused one. Men, so long as they are truly human, are bound to deal with the ultimate questions, but it is blasphemous to deal with these by slogans and catchwords and cliches.

—Elton Trueblood, *The Incendiary Fellowship*, p. 57.

What picture of Christian society does the New Testament provide?

The pictures of the church carried in our minds are obviously out of date. They have been painted in an earlier day, often by those who have not glimpsed the glory now seen. They have been set in a frame too small, a frame no larger than private experience in particular parishes. Our images of the church have been determined too much by our puny minds and provincial prejudices, not enough by the wide-horizoned story of God's people.

Accordingly we look for more adequate images, not so much that we may be deceived by their greater glamor as that we may be rightly instructed by their overarching validity.

These impulses find their way not only into the work of theologians but also into the work of historians, particularly of biblical historians. Nor is this strange. Virtually every Christian communion recognizes the Bible as an authoritative standard for faith and action. To be sure, this recognition may be formal rather than real, official rather than actual. Even when a communion takes seriously its avowed norm, it often cautiously limits the range of concerns to which it applies this norm. For example, when a particular practice such as baptism is challenged, a communion may appeal immediately to passages in the New Testament which appear to justify its practice. But this communion may not listen so intently to the same New Testament to discover new light on what the real church actually *is*. Whether our sacramental practice is biblical is ultimately less decisive than whether our understanding of the church is biblical. Do we have an image of the church which is recognizably the same as that which is found in the New Testament? That is the more difficult and the more humbling question. Before we will be in a position to answer it, we need to pose a prior query: What comprehensive picture of Christian society does the New Testament itself provide?

—P. S. Minear, *Horizons of Christian Community*, pp. 9–10.

Have you considered consulting the Bible for an answer?

The Church is more than an activity in history. It has a distinctive form and a particular kind of corporate life, in addition to its mandated activity of service and mission. Obviously any church body which is preoccupied with itself, ceaselessly contemplating its image in a mirror in order to understand what it really is, is a defective church. It is doomed to answer to the description which a rural church in Tennessee inadvertently gave of itself when, for purposes of postal reduction, it actually stamped on its envelopes: 'A non-prophet organization.' But conversely, a church which has no regard at all for knowing its own nature can become engulfed, and finally exhausted, in its own activity.

The New Testament poses many questions and leaves most of them only partly answered. What is the Church? What must it do to be faithful? How should its life be lived? The answers are only pointed to, but not defined. So Christians today are increasingly disposed to return to the New Testament and reflect upon its witness in the light of past centuries of tradition and of present problems. In this they are discerning more clearly the lineaments of a local church which is both apostolic and contemporary, both consistent with the life and pattern of the earliest Christian community and yet vitally effective today.

In this book I have attempted to find concrete guidance for the present life of the Churches in the simple but very suggestive words of the Acts of the Apostles 2:42. The four elements which are set forth there provide an admirable opportunity for discoursing on some of my chief concerns about the congregations of Christians now alive, and especially those of Protestant character in America.

—J. R. Nelson, *Criterion for the Church*, pp. 7–8.

"Church—know thyself!"

Rather than beginning with analysis and prescription, which is the common procedure, we need to give deliberate attention to the biblical understanding of the church. We must ask: Who are we? What is our mission and purpose? How do we go about accomplishing this mission and purpose?

We have not been giving adequate attention to these important questions. Yet both what we do and the manner in which we do it should spring from our understanding of who we are. Thus we can keep the proper balance of activities in the church and also increase greatly its total contribution. Preaching, teaching, baptism, the Lord's Supper, fellowship, missions, evangelism, social service—all that the churches do—will be properly understood only when viewed in relationship to the New Testament understanding of the church.

But someone may inquire, "Why is it so important to *begin* with an understanding of the church?" Precisely because self-understanding will give the maturity necessary for coping with the tremendous problems now facing the Christian church. In a sense, self-understanding and maturity are almost synonymous. Perhaps Socrates was not far off the mark when he challenged, "Know thyself." At any rate, the mature person will know as much about himself as he can. His maturity lies not so much in perfection in all faculties as in a correct assessment of the strengths and weaknesses of those faculties.

—E. Glenn Hinson, *The Church: Design for Survival*, p. 20.

1. Confused Images of the Church

The "peace of mind" trap.

Applicants for church membership in four Pacific Coast Presbyterian churches, in answering the question of their intent upon joining, tended in the majority of cases to answer, "The church fills my needs," or "The church helps me to be a better person." Whether these remarks can be trusted to be articulate and accurate may be questionable; they do, however, reveal a rather general attitude that the church exists primarily as a ministry to subjective inadequacies rather than a stimulator toward obedience and a strengthener of social values.

—Wesley C. Baker, *The Split-Level Fellowship*, p. 27.

Our "earthly bosom" complex.

"She," we called the church. The sympathetic feminine, the perpetual mother who shelters us in our hurts, who warmly accepts us as we are, and who weeps over our failures, she is our all-inclusive community. *Qahal* and *ekklesia*, the bride of Christ (II Cor. 11:2; Rev. 19:7), the subject of John XXIII's *Mater et Magistra*, no one would have the poor taste to ascribe masculinity to the communion of saints.

This may be a serious symbol confusion. The issue is not related to the actuality of male-female characteristics, whatever they may be, but the imagery and its appeal to widely held association. Femininity popularly connotes passivity, nonauthoritative guidance, a readiness always to reflect in softened tones whatever the prevailing values of the masculine world may direct. In requiring the motherly role of the church, the generations have made her to be submissive and obedient when the times called for the lonely but effective masculine cry of the prophet.

—Wesley C. Baker, *The Split-Level Fellowship*, p. 19.

Pure congregationalism is an inadequate image.

No conceptualization is more misleading than the persisting one which insists that the local congregation is the only viable expression of Christian mission. The social realities of our day make pure congregationalism obsolete and ineffective in confronting existing problems which must be solved on a city-wide basis. Yet Protestantism still tends to be overly dependent upon congregational initiative, in a society so highly organized that congregations can be only part of the decision-making process.

—Richard E. Moore and Duane L. Day, *Urban Church Breakthrough*, pp. 22–23.

The Church suffers from a local "edifice complex."

There is then a strong case for rejecting the conclusion that the residential congregation is necessarily the normal form of church life. It seems possible that the deep attachment to this view is holding the Church back from the freedom it needs to be re-formed in such a way that the presence of Christ can inform the secular patterns of everyday life. Hans Schmidt speaks of attachment to the view that the residence congregation is the norm, as "morphological fundamentalism". . . .

The case for saying that the Church is suffering from a local "edifice complex" seems very strong. Moreover, it would seem that the form of the local residence congregation is so turned inward, that it is often well-nigh impossible to reverse its direction in order that its life may flow outward into the structures of the world's need.

—Colin Williams, *Where in the World?*, pp. 11–12.

2. Marks of the Church

Sustained by hope in the face of impossible tasks.

As the individual in dispersion is sustained by hope, so for the congregation in its united witness its faithfulness depends upon hope in spite of the impossible tasks it faces in the midst of the modern city. No longer does the imagery of a mighty conquering army or of a world won for Christ in this generation sustain the congregation. Now the metaphor of salt or leaven is more relevant. The inner-city congregation is called to flavor, preserve, and leaven its situation, while trusting in the ultimate faithfulness of God. The gospel, in calling men to God's work, demands realism. So also, in continuing to trust in God in the midst of all discouragement and conflict, the congregation is allowed no cynicism, for it trusts in the Resurrection. Living in the midst of the world, but part of the invisible kingdom of Christ, the congregation endures, suffers, watches, confesses, perseveres, overcomes, and resists the powers of darkness. The congregation continues in its missionary task, not because in some ways it finds that conditions are gradually improving or the kingdom of God is being achieved, but simply in patient waiting for the great acts of the full revelation of the kingdom and its Lord, for a new heaven and a new earth that are the final glory of God.

—George W. Webber, *The Congregation in Mission*, p. 189.

Love is the final mark of the Church.

The nature of a true Christian society or Church is so rich that it cannot be fully expressed in a single idea. Love is not the only mark—it is merely the final mark. Though the marks of the true Church are many, a particular mark may, with logical consistency, be recognized as more important than the others. When we truly become a Company of Christ's Committed Ones we exhibit a number of features which fit together into a total complex of greater and lesser features. In such a society there is *commitment,* and *enlistment,* and *witness,* and *penetration* of common life, and *caring,* but the greatest of these is *caring.* The Church of Jesus Christ is not merely a society of love, for love is conceivable in any historical tradition, but if the Church is genuine, it must always involve love as the most important single attribute.

—Elton Trueblood, *The Company of the Committed*, pp. 97–98.

Inspired by love, guided by the Holy Spirit.

Fellowship, gospel, liturgy and ministry—these are ways in which the love of God known and accepted in the Church is expressed. Only in so far as they are in direct contact with their origin in love can they be saved from abuse. And they have been abused in the past. Fellowship can become a close, introverted circle; gospel can be a monologue towards the world to whose needs the Church will not listen; liturgy can become a private service for the benefit of the spiritual *elite;* and ministry can become a means of self-service, of salving conscience, and of patronizing people. These can only become instruments of the mission of the Church as long as they are controlled by real love. And real love is ultimately something more than human. It originates with the Holy Spirit to whom the Church must always turn for the direction of its mission. Even mission, that outward-going, world orientation which the Church needs so desperately today, can fail to be an expression of the true 'sentness' of the Church unless it is always inspired by love and guided by that wisdom and understanding which is of the Holy Spirit; unless it is grounded in that true holiness which is sustained by prayer, by the word, and by the sacraments, in the midst of the turmoil of life.

—B. N. Y. Vaughan, *Structures for Renewal,* pp. 61–62.

Joy! Joy! Joy!

It is also true that a church, participating in one another's lives through participation in Christ, knows joy as well as estrangement. This joy is not the tinkle of well-bred laughter over a ministerial joke. It is the sense of relief that comes from not having to pretend any more. To know that you are known by God must surely fill you with shame and the need for confession, but it also fills you with relief. The pure joy of escape from "antennae adjusting" is Christian joy. The contrast between the earthy humor of Martin Luther as reflected in his sermons of later life and the tormented fear of God in his early life is a good illustration of the meaning of Christian joy. Then the mood changes from one of apprehension that you may not be quite fitting the mold of your level of society to expectancy that God will provide surprising opportunities every day to a church that holds to him in faith.

This sense of estrangement and of joy is the fruit of the life of faith. A church must know itself to be a separated people, a royal priesthood, a household of God.

—Robert W. Spike, *In But Not Of The World,* pp. 15–16.

The realized presence of God.

If we are completely immersed in the stream of human history, there is little for man to be cheerful about. Only if we include another dimension to life besides the horizontal flow of history can there be found a true basis for Christian hope. God gives each moment in the flow of history a new look. A new perspective is added. Some of the confusion and all of the hopelessness is removed, and interest in God and the vertical dimension of history which His inclusion adds must not be substituted for the active and vital concern of Christians for what goes on in the ordinary affairs of the world. Jesus did not say, "Be of good cheer, the world is unimportant." It is always wrong to replace the horizontal measurements of history with the vertical. This is an ever present danger of any religious understanding of life. Ever and again, especially when events promise disaster, religious people are tempted to flee the world.

Jesus did not say, "Be of good cheer, things are not as bad as they look." A second and perennial danger of religion is to sentimentalize. It will do us no good to suppose that the historical issues we face are any less desperate than they appear.

Jesus said, "Be of good cheer, I have overcome the world." He had overcome the world because, although fully immersed in the stream of history, He had and offers a vital relationship to the eternal God, who is both the Lord of history and yet is also before and after, above and beyond all history. Our essential trouble is that we do not really believe in God. We talk about Him, we think we have adopted Him as our theory, but we are apt either to put Him off into the past or to hope for Him in some far-off future. But too often God seems to be nothing to us now. It was because of the realized presence of God that Jesus was able to say to his Disciples, "Be of good cheer, I have overcome the world."

—Eugene Carson Blake, *The Church in the Next Decade*, pp. 13–14.

New men are seeking renewal and being renewed.

If we look at the passages which speak about newness of life and renewal we find that some of them speak of the new life as an established fact, some of them speak of it as a task to be accomplished and some of them contain these two perspectives together. These last passages show us the way to an understanding of the relationship between the affirmation: 'You are new men' and the exhortation: 'Be renewed.' Thus in I Cor. 5.6–8 the Corinthians are warned to cleanse out the old leaven so that they may be fresh dough, but this exhortation is confirmed by the affirmation that they *are* really unleavened. In other words St. Paul says: renew yourself for you *are* new people. Similarly in Colossians (3.9) the imperative, 'Do not lie to one another' is supported by the argument that the Colossians *have* put off the old nature and put on the new nature. But here a further explanation is given namely that this new man *is* being renewed. In other words we have now three statements: the Christian is a new man; he is to seek renewal; he is being renewed. Other passages in the New Testament emphasize one or the other of these three aspects. (See Rom. 7.6; Eph. 4.23; II Cor. 4.16.) Thus it is clear that these three statements are meant as complementary truths.

—W. A. Visser't Hooft, *The Renewal of the Church*, p. 34.

Unashamedly supernatural.

Here we approach one of the anomalous embarrassments of the church. Loyal as it is to institutional rationalism, the church cannot hide the fact that it is based upon certain supernatural assumptions or revelations. The more mysterious aspects of faith, prayer, belief, the difficulties of interpreting certain nonrational passages in the Bible, and the problem of even discussing the theological anthropology of Jesus, usually constitute the insolubles and divisive predicaments of parish life. Where the leadership of a local church is theologically sophisticated, capable of euphemistic interpretation, and courageously deals with human involvement in "things unseen," here is the church that has the most questions raised, and by far the most questions left unanswered. Official boards are usually embarrassed to clutter up their deliberations with any implications of Bible study, and elected church leaders are most often threatened by the implication that they should also be religious leaders and teachers. The fringe groups of Protestantism usually solve this problem by being unashamedly supernatural, and content to express this aspect in simplified formulas and prescribed devotional activities, asking fewer rational questions and participating more intensely in emotional expression and simplified, austere moralistic behavior.

—Wesley C. Baker, *The Split-Level Fellowship*, p. 28.

Commitment—believing "in" vs. believing "that."

The crucial question today is not whether we must have a fellowship, for on that point we are reasonably clear; the crucial question concerns the *character* of the fellowship. The more we think about it the more we realize that it must be a fellowship of the committed. This is because mere belief is never enough. . . .

There is no better way, in contemporary thought, of approaching the meaning of commitment than by reference to Marcel's distinction between "believing that," and "believing in." To be committed is to *believe in*. Commitment, which includes belief but far transcends it, is determination of the total self to act upon conviction. Always and everywhere, as Blaise Pascal and many other thinkers have taught us, it includes an element of wager. This is why in great religious literature, including the New Testament, the best light that can be thrown upon commitment is that provided by marriage. For everyone recognizes the degree to which marriage is a bold venture, undertaken without benefit of escape clauses. The essence of all religious marriage vows is their *unconditional* quality. . . .

One way of stating the crucial difference between belief and commitment is to say that when commitment occurs there is attached to belief an "existential index" which changes its entire character. . . .

We shall not be saved by anything less than commitment, and the commitment will not be effective unless it finds expression in a committed fellowship. If we have any knowledge of human nature, we begin by rejecting the arrogance of self-sufficiency. Committed men need the fellowship not because they are strong, but because they are—and know that they are—fundamentally sinful and weak.

It is generally recognized that though commitment is of the first importance, men may have more than one object of their commitment. The full commitment of millions of Germans, prior to and during the Great War, was to Adolf Hitler and *his* cause. Other millions are today committed to Marxism. This is why it is now recognized that Marxian communism is fundamentally a religion rather than a mere economic or political system. The fact that it denies God does not keep it from being religious. Christians have no monopoly on commitment; they simply have a different object. A Christian is a person who confesses that, amidst the manifold and confusing voices heard in the world, there is one Voice which supremely wins his full assent, uniting all his powers, intellectual and emotional, into a single pattern of self-giving. That Voice is Jesus Christ. A Christian not only believes *that* He was; he believes *in Him* with all his heart and strength and mind. Christ appears to the Christian as the one stable point or fulcrum in all the relativities of history. Once the Christian has made this primary commitment he still has perplexities, but he begins to know the joy of being used for a mighty purpose, by which his little life is dignified.

—Elton Trueblood, *The Company of the Committed*, pp. 21–23.

A visible community of broken barriers.

It is the sense of its chosenness by God that enables a community to address God, to seek after His word in their history, in the individual events of life, in conversation and dreams and visions. We cannot talk about the Church being in the world today without talking about a community whose life coheres in a Servant Lord. A new positioning of the Church in the world, which all renewal literature asks for, is needed, but this will not convey the new creation. Only a visible community where one can experience the breaking down of the dividing walls within oneself will make witness to a God who calls us out of estrangement and isolation.

—Elizabeth O'Connor, *Journey Inward, Journey Outward*, p. 104.

An open-ended search for God's will.

What the Church represents is not a repository of unchanging truth, but an open-ended search for God's will in our lives, both individually and in the redemptive fellowship. Instead of an unchanging certainty of the kind presumed by those whose faith is a collection of infallible proof-texts, finite men have the awesome responsibility of sharing in the possession of the liberating keys. What is laid upon us is neither a peculiar wisdom denied to others nor a doctrine in which we can take pride, but a responsibility to share in a difficult task.

—Elton Trueblood, *The Company of the Committed*, pp. 27–28.

The inward awareness of holiness.

Anything which we do as a church and anything we do publicly in our city, first of all, will grow out of an inward awareness and holiness. It is fundamental to everything which we do as Christians, that we personally develop a style of life which is recognizably Christian. This means that in our family groups, in our businesses and our government offices, when we walk in, a light goes on. This style of life will be recognizable in all of our personal contacts with public servants in transportation, mail, laundry, and milk; with servicemen, salesmen, telephone operators, trash collectors, janitors, hospital attendants, elevator operators—to anyone who serves us in any way. We shall mediate something to every person we meet.

—Elizabeth O'Connor, *Call to Commitment*, pp. 160–61.

You look best when dressed in humility.

The Church is most true to its own nature when it seeks nothing for itself, renounces power, humbly bears witness to the truth but makes no claim to be the *possessor* of truth, and is continually dying in order that it may live.

—J. H. Oldham, *Life Is Commitment*, p. 103.

The fellowship of the forgiven.

A quite secular analogy to *koinonia* is felt in a meeting of Alcoholics Anonymous. AA is open to anyone who is an alcoholic and knows in fact that he is powerless by his own efforts to defeat his problem. Only when he recognizes his utter bondage to his problem and is willing to rely absolutely on the power of God and the support of his brothers can he really be part of the organization. Even when he has been able, through the organization, to maintain his sobriety for a long period of time, the alcoholic never forgets that he is still in bondage to this problem. It is still a very real threat, in spite of his present triumph. A testimony at an AA meeting always begins, "I am an alcoholic," even though you discover that he hasn't had a drink in fifteen or twenty years. Alcoholism remains his continuing problem. The alcoholic lives one day at a time, praying only that he may have the strength to live that one day without a drink. He is always available day or night to assist a brother alcoholic. Here the crucial element of unity lies in common human bondage, whereas for the Christian unity comes from the common Lordship of Christ. But the analogy to *koinonia* is impressive.

—George W. Webber, *God's Colony in Man's World*, pp. 54–55.

Tune in to the frequency of Christ.

What we have been discussing might perhaps be expressed in this single image. If one of two tuning forks, which have the same frequency and are close to each other, is struck, the other begins to vibrate sympathetically. In principle, every object has its own natural frequency or pitch, and when we find and create that pitch, sympathetic vibrations are set up in the object.

To apply the analogy: Jesus of Nazareth represents the authentic frequency of man's life and as such has been sounded and is setting up sympathetic vibrations throughout creation. Wherever this life emerges in individuals (in good Samaritans, atheistic revolutionaries, and anti-ecclesiastical integrationists as well as in official saints) or in institutions (in the growth of governments and technology as well as in Apostolic Succession), then the phenomenon of its sympathetic vibration is manifest. Man's natural frequency is, of course, more or less muffled—laid over with sound-deadening material—from its activating source, and so our lives often betray a kind of deaf aimlessness. But it does happen that when some persons and human institutions are more or less stripped of this mufflement, they respond more clearly to the frequency that is in Jesus. The task of Christians—as we shall consider it in this chapter—is simply to become increasingly open to the frequency of life, which vibrates in him.

—Myron B. Bloy, Jr., *The Crisis of Cultural Change*, p. 114.

The willingness to risk making mistakes.

The second source of the church's power in the struggle has been the willingness of the established institutions to take *risks*. That is what convinced the Negro civil rights leaders that some trust was possible. It is what convinced legislators and other government officials that the church might be worth listening to at this juncture. If the leaders of the church, which is seen popularly to be so related to middle-of-the-road and even conservative opinion in this country, were willing to risk making mistakes that might lead to embarrassment, then the issue simply must be serious. That was what underlay so much of the possibility of action. The glimmer of evidence that the churches might be taking the gospel somewhat seriously—a gospel which involves a Cross, suffering for the sake of one's brother—this gave the church power. So many people have experienced the church only as exhorter to be and to do things which did not threaten the minister or the church as an institution. More and more laymen are aware of how desirous they have been of keeping the real power of the church under proper control—namely, the appeal of Christ to risk one's self for the sake of the brethren.

—Robert W. Spike, *The Freedom Revolution and the Churches*, p. 113.

The Church is both a divine community and a social institution.

If the layman seeks, as he must, to bring together the Christian faith and the modern world, he has to recognize at the outset the *double aspect* of the Church. On the one hand the Church is the divine community, called into being by Christ. This is its theological reality. The Church is part of the Christian faith. "I believe in . . . one Holy Catholic and Apostolic Church." I belong to and worship in a particular church *because* I believe this, and not because social conformity demands it, or because I think the Church is a useful welfare organization. But, on the other hand, this divine community exists here on earth in the form of a social institution— companies of people meeting in buildings; orders of ministry regulating worship and doctrine; organized denominations; church institutions. This is a matter of *fact,* and the Church thus organized may be explored by historians and sociologists using the tools of scientific study.

—Kathleen Bliss, *We the People*, p. 10.

The Church is a minority instrument of the kingdom.

But this I believe needs questioning in the light of the Bible. For while the New Testament holds out as the consummation of all things the vision of *Christ* as all in all, it never suggests that all men will be in *the Church*, at any rate within this age. In fact, right through to the Book of Revelation, it continues to visualize the covenant people as a minority instrument of the Kingdom.

Perhaps the closest modern parallel is the relationship between the Communist party and the state in Soviet Russia. As is well known, the Communist party is a small minority in Soviet society, and by no means is its only function to make more communists. Without the party the regime would indeed collapse, but its tactics are not based on the assumption that all Russians will become communists, in the sense of acknowledging a conscious ideological commitment and discipline. Its policy is geared to making Russia and eventually the world a socialist society.

To transfer the analogy to the Christian mission, it is possible to regard the "latent Church" either from the point of view of the "manifest Church" or from the point of view of the Kingdom of God. Evangelism in modern parlance has come to be seen almost exclusively in the former perspective: it means drawing individuals across the line into the camp of committed Christians. But from many of those for whom the Kingdom "drew near" in the ministry of Jesus he sought to elicit no such commitment. For the Syrophoenician woman, for instance, the good news of the Kingdom—the Gospel—was precisely that he was able to meet her *where she was,* as the gracious neighbour, in answer to her absolutely elemental human need— despite the fact that she was not even one of the lost sheep of the house of Israel.

Today, I believe, the main work of the manifest Church, certainly in terms of sheer numbers, is probably to make it possible for men and women to be met by Christ *where they are*—that is, within the context and thought-forms of the latent church. It has to ask itself whether what it really cares for most is that "the poor *have* the Gospel preached to them"—if need be in the entirely non-religious terms announced by Jesus, of release for prisoners and recovery of sight for the blind—even if they never say, "Lord, Lord." If so, then it must, for the greater part of its work, be prepared to *respect* rather than remove (which is its instinctive urge) the incognitos under which the

WHAT IS THE CHURCH?

parable of the Sheep and the Goats alone shows it possible for the Christ to meet and to judge the mass of men. And the incognitos of that parable are those of *humanity* and *secularity:* the Son of Man wills to be met in an utterly disinterested concern for persons for their own sake, and in relationships that have nothing distinctively religious about them.

—John A. T. Robinson, The New Reformation, pp. 48–50.

A city set on a hill, and leaven in the world.

Balthasar emphasized the role of the church as a separate institution showing in its own life the signs of God's purpose for all life. The church is called first to be a city set on a hill. Hoekendijk stressed the need for the church to point away from its own institutional life to the places where Christ is working out his purpose in the struggles for true human life within the other institutions of the world. The church needs its separate life—house churches in which believers are trained for their servant role in the world. But this life must be humble and unobtrusive, with the church community making itself available to Christ in his struggle for true community within the structures of the world. The church is called to be leaven in the world.

Perhaps the Ephesians letter gives us a clue as to how to handle this vital difference. In the early church situation the Balthasar emphasis was primary. The life of the church itself was a sign that a new community life is available: that it is possible for conflicts of race, culture, class, and sex to be overcome and for a fellowship to emerge beyond the death of these ancient hostilities. At that time, penetration of the structures of the world was limited, but nonetheless important. Christians had major access to family life, and they made the most of that opportunity to show how the servant way of Christ could transform it. They had a limited access to the master-slave relationship —not enough at that time to break through the massive institution of slavery, but enough to begin to transform the superiority assumptions that lay behind it. In those days, then, the city-set-on-a-hill role was predominant. But later as the church grew, so its access to the other institutions increased. As a result the leaven role became increasingly important.

What then is the relation between the two roles today? Both are still vital, but in different situations the balance may vary considerably. In some countries the church is in a situation similar to that of the first century, with little access to the other institutions. But in others it has considerable opportunity to join Christ in his struggle for a truly human existence within the institutions of the world. Then, Hoekendijk rightly insists, it must train its members to fulfill that servant role in the world, humbly pointing away from its own life to those places on the frontiers of life where the key struggles for human community are going on. This does not mean that the role of the church as a city set on a hill disappears. There is still need for the church to seek to serve Christ as a demonstration community, where the way of the future is being tested. But what the extent of this separate life should be and how far the church should go in seeking to disperse that life of demonstration of the servant way into the other institutions—these are points where real differences of judgment will continue to exist.

—Colin Williams, *The Church*, pp. 90–91.

The incendiary character of the fellowship.

The miracle of the early Church was a partial fulfillment of Christ's expressed purpose about setting the earth on fire. Of course this did not involve all of mankind, but there is no doubt that the fire burned brightly enough, in the lives of those who were involved in the Movement, to make a miraculous difference in the culture of the ancient world. What we know is that it was the incendiary character of the early Christian fellowship which was amazing to the contemporary Romans and that it was amazing precisely because there was nothing in their experience that was remotely similar to it.

—Elton Trueblood, *The Incendiary Fellowship*, p. 107.

3. The Integrity of the Church—Patterns of a Disciplined Life

Discipline is the procedure by which we learn.

You are a minister; therefore be secretly disciplined. A mature man is disciplined—secretly.

The word "discipline" has disagreeable connotations for most Americans. There is no need for this. The root word means "to learn," and the derivative from which the word comes directly means "to train" or "to teach." Discipline, therefore, is the procedure by which one learns, by which one is taught, or by which one trains oneself. Graphic evidence of discipline and the lack of it can be seen at a square dance. A young beginner enters into the festivities with vigor and enthusiasm, resembling a man trying to stamp out a brush fire. He misses the calls and snarls up everybody in his set, which is amusing—for a time. However, an old-timer, who may be fifty years the beginner's senior, will still be going strong and thoroughly enjoying himself long after the younger man has collapsed from exhaustion on the side lines. One is a disciplined, the other an undisciplined, dancer.

It is impossible to overemphasize the need for discipline. Without it, no man can realize his potentialities; certainly, none of the other elements of style discussed above is possible. Without discipline, affirmation of life becomes the rigid overemphasis of a fraction of life or the formless indulgence in one's latest whim. Awareness is reduced to a few fragments of knowledge understood and appreciated only by a small group of equally lazy people. Responsibility becomes willful "do-goodism" and irresponsible activism. The very thought of suffering causes panic. Without discipline, a man ceases to be a man; life becomes shattered and chaotic.

—Francis O. Ayres, *The Ministry of the Laity*, pp. 117–18.

Inner controls are indispensable.

Commitment is a necessary beginning, but it is far from being the end. Beyond commitment there is a vast amount of necessary toil, which cannot be accomplished without the glad acceptance of personal discipline. The renewed Church must be the disciplined fellowship of disciplined persons. The Christian who rejects inner controls, supposing that free self-expression is the essence of the Gospel, will never contribute to the renewal of the Church.

—Elton Trueblood, *The Incendiary Fellowship*, p. 74.

Seven steps for beginners.

A program which tells how many have found in the Christian Witnessing Fellowship a new faith, joy, effectiveness and purpose in daily living:
1. We acknowledged a problem or a concern which made our lives ineffective or unhappy.
2. We met regularly with others who understood our problem to share our experiences in Christian fellowship.
3. We had awakened in us a belief and a faith that God could accomplish in us and in our world what we could not do for ourselves.
4. Having been convinced that a new way of life through Christ was desirable and possible for ourselves and for mankind, by an act of our wills, we gave ourselves to God as we began to know Him in Christ.
5. We made a thorough check of our present and past lives against God's purpose for us as we saw it in the Lord Jesus Christ.
6. We confessed to God in the presence of one of His ministers such guilt memories as remained unhealed after we had repented and sought God's forgiveness through Christ.
7. We were baptized in obedience to Christ, and so became members of the Church.

Having come into awareness of Christ's presence through the Holy Spirit in us, we now seek to live daily as obedient children of God in the fellowship of His Church.

—Claxton Monro and William S. Taegel, *Witnessing Laymen Make Living Churches*, p. 64.

Learn to travel light.

If we are to take seriously the transformation of the Church as we know it into a genuine order, we must voluntarily accept an agreed discipline. Once a Christian has become a member of Christ's company he must be ready to give up some of his personal freedom, much as any soldier—and even as any Communist—does. He may, for example, no longer be the sole arbiter of his own time and energy; and he cannot be free to use all of his money on his own self-indulgence. He may have to give up his own personal plans in order to engage in a contemporary equivalent of Timothy's hurried return to Thessalonica. He is almost certain to give up some connections with clubs and societies which, though they may be innocent or valuable in their aims, are far too numerous in most modern lives. There will always be a sense in which a person who takes seriously his commitment to Christ will have to learn to travel light, giving up some particular involvements in order to make other involvements more truly revolutionary.

—Elton Trueblood, *The Company of the Committed*, p. 40.

Batting averages are known only to God.

In a Christian style of life, in conforming to Jesus Christ, in one's responsibility to God, batting averages are not known except to God—and he's not saying. Evidently, God is not too concerned. A man is free to do poorly or to fail completely. God seldom leaves a man without some sign of accomplishment—though he never grants the encouragement that men in their pride and weakness demand. What interests God seems to be intention, readiness, openness, faithfulness, perseverance. In other words, God calls men to obey him in fighting against evil and in conserving the good, and he has revealed to men that he will use whatever they offer him. Trust and obey. You are a minister; therefore be responsible.

—Francis O. Ayres, *The Ministry of the Laity*, p. 107.

He goes responsibly where he is sent.

You are a minister; therefore be responsible. You are called, freed, given gifts, and sent, in order that you may be responsible to God. A characteristic of mature manhood is responsibility to God for the world in which one lives.

From the Biblical point of view, all men are responsible to God. Created by him, they have been placed in the world and given dominion over it. They are answerable to God for what transpires there. However, baptized persons are responsible in a much more profound way. They (or others acting for them) have entered into a solemn engagement, a covenant, acknowledging and accepting their responsibility. In baptism, a man says Yes to the call of Christ. He goes responsibly where he has been sent. He says, "God is, I am: therefore I will obey God's will," and he knows that God's will, in Bonhoeffer's words, "is not an idea, still demanding to become real; it is itself a reality already in the self-revelation of God in Jesus Christ."

—Francis O. Ayres, *The Ministry of the Laity*, p. 98.

A one-month trial run.

One important fresh development, which began in the John Wesley Methodist Church of Tallahassee, Florida, and which has subsequently spread to other cities, particularly to Louisville, Kentucky, is that in which the hard disciplines are accepted, in the beginning, for only one experimental month.

The psychological advantage of this is apparent, because there are many sincere persons who hesitate to accept a discipline for all the rest of the time, yet will gladly try it for thirty days. It was found. in the Louisville experience, that a number of Christians who hesitated to tithe all year, were perfectly glad to give one tenth of their total income during the month of August. The happy outcome is that a considerable proportion of the experimenters have voluntarily decided to continue a practice which meant much more than they expected it to mean. They found that they were glad to be part of a movement in which discipleship really meant something, and a surprising proportion of these have now gone on from mere discipleship to apostleship.

—Elton Trueblood, *The Incendiary Fellowship*, pp. 74–75.

Awareness is the mark of a mature man.

You are a minister; therefore be aware. Knowledge, judgment, sensitivity, discernment—all are implied in awareness, and all are to be found in a mature man. Awareness has been chosen because it retains a freshness which knowledge, for instance, has lost and because it seems to point more directly to what the Bible holds as essential to man. . . .

Awareness as revealed in Jesus Christ incorporates a wide knowledge of, sensitivity to, and discernment of men, events, the world, and oneself. It is inseparably linked with action. It indicates a view of everything from the perspective of God's purpose—not only a conviction that "He's got the whole world in his hands," but also some understanding of what he intends it to be. Awareness is a part of being conformed to Christ, an element of a Christian style of life—in short, a characteristic of man and an essential ingredient of ministry.

—Francis O. Ayres, *The Ministry of the Laity*, pp. 88, 90–91.

Seven disciplines for Church members.

To glorify God, to strengthen the Church, to help the world, to grow in my Christian life, in the name of Jesus Christ our Lord, as an expression of my love for God, I will do my best to:

1. Seek God's plan through a daily time of listening prayer and Bible reading.
2. Worship weekly in the Church with emphasis on Holy Communion.
3. Participate regularly in a weekly group for Christian sharing, study, and prayer.
4. Give regularly a definite grateful share of my income to the spread of God's Kingdom through the Church and in the world.

And, as an expression of love for my neighbor I will do my best to:

5. Pray daily for others with thanksgiving.

6. Exercise faithfully the particular ministries to which God calls me in the fellowship of the Church and in the world.
7. Speak and act so that my daily life is a witness to the love of God in Christ as I have come to know it.

So help me God.

—Claxton Monro and William S. Taegel, *Witnessing Laymen Make Living Churches*, p. 78.

Free to be the slave of all.

To become and to be a Christian is not at all an escape from the world as it is, nor is it a wistful longing for a "better" world, nor a commitment to generous charity, nor fondness for "moral and spiritual values" (whatever that may mean), nor self-serving positive thoughts, nor persuasion to splendid abstractions about God. It is, instead, the knowledge that there is no pain or privation, no humiliation or disaster, no scourge or distress or destitution or hunger, no striving or temptation, no wile or sickness or suffering or poverty which God has not known and borne for men in Jesus Christ. He has borne death itself on behalf of men, and in that event He has broken the power of death once and for all.

That is the event which Christians confess and celebrate and witness in their daily work and worship for the sake of all men.

To become and to be a Christian is, therefore, to have the extraordinary freedom to share the burdens of the daily, common, ambiguous, transient, perishing existence of men, even to the point of actually taking the place of another man, whether he be powerful or weak, in health or in sickness, clothed or naked, educated or illiterate, secure or persecuted, complacent or despondent, proud or forgotten, housed or homeless, fed or hungry, at liberty or in prison, young or old, white or Negro, rich or poor.

For a Christian to be poor and to work among the poor is not conventional charity, but a use of the freedom for which Christ has set men free.

—William Stringfellow, *My People Is the Enemy*, p. 32.

Inner piety follows the form of outer mission.

To defend piety as an important aspect of the Church's life is not to propose that our immediate task is to cultivate a piety appropriate to metropolis. This is the mistake of most of the renewal movements in the churches. True piety emerges in the engagement of the Church with the world. *True piety is the subjective expression of the objective ministry of the Church in the world.* Only as the churches become the servanthood of the laity in the metropolitan areas will a piety emerge which is appropriate to metropolis. The Christian style of life is not the means to engagement in the world but the consequence of a ministry in the world. Christian virtues and perspectives enter into every ministry, of course, but the task of the Church can never be understood as the cultivation of such subjective attitudes and virtues. The Church is in the world to proclaim to the world its place within the saving history, man's history with God. The Church is not in the world to cultivate the emotional and moral integrity of its membership. The Church is not a spiritual culture society nor is it an ethical culture society, despite the appropriation of this name by one of the liberal churches of our day. The Church proclaims and lives a message of deliverance, freedom and hope in a world which finds itself caught in bondage and hopelessness. In that ministry and witness, Christians and the Christian Church manifest a piety, devotion, consecration and commitment which are appropriate to their witness in that particular moment of history. One can look for a new style of piety as the servanthood of the laity becomes the ministering reality of the Christian Church.

—Gibson Winter, *The New Creation As Metropolis*, pp. 25–26.

Poor sticks make a grand fire.

The metaphor of the fire would be meaningless without the fellowship, because it has no significance for merely individual religion, as it has none for merely ceremonial religion. Though it is, of course, impossible to have a committed Church with uncommitted members, the major power never appears except in a shared experience. Much of the uniqueness of Christianity, in its original emergence, consisted of the fact that simple people could be amazingly powerful when they were members one of another. As everyone knows, it is almost impossible to create a fire with one log, even if it is a sound one, while several poor logs may make an excellent fire if they stay together as they burn. The miracle of the early Church was that of poor sticks making a grand conflagration. A good fire glorifies even its poorest fuel.

—Elton Trueblood, *The Incendiary Fellowship*, pp. 107–8.

Brace yourself for suffering.

You are a minister; therefore be one with Christ in his sufferings. There is no more integral part of "human form" as revealed in Jesus Christ. . . . If being conformed to Jesus Christ is what it means to be a man, sharing in his sufferings is the basic test of manhood.

—Francis O. Ayres, *The Ministry of the Laity*, p. 108.

B. Called To Be a Servant—The Mission of the Church

"Church is mission." An emphasis, not a formula.

But in its simple form, "The church is mission," it leaves many questions as to its meaning and application. The very need for self-correction in the church can readily lead to a certain sloganizing that itself is a source of misunderstanding. "The church is mission" must thus be seen in the consensus as an important emphasis, but not as an absolute and all-inclusive formula.

—George W. Webber, *The Congregation in Mission*, p. 67.

Servant humility is the new way of mission.

The Church's mission must take the same form as Christ's own mission; it must take the form of a servant. This is the new way of mission, the way of the servant and the way of humility. It is the way of dying to the cultural and ideological forms in which Christianity has been clothed, so that the Church may grow up through the new structures of society. It is the way of Calvary, the way of the cross and death, leading to a new life. How can the Church find the form of a servant? This is the basic problem of the structures of mission and the renewal of the Church.

—B. N. Y. Vaughan, *Structures for Renewal*, p. viii.

What is the mission of the Church?

Some years ago, when I was president of the National Council of Churches, I paid a Christmas visit to the troops at Thule in the far north of Greenland. As I remember it, there were some ten thousand men stationed in that cold, twenty-four-hour darkness. Why were they there? Most of them were struggling to keep each other warm, housed, fed, and entertained. The *mission* of the base was to keep at twenty-four-hour alert a small wing of fighter planes to intercept any bomber force which might be sent across the pole from Russia to attack the United States. The Christian Church, without its mission, could very well be compared to the Thule military base without any fighter planes.

What is the mission of the Church? It is to proclaim by word and act the good news to all men that God was in Jesus Christ reconciling the whole world to Himself. Unless the Church is doing that job, it had better be liquidated. History does not reveal a pretty story about the Church. Again and again in various crises, the Church has been false to God and betrayed the true saints among its members.

—Eugene Carson Blake, *The Church in the Next Decade*, p. 104.

The Church is a servant of the majority from a minority position.

Hawthorne House is a nonprofit, nondenominational, community-based "thing," which might be called a "counter-sign" of hope and purpose and creative activity. It is not an ecclesiastical institution, its primary focus has nothing to do with a congregation. Yet it means the Church is present to this city today in a special way. And perhaps this is what the Lord intends in this age for his Church. Perhaps it is just to be the servant of the majority from a minority position, the unknown and uninvited fellow traveller on the road to the New City. This means that we rejoice to be his inadequate, unrecognized, even suffering servants, few enough to be a gathering, a community without a resting place who on occasion assemble, knowing and celebrating the love and wisdom of the Incarnate Word, collaborating with every brother to make a new worldly neighborhood.

—Michael F. Groden and Sister Miriam Clasby, "Church As Counter-sign: Process and Promise," *The Underground Church*, ed. Malcolm Boyd, p. 114.

A doctrine of the Church—a product of mission.

What is required is to move ecclesiology out of the center of theological concern, for as soon as ecclesiology becomes central it is falsified. The way to a true ecclesiology must be indirect, for the church is meant to be not an end in itself but the servant of God's mission to the world.

—Colin W. Williams, *The Church*, p. 16.

Servant ministry—a clue to the world's destiny.

Certainly the church itself needs to become a demonstration community in which the world can see how the forces that bar the way to true community are overcome by the power of servant love. But a demonstration community exists precisely so that what is being demonstrated can then be accepted elsewhere. Thus, the church has its second task: training members to take this way of Christ into the other institutions of the world so that they can find their God-given ministries. Then the church and the other institutions alike can find in the servant ministry of Christ the clue to the world's destiny. They can discover that this weak way of servant love has been shown by the surprising Christ of the cross to carry the secret of God's power to save the world.

—Colin W. Williams, *The Church*, p. 99.

The distinctive shape of Christian service.

From these concrete examples perhaps we can generalize concerning the "difference" between humanitarian services and the witness of a Christian servant. There are at least three distinctive aspects of the shape of Christian service.

1. *Motivation.* One may do "good deeds" for a variety of motives. A humanist may be motivated by his reverence for and gratitude to life itself. The Christian servant is motivated by his reverence for and gratitude to the Lord of life, Jesus Christ. It is the knowledge of Christ's love that drives a Christian servant to serve others as Christ has served him (John 13:1–15). The humanist may indeed be a superlative person with great compassion. But only the Christian goes forth because he has been sent by Christ, to offer the love of Christ. . . .

2. *Resources.* The humanist brings the depth of his own concern. The Christian servant comes primarily not in his own strength but in the strength of Christ. The Christian servant, and only he, can point to Christ, who is the hope of finding meaning in suffering that is beyond stoic endurance. The Christian can bring the promise of resurrection, and the living hope of an inheritance which "nothing can destroy or spoil or wither" (I Pet. 1:4, NEB).

3. *Fellowship.* The humanist comes by himself, speaks for himself, and offers his own services. The Christian servant comes as a representative of a witnessing community, a corporate life that includes him but goes far beyond him, that bears him up and gives him power and joy. The fact that there are, at any one time, several Aldersgate people engaged in this ministry together is dramatic expression of the truth that the *church* is there in their servanthood. The possibility of sharing in the community of faith, through this kind of conversation and in wider fashion through prayer, is something only the Christian brings.

Changes take place in those Christian witnesses that are sometimes highly visible to those who know them well. Their friends and family can see something new happening in them, interpret it as they will.

—Robert A. Raines, *Reshaping the Christian Life*, pp. 73–74.

The only thing we have to offer is Jesus Christ.

The content of our service is the love of Christ, poured out freely wherever there is human need. Whatever the wineskins by which we seek to serve our brothers, the only thing we have to offer is Jesus Christ. That fact alone distinguishes the work of Christians from all others who seek to help their fellow men.

—George W. Webber, *God's Colony in Man's World*, p. 90.

Existing only to pour out its life.

This concept of the church as servant ought to make us cautious about using the oft-employed image of a church militant. The church does not exist in order to conquer its foes; God does that for it. On the contrary, it exists in order to pour out its life in service—healing the sick, casting out demons, cleansing lepers, restoring sight for the blind, providing food for the hungry, giving rest to the weary, making homes for the homeless, bringing comfort to the distraught, preaching peace to those near and far. Like Jesus himself, it lives by dying, pouring out its life to satisfy human need wherever and in whatever form it finds it. It does not strive to guarantee its own future even; rather, it lives by God's grace, seeking only to magnify him and his rule (Matt. 16:25).

—E. Glenn Hinson, *The Church: Design for Survival*, p. 35.

Either an evangelist, or getting ready to be one.

No person is really a Christian at all unless he is an evangelist or is getting ready to be one. The person who supposes that he can be a Christian by observing a performance, whether of the Mass or anything else, has missed the whole idea. There is nothing wrong with watching a performance, providing the watching serves to make the daily apostleship more real, but there is terrible wrong in watching a performance whenever this serves as the *end*. The Church, however large its buildings and however grand its ceremonies or vestments, is a denial of Christ unless it is affecting the world—in business and government and education and many other segments of human experience.

—Elton Trueblood, *The Company of the Committed*, pp. 70–71.

The Church is unique. She exists for the salvation of men.

In the matter of mission, the Church of Jesus Christ is absolutely unique in history. She exists for the salvation of men. No other organization or institution has this mission. There are hundreds of organizations, in addition to government itself, which exist for the social welfare of men; and incidentally, these organizations are manned in great part by church people and receive a great part of their financial support from church people. And they are doing what they are designed to do. But, their purpose is not directed to the eternal spiritual welfare of men. If the Church fails here, there is no organization that will fill the breach. The Church cannot, must not, default in this mission, however busy she may be in her care and concern for men.

Humanitarianism is not Christianity. The central purpose of the Church and of every individual Christian is to witness to the Lordship of Jesus Christ as the Savior of everyone who will accept Him as the Lord of life in this world and in the world to come—beyond the grave. This is relevant.

—Richard C. Halverson, *Relevance*, p. 42.

The difference between mission and missions.

Our confusion about the mission of the church comes to the surface almost any time we talk about missions. In the town and country parish there is precious little awareness that the local parish is God's cutting edge against the world, that "the end of the world" for anyone can be measured spiritually by the distance he is from Christ. Since the parish, in common thinking, is primarily an organization, missions must be some sort of extension of our organization: missions are what we *do* above and beyond what we *are* as a parish. Thus missions are pigeonholed to mean work far away or work among people less fortunate.

—Paul R. Biegner, "In Town and Country," *Death and Birth of the Parish*, ed. Martin E. Marty, p. 61.

The softness and toughness of good diplomacy.

Being an ambassador for Christ means that we are in the world to represent the best interests of our Lord. But some of us are so undiplomatic, so obvious, so naive, so violent, so arbitrary, so brittle, so inflexible, so self-willed. May God give us the softness and the toughness good diplomacy requires. . . .

What is required of us as ambassadors of Christ? Paul reminds us "That he died for all, that they which live should not henceforth live unto themselves, but unto him which died for them, and rose again." This is very plain language. In the light of this requirement it is not difficult to understand the absence of power of the Church in the world. How pathetically self-centered we are. How desperately self-seeking. How defensive of self. How protective of self. How ambitious for self. Think what would happen if every Christian really gave himself away to Christ and began to live, not for himself, but for his Lord.

—Richard C. Halverson, *Relevance*, pp. 50–51.

The first century Church would recognize our situation.

He makes the point that in actual fact the missionary task of the church in the twentieth century has more parallels with that of the first century than with any other era of Christian history.

—George W. Webber, *God's Colony in Man's World*, p. 63.

The suffering servant.

The most disturbing experience for church members in our time is to find their confessional assemblies divided over public and economic issues. Men and women today look to the local congregation as a haven from conflict and tension. Clergymen view their work as the maintenance of harmonious relationships within the flock; the frictionless machine is the ideal image of the congregation. The creation of such *harmonious enclaves* is an indication of the utter dislocation of the Church in our society. The Church is intended to be a *suffering body* in the world, showing forth the Lord's death until He come. This community in Christ is not called to sacrifice its ministry of reconciliation in order to preserve its inner tranquillity. This body is called to bear within itself the sufferings imposed upon it by a ministry of reconciliation within the broken communication of the world. Reopening broken communication will inevitably tear and disrupt the internal life of the Church, but that inner suffering is the essential nature of the authentic presence of the New Mankind in the world. The work of the clergyman is not to spare the ministering fellowship from internal suffering by diverting it from its ministry; his task is to open new possibilities of ministry to which the servant

Church is summoned, deepening the reflection of the prophetic fellowship in the course of its sufferings. There is no Church without such a ministry.

—Gibson Winter, *The New Creation As Metropolis*, pp. 127–28.

The dangers of servanthood.

Churches that are always aware of their relation to God and the world as a disciple-servant relationship safeguard themselves from the corrosion which inevitably results from a sharp separation of the time of learning and the time of doing. When Churches feel that they have learned once for all and thus enter upon their time of service, they are sure to shift in time from an inquiring concern for the tasks in which they are engaged; they are sure to shift to a self-confident authority and certainty about the validity and suitability of the ways they have chosen to do their work. Not only do they cease to grow but they lose whatever imagination, dynamic, and creativity they once had.

It is not inconceivable that when Churches think only in terms of servanthood, that is, of a performing ministry learned once for all, they may actually come to the time when they serve the world with an authoritarianism and unresponsiveness which are the properties, in the extreme sense, of bigotry and fanaticism resulting from the absolutizing of specific forms of ministry and the self-idolization of the performer. It has not been uncommon in history to find the creative, devout, and strict observer of religious duty changing the prophet's robe of righteousness and sensitivity to the will of God for the Pharisee's garment of self-righteousness and self-will.

Ignorant of the changing needs and demands of the present generation, such Churches alienate the world to which they have been sent. And how quickly they condemn inquiring needy people of sin when these people look in other directions for the fulfillment of their needs!

The servant Church must also be a disciple, learning through its contacts with those whom it serves. It learns the extent to which it is meeting the real needs of the present age, and how it should adapt its presentation of the Gospel to new conditions and circumstances. Its disciple-servant relationship, however, must remain a dynamic one to meet the unforeseen changes of our urbanized and industrialized society with creative, imaginative, even hitherto untried, forms and structures of ministry.

—Jesse McNeil, *Mission in Metropolis*, pp. 41–42.

C. The Location of Service—The World

The Church lives its life in the world, still largely unrecognized.

However, the fact that the church lives most of its life in the world is still largely unrecognized. This explains why it is so hard to see the church's people when we look closely at the urban scene. They live on every city block, work in every office building, belong to almost every organization, vote in every election. Yet, they have failed to see that they are Christ's ministers within the metropolitan region. In fact, they have often been among those who have turned in horror from the complexities of the city's problems and its sinful neglect of proper worship to God. Repelled by the overwhelming task facing those who seek to maintain or criticize or reconstruct the *status quo*, they have neglected the very ministry to which they were called by Christ—preaching the gospel to *the whole creation*. Unlike Jesus, who himself ate with tax collectors and sinners, the churches gathered in his name refuse to acknowledge that God's redeeming love is sufficient for the multitudes of the metropolis.

Some churches in America's cities are beginning to recover the power of their Lord's command. Turning from a concept of mission that would see their main task to be filling the pews of the sanctuary on Sunday or crowding the building with activity every day of the week, they have called their members to the realization that the church's main ministry is carried on in the world, in the life of every day, in that which finds its focus outside the walls of the meetinghouse. The Christian is being helped to see that his daily work, no matter how prosaic or humble, is a part of his worship to God. The janitor and school teacher, the bank executive and factory worker, the postal employee and housewife—each in his own way shares in the God-given task of creating community through the *status quo;* each in his own way bears a portion of God's judgment upon the powers that be through challenge and criticism; each in his own way responds to God's redemption of the world in Christ as he takes part in the task of social reconstruction. The daily work of the church's members is a part of its ministry.

—George D. Younger, *Church and Urban Power Structure*, pp. 76–77.

The tension of being "in" but not "of" the world.

A church that is not *in* the world has forgotten what the incarnation is all about; but a church that is *of* the world has forgotten both the divine judgment that is being passed upon the world and also the promise that human life can be made new. It is not surprising, however, in view of the double requirement to be *in* the world yet *not of* the world, that throughout the history of the church large numbers of Christians have emphasized one aspect of this relationship to the exclusion of the other. On the one hand, many churches, seeking to remain uncorrupted by secular society, have chosen the path of *withdrawal* from culture. Others, remembering only the requirement that they be in the world, have become *folk churches;* as such they have viewed themselves as the guardians of the particular cultures in which they have been set. But from the beginning there has been a third group of churches which have endeavored to enter into the life of the world and bear witness to the relevance of Christian faith for the totality of human existence without themselves becoming captive to the values and idolatry of the world. Such churches have understood the normative relationship between the church and the world in terms of creative *tension* or polarity.

—E. Clinton Gardner, *The Church As a Prophetic Community*, p. 182.

The Church has difficulty seeing God in the secular.

If it is a difficult feat of imagination for contemporary Christians to see how the power of grace emerges in a Samaritan or in individuals who are atheistic revolutionaries, the difficulty is compounded when we are called to discover this life as it manifests itself in secular institutions and broad historical forces.

—Myron B. Bloy, Jr., *The Crisis of Cultural Change*, p. 81.

Christians and the growth of a healthy culture.

Turning now to the present, it may be said that Christians today have a twofold task to perform with respect to culture. First, by taking the risk of commitment and submitting that commitment to judgment, Christians encourage their neighbors to undertake such a risk too. For courage is, hopefully, contagious even when the loyalties and commitments are dissimilar. Secondly, Christians should describe as imaginatively as possible in act and word the relevance of their commitment to the present cultural crisis, offering their own viewpoint as a possible focus of self-identity to the culture. Thus, implicitly and explicitly, they have a crucial role to play in the growth of a healthy culture.

—Myron B. Bloy, Jr., *The Crisis of Cultural Change*, p. 43.

The Church is often a little island of irrelevant piety.

One day several years ago I was sitting in a dentist's chair and my good friend, Dr. James Sheets, was working on my teeth. He had just been asked to serve as president of the Inglewood, California school board. Recognizing the fact that such a responsibility would force him to drop much of what he was doing in the church, he asked for my opinion. As he talked, I felt a deep sense of resentment welling up within me. The very idea! What right did that board have to rob "my" church of one of its finest leaders? Fortunately, my mouth was propped wide open and I could not respond immediately to his request for advice. As the moments passed, the Spirit of God began to deal with me, and when I was able to speak, I said something like this: "Jimmie, I can't imagine anything more wonderful than for a committed Christian like you to be president of a board of education in a thriving and growing city."

What a contrast to my previous reaction! When I began my ministry twenty-three years ago, I planned and labored as though the work of the church consisted in the maintenance and in the prosperity of the establishment . . . and incidentally—my personal success. The work of the church was what we did in the building and for the institution. In short, the work of the church was . . . the PROGRAM. In those days I had one simple criteria for a good member: it was his involvement with the establishment; his attendance at stated meetings; his work for the building and the program. Obviously, a person who attended Sunday school, morning worship, Sunday evening groups, evening service, and mid-week prayer meeting was five times the Christian that someone was who attended only on Sunday morning. I actually resented all competition with community and civic organizations . . . and, above all, other churches. Everything outside "my church," including other Christian organizations, constituted a threat to my success. If P. T. A. met on Wednesday evening, it was understood that prayer meeting would be the choice of the "dedicated" Christian. It was absolutely unthinkable that any good member would let Rotary, or the Chamber of Commerce, or a union meeting, or a school function interfere with his proper "commitment."

What has been the result of this kind of thinking and practice? The church has succeeded in pulling Christians out of the world—out of society—out of community and civic affairs. So often it is a little island of irrelevant piety surrounded by an ocean of need. And our preoccupation with the establishment has been so complete that we have been unable to see the ocean . . . except, of course, if there is someone out there that we want to recruit for the program. The congregation has become an exclusive little system of satellites orbiting around the program . . . or perhaps, it would be more accurate and honest to say, orbiting around the pastor. In the meantime those "secular" institutions out there in the community, lacking leadership which takes God seriously, are so frequently being led by persons who have little or no time for the church. Now we bemoan the fact that labor unions, service clubs, chambers of commerce, school systems, and the government itself have been so thoroughly secularized that the church is on the outside, without influence.

The blasphemous contradiction of this concept began to dawn on me several years ago when I recognized the frustration of good men in the church with nothing to do. For example, Hollywood Presbyterian Church, where I served for nine years, had about 1,750 men on the rolls, but needed not more than 365 to run its affairs. The church I now serve has nearly 300 men and needs only 65 to run the establishment. The sheer absurdity of this caricature of the work of the church comes to light when one sees how busy some pastors are trying to "find jobs" for members . . . and the best they can do is to challenge them to go down to the church on Tuesday evening and paint the chairs in the primary department.

—Richard C. Halverson, Relevance, pp. 73–75.

God is not a stranger in the world.

As I reflect upon these controversies, what they amounted to were reflections of the differences within American Protestantism at large as to the meaning of God's concern for and presence in this world. From my own vantage point and experience on that issue, the Christian faith is not about some god who is an abstract presence somewhere else, but about the living presence of God here and now, in this world, in *exactly* this world, as men know it and touch it and smell it and live and work in it. That is why, incidentally, all the well-meant talk of "making the gospel relevant" to the life of the world is false and vulgar. It secretly assumes that God is a stranger among us, who has to be introduced to us and to our anxieties and triumphs and issues and efforts. The meaning of Jesus Christ is that the Word of God is addressed to men, to *all* men, in the very events and relationships, any and every one of them, which constitute our existence in this world. That is the theology of the Incarnation.

—William Stringfellow, *My People Is the Enemy*, p. 97.

Mission is not to bring the world into the Church.

The church's mission is not primarily to bring the world into the church but to *be* the church in the world. We are a world-oriented people. Our task is to participate in God's mission there—the God who so loved the world He gave His Son, who sent the Son not to condemn but to save the world, who was in Christ reconciling the world to Himself. Jesus told the disciples that they were the salt of the *earth*, the light of the *world*, the leaven of the *lump*, sheep in the midst of *wolves*. We are sent-people, apostles, missionaries. The world is the field of our mission.

—Robert A. Raines, *Reshaping the Christian Life*, p. 34.

Mission is shaped by the world's needs.

The Church is discovering that it is called not only to reunion but also to renewal of its mission to serve the world. Those who listen closely at the places where the world's needs are crying for help, where the crises of change and growth ask for guidance, or where the danger of divisions calls for the presence of a reconciler, find that it is not only the problem of the reunion of the Churches which must be faced, but also the question of how unity, when it has been rediscovered, can be used to serve the true needs of the world. When we have listened to the agony, the fear and the hope of the world and had the demand for our own reconciliation as Christians laid upon us again, we still have to answer the question of how the Church can perform its mission to the world which it has begun to rediscover.

This is why we have to face the question of what has come to be called 'Church,' or better, 'missionary structures.' It is the question of how the Church should marshal its forces or deploy its ministry to meet the needs of society today. And we use the term 'structures' here without the definite article, as Hans Kung does in his *Structures of the Church* to differentiate those structures which the mission of the Church adapts to the social changes, from 'the structure' of the Church itself which is unchangeable. For we must distinguish between the shape which sociological facts impose on the mission exercised by the Church from what A. G. Hebert calls 'the form of the Church' itself which is theologically determined and constant.

On this question of structures, which is basic to the renewal of the Church, it is becoming increasingly clear that the shape of the future mission of the Church will only be adequately determined by listening to those at the places where the world itself is taking new shape, and by exposure to the new as well as the old forces which are at work there.

—B. N. Y. Vaughan, *Structures for Renewal*, p. v.

"Holy worldliness" as a style of life.

Our search for a style of life in our day will not focus primarily on a new piety, however, but on preparation for witness and service in a world which has rejected God. A fine phrase often used to describe a style of life for our day is "holy worldliness." We can readily understand what is meant by "holy otherworldliness" or "unholy worldliness." We expect the church to live in one of two different worlds and like to keep them honestly separated. The style of life for the church in the twentieth century involves learning once again to live a holy life in the midst of the world. The missionary congregation is called so to live that it is able to dirty its hands in the life of the world where God is at work and at the same time to share in the joyous liberty of Christian freedom.

—George W. Webber, *The Congregation in Mission*, pp. 114–15.

A colony of the King.

In such a colony three basic facts of their existence were "existentially" apparent. First, the colony was utterly dependent upon the homeland if it were to be sustained in the middle of a hostile world. Only the infrequent ships bringing supplies and new personnel along with encouragement from the homeland made it possible for the colony's life to be continued. It was the lifeline to the homeland which could not be severed if the colony were to continue in strength during those early years. In the second place there was an unmistakable unity which surrounded the lives of the colonists. They were all in the same boat. If a child contracted smallpox, the lives of everyone were in danger. If the Indians attacked, all had to come to the defense of the colony. They were, in a unique sense, made into one family. Finally, the colony recognized that its only reason for existence was its work in the world. Although by night it was necessary to withdraw behind the stockade for protection from the Indians and the marauding beasts, the work of the colony was outside the fence, in the tasks of subduing the wilderness and bringing it under the lordship of the colony's own king. The work of the colony was in farming the land, fishing the streams, and colonizing the Indians. The colony in its own interior life existed only to make possible the task of the colony in its dispersed life in the world.

—George W. Webber, *God's Colony in Man's World*, p. 45.

Interpreters of Christ's presence in the world.

It is all very well to speak of the church involving itself in these new areas of decision: but in what way? Many shudder at the thought of the church as an institution trying to regain control of the world; and insist that the church can only truly witness to the Lordship of the humble Christ when it respects the freedom of the secular world from this institutional control. For that reason we often speak today of the 'scattered church' and of Christian witness being given to the laity in dispersion in a way that fully respects the autonomy of these realms from the church whose institutional task is to train Christians for their life in dispersion.

That there is real truth here we can acknowledge; but in this way also lie grave dangers. One popular metaphor speaks of the laity being trained to light their candles from the central candle in the church so that they may then spread out into the secular realms taking with them the light of Jesus Christ. But what if our task is to be not so much the *source* of light for the world by bringing it *from* the church, but to be those who are to discern the light that is shining in the darkness of the world? Then our task as the church is to be out there learning what Christ is doing in the world, and seeking to be his interpreting presence—shining as lights by reflecting the continuing deeds of the living Lord as he is working out his purpose in the events of history.

—Colin Williams, *What in the World?*, pp. xix–xx.

Give to society its proper shape.

Ever since the apostles looked for "seven men" to take care of the business matters in the church, the church has been involved *officially* with the physical and social concerns of society. In early times, the church was the first organization to provide hospitals, orphanages, old people's homes, and other such facilities for local communities. It fought for the humane treatment of prisoners, and it boldly rebuked emperors when it thought they were intruding upon the freedom of their people. "Love of the brethren," "seeing Christ in every man"—these were the profound attitudes which propelled early Christian leaders into the center of community life, and inspired them to shape that community life as no other group of people has ever done before or since.

So it is, and must always be, a characteristic function of the church to shape society, to be effective in the creation of human communities.

The church's disorientation from the modern community is therefore something unnatural to it—its concerns are too limited; its resources are too largely neglected.

—Perry L. Norton, *Church and Metropolis*, pp. 75–76.

Keep your eyes open for grace.

The individual who has discovered in Jesus of Nazareth the power to be a man and comes to celebrate this fact with others who have made the same discovery will—if his imagination is not barred from that expectation—grow increasingly sensitive to the movement of this power in the "secular" world. Just as the seasoned gambler seems to have a sixth sense for the game where the stakes are highest, so the Christian growing in grace will develop a special sensitivity for these crucial manifestations of grace, of authentic existence, in the world. Grace manifests itself in many simple, silent ways, to be sure: but it is also inevitably present in the midst of issues that touch crucially the growth of mankind into its adulthood. For example, when the late Senator McCarthy mounted an attack on our traditions and institutions of individual freedom and evoked a slavish fear in all too many hearts, only a few men defended these bastions and turned back the demonic attack. To stand, in that case, with the power of grace was to stand in a conserving or defensive position. Yet just as often our spiritual growth is the real issue in movements of revolutionary change, and in this connection we have already taken note of the Freedom Movement. Wherever man's adulthood as we see it revealed in Jesus of Nazareth is being attacked or is on the move, *that* is where "the action" lies for Christians, *that* is where Christians are called to celebrate the power of grace in the world by placing themselves in its presence, by affirming and holding it up so that others may recognize its life-witnessing power, too.

—Myron B. Bloy, Jr., *The Crisis of Cultural Change*, pp. 125–26.

One may hear God speak in a movie.

Affirmation of life means to enter fully into everything God has created, into all that man with God's help has created. This in no way negates the true purpose of men, companionship with God and each other, but it asserts that God is met in the midst of life and that God always talks with men in terms of their life in the world. One does not go to a movie, announcing, "I am going to meet God." That would be unbearably pious and presumptuous. One goes to a top-grade movie because it is a product of God's Creation and, consequently, is to be enjoyed by man. Nevertheless, there is always the possibility that one will meet God in a movie and hear him speak.

—Francis O. Ayres, *The Ministry of the Laity*, p. 81.

God is engaged in politics.

The Bible confronts the church with the political perspective in a developed form. From beginning to end God is engaged in politics—ordering the destinies of men and nations. The Bible is full of political images—covenants, kingdoms, rulers, judges, and finally a Messiah who heralds the onset of a new kingdom establishing God's rule on earth. The climax of the story of redemption is political through and through. The Son who was born brings about God's rule in men's hearts; that is, makes them truly human according to God's purposes by reconciling them to their creator and to one another. God is at work in his Holy Spirit, not only to make, but to keep men truly human. In Christ we discover our true humanity. Thus the gospel is a "secular event." It is for the world and about the world.

—George W. Webber, *The Congregation in Mission*, p. 52.

Watch for God among the pagans.

When the Church sees itself as a piece of the world used by God to approach the world which he would redeem, it also is rescued from the temptation to think that God speaks only within the institution of the Church. Knowing that God's purpose enfolds the whole world, and that the Church is a segment of the world which exists for the world, it also knows that God is at work in the rest of the world outside the Church; that he speaks to the world also through pagan witnesses, and that the Church must therefore watch for the signs of God's presence in the world, ready to reach out to work with God at the points where he is at work and to be open to "humble dialogue with pagans."

This attempt to describe the Church in dynamic terms drawn from its role as a servant of God's mission to the world, even to the point of seeing the lines which mark the boundary of the Church's relation to the world dissolve, is one which cuts beneath the unfortunate separations between the Church and the world and forces the Church to seek continually for forms of life which will enable it to maintain situations of dialogue in the world and lines of service within the institutions of the world.

—Colin Williams, *Where in the World?*, pp. 48–49.

Needed: a sociological study of church life in the New Testament.

It is in terms of the "outsider," the hearer of the Gospel, that the life and proclamation of the local Christian community is to be judged and conceived. The basic truth of this affirmation is that even the most solid of church members is himself an "outsider" and that every element of church order is but a provisional and limited response to specific situations. Every attempt to codify and institutionalize this response denies both historical change as well as social and institutional variety. By separating itself from the social and historical processes of the world, the Christian community unfailingly demonstrates its profoundest worldliness. On the other hand, when the Christian community recognizes that its authenticity depends not on given forms of order, worship or service, but on God's own action of calling, sustaining and forgiving, then it will be free to reshape its life and worship in terms of the particular historical and social reality in which it must bear its witness.

Consequently, what is needed is a thoroughly sociological study of congregational life within the New Testament, which would indicate precisely how the life of the "outsider" (by this term I imply the general cultural and social milieu) did—and often did not—dictate the forms of congregational life in different areas of the New Testament world. Such studies have already been carried out with respect to the specifically theological traditions of the New Testament. But we must recognize that theological reflection does not exhaust the life of early Christianity. This reflection was but one element among others in the life of the community. The shape of the community, as well as the shape of its theology, was created by a concern for authentic existence in a given—undoubtedly unique—historical situation. Once we have recognized this fundamental principle, we will be set free *from* slavery to the specific forms of the church in early Christianity and set free *to* discover their more fundamental theological and historical significance for our own Christian communities.

—John G. Gager, "The Local Christian Community in the New Testament,"
Planning for Mission, ed. Thomas Wieser, p. 152.

To the critics: the Church is already in the world.

One consequence of the future changes, we are always being told, is that the Church must descend from the ivory towers which it is said to inhabit and, instead, immerse itself in the whole life of the world. Since, on Christian terms, the world is God's world, the advice seems evidently sound, but it is also singularly vague. What does it mean and who is to be thus immersed? Clearly, the Church must so present the Gospel that it infiltrates into every part of the world. Clearly, also, there are many parts of the world's present life where this is not being done. But it is really rather stale news to tell us that God is just as interested in what goes on in the factory as in what goes on inside the church. It is something which no one doubts. All the many experiments which we have made in recent years to immerse the Church in the world do not seem to have gone very far. Plainly something much more far-reaching than a few industrial chaplains, still fewer worker priests, and the suggestion that young laymen should be trained to bear their Christian witness in their trade union branches rather than by teaching in the Sunday school, is needed.

The best way of approaching a very difficult problem is, perhaps, to remind ourselves that the Church is already in the world and, if it is God's world, then the Church and all its people are part of it now and already immersed in it to a considerable extent. The Church is indeed not synonymous with the world, nor is it yet the whole of the world, even though it must permeate the whole. Therefore, the immersion of a Christian in the Church and his absorption in the life and work of the Church is not necessarily a withdrawal from the world.

—Roger Lloyd, *The Ferment in the Church*, pp. 113–14.

D. The Agenda of the Servant Mission

Christ's pattern of engagement with the world.

The basic clue for missionary structures at this point lies in seeking as laity to follow the pattern of Christ's own engagement in the world; Incarnation (presence as a true man in the world), Crucifixion (ministry to the human needs of the world), and Resurrection (witness to the ultimate power and victory of God over the world).

—George W. Webber, *The Congregation in Mission*, p. 138.

Restorationism of New Testament forms is a mistake.

The apostles lived their allotted years during the first century, subject to the social and cultural conditioning of their time and place. So how, it is often asked, are we Christians able to recapture the life and character of the apostolic Church? The answer proposed by some Christians today is disarmingly simple: Let the Church take the form it had in the time of the apostles. This is appealing. There is a tendency among Christians to be inordinately sentimental about certain 'golden ages' of the Church's history. According to the varieties of their interest, they idealize the New Testament community, the Church of the first five centuries, the thirteenth century, the Church of the Reformation, the movement of the Wesleys, or the little brown church in the vale. But there is little practical help for the improving of church life today which can come from the indulging in sentimental thoughts about the churches of yesterday.

The Christians described in the Acts of the Apostles did not live in an ecclesiastical Garden of Eden. There was never a time when they could live in community with a shameless disregard for such metaphorical fig leaves as might cover the defects in their faith and service. Heaven may have lain about the Church in its infancy; but the clouds of glory which came trailing after did not long persist after the first few years. Not even in the days of the apostles could the Church be described as a colony of heaven which perfectly reflected on this planet the way of life in the homeland.

In calling for the renewal of the churches according to the criterion of apostolicity, therefore, we need not embrace the doctrinaire position of New

Testament restorationism. There is a partial validity to this view in so far as it emphasizes precisely some basic elements for which we have been contending: namely, the normative truth of the apostolic message, the pristine sense of community, and the personal life of faith in Jesus Christ. But the unconvincing error of restorationism is its notion that the churches of the twentieth century can readily and exactly assume the form and character of the Church of the first century. The inevitably unsuccessful efforts to do this have led some Christians into a state of self-delusion and hypocrisy.

—J. R. Nelson, *Criterion for the Church*, pp. 27–28.

Basic characteristic of the Church-world relationship.

A preliminary question, however, requires our attention: If we seek to develop forms of Church life within these structures of the world, *what should be the basic characteristic of the church-world relationship?* Are we there primarily as informants (how can they hear without a speaker?) or as servants (that they may see your good works)?

—Colin Williams, *Where in the World?*, p. 85.

Missionary structures emerge from the dialogue with culture.

There is no "missionary structure" but countless structures through which congregations in various times and places will fulfill their function as God's instruments in the world. Our contention is that missionary structures are neither "given" in the Bible or tradition, nor are they simply the church's response to its particular situation. Rather, missionary structures must always emerge from the dialogue, continuous and necessary, between the faith of the church and its cultural setting.

—George W. Webber, *The Congregation in Mission*, p. 197.

The shape of the congregation in the world.

This understanding of the Church as Body has profound implications for the residential congregation, implications which are seldom adequately explored or followed out. The basic role of the minister is not to persuade people to serve him or the building or the institution or even one another. The role of the residential congregation or any other expression of vital Christian community is not simply to turn out better ushers, Church-school teachers, and lay assistants to the minister. The goal is to develop better fathers and wives and factory workers and politicians and citizens, who draw basic insight and strength from the beloved fellowship of the Spirit. The residential congregation, like the specialized ministries to be described in later chapters, must take on form and extension where men pull switches and voting levers, push brooms and bowling balls. And as the congregation takes shape it exists in these situations just as surely as in the colonial structure on the corner.

—Richard E. Moore and Duane L. Day, *Urban Church Breakthrough*, pp. 31–32.

Give up structures when they fail to meet a need in the world.

As I write this, those who have been the core members of the Workshop are leaving to pursue their work in new areas, and we are reminded that we must be willing to give up structures not only when they fail to meet a need in the world, but when they no longer provide the framework that lets us be on the "immense journey" of becoming. A call which is valid at one time in a person's life will not necessarily be valid at another time. The young parent may need a structure for his growing and giving entirely different from what he needed as a young single person. The gifts of middle age will have their specialness. The task one is called to in old age will not be that which called us in youth. If we are people on an inward journey, the goal will be more clearly perceived. Also, as we come to know ourselves at new depths, our values and emphases and direction may radically change.

—Elizabeth O'Connor, *Journey Inward, Journey Outward*, p. 35.

Read the Bible. Read the newspaper.

On the one side we need careful Biblical and theological study on the question of how we are called to seek the signs of God's presence in the world. At the same time we must watch what is happening on the moving edge of the church's relation to the world to see what God may be teaching us out of the struggle for contemporary obedience in the world.

—Colin Williams, *What in the World?*, p. 72n.

Define your mission field; equip your servants.

The purpose of our life together as Christians is to prepare us for effective Christian living in the world. It is the task of the church to equip its people for congregational and personal mission. There are limits to the mission fields for which the local church should prepare its members. Each congregation needs to define the missionary areas of its primary competence and responsibility and to perceive its peculiar vocation in the unfolding purpose of God. It is then free to rejoice in the specialized ministries, both traditional and experimental, provided for in mission fields outside its own purview.

At the same time, the local church should rightly seek to expose its people to the whole of life in its cultural setting. In appropriate ways every church must seek to enable its members to be whole persons in the variety of ministries they perform in daily life and work. The particularity of the mission fields responsibly chosen by a local church will depend upon such factors as its size, location, congregational make-up, etc. *Every local church needs to define its own mission fields and appraise its congregational program in terms of its effectiveness or irrelevance to the task of equipping its people for mission.*

—Robert A. Raines, *Reshaping the Christian Life*, p. 41.

Judged by the twin tasks of worship and witness.

The Christian community, a body of those called from darkness into light by the power of God's grace, exists to *worship* and to *witness*. The whole life of the church must revolve around these foci. To give glory to God by its corporate worship and sacramental life and to serve his purpose by its existence as a colony in the world—these define the whole meaning of the church's life. The wineskins which are appropriate for the life of a colony must be judged by their capacity to contain these twin tasks of worship and witness.

—George W. Webber, *God's Colony in Man's World*, pp. 51–52.

The local church is the real Church.

There is a way, I think, by going at the ecumenical movement from a completely new direction—from the direction of its "low" side, rather than from its "high" side. It is just conceivable that in looking at the ecumenical movement from this perspective, we might discover that the "low" churches have something very "high" about them and that the "free" side has something very "authoritative" in its life.

What I would make bold to suggest here is a new look at the church, and the consideration by those who care, of a new basis for Christian unity. I think it could help to provide the new appreciation for each other about which we have all been talking, as well as an alternative plan toward that new unity in the church for which we all are seeking.

I would unashamedly ask here for a reconsideration, among ecumenical leaders and among the hosts of those who are concerned, of the principles of free churchmanship which have within them the seeds, at least, of a life common to all our traditions.

If the church is to live anywhere, if it is to become a reality anywhere, it must become a reality and live at the local level. There is no real church without somewhere, at some point, the gathered church—the church which Christ has gathered together in one place to live for him and to be faithful to him.

If the emphasis can be put on the power of the church at this local level to be really the church, really to be used by the Spirit of Christ, and if all the various traditions could center their thinking and conversation upon this vital level of the church's life, they would find, I am convinced, an increasing sense of unity, an increasing awareness of common heritage, and increasing excitement about the vast possibilities of a church united in heart and spirit at this level of day-to-day life.

The genius of such a view of the church is that a truly "Spirit church" becomes inevitably a reconciling church, in its internal life and in its life in the world; and as a reconciling church it can be nothing but a unifying and united church.

The key is the Spirit, and the willingness of all the churches and denominations to look to the Spirit as the heart and the hope of their new life. And
the gathered church could make it possible.

—Arthur A. Rouner, Jr., *The Free Church Today: New Life for the Whole
Church,* pp. 135–36.

How much can, and should, the local congregation do?

In such a situation as that of our day, we have to ask 'Why the local congregation at all?' and 'What is the inescapable basic minimum?' We are
moving now out of a period in which it was generally considered that a
congregation should do as much as possible, filling every moment of Sunday
and every week evening with activities, into one of asking: 'What must be
done in a gathered congregation and how much is better done elsewhere?'

—Kathleen Bliss, *We the People,* p. 125.

The "friendly enemies" and how they minister.

God has something significant for everyone to do as long as they do not
completely frustrate his primary business. It is, therefore, not our purpose
to dismiss from the church these "marginal members" whom God himself
has not dismissed. All we wish to say is that there is a danger here. These
people are the "friendly enemies" of the mission of the church as we have
described it. They are dangerous in the sense that their ignorance of the
meaning of the church weakens everything it does in the world, that even
when this ignorance is dispelled by "Christian education," they will not
tolerate a church that gives up spiritual things to mix itself up in the business
of the world. They will not break through the walls of their socioeconomic
ghettos and chummy coteries to contact and enter into dialogue with the
unconventional or alienated people of the community.

Nevertheless, the marginal members are also the church. They are indispensable to the mission in the sense that, for all their often reactionary
attitudes and peripheral involvement, they continue to be the main pool from
which the lay apostolate is recruited. Moreover, in so far as they continue to
identify with the institutional church and present to the powers that be, the
image of a "church public," they are important for the social mission. This
is, perhaps, not enough to say for people who are loved by God and members
of his household, but it is something. Their role in the American churches
today is extremely ambiguous. For that reason it is not inappropriate to call
them the "friendly enemies" of the church in its secular posture.

—Gayraud S. Wilmore, *The Secular Relevance of the Church,* p. 64.

Changes in mental, institutional, and community structures.

The conviction of those who are pressing towards a major re-shaping of
the relation of the church to the world can perhaps be summarized by point-

ing to three levels of change which they believe to be necessary—changes, also, which they believe to be already occurring.

First, they believe we are in the midst of *a massive restatement of the gospel,* with the need for the discovery of a new language of interpretation in order that we may fulfil our missionary task. This we have called the problem of "mental structures."

Second, they are sure that we are on the threshold of *a major realignment of the forms of the church's life;* spurred by the necessity of discovering new forms of Christian presence in the world if we are to fulfil our missionary calling. This we have spoken of as the problem of "institutional structures."

Third, they speak of the necessity we are facing for fashioning *a new Christian style of life,* centering upon the necessity of discovering ways in which the laity can discover their secular ministries—learning to live within the structures of urban technological society in such a way that they can fulfil their missionary task of witnessing to the shape of the kingdom of God as it breaks in upon the kingdom of this world. This problem we may describe as the search for "personal and community structures."

—Colin Williams, *Faith in a Secular Age,* p. 107.

The free church tradition is the most exciting and the most dangerous.

The belief of the free churches of the gathered tradition is that it is in fact possible for a congregation of God's people to live faithfully under the sole authority of the Holy Spirit—and that it is possible for such congregations to live without any other human authority.

They are well aware that theirs is the most dangerous of church traditions. But they also believe it is one of the most exciting of church traditions. They believe it contains within its life much of what modern man is most eagerly looking for in church life: true democracy, seeking, pilgrim spirit, and equal, even exalted place for the laymen, the necessity of an attitude of humble devotion, and most particularly, an authentic new authority.

—Arthur A. Rouner, Jr., *The Free Church Today: New Life for the Whole Church,* p. 130.

Who shall make the decision about mission structure?

Who shall make the decision? Wary of lopsided authority within the church, and tired of humans presuming to know the divine will, Protestantism has built within it a reluctance to say that any worldly system should point out the ground rules of Christian discipleship. But this is not to say that we have avoided the subject, nor that we are unprepared politically to deal with it. The constitution of the Presbyterian and Reformed churches, for instance, contains the clear mandate that there are ascending courts of authority, and that this very question, namely, membership, belongs squarely in the laps of these judicatories. Most immediate and responsible of them is the session, or board of elders, or consistory, in which the presbyters of the local congregation are clearly charged to examine every applicant for membership on the basis of his preparation to serve and follow Jesus Christ. To put into effect a realistic grappling with factor Beta, the Presbyterian Church for one does not need to change a single word of its already established law. In churches of episcopal power, the presiding officer may or may not have to consult with the ecclesiastical parliament under him, but in most cases is quite capable of clarifying and defining all who would be Christians in his diocese. In the Episcopal Church, where the bishop assumes personal responsibility for confirming every member in the entire diocese, he may, and is constitutionally enabled to prescribe standards upon which he will consent to confirmation. So very little needs to be added to this type of church to determine the seat of decision, and originate a sensible definition.

In churches of congregational government, this will tend to be considerably more difficult, for no authoritative voice comes from outside the local parish. Individual heroic congregations, stimulated by the leadership of their more connectional brethren, may erect such standards of local parish worth as to inspire other churches of similar government to respond in kind. Here, as in so many historical developments down through the ages, it will depend on the churches of more centralized and efficient authority to set the pace, to color the prevailing characteristics of Protestant Christianity to the end that other individual congregations will be enlightened and inspired to follow.

—Wesley C. Baker, *The Split-Level Fellowship*, pp. 62–63.

The Establishment and the Servant are not incompatible.

But establishment itself is not incompatible with the role of the servant. In fact it can be the truest structural expression of it. When the Church has an external relation to the state, there is the greater temptation for it to build its own independent institutions, instead of serving in the house of another. Theologically, too, there is for the Christian no antithesis between the role of the Servant and that of the King. Paul Tillich, after a penetrating discussion of the priestly and prophetic relationships of the Church to society, goes on to insist that, like its Master, it also has its royal office. No position can be, or has been, so easily abused. But this does not release the Servant from responsibility.

—John A. T. Robinson, *The New Reformation*, p. 30.

Give up professional ministeries, real estate, and the local congregation.

Death by crucifixion was the world's way of getting rid of a disturber. Christ made himself vulnerable to the world. The Church is to be vulnerable to the world. It is to take the shape that the world needs. We are not to be protected by our own power structures which are so strong that the world cannot crucify us! Our faith says that the only way there can be rebirth is by death and that the Christian must always think in terms of death and resurrection.

The Church is in the world to die, not to develop power structures which protect it from any form of crucifixion.

The shape of the Church will be determined by the changing nature of the world itself. The Church must flow into the world, and its flow will take the shape of its channels. We must be willing to entertain wild hypotheses and fantastic possibilities. This is a very important frame of mind for people going into the wilderness.

Entertaining any possibility is quite different from recommending it; it is not saying, "This is what we must do." But several things occur to me.

  • I think we ought to be open to the giving up of all professional ministries. It may be that I ought to earn my livelihood another way. Perhaps all of the ministers of a congregation should be engaged in a tent-making ministry and do their job in the life of the world.

  • Another possibility is that of giving up all real estate. I think our present real estate serves us, but I think that a pilgrim people ought always to be open to the possibility of giving up all its real estate. If a bomb were to fall on this area we would have to be the Church without any real estate. The Church was the Church during the most vibrant period of its life, several hundred years, without real estate.

  • Another possibility is that the Church might carry out its mission through small bands of people, just two or three or four or five, who would live out their lives in the midst of the world of business, the world of government, the world of mass media, the medical world, the educational world— out there where they are making their tents, earning their living. Such little mission groups would be working at the problems of mass media, or on the issues relating to peace and prevention of war, or on race relations and housing, or with the poor, perhaps taking a vow of poverty.

I am not talking about little functional groups related to the local congregation. These mission groups of which I speak would *be* the local congregation. We need to redefine the meaning of congregation. "Where two or three are gathered together in my name, there am I in the midst of them."

—Gordon Cosby, "Not Renewal, But Reformation," *Who's Killing the Church?*,
ed. Stephen C. Rose, pp. 55–56.

Criteria for selecting areas of ministry.

By what criteria, then, will it select areas of ministry?

Without claiming to exhaust the possibilities, I would suggest three criteria for judgment.

1. *The church must determine priorities according to need.* Where other institutions—for example, the federal, state, or local governments—assume

the burden of work, the church can relinquish its tasks and allow these to assume them in order to concentrate its resources on areas of greater need. Undoubtedly, its decision will be influenced first by whether or not it sees an opportunity to render its *unique* ministry, that is, announcing the "good news" of Christ's reign, which distinguishes the church from all other institutions.

2. *The church must lead the way into new areas of service.* The true servant church should have a sensitivity to human need which is unmatched by any institution created for purely humanistic reasons. Not only should it share in human suffering and need more empathetically, but it should have the wisdom to get to the underlying roots of them. It should perceive the *real* problems in the illnesses of society and minister to them accordingly. . . .

3. *The church must serve as the prophetic voice which calls attention to human need.* This is necessary in that the church's resources will never go far enough. From its pulpits, through its news media, in its discussions, wherever it has opportunity—the church must quicken the conscience of society with a cry for reform. By the sometimes feeble effort it puts forth itself in correcting abuses and filling needs, it also may jar society awake.

What the church must avoid at all times is the attitude that its tasks remain the same and that it must retain all institutions it has designed to do these. The church's *mission* remains the same—to satisfy human need wherever or in whatever form it encounters it. But the mission and the tasks are not synonymous. The tasks will change, even though we have some of the same tasks with us always. Changing times bring new challenges and new problems. They frequently leave behind old ones.

—E. Glenn Hinson, *The Church: Design for Survival*, pp. 44–45.

Four ingredients in a realistically shaped mission.

It becomes increasingly obvious as one listens to these contributors that the Church has to take account of at least four things if it is to face realistically the task of shaping its mission for the modern world.

First, it must rediscover its ecumenical dimension. By ecumenical here is meant universal or worldwide. For many centuries the Church's mission has not only been denominationally but also nationally structured and some would say structured also by other factors such as economics, power, class and so on. This has led to a narrowing of perspective for Christians confined within Churches structured along these lines, so that the needs, agonies, abilities and insights of one another have not been shared. Now that we are acquiring an ecumenical perspective through The World Council of Churches, The Second Vatican Council and the programme of Mutual Responsibility and Interdependence in the Body of Christ in the Anglican Communion, as well as similar ecumenical programmes sponsored by other world confessional Churches, this must be allowed to influence the way in which the Church performs its mission.

Second, the Church's main mission to society must continue to be that of a reconciler. With the menace of divisions between East and West, and now between North and South, between black and white, between underdeveloped and developed, between culture groups as well as within fragmented areas of technological culture, the Church must find a structure to minister the gospel of reconciliation. This it cannot do when it is itself divided.

Thirdly, while the Church cannot provide the technological, political and cultural answers to the problems of modern society, it can provide guidance about human life by presenting society with a style of true human living. The Christian community and its genuine style of life in the Holy Spirit speaks a language which cuts across the divisions of men in the city of Babel. It provides a modern Pentecost to a fragmented humanity in the secular city.

Fourthly, the Church cannot attach itself to any ideology. Ideology may or may not have a proper place in some Eastern societies now passing through a period of loss of meaning, as a result of the desacralizing process of modern technology. But the Church cannot attach itself to any. The Church must be free to speak the Gospel to the people of any and every ideology. The Church is an eschatological society which anticipates, and in some measure already enjoys, the fulfilment of man's destiny. Therefore the Church speaks from that eschatological dimension in judgement upon all human pride and in hope for human creativity which God accepts in mercy at the hands of his children.

—B. N. Y. Vaughan, *Structures for Renewal*, pp. vi–vii.

The place of evangelism in mission.

Evangelism needs to be placed in the midst of the struggle to discover the new shapes of Christian obedience within the human communities of our time—in inner cities, in town and country; in the decision-making structures; in the worlds of international affairs, of politics, mass communications, leisure and the rest. In this way it is affirmed that the call to decision for Christ should be related to the ways of obedience that now must be fashioned in order that the church may be present with Christ in the communities of the world, raising the signs of the coming kingdom.

—Colin Williams, *Faith in a Secular Age*, p. 122.

How does a witness point to Christ?

When, in dispersion, the congregation enters into the life of the world they also pray that there there may be a witness that points to Christ the Lord. This emphasis rightly comes in the last place, for in a world of constant talk, where men too easily chatter aimlessly or assume the role of spectator, the church does not dare add its own chatter or talk irrelevantly in words the world no longer understands nor cares to hear.

The forms of pointing which one hears mentioned in our consensus involve first of all "gossiping the gospel." This is the natural response to Christ of men who have been made captive to him. Something of such overwhelming importance has happened to them that naturally, without sounding forced or intruding into the lives of others, or even seeking any response, they "gossip" about that which is of ultimate importance to them. This theme was the subject of Lenten Bible study in inner-city parishes in Lent, 1962.

A second aspect of pointing is to stress the need for Christians to enter into conversation first at the level of their common humanity with others. In learning to be human with other men, to converse at the level of genuine meeting, the way is prepared for communicating the meaning of faith. This is the point of Kraemer's widely read book on communicating the Christian faith. Said another way, it means keep quiet until the world asks the questions. This need not contradict the idea of "gossiping the gospel" but serves to remind the Christian that he must be sensitive to the other person, not an intruder.

In the third place, the congregation is concerned in all it does to point to Christ and not to itself. "Let your light so shine before men, that they may see your good works and give glory to your Father who is in heaven." (Matt. 5:16.)

Fourth, the congregation awaits the end. Its mission of witness is until the Lord comes. This eschatological note has clearly intruded itself, as we suggested earlier, into the inner city enterprise in this country. It is the hope of Christ that makes possible strenuous efforts to share in the heartbreaking work of Christ, and yet does not depend upon results.

Finally, to point to Christ is to trust that he alone converts and calls men. He is the evangelist. Men only share in his work.

—George W. Webber, *The Congregation in Mission*, pp. 71–72.

Too concerned about social problems, too little about conversion?

But there is *one problem* in all this that is *causing deep worry in the churches.* The worry is expressed in various ways; but the variety of expression points to a common concern. Are our churches now too concerned about social problems and too little about conversion? Are they too involved in politics and secular affairs, and too little engaged in the central task of the church—evangelism and spiritual life?

The reason for this question should be clear: it lies in the realization that a major change is occurring in the missionary strategy of our churches and there is an uneasy feeling that by widening our concern to the circumferences of life, we are in danger of vacating the central emphasis upon the one thing needful—the emphasis upon the need to call sinners to repentance and to new life in Christ.

There is no doubt that we are here at the nub of it all. Why is there this drastic change in missionary strategy to-day? Why is pietism now denigrated? Why is appeal to individual conversion not kept unwaveringly at the centre?

The answer here must be sought in the changed historical situation in which we find ourselves. It is easy for us to forget that the evangelism with which most of us are familiar is itself the outcome of a quite drastic revolution in missionary strategy. . . . Consequently a missionary strategy was developed: a strategy of concentrating upon the moment of decision; of calling upon the hearer to become what he already believed himself to be; and to appropriate the truth which he already assumed to be the truth of his life.

The development of this new evangelical strategy was one of the great moments of Christian history. From it new life broke forth from the old Christendom: new freedom for Christ that streamed out into the mission fields, the new lay movements, and the new social concerns of that time. But now we are in a new situation. Let me mention just two factors.

i. We do not live in Christendom: where the Christian tradition is assumed to be true; where the masses believe themselves to be Christians. We live instead in a world where vast new powerful secular forces are sweeping across our world bringing the incredible changes to which we have already referred. And we must ask: What does it mean to-day to call people to Christ? Has it not become clear now that to call them to conversion; to call them to accept Christ as Saviour without helping them to see the nature of the changed life that is required by Christ as Lord, is in fact one of the grave dangers for the church to-day? . . .

ii. This links with the second factor. In the 18th and 19th centuries where the older pattern of evangelism was forged, the more individual patterns of village life made it easier for individuals to grasp immediately the responsibilities of the life of discipleship. But the rise of the complicated patterns of urban society makes it increasingly important that the new forms of evangelism to-day should enable the call of Christ to come to the bearer in such a way as to enable him to count the cost of discipleship within the structures of his secular life.

. . . The result is that now our residential congregations no longer 'see' their responsibility of ministry to the outcast individuals, and the evangelism that takes place inside the communities of our congregations—communities from which these needs are by and large excluded—no longer is able to point its converts to the missionary responsibilities involved in discipleship. For the convert to understand this, he must be helped to see the new shapes of need, and he must be helped to search for new forms of church life which will reveal his responsibility within these worlds of need.

What we are called to to-day then is an evangelism in which calls for decisions for Christ (and these we must make) are related to calls for decisions 'in Christ': to a call to be free for the presence with Christ within the struggles of our time where Christ is working to overcome prejudice and poverty and political irresponsibility and international tribalism in order that all men may grow up together as one new man in Christ.

—Colin Williams, *Faith in a Secular Age*, pp. 115–18.

Theology needs sociology.

Theology, in other words, must relate the continuing shape of Christ's presence and of the church's service to Christ to the changing shapes of our daily life. Since those shapes of our life are highly complex, the task can be fulfilled responsibly only when we avail ourselves of the skills of the trained social observers.

—Colin W. Williams, *The Church*, p. 151.

Secularization need not be godless.

The notion of secular refers to a sphere of work in the world, and secularization means a shift of responsibility from religious authority to worldly authority. Both terms suggest a loss of administrative control by the church, but this loss of direct administrative control never implied godlessness. To be sure, secularized lands might be administered by godless principalities who exploited them, but the same can be said of lands which were administered by religious authorities in medieval Europe solely for the benefit of avaricious bishops. There is no principle by which secularization need lead to godlessness any more than administration by religious authorities would have to lead to godly and just administration. This applies as well in the twentieth century as in the twelfth; for example, the pay scale and working conditions in religious establishments in the United States are notoriously unjust by the standards of compensation and work in industry.

—Gibson Winter, *The New Creation As Metropolis*, pp. 35–36.

Heal now, preach later.

Early in the history of the East Harlem Protestant Parish a group of men and women from the very poor tenement building next door to the first store front church came to see Don Benedict to say that for several days they had had no heat in their building. The landlord, trying to save money, had set the thermostat located near the oil burner at 50°. As a result the families in the building had been without any heat whatsoever during a very bitter December week. This had happened a number of times before, but the tenants had been terrified to make any protest. Even now it had taken considerable courage to come and ask Don if there was anything he knew they might do. He suggested they get the facts by each getting a thermometer or two from the ten cents store and for the rest of the day keeping track of the temperature in their rooms. They were to return the following morning. The temperature readings, when produced the next day, were a pretty sorry picture. Don at once called the city Department of Housing, and, before he could be shunted off to some other department, told the bureau that the tenants were all on welfare, would all certainly come down with pneumonia, and would cost New York a great deal of money if they didn't get an inspector up right away. For whatever reasons an inspector did come up that very day, and after taking a look at the thermometer readings, he set the thermostat at 80°. Shortly thereafter a summons was issued for the landlord to appear in court. It was a great day for the tenants when they and the minister together went to court to stand up before the judge and testify to the injustice to which they had been subjected. A kind of self-respect and integrity seemed to have been granted to them at last. However, on the way out of court one of the men said to Don, with real bitterness and considerable sadism, "This is really terrific. We've got that old so and so over the barrel now. We're really going to make the landlord suffer."

In a very real sense the church had been helping the tenants face a problem of their palsy. Now had been developed a relationship between the minister and this man which at least enabled them to talk at a new level of comradeship and understanding. In a direct way the man had poured the bitterness and hatred in his heart out where it could be seen. Now that the manifestation of palsy was beginning to be dealt with, the underlying problem of sinfulness, in its form of bitterness and hate had been exposed. Now there was a real opportunity for the ministry of proclamation to begin as a result of the ministry of healing which had taken place.

—George W. Webber, *God's Colony in Man's World*, pp. 106–7.

Stand with the world in its struggle for betterment.

The misconceptions about Christian mission, which come of failing to grasp the fact of Christ and what is revealed in him, are manifold. In one city, for example, it is quite clear that the groups most ardently and effectively struggling for racial justice are made up largely of non-Christians, and that nonreligious Negroes and Jews are providing the best leadership. Yet the strategy of many Christians concerned with civil rights has been to attempt to form church groups to undertake the same tasks that are already being effectively performed by secular groups in the same neighborhoods. Why? Apparently these Christians assume that the power of grace will not be brought to bear on the racial dilemma unless *they* gather together and carry it into the situation. The fact is, however, that this is nothing short of spiritual arrogance. The power of life and grace is already bending history to its true end, carrying mankind into its adulthood, and, in this instance, through the secular groups. The task of Christians (lately awakened to the evil of race prejudice), therefore, is not to fragment and weaken the struggle for justice by creating yet other groups but to rejoice and stand with the grace-full power being exercised *already*. Similarly, it is only rarely, and in very unusual situations, that there is justification for the founding of church schools or colleges, church hospitals, or church political parties; but there is an obvious imperative for Christians to stand with life in the world as it struggles to bring into being (or improve the existent) schools and colleges, hospitals, or political parties which will help men move toward maturity.

—Myron B. Bloy, Jr., *The Crisis of Cultural Change*, p. 116.

The job is an appropriate area for mission.

The present activism of the local church fails to recognize that one's job or one's involvement in broad secular associations is, for many laymen, the most appropriate area of mission. Laymen so involved *are* the Church, even as those who minister in the local neighborhood are the Church, even as those who support the traditional ministries of chaplaincy and teaching are the Church. Such laymen would be considerably more loyal to a church that demanded not institutional allegiance but allegiance to the imperatives of servanthood in the world. They would no longer feel that *their* work, *their* interests, and *their* complex decisions were something isolated from the Church's life. The new structure would provide for those who have no desire to be "active" in the traditional sense, and for those who do.

—Stephen C. Rose, The Grass Roots Church, pp. 77–78.

Politics can be the path of relevant love.

It is an obvious fact in American life that most of the problems which warp and limit human life, which create helplessness in men and women, can most effectively be dealt with through political channels. Here lies the path of relevant love. The naivete of Protestants about politics is overwhelming. Politics has even been identified as the real source of evil in American life and is something which good Christian people too often avoid with a real sense of superiority. Can one not on the contrary argue that to be a Christian citizen in a democratic society makes participation in politics an absolute necessity? We have no right to be the odd man out, avoiding responsibility for the structures which make our common life in the world possible. Furthermore, much of our service degenerates into sentimentality if we do not seek to use the channels of political life.

—George W. Webber, God's Colony in Man's World, p. 93.

To show the world what true community means.

Our firm belief is that it is part of the calling of the church to show the world what true community means: a fellowship of free persons bound to one another by a common calling and a common service. Only in Christ can we solve the tension between freedom and authority, between the right of the individual person to attain fullness of life and the claim of the community as a whole on each of its members. For in and through him we learn what it means to be perfectly free, yet obedient unto death; to come as a servant, yet through this very self-abasement to attain fullness of life.

We must, therefore, ask ourselves the questions: How far is the local congregation, how far is the church as a whole, this exemplary fellowship which by its very existence should be a constant challenge to the world? How can we help to heal the strife and tensions of the world, if the same divisions and tensions exist in our midst?

—Suzanne DeDietrich, The Witnessing Community, pp. 13–14.

Marching orders to the city of Dallas.

In searching for an answer to the questions "where" and "how," we must start with the "where," for the church is never the church in general but is always in some concrete and specific place. This meant that for Northaven we had to begin with the geography, culture, and power centers of our own physical location. I would assume that this is equally true for any other congregation. While in one sense we existed for the whole world, Northaven's marching orders were primarily to the city of Dallas. Our cosmopolitan posture must include a comprehensive knowledge of our particular metropolis, and we are less than cosmopolitan if we ignore our own address for the more colorful or dramatic doorsteps of distant places (though we must be prepared to go to Selma and other focuses of history wherever and whenever they may call).

—W. A. Holmes, *Tomorrow's Church: A Cosmopolitan Community*, pp. 156–57.

The enemy can be defeated in principle, but still be dangerous.

The most helpful analogy I have come upon is that of the situation during a war when the peace treaty has been signed, the victory won, but the enemy continues to fight on. Thus Japanese troops on Okinawa continued to fight long after the peace treaty had been signed in Tokyo Harbor. The American troops, well aware that a victory had been won and the war was over, were nevertheless engaged in a deadly encounter with an enemy, defeated in principle, but still vicious and dangerous. This is the position of the Christian in the world. Confident that the victory of Christ is real, he can continue to face the manifold threats of the principalities and powers of evil which still rage so furiously in the world. This kind of affirmation permits the Christian in the city to face its problems with hope.

—George W. Webber, *The Congregation in Mission*, pp. 186–87.

E. The Church Hesitant—Resistance to Change

Unready for such adventures.

When we tried to pinpoint areas of worldly need in our community we discovered our ignorance and inexperience. It is easy to make a conventional list of problems drawing on newspaper editorials, and to talk about accepted ways of handling them. But it soon becomes evident that we talk in terms of social work and not at all of redeeming power. When we try to go further a deep silence falls.

We confess with concern that we do not know where to start. In this, we believe, we are no different from most other suburban church members. The reason for our ignorance is that we have not taken either our mission or our world seriously for a long time.

Before our mission in Milford can come alive we will need to recognize the areas of need. For that to happen we need a deeper knowledge of ourselves and our world in the light of the Gospel, than we once thought necessary.

—Colin Williams, *What in the World?*, p. x.

Resentment from the clergy.

The suggestion that the present congregational structure is inadequate to the contemporary task of mission has often brought forth deep resentment— far more often from the clergy than the laity. One reason for the initial resentment is undoubtedly misunderstanding—based upon a feeling that when those who are participating in the study speak of the *inadequacy* of the residence congregation, they are really suggesting that the residential congregation must now be *abolished*. Since no documents or statements issuing from the study have suggested this abolition of the residence congregation, we must ask why this fear has been expressed so regularly. Does the very existence of this study bring out a hidden fear in many now working in the residence congregations that the study may discover that their form of present commitment will have to be abandoned? Does the study stir up the frightening thought that the missionary calling today is leading us out with Abraham into the institutional unknown? There is sufficient open expression of this feeling amongst theological students—a considerable number of whom are declining to enter the parish ministry on the grounds that the residence congregation is alienated from the true centres of the world's life—and amongst a wide variety of laymen to make it imperative for us to ask such questions as: What is the place of the residence congregation in the contemporary mission of the church in the world?

—Colin Williams, *What in the World?*, pp. xv–xvi.

Many fear renewal will destroy the family unit.

The deep fears that are awakened when the adequacy of the residence congregation is questioned are not to be explained just by the fear of being separated from our familiar church ways. Behind it apparently is the deeply rooted anxiety that any alienation of the churches from the primary association with the residence community will remove the last bulwark against the imminent collapse of *the family* into final chaos. Time and again those who have expressed strong resistance to the study have given expression to the view that the primary relationship of the church must *always* be to the family. It is from the family, they have claimed, that the values that create society emerge, and it is through the church's relationship to the family that the way is found for the radiation of the gospel out into the many structures of society.

—Colin Williams, *What in the World?*, p. xvi.

But the New Testament was not concerned with social issues.

A second major fear is that the literature of this study, when it speaks of penetrating the public worlds—industry, commerce, leisure, politics—is forcing the gospel outside its New Testament range of concern, and is in danger of repeating the old mistakes of the social gospel. It is admitted that in the New Testament we are told of a new heaven and a new earth in which all things will be renewed in Christ. But it is suggested that it is not the task of the church to carry out the direct translation of the final goal of the Kingdom of God into the social structures of secular life. That final translation is the work of Christ when he returns. Our task as a church is more humble. We are to witness to Christ as King and Saviour; we are to reveal the redeemed life of the Kingdom in the quality of our community life as the 'called out' people of God and in personal relationships with others—in the family, in relationships of employers and employees, and in servant love to those whose needs come before us. But the New Testament, it is claimed, does not place the state or secular institutions within the realm of redemption. They are within the realm of providence and are under law, not grace. New Testament ethical instruction for Christians is personal, and it teaches us to wait until Christ returns before his Lordship over the secular world will be manifest.

—Colin Williams, *What in the World?*, p. xvii.

Powerful vested interest works against change.

It would be senseless to refuse to acknowledge the powerful vested interest against change: material, because of the vast institutional investment in the forms of past obedience; emotional, with the great reluctance to leave the world of the familiar; professional, with the fear of leaving the forms of church life for which we were trained, to venture out like Abraham into the unknown. The strength of this natural conservatism poses real problems of strategy for would-be reformers.

—Colin Williams, *What in the World?*, pp. 71–72.

Leave us alone in our popular irrelevance.

There is, in this land, a still greater block, the powerful myth of the 'private'—the feeling that our 'real' life is not in those public worlds, but in the private world of the home. This myth lies behind the powerful bourgeois attempts to maintain, in the outer suburbs, the disappearing forms of family and community life. The business and political life of the outer suburbanite is separated from the home; but in this disturbing world of rapid transition, he still wants the feeling that the old-time values of the home abide; and that this abiding 'private' world is the real world—the eternal world to which he can retreat from the exciting but frightening world of rapid social change. In this attempt, bourgeois man has found in the church his main ally. It has gone with him to his separate residence world. It has assured him that the home is what really matters. And so, ironically, it would appear that it is precisely *because* the local church is *separated* from business and politics and the pressing problems of society in transition, that bourgeois man has found himself 'at home' in it. We therefore have this ironic but tragic fact, that in many instances the residence parish congregation is popular precisely because it is irrelevant!

—Colin Williams, *What in the World?*, p. 12.

We prefer to keep the Church feminine.

It would be wrong, of course, to make the church exclusively masculine. The twin functions of priest and prophet have the polar relationship of the genders, and the ministry of the church includes both. But just as all life will tend to wax sentimental over mother, and distantly respectful (or resentful) about father, so will the Christian community love its priestliness and rationalize its prophethood. We appreciate the term "pastoral care"; we recoil from Calvin's "churchly discipline." We praise the church when it upholds our values; we feel alienated and bitter when it dares to judge us.

In short, we prefer to keep the church feminine. This is a rough-and-tumble, dog-eat-dog, man's world. The church, we imply, would be embarrassed to know the real vulgarities of life; "twere well," for her sake, she be protected from the harshness of reality and kept in her place. Even John Calvin stated that church is mother of all who have God for their father.

—Wesley C. Baker, *The Split-Level Fellowship*, p. 22.

Perpetuating the social status quo.

Just as some kind of social stratification is probably inevitable in any complex society, so it is probably inevitable that the social structure that prevails in society as a whole will manifest itself in the churches in various ways and to various degrees. The problem of class and social status is one of the continuing problems with which Christians in all days and ages have to wrestle. Just as complete equality in the political area is never fully achieved either in a democracy or in a communist state, so it also eludes the churches since they are composed of people who differ in native abilities, values, education, and income.

Yet the church is the one voluntary institution in society that is committed to the service of all men without regard to these relatively accidental or secondary characteristics. When it is true to itself, it must always feel a tension between the norm to which it is committed and the existing institutional churches insofar as the latter are class-oriented and exclusive. It is not that the values that the middle- and upper-class churches pursue are bad or evil per se. Education, economic security, comfortable homes, attractive neighborhoods, and vacations are goods rather than evils. The problem, as far as the membership of the churches is concerned, is not that some people have access to these things; rather, it is that most of the world's people are deprived of them, and even of the barest necessities of life. As a consequence of this fact, the people who possess these goods are separated from the people who do not possess them, and thus the community that all men share with each other under God is effectively denied. Moreover, insofar as the churches of the privileged groups sanction the *status quo*, they help to perpetuate the divisions and the underlying social injustices of which the less privileged classes are the primary victims.

    —E. Clinton Gardner, *The Church As a Prophetic Community*, pp. 48–49.

The tension between adventure and security.

Curiosity, if nothing else, should move us to wonder how the new congregations are responding to this tension between adventure and security. Sociologists and informed churchmen might well be concerned for weightier reasons. The new congregations are prime examples of organizations forced to maintain a precarious balance between the energies devoted to their own security and the energies devoted to the accomplishment of their formal purposes. Numerous studies of educational, medical, political, religious, and governmental groups have shown how organizations under less trying circumstances can be diverted by secondary interests from the accomplishment of their expressed goals.

—Donald L. Metz, *New Congregations: Secular and Mission in Conflict*, p. 16.

Why are some church members afraid of renewal?

Of course it goes without saying that any significant change in a parish program will be deeply and sincerely opposed by some church members. This is a scary world we are living in for a good many people. Think about it. Some members came stumbling into the church years ago out of some personal terror or private pit of guilt, or a hell on earth about which they have never told. And hearing that God would forgive them or even that a loving God "backed this club," they joined and found some sort of peace and security in a frightening world. They may never have heard about a personal faith in terms that seemed relevant to them, but the public worship—just as it is, or the quiet guild meetings, may have become the only recurring, dependable events in a life of chaos inside for them. And when some bright eyed young business people, or ministers, start talking with enthusiastic seriousness about a "more committed" way to live, the old parishioners may perceive this "new life" as a demand to give up something or confess openly some sin they have held back from God for years and do not want to change. Or this new approach might signify to the average parishioner a grim disciplined life with which he cannot begin to identify. He may sense that the new approach is going to do away with the stability of the psychological adjustment he has made with his terror or guilt. And if this new program gets *in* and he can't go along, then he may be on the "outside" again. Anyone who has ever really been afraid and alone and then found security, however tenuous, will understand why these people put up no small objection to a new approach which they don't understand or with which they cannot identify. Other church members remember a certain religious excitement surrounding their own joining of the church, but since it "wore off" for them, they assume it will for this new bunch. Of course some people are simply reactionary and do not like change. Still others have taken a cool look and do not agree that a change is necessary. But I believe that the problem is deeper than any of these kinds of objections. I believe that we have made a significant historical mistake in our approach to renewal in the Church.

—Keith Miller, *A Second Touch*, pp. 148–49.

The loss of the prophetic stance.

Seen in the light of the radical monotheism of Biblical faith and the New Testament conception of koinonia, the church is in its very nature a prophetic community. It exists in the world, but its purpose is to point men to God, the true center of their existence and the ultimate ground of meaning and value. Viewed from the perspective of a Biblical understanding of the church, it is evident that the church today as it actually exists in the form of local congregations and denominations is in need of radical transformation and renewal. Instead of reshaping the communities in which they are set, the churches tend to reflect and deepen the divisions of secular society and to sanctify the prevailing values and patterns of culture. They have lost their capacity to leaven society and to give light in the midst of the world's darkness. Because they have become captive to the particular cultures and subcultures in which they are set, they appear to be irrelevant and even hostile to the deepest interests and needs of people with different cultural backgrounds. Thus, they have often become agents of conflict between classes, races, nations, and warring ideologies, rather than agents of reconciliation.

—E. Clinton Gardner, *The Church As a Prophetic Community*, p. 180.

Foot-draggers deserve to have their needs met.

Those who are entrenched in the older ways of the Church, even when the world itself around them has changed, deserve to have their needs met and their views heard. It is, in fact, good to be reminded in the midst of all this talk of change that there are certain things which are changeless and essential to the mission of the Church. It is very often to these that the older school is firmly attached and it is these which at its best it fears to lose. And in fact, without these, the Church could not do its essential work. Any reform which is to take place must, therefore, take account of these.

—B. N. Y. Vaughan, *Structures for Renewal*, p. 43.

Virtues which belong to the older era must be preserved.

There is some reason to fear that, because we have heard a great deal about the virtues of the new secular era, not enough respect is going to be paid to those virtues which belong to the older era. Three points need, therefore, to be made. First, the mission of the Church is as much to the old structures of society as to the new. People have to be ministered to where they are, and the old structures of the Church must continue wherever the old structures of society in their many forms continue. Many, especially rural, areas will change very little in spite of great changes in industrial centres. Secondly, the tradition, wisdom and resources which belong to the older structures will be greatly needed in the mission of the Church, and must be respected. Thirdly, and most important of all, the quest for unity must not be at the expense of new divisions. It would be as much a contradiction of the ministry of reconciliation if we were to produce and allow new divisions between the old and the new as it is to condone the present divisions of the Church. The task of unity, as the last chapter tries to show, involves creating the right attitudes between the old and the new.

—B. N. Y. Vaughan, *Structures for Renewal*, pp. vii–viii.

IV

The Internal
Renewal of the Church

Some Emerging Strategies
of the Journey Inward

Renewal involves engagements with self, God, and others.

"Inward journey" and "outward journey" are familiar terms in our community. We use them to describe what the Christian life is all about. We use them to describe the meaning of membership in the Church of the Saviour. As a community of faith we are committed to being a people on an inward journey and a people on an outward journey.

The inward journey involves us in three engagements. These Gordon Cosby has held before the community since its founding. Not only are they subjects of sermons, but the whole of the church's life is structured to make them possible.

The first engagement is with oneself. We have come increasingly to see the need of consciously moving toward self-knowledge. We had some understanding of the injunction of the ancients to "know thyself" and the writings of depth psychology about the vast unconscious in each of us, but more than this was necessary to begin with any seriousness a journey into self. We needed the collaboration of our own experience in a community to understand that self-examination was essential. if we were to have a life together and to be in any meaningful way the Church in the world. . . .

The second engagement is with God. Whereas no one can know God who does not know himself, it does not follow that knowledge of self is knowledge of God. God speaks through the self, but He is not the self. He can come to us through the revelations of the unconscious, but He is not the unconscious.

The third aspect of the inward journey is the engagement with others.
This is bound up with our whole concept of the church as a people committed
to God in Jesus Christ and to one another. . . .

Engagement with others in depth is always difficult within the church,
which is probably why so few try it and why there is so little genuine Christian community in the world. In other groupings we choose those we want
to be close to and those whom we want to hold at a distance, which means
that any relationship in depth is on the basis of human affinity and the
standards set for friendship. The church is the only place where this does
not happen. A person is not received into the membership of the church
because he is a certain type or because he has arrived at a certain place in
life, but because he can say Christ is Lord. We do not do the calling. Christ
does the calling, and this is very threatening if we belong to his Church,
because the people he calls are the people with whom we are to have intimate
belonging. This gives us a strange assortment of people to be with. They are
often not our idea of the ones God should be using to proclaim his Kingdom.
Even when we finally get hold of what the Church is all about, we struggle
for a long time with pride. At the Church of the Saviour we are aware of this
when Christian brethren visit from other churches and ask to meet the members, like people asking to meet spiritual heroes. Under the pressure of wanting to live up to their expectations, we confess our feeling is often "Someone,
quick, hide the rolls!"

Whereas Christian community is the most difficult to be involved in, it is
the most rewarding and the most essential to those on an inward journey. As
we grow in depth relationship with those whose values and experiences are
different from ours, the horizons of our little worlds are pushed back—our
Umwelts are enlarged. Life comes to have a variety and a richness that was
not there before.

　　　—Eliabeth O'Connor, *Journey Inward, Journey Outward*, pp. 10–11, 16, 24–25.

A. Seeking a Regenerate Church Membership

There are many illegitimate members.

Integrity of membership requires live births—dead babies don't grow. It
requires spiritual nurture—abandoned babies soon die. A more painful requirement is discipline—the mark of all true children of God. "If you are
left without discipline, in which all have participated, then you are illegitimate
children and not sons" (Hebrews 12:8). Our present churches have many
illegitimate members.

　　　—Russell Bow, *The Integrity of Church Membership*, p. 89.

Five factors contribute to the current admission problem.

Without seeking to separate causes from symptoms, James Leo Garrett lists five factors related to the problem of admission to church membership that have contributed to the current condition. First, there is the failure to have any serious or vocal confession of one's faith when the candidate applies for membership. Instead, there is the practice of the pastor's confessing faith for the applicant to the congregation—"a strange proxy method for Baptists!" Second, there is a lack of any serious doctrinal or ethical standards as pre- requisite for membership. A third factor is the "subtle pressures toward quantitative or numerical gains in church membership." Too often success is measured by the number of additions reported. From many sources the pressure is on the pastor "to produce results!" Fourth, there is the use of questionable methods to provoke premature professions of faith by young children. Fifth, "there is the widespread practice of taking the congregational vote on new members immediately after the applicant presents himself for membership."

—Findley B. Edge, *A Quest for Vitality in Religion*, p. 203.

The fallacy of the lowest common denominator for membership.

Factor Beta means that the local parish, and this seems to be most acutely true in the Protestant setting, only achieves any kind of unity or comity on the level of the *lowest common denominator*, and will always be limited to this as long as the factor goes unfaced. Someone has said that the Protestant Church is antiurban; I would say it is antireality. Dreams of improving this by programmatic innovations, such as theologically enlightened study groups, will only serve to increase the intracongregational tensions and *put the sharp- ness of the conflict within the church when by all rights it should be between the church and the world.*

The problem is one of definition. The church is called the fellowship of believers in Christ. But we fear with a monumental dread to deal critically with just what is meant by a "believer." And since the essence of local parish life is unconsciously dedicated to the proposition that the only safe judgment on this is subjective, we enforce and support a passive vagueness that rests entirely on the assumed and unspoken.

I see no compromise whatever with Protestant principles in dealing with factor Beta. As a matter of fact, the predicament of the parish church is the result of our cowardice to be honest to our own standards. Simply put, I suggest we move the believers (which will necessarily mean only those who are willing to go) out of the nave and into the chancel. Then, significantly, we must turn around and give some kind of theologically respectable recogni- tion to those who stay in the nave. If the necessary support comes from the authoritative higher church courts, we *can* erect meaningful standards for membership. Admittedly, this will thin the ranks, probably by considerable numbers, but I seriously doubt if our institutional securities really do depend on a broad base of popularity. Since the real area of bewilderment here is what to do with those who are left behind without seeming cruelly exclusive, we need to consider reviving the old "learner" or catechumen classification of premembership (or nonmembership) and let it have the status of being a majority group. Then let the church be *the church!*

—Wesley C. Baker, *The Split-Level Fellowship*, pp. 41–42.

There are two types of membership: professing members and full members.

To implement the practice of a period of waiting, it is further proposed that the church should have two types of membership. "Professing members" would be those who had been received on the basis of their "profession of faith." "Full members" would have demonstrated by "credible evidence" the reality of their profession.

—Findley B. Edge, *A Quest for Vitality in Religion*, p. 204.

Dealing with the delinquent.

Dealing with the delinquent members is the most difficult step the church must take toward integrity of membership. It will fail unless spiritual vitality has already been realized by the renewal of a remnant at the heart of the church; unless there is a warm spirit of love within the fellowship; and unless it is undertaken under the leadership of the Holy Spirit.

—Russell Bow, *The Integrity of Church Membership*, p. 98.

Church discipline should win them back.

The emphasis on church discipline should not be in removing negligent members from the roll; but in winning them back.

—Russell Bow, *The Integrity of Church Membership*, p. 94.

A live chicken under a dead hen.

Spiritual nurture is a necessity for all church members. Newborn babes require special care. One of the reasons for the failure of the church to provide Christian nurture for its new members is the low spiritual temperature of the old members. Instead of warm cradles of love, we put our babes in Christ in spiritual refrigerators. Samuel Shoemaker has said, "Putting an eager seeker after Christ into the conventional church is like putting a live chicken under a dead hen." We can never achieve integrity of membership in our present churches if our only approach is at the point of entrance. No matter how healthy our spiritual babies are at birth, they will not live if we put them in an icebox.

—Russell Bow, *The Integrity of Church Membership*, pp. 75–76.

Cleaning up the roll for efficiency is a questionable practice.

The practice of "cleaning up the rolls" for the sake of efficiency must be called into question. To legalistically exclude the weak brother is to exclude Christ's opportunity for us to serve the weak. The practice of having a standard set of procedures mechanically starting with a form letter and concluding with a notice of termination seems much more a method of efficient business operation than of personally and lovingly dealing with one who is weak. To identify the weak brother with the unrepentant sinner of Matt. 18 is a practice not worthy of the parish, which is committed to bringing repentance and life to a world of sinners.

—Roy Blumhorst, "In the Suburbs," *Death and Birth of the Parish,* ed. Martin E. Marty, p. 115.

Maintenance and edification of membership.

The maintenance and edification of the membership offers an even greater challenge. One of our weaknesses is that we have not developed so well the qualitative criteria in addition to the quantitative criteria for church life. Some Baptists have taken growth to mean solely multiplication and seldom maturation. The conditions which produced the charge that Baptists "dip them and are done with them" are not altogether removed. New converts must not have the live option of a stunted Christian growth and second-class discipleship. Furthermore, we must deal with the non-resident member and the inactive member problems more thoroughly and regularly. The First Baptist Church of Alexandria, Virginia, for example, periodically sends to its inactive members a letter which affords to such members four clear alternatives or options. First, a renewal of active membership as evidenced by participation in the worship services of the church and in the financial stewardship of the church may be made. Secondly, there is the option of maintaining church membership despite one's inability to attend services regularly and to contribute and with a request for a pastoral call—an option designed for the elderly and shut-ins. Thirdly, a statement that one has already united with another church, the name and location of which are given, may be made. Finally, one may indicate a definite decision to seek a transfer of membership to another church, whose name and location are indicated, together with the request that one's name and address be sent to such church. Indeed the church letter among us, like Confederate money, has depreciated. We must find a way to differentiate between letters of dismissal for active, committed members and letters for members long inactive and indifferent. Following Paul's metaphor, we must be willing to acknowledge that some have not been "members" of the "body," only disjoined arms and separated legs. Can Baptist churches that have abandoned the negative aspects of congregational discipline restore the same without some of the abuses of the past? Are there really some limitations to Southern Baptist churchmanship besides "alien immersion"? Should a member who sells liquor be removed if he refuses to abandon such a business? A recent inspiring example in the Walnut Street Baptist Church, Louisville, Kentucky, seems to answer in the affirmative. But what of the member who sells no liquor but only peddles race hatred, prejudice, and violence?

—James Leo Garrett, "Seeking a Regenerate Church Membership," *Southwestern Journal of Theology* 3, no. 2 (April 1961) : 35–36.

High standards at the threshold.

On the other hand, a formal period of membership training is not the complete answer. The important thing is to lift up a new standard, to create a new image of what membership involves. It is important that new members face up to the high demands of discipline at the time of joining. It is difficult, and sometimes may seem unfair, to ask more of new members than is practiced by many already on our rolls. This is why it is important to work for integrity of membership at other points suggested in the following chapters while we are seeking integrity at the point of entrance. However, new members may be more willing to accept high standards at the threshold of membership than later. It is essential that new members know exactly what is expected of them.

—Russell Bow, *The Integrity of Church Membership*, p. 65.

The way to renewal is the regenerate Church seeking to win the uncommitted Church.

Two great traditions within Christendom have become the heritage of all Protestantism—the church as a gathered community and the church as parish. The view of the church as *koinonia* is fundamentally the process of finding itself as a gathered community, but this must never be done to the exclusion of its parish responsibility. What must be discovered in the local church is a way to express its life as a unique special people without fostering the implication that this is a specialness of pious superiority. Some modern adaptation of the relationship between catechumens and the baptized in the early church must emerge. It is necessary to think of every church in terms of concentric circles. The widest ring includes all those who are somehow related to the church, either by marriage, or through some superficial contact with the church. It includes both the people who, if pressed for religious affiliation, would name the church as theirs, and also the people who might not own it. The next ring includes the nominal members, and also those who are seeking. The inner ring is the fully gathered church, those who know Whom they have believed, those in full communion. These circles can never be too rigidly defined. But the heart of the church, the gathered ones, must be aware of these groups, and must constantly be seeking to draw people closer to the heart of the church. The whole organism is in some larger sense the church, but the heart which is the generator lies in the center. A regenerate church membership is the corporate life of the ones who are in full communion with God and with one another. The enlargement of that group, through the magnification of the witness of the life that is there, is the way to proceed toward a regenerate church.

This is a delicate art, and is the essence of pastoral responsibility. This does not mean that it is solely the responsibility of the minister. It should be increasingly the shared work of those who know *koinonia* in its deeper dimension.

—Robert W. Spike, *In But Not Of The World*, pp. 18–19.

The advantages of a period of waiting before church membership.

There are several reasons why this period of waiting is desperately needed in the life of the modern churches. First, it is needed so that the church itself will come to understand more clearly that growth is essential for the one who has just made a profession of faith. The church has paid lip service to the idea of Christian growth. A waiting period will serve as a prolonged reminder to the church that it must express an intensive and continuing concern for the individual after he has made his initial decision. . . .

In the second place, this period of waiting is needed so that the individual who makes a profession of faith will understand that growth in the Christian life is essential. The church must not be deceptive at this point. Both church and convert must understand more clearly the radical nature of the call of God to discipleship. . . .

This period of waiting is the church's way of saying that growth is not optional. Growth is essential. The current "loss" within the membership of the church cannot be allowed to continue. It is a sin against those who are thus "won"—and, perhaps, deceived. The church cannot rely exclusively on a "profession" as the *sole evidence* of one's salvation. Its validity can be demonstrated in obedience.

The present status of religion in society and in the life of the churches is another reason a period of waiting is necessary. . . .

The very "religiousness" of our culture is a serious handicap to the church in seeking to recapture the true vitality of the Christian faith. The early church developed in a culture that was highly "religious." . . . A person growing up in modern "religious" America does not necessarily come to understand the true nature and meaning of the Christian life. Rather, quite the opposite would more likely be the outcome. He might easily get a distorted and inadequate concept of the Christian faith.

When we turn to the church, the argument that those growing up in the church would not need a period of waiting would be valid if the life lived by the church were a true demonstration of New Testament Christianity. However, if the Christian life is understood in terms of undertaking a mission and fulfilling a ministry for God in the world, then the life lived by a majority of the present-day church members is such a shallow, superficial representation as almost to be called "pseudo religion." . . .

This suggests a fourth reason. Because the life lived by the church is such a powerful educative force, the church must strive toward vitality and purity in her life. The influence of the life lived by the church as an educative force has not been adequately understood nor sufficiently emphasized. Although no statistical studies have been made that can be cited to substantiate this claim, it is quite probable that the most powerful teaching force in the entire church is not the pulpit, nor the Sunday school, nor any other educational agency. It is the life lived by the church. . . .

The life of the modern church stifles rather than encourages daring Christian living, in spite of its preaching and teaching to the contrary. Thus, these impulses eventually die, and the individual settles down simply to being good and attending the services. The church tends to mold the new members in its own image. In doing so, the expression of the Christian life deteriorates into the observance of external forms and the church continues toward institutionalism. If the church is ever going to approach the ideal of a dynamic, experiential faith, it must make sure that its life shall be as accurate an expression of the vitality and purity of the New Testament faith as possible.

Another reason for the waiting period is so obvious that it needs only brief explanation and defense: to insure a regenerate church membership. This reason has two facets to it. First, when there are unregenerate members in the church, it is difficult for the church to give its witness to God and for God, particularly when this witness would challenge the *status quo* about some evil that is accepted by society. . . .

The second facet is that with an unregenerate membership the witness of the church to the world is ineffective. The inconsistent lives of its members handicap the witness of the church. . . .

A period of waiting is needed, in the sixth place, because our present practice of granting "full membership" to candidates immediately upon their profession of faith, especially young children, actually presents a serious theological problem that has not been faced realistically. Church statistics indicate a rather significant "falling away" from the church during the period of middle adolescence. If one holds the doctrine of "once saved, always saved," what is to be the verdict concerning these who "fall away"? It is true that some of these who leave the church during this period later return. But the fact remains, many do not. What of these? Surely it cannot be said that an individual was saved on the basis of a profession he made when he was a small child, while his whole later life is a denial of any genuine relationship with Christ.

—Findley B. Edge, *A Quest for Vitality in Religion*, pp. 205–11.

A regenerate Church membership—Georgia style.

Renewal theories are building up a head of steam in numerous denominational circles, and yet few have provided enough impetus to put a local church in step with the youth-geared twentieth century. A couple of churches in the Convention, however, have pulled into the speeding traffic—like First Baptist Church of Decatur, Ga. . . .

For example, revolutionary membership procedures were adopted. "When a member presents himself on Sunday morning, he is not voted into the church on-the-spot, but receives a very hearty welcome," Lancaster explained. Henceforth, this person is identified as an applicant until he has attended a series of membership seminars accompanied by a pair of friendly "sponsors."

"Ideally, the applicant reviews the history of this church as well as Christian mission, and is crystallizing in his mind a vision of his talents and how he fits in," Lancaster said.

At the conclusion of the seminar, the applicant is asked if he is willing to commit himself to the church and the ministry that has been presented. If he is, he once again is presented on Wednesday evening; a vote is taken and if he is voted in (by majority), he later is presented with a Bible inscribed with the date that he was received into the membership. . . .

The bulletin-like literature distributed at the first new membership seminar further indicates this search for a new commitment.

"It is (our) hope . . . that new-member orientation will provide both the stimulus and the direction of those coming into the church to understand what the church is all about and to find their own personal sense of mission in it. Our objective is not to make membership harder to achieve but to make membership more meaningful. . . ."

New membership procedures apply to all newcomers except former members, who can elect whether or not to participate. Existing members also may participate in the seminars.

When a person becomes an applicant, he is assigned "sponsors"—a couple generally in his own age bracket. Before Wednesday night this couple visits in the home to take printed materials about the church, to answer some questions in the person's mind and to begin getting to know the applicant on an intimate basis. Thereafter, they are with the applicant at every service he attends for the first month (no more getting lost in search of a classroom or being discouraged and lonesome because you really don't know anyone).

The first Wednesday after a person has become an applicant, the sponsors go with him to the services, reintroducing him and telling something about him—education, employment, interests. The next Sunday evening the trio begins attending the four-week seminar: "Our Church: Past, Present and Future"; "The New Testament and the Christian Life"; "What Baptists Believe and Practice" and "Missions: Growing up and Reaching Out."

—Sue Miles Brooks, "Depth Through Discipline," *Home Missions*, April 1968, pp. 12–13.

B. Bible Study As Controlling the Life of the Congregation

Now that you have seen the movie, read the Book.

We are fortunate that so many movies and books have been made of Bible stories; however, a serious student cannot allow the combined artistry of Cecil B. DeMille, John Huston and Fulton Oursler to be a substitute for the reading of the Bible itself. Now that so many have seen the movie they ought to read the book.

A very talented young minister friend of mine was quite eager to stimulate his congregation's interest in the reading of the Bible. He announced that on a certain Sunday night there would be a vote taken to determine what portions of the Bible would be left in and what portions would be taken out. The poll was made, not on the basis of what they believed, but on the basis of what they had read. Those passages which the majority of the people had read during the previous year would remain, but those passages which the majority had not read would be removed. They began with Genesis and moved all the way through the Bible. It was a rather traumatic experience for the congregation. Genesis I, the Ten Commandments in Exodus, one or two favorite passages from Isaiah, the Twenty-Third Psalm, portions of the Sermon on the Mount, the third and fourteenth chapters of John, and First Corinthians 13 were the passages which survived.

The congregation got the point. It is not the Bible believed, but the Bible believed and read which has the potential for changing lives. One individual rushed up to the minister after the service and said, "I deplore your tearing pages out of God's Holy Word in front of the church." Evidently the mutilating of the pages bothered her more than the neglect of the reading and the teaching of the Scripture.

—Kenneth Chafin, *Help! I'm a Layman*, pp. 46–47.

Renewal goes hand-in-hand with Bible study.

Historically we have evidence that whenever there has been a renewal of life within the church there has been a fresh confrontation with the Biblical message. This provides us with a major clue for the recovery of genuine life in the church today, and a clear indication of the lines along which religious experience may develop. A dialogue with the Word of God in the context of a dialogue with one's neighbors is the community to which the Holy Spirit is given.

We are all aware of the appalling Biblical illiteracy among modern Protestants, but the problem is much more serious than simply the lack of information among church members. As our churches are now structured personal relationships are almost exclusively at a superficial level. This has the more serious consequence that the message of the Bible and Christian doctrine can not be experienced in our churches today. The Incarnation and the Resurrection remain sterile dogma, even if there is an academic knowledge of the doctrines. Our real need in the church is to provide the medium through which the Biblical proclamation may be experienced. Small, personal groups, where men and women are wrestling with the Biblical message, provide the opportunity for such experiences. We have found this to be true at Plymouth Church for those who have been willing to devote the time, but there has never been a large response by the congregation to participation in small groups. The church has its membership frantically engaged in many, many activities and one more thing is just too much for some people. For me, this calls into question the whole organizational structure of the Protestant Church today.

Where there is engagement with the Biblical Word in a group situation there is opportunity for genuine religious experience. An outgrowth and necessity of this is commitment—absolute, unqualified commitment to Jesus Christ wherever the Spirit leads us. This is radical, and when church members are confronted with this as a serious choice they are appalled. It is radical because however much we may speak about Christian America there is the immediate realization that our society does not live by Christian standards. Therefore to take Christ seriously means to take His cross into our lives. And Thomas a Kempis is still right, "God has now many lovers of His heavenly Kingdom, but very few bearers of His cross."
—Harold R. Fray, Jr., "The Search for New 'Wine Skins,'" *Union Seminary Quarterly Review*, 16:318–19.

How does this biblical truth apply to my life?

The natural tendency of all of us is to study the Bible without asking the question, "How does this truth apply today to my life?" Because the Bible was written so long ago and so far away, there is a tendency not to relate it to problems we are facing now.

One summer I was teaching the book of First Corinthians to a group of students at a church camp. The first day we studied divisions in the church and they couldn't have been less interested. The assigned chapter for the next day dealt with discipline in the church. They were not too enthusiastic. Before we began the study I posed a problem being faced by a church in the community. A man's wife had died. The man had broken up the marriage of his son and daughter-in-law and had married the daughter-in-law. I asked the class what they thought the church ought to do.

One by one they responded with interest and some resentment that I should even suggest that anything ought to be done. After they had committed themselves I read the very plain statement that Paul made to the church at Corinth about disciplining the ones guilty of immorality. To my amazement, while before I read the passage they were a bit upset with me, afterwards they were upset with Paul *and* me. Afterwards one young man came around and made this confession. "I have always said that I believed everything in the Bible. But today I realized that the reason I can so easily say that is that I do not know everything in the Bible and I have not tried to apply it to life." If the truths of the Bible were to be dressed in a single-breasted suit and marched into the midst of life many of those who claim to believe the Bible would find themselves opposing its teachings. But the Bible must be applied to life. It has power to change lives and situations.

—Kenneth Chafin, *Help! I'm a Layman*, pp. 52–53.

Pastors, teach the Bible.

Thus if the biblical word is to be an authority in our churches—if they are to be Bible churches *in* culture—there must be theological instruction in the church: instruction in the Bible, its history, and its meanings; instruction in its theological ideas of God, man, and the cosmos, and in the history of those ideas in the life of the church; instruction in the relation of those ideas to our contemporary scientific and philosophical concepts; and finally, instruction in the ethic of the Bible and its relevance to our own current problems. Only thus can the intelligent layman come to realize the authority of the Bible over his own mind and life—for only thus did each of the clergy, in so far as he can now read the Bible with comprehension and devotion, come to understand, appreciate, and live under that authority. If this seems to mean adult classes and catechetical instruction of young people in the churches, the inference is correct—it means exactly that. The role of the minister as *teacher of adults* and as instructor in Christian ideas and values to every entering member of the church, is as old as the early catechetical classes for candidates coming to the church out of the pagan world. It is as old as the assumption that a man or a child must *learn* Christian beliefs, since he comes to them neither by nature nor by birth. The only reason the sects formerly believed they could dispense with this regular instruction was because each member lived in the world of these ideas and immersed himself and his family in the Scriptures through daily readings. Neither activity is characteristic of our laity today. The result is that, unless we teach them in the church, the laity will become progressively more and more ignorant of the beliefs and doctrines as well as of the ethical standards of Christianity.

—Langdon Gilkey, *How the Church Can Minister to the World Without Losing Itself*, pp. 97–98.

Bible study effects a second conversion.

In the first place, Bible study provides a context in which *koinonia* may be discovered. In the context of regular Bible study men and women find it hard to maintain their disguises. . . . Another often reported effect of Bible study is what John Wesley called a "second conversion"; that is, a new and perhaps deeper appropriation of faith. . . . Again, Bible study has the effect of bringing the biblical perspective to bear on the problems of daily life and sending men forth in mission.

—George W. Webber, *The Congregation in Mission*, pp. 80–82.

Biblical norms for missionary structures.

In the inner city, clergy and laity are turning to the Bible, not only for devotional help or sermon material, but for insight into missionary structures. Men are affirming that in the New Testament are patterns for the life of a congregation which must be taken as controlling or in some sense as normative.

—George W. Webber, *The Congregation in Mission*, pp. 53–54.

A five-year plan of adult education.

It is helpful to try to envisage what some of the adult courses might be and to arrange them in a series, so that, at the completion of the series, the average lay minister would have a right to feel a certain competence in his preparation. One five-year plan, including courses designed for local churches and largely taught by local pastors, is as follows:

The First Year, The Hebrew Prophets.

This course would introduce many students to the scholarly study of the Bible, with documents read in historic sequence. The Biblical material would be carefully read in large units and studied with the aid of the best commentaries, including the *International Critical Commentary*. Older works like those of George Adam Smith would be mastered as well as contemporary interpretations. A useful procedure would be to read, during the year, the Biblical material in the following order, *Amos, Hosea, Isaiah 1-39, Micah, Jeremiah, Ezekiel, Isaiah 40 ff., Jonah.*

The Second Year, The Synoptic Gospels.

Each of the Synoptic Gospels would be read slowly, first Mark, then Matthew and finally Luke. The similarities and dissimilarities of the three accounts would be carefully observed, the chief documentary theories about the oral discourses would be considered and students might be encouraged to produce, with the aid of scissors and paste, their own harmonies, in three parallel columns. A general grasp of the life and teachings of Christ might be expected from this study, far more profound than anything known in previous experience.

The Third Year, The Christian Classics.

This course might follow the essential techniques of the Great Books Movement, but concentrate on acknowledged classics of Christian thought and devotion. Since this is a field in which the average Christian is even less at home than he is in Biblical studies, interest may confidently be expected to be high. A good method is that of using the full time of class for discussion of the interesting material already read, with little or no time given to lectures. A tested selection of books is as follows: *Augustine's Confessions, The Little Flowers of St. Francis, The Imitation of Christ, The Prayers and Devotions of Lancelot Andrewes, Pascal's Pensées, John Woolman's Journal* and *The Prayers of Doctor Samuel Johnson.* This makes an exciting study for one year, all volumes being easily available in cheap editions, so that each student can own and mark his personal copy.

The Fourth Year, The Intellectual Understanding of the Christian Faith.

In this more mature study the class should consider all of the major and cumulative reasons for believing in God as well as the questions concerning God's nature and the Christian revelation. The hard problems, including those noted above, should be faced without hurry, and every effort should be made to arrive at a coherent system of belief. The reasons for believing in immortality and the doctrine of the resurrection should be handled *after* the other major subjects of the course have been studied.

The Fifth Year, The History of Christian Thought.

The greatest gap in the knowledge of most concerned Christians is the historical one between the Bible times and the recent past. Countless classes in Sunday School have studied various parts of the Old and New Testaments year after year, but very few have ever studied Christian history. The rise and decline of various heresies, the growth of the Papacy, the beginnings and completion of the Reformation, the origin of contemporary denominations, the conflict with science, all these and many more topics can be exciting for both teacher and student alike.

—Elton Trueblood, Your Other Vocation, pp. 119–22.

Objections to Bible study.

First, are men and women willing and able to undertake such regular and disciplined study? . . . The second objection arises from ecclesiastical rigidity and denominational pressure. The moment Bible study becomes one of the basic foci of the gathered life of the congregation the traditional "table of organization" with its great variety of groups and activities is badly undercut. . . . Another obvious objection arises from the radical differences between the world of the Bible and the life of the modern city. How can we expect to get across the talk of lambs and vineyards and flowing streams to city children whose experience is limited to tenement streets and crowded subways?. . . Another objection arises out of the mobility, either real or expected, in urban life. How can any congregation talk about "long-range, consistent, continual" Bible study?

—George W. Webber, The Congregation in Mission, pp. 85–87.

C. CREATING A COVENANT LIFE IN THE CONGREGATION— ELEMENTS OF THE NEW STYLE

A distinct style of living.

The Christian will be free, poised, integrated, and alert. Of course, the peculiar quality of the Christian life could be described with other characteristics. Then, too, Christians fail frequently. They are not superior to other men. They often cut themselves off from their resources. Yet God has given them gifts which enable them to contribute through their lives a new dimension within the daily round. They can develop a responsible way of living that becomes a distinct style.

—Frederick K. Wentz, *The Layman's Role Today*, p. 56.

The new life is like the stages in a marriage.

Looking back over the past few years, one can see that the new life that has come to Salem has produced three stages of growth, much like the usual stages in a marriage. Just as the wedding is followed by a honeymoon and then by the serious business of building a family, so the new life that comes in response to the love of God in Christ, beginning with a definite commitment, is likely to be followed by a honeymoon of inexpressible joy and peace, but leads eventually into costly involvement through witness and sacrificial service.

This is what is happening in Salem. It began with a cluster of conversions and rededications that occurred almost simultaneously. The ensuing joy of fellowship created a true expression of the "Body of Christ," and many have been so overwhelmed by God's personal concern for them as individuals that they have just reveled in the joy of "Jesus and me." But for some the honeymoon is over, and they are responding to God's call to salt every area of their community's life in costly service.

—Walden Howard, *Nine Roads to Renewal*, p. 18.

The new piety of adventure and risk.

The piety of our time is no longer to be vertical but horizontal in its emphasis. It is an adventure, a risk, an experiment. It has many surprises in store for us but it will also bring with it new certainties, new attitudes with which we shall find it quite possible to live.

—Hans Jurgen Schultz, *Conversion to the World*, p. 65.

The power to confess phoniness.

As I saw more clearly the sickness and self-centeredness in my own life, I also began to see the sickness and self-centeredness in our corporate church life. The difference was that, personally, I was becoming free to confess my phony ways, when I could see them, and find acceptance and forgiveness. And this was freeing me to take risks and, for the first time, to think creatively about relationships and purpose in church programs. Consequently, I began to shake off activities which, for me, were unreal. I saw that *life did not have to be the way it always had been.* My life was becoming an adventure. I became interested in people's needs and actually cared about some of them. But in the organizational life of the Church, no one seemed to see that there was even anything wrong, much less that a *whole new experience of living was waiting just outside our humdrum life together.*

—Keith Miller, A Second Touch, p. 110.

1. Habits of Discipline

We are afraid to let our true selves be known.

In short, I believe that we deceive ourselves about our selfishness and egocentricity because we are afraid a revelation of our true nature would alienate us from our chosen associates. Further, we cannot face the Biblical implication that the true nature of man is such that each of us is really engaged (however unconsciously) in the building of the Kingdom of Keith or Joe (or whatever *your* name is). We must find an appropriate audience because a kingdom with no subjects to respect the king is untenable. (And this is true whether one is a man or woman or whether one's audience is a national one or only a single husband or child.) To build up our images, and our kingdoms, we are subtly dishonest about any thoughts or desires or habits we have which do not fit our projected image for fear our subjects will discover our secret: that inside, behind the facade, we are not really kingly or queenly at all; but instead, in our intimate actions we are the servants, the slaves, of our resentments, our jealousies, our lusts, and our anxieties and insecurities. The more kingly, the more self-sufficient an image we try to project, the more we must dishonestly deny in a hundred ways that we are self-centered little children at heart bent on our own self-gratification.

—Keith Miller, The Taste of New Wine, pp. 26–27.

Commitment is an ongoing process.

All of us knew a call to commitment, but what our pilgrimage with a people told us so well was how imperfectly we had responded to that call. The witness of the Church of the Saviour is to a God who makes wondrous use of even the little that we give Him. This has given us reason to imagine what might be the miracles, if we could be wholly surrendered.

It is not that we are blatantly untrue to our commitment, "I unreservedly and with abandon commit my life and destiny to Christ." It is simply that commitment is never understood once and for all. It is a basic fallacy to suppose that the dream is always ours, the mission always clear. Participants in great visions are always in danger. Love can go, and it can go in little ways without our even knowing it. We are all children of Israel. It is possible for anyone to take the richness and the profusion of the gifts of God and look on them as commonplace. We sometimes take even His people for granted.

—Eliabeth O'Connor, *Call to Commitment*, pp. 92–93.

My fellow sinners.

So on and on we train our children to *look* happy and successful, to hide their true feelings, their true needs. By the time they are grown, their natural reaction is to put forth immediately the image expected of them in almost any given situation—regardless of how they may honestly feel about that situation.

The result is our churches are filled with people who outwardly look contented and at peace but inwardly are crying out for someone to love them . . . just as they are—confused, frustrated, often frightened, guilty, and often unable to communicate even within their own families. But the *other* people in the church *look* so happy and contented that one seldom has the courage to admit his own deep needs before such a self-sufficient group as the average church meeting appears to be.

What am I suggesting?—that we suddenly drop our masks and reveal ourselves naked to each other and the church with all our secret greed and lust and hate and resentments? No, but I am suggesting that we must realize that our fellowship is incurably crippled until and unless we recognize and face squarely the nature and extent of our deceitfulness with God, with each other, and with ourselves.

—Keith Miller, *The Taste of New Wine*, pp. 22–23.

Confess your sins to one another.

I realized experimentally that the Incarnation means that God has made the material world of people and things His concern and that we must make it our concern for Him.

But there was a fly in the ointment. I found that although I had believed God could forgive me for all my selfishness and sins, I discovered that I could not forgive myself for one of them in particular. After months of inner anguish and continued confusion I was talking to a close Christian friend. In a prayer I confessed this sin aloud to God before this friend. And within a few days, I could accept God's forgiveness. As a Protestant I had always been repelled (and frightened) at the idea of revealing my true self before another person. But now I realized why Luther made the admonition in James to "confess your sins to one another" (James 5:16) a part of the Priesthood of all believers.

This experience opened a whole area of my Christian life. I realized that once a man has confessed his most awful sins to God *before another person,* he can never again pretend (comfortably) that he is righteous . . . however famous he may become as a Christian. He can quit wasting so much of his energy explaining himself and making sure that everyone understands that he is a good man. Because now he knows that at least one other fallible human being knows that he is not. He is a selfish sinner. I am not recommending this to anyone. I am merely saying that *I* was trapped with some terrible anguish; and through this kind of specific confessing with a trusted friend (whom I knew might fail me), I found myself in a position in which I had to trust God with my reputation . . . and I found a new freedom. I could begin to be my true self with other people, realizing that as awful as I am, Christ loved me enough to die for me and people like me. Now I really *wanted* to be different in my life *out of gratitude.*

At this point a new honesty crept into my prayers. Before this, I had always started out by saying "God, I adore you" (whether I really did or not that morning). Now I could say, (when it was true), "Lord, I am sorry but I am tired of you today. I am tired of trying to do your will all of the time, and I'd like to run away and raise hell." But now I could also continue; "But, Lord, forgive me for this willfulness: and even though I don't 'feel like' it, I ask you to lead me today to be your person and to do your will." This was a real act of *faith,* because there was no religious feeling involved. My days began to take on the character of adventure.

—Keith Miller, *The Taste of New Wine,* pp. 60–61.

The motivation to search.

I do not believe the average layman's problem is a lack of information anyway. It is a lack of *motivation.* And if a man truly changes his direction and begins to try to live his *whole life* from Christ's perspective, he *will, on his own,* begin to seek to learn more about his faith—until he gains something of the breadth, wholeness, and balance God has for him. And, on his own, he will call for books and seminars and set them up—as laymen are doing all over the world today. But until he finds a continuing *motivation to search,* through a life which daily brings up new and threatening problems, I do not believe he will pay the price to seek, because the focus of his attention will be elsewhere.

—Keith Miller, *A Second Touch,* p. 133.

What is involved in suburban spirituality?

Andrew Greeley proposes a "spirituality for suburbanites" which might well put specific meaning to the commitment. He suggests first of all *self-denial.* Suburban affluence can easily become suburban avarice. Can a person keep balance among all the gadgets without finding it necessary to deny himself some of them? The spirituality would include *generosity*. The suburban person can easily fit into Jesus' story about the rich man and his success. Jesus concluded with a warning to those who lay up treasures for themselves and are not rich toward God. Greeley also suggests real *engagement* with the world. It is easy for the suburbanite to write off the slums, the bad politics, and the neighboring communities as no problem for him. Commitment to Jesus Christ will not let him off so easily. Finally, Greeley proposes an emphasis on *reading*. If suburban people have both the ability and the inclination to read, can we not foster a higher level of Christian commitment by making such literature available? In many parishes the only library is composed of donated books in dusty corners. But a library is not the only possibility. One role for the pastor would be to suggest literature to the people with the goal of deeper commitment in mind.

> —Roy Blumhorst, "In the Suburbs," *Death and Birth of the Parish*,
> ed. Martin E. Marty, pp. 110–11.

Coming to God at the center of one's life.

I have become convinced that the things which keep us from a live relationship to Christ are often not the "bad" things in our lives, but the good things which capture our imaginations and keep them from focusing on Jesus Christ. I think this accounts for a good bit of our frustration as churchmen. We look around in our lives and say, "No stealing, no murder, no adultery! Why, God, am I so miserable and frustrated in my Christian life?" But we have not seen the fact that we have never really offered Him the one thing He requires—our primary love.

What does one do when he finds out that he loves something more than God? For me it was rather terrifying, because the thing which was keeping me from the freedom of Christ was *my desire to be a great minister!* Because one's decisions will ultimately be made to conform with the shape of whatever has truly captured his imagination, my own decisions and sacrifices were not being made purely to love and feed Christ's sheep out of obedience and love of Him; but rather my decisions were made to help "the church's work" (*my* work) to its greatest fulfillment. This led to chaos and frustration.

When one sees, and can honestly face the fact, that his world is really centered in something besides God, in one's self in fact, I think he faces the most profound crossroads in his life (whether he is a layman or a Bishop). Because this is to recognize that one has separated himself from God by taking God's place in the center of his own little world.

What does a person do? The answer is paradoxically the simplest and yet the most difficult thing I have ever done. In our age of complexity we want a complex answer, but Christ gives us instead a terribly *difficult* one. I think there are basically two things involved in coming to God at the center of one's life: (1) To tell God that we do *not* love Him most, and confess specifically what it is that we can not give up to Him. (2) To ask God in the personality of Jesus Christ to come into our conscious lives through His spirit and show us how to live our lives for Him and His purposes . . . one day at a time.

But what if you recognize that you *honestly do not* want God more than whatever is first in your life? I think this is where a good many perceptive Christians find themselves. In that case I would recommend that you (1) Confess (as above) and then (2) tell Christ that your honest condition is that you cannot even *want* Him most. But tell Him that you *want to want* Him most (if you do), ask Him to come into your life at a deeper level than you have ever let Him before, and give Him permission to win you totally to Himself. This may be your first honest encounter with Christ, and He will take you wherever you are. As a matter of fact I believe this is really all *any* of us can do . . . give God *permission* to make us His. We certainly cannot be His by our own strength of will.

And if you made this new conscious beginning in a conversation with me, this is what I would tell you: that from now on you are not responsible to exert the pressure, the burden of muscling yourself up to be "righteous." You are not *promising* to change, or to *have strength*, or to be a *great* Christian. You have only confessed your need and turned your life over to Christ. What a relief! If He wants me to change, He will furnish the motivating power by giving me the desire to change, and then the strength to do it.

—Keith Miller, *The Taste of New Wine*, pp. 98–100.

Three possible approaches to effective discipline.

One is to ignore it altogether and see what emerges as the shape of the lives of its members as they participate in the dialogue between God and his world. This is a very attractive approach in our time, because we are so afraid of any type of piety or planned style that will separate us from life in the world. Thus a task force group in city government may decide to concentrate on listening and learning and let the questions of discipline and style remain questions as they get on with the work. This is an honest approach because, indeed, we have only a few hints about what it might mean to live as a secular Christian in a secular world. However, the danger of this procedure is that the nurture of a witnessing community depends on the willingness to keep our lives open to Christ as well as to the world, and ignoring the question may result in a kind of style that tends to close off opportunities to hear and see God's mission. No matter how much a community refuses to adopt a conscious style of life, the question cannot be completely ignored, because a style emerges out of their daily habits of living and serving together, and they have to consider whether this style, be it one of complete individualism, assists them in their task of mission.

A second possible approach to discipline is to make certain requirements for membership in the witnessing community that consciously seek to set the style of the group. This, for instance, is the approach of the group ministry in East Harlem, and of the Church of the Saviour in Washington, D.C. But this approach is only valid if the discipline is seen as an essential form of equipment for a particular mission. The East Harlem Group Ministry has a discipline because they know that there is no possibility of being responsible human beings in the tasks that they have to perform without regular periods of Bible study, retreats, worship, and involvement together in issues of social action, economics, and vocational commitment. The disciplines are *ad hoc* to this task, the task that all the members, both lay and clergy, of the group share in common, that of working as staff in one of the Christian communities serving the area of East Harlem.

A third possible approach to discipline in a witnessing community seeks to take discipline seriously while recognizing that the main way that it shapes people's lives is through their participation in a witnessing community. Thus the witnessing community will take real thought as to the pattern of its life together that will help it to be most open to Christ and God's mission in the world, but it will not make this pattern a requirement for participation in the community. Rather, it will seek to help shape each person's life as he participates, letting each person grow in his habits of Christian obedience in the same way that a child grows in a family. In this way, participants are loved into loving, helped into helping, served into serving until they are "hooked" on a particular pattern of life. The danger of this approach is that it has to be able to take a positive group approach to learning by participation, without taking the negative approach at the same time, which assumes that those who do not learn by doing and adopt a certain pattern are wrong or to be rejected.

Variety in approach to discipline is a given in a situation where discipline is functional and grows out of involvement in God's mission.

—Letty M. Russell, *Christian Education in Mission*, pp. 117–19.

A thirty-day experiment in Christian commitment.

There also is a 30-day experiment in Christian commitment called "Depth Through Discipline," designed to regenerate "old" members to the same type of commitment to the church and its ministry required of new members.

The voluntary experiment requires (1) rising 30 minutes early for prayer and meditation, (2) searching out during the day some opportunity for service, (3) giving two hours a week to some definite mission and (4) meeting in small groups to share experiences of trying to live the disciplines and to discuss the church and its ministry. Each group meets weekly in someone's home, with the exception of a group of businessmen—the only all-male group—who for convenience have a weekly luncheon in a commercial office building.

Recently the early meditation period caused one man (There are 300 in this experimental group.) to miss his bus to work. "I got in the car to drive to catch the bus at another place and I missed again. By this time, I was beginning to lose the spirit I had gained in earlier meditation, but I kept reminding myself that I had prayed for an opportunity for service and maybe this was the way it was coming."

Then he spied what he thought was the opportunity—an old Negro man wearing a T-shirt and worn-thin pants lay on the sidewalk freezing in the 20-degree weather. But the opportunity really came in a chance to witness to a young Negro man who helped get the old man into the car and to a hospital.

"What's with you? Why did you stop?" the Negro youth questioned. And the long-time Baptist caught up in a new experience of commitment answered: "I prayed to God this morning that I would find you."

—Sue Miles Brooks, "Depth Through Discipline," *Home Missions*, April 1968, pp. 11–12.

Intercessory prayer is the most important rediscovery.

We need ever to be intercessors for one another and intercessors for our groups that we may be open to the receiving of this gift of the Holy Spirit, and something can break in our lives and in the lives of our mission groups and they can be channels of His power. Intercessory prayer is not a new discovery, but it is the most important rediscovery of the church in our time. We stand on the threshold of a New Reformation, but it will not come except as we are intercessors, congregations which gather to pray, to look into the face of Christ and to give praise. There will be no revival, renewal, or rebirth without worshipping, praying congregations. This is the mainspring of the Ecumenical Movement, for here we discover our oneness as a congregation and our oneness as the church of Christ in the world. We become ecumenical as we enter into depth commitment and as we deepen the life of worship and adoration. The church is not organized into unity. The merger takes place in mind and heart and spirit as a people gathers and the Holy Spirit is given as it was at Pentecost. It is then that we are empowered to take a gospel to the world. Again we do not try to unite in order that we can be on mission, but it is as we are on mission that we move into the unity which has been given us in Jesus Christ.

—Elizabeth O'Connor, *Call to Commitment*, pp. 182–83.

Prayer drives us beyond our circle of friends.

It dawned on me with a sudden jolt that real prayer, Christian prayer, inevitably drives a man, sooner or later, out of the privacy of his soul, beyond the circle of his little group of Christian friends and *across the barriers between social, racial and economic strata to find the wholeness, the real closeness of Christ in that involvement with the lives of His lost and groping children whoever and wherever they may be.*

But behind and woven through all of these outer problems and adjustments had developed a new inner prayer life. There was a sense of active adventure.

My prayers were no longer vague mystical "feelings." I was communicating with a God who was *alive*, about real issues and real people in my days and nights. God was trying to give me an abundant new experience of life, when and if I would take it . . . a day, an hour at a time. When my regular morning prayers would start out "dry" I learned to read devotional books (like *My Utmost for His Highest* by Oswald Chambers or *The Imitation of Christ* by Thomas à Kempis) to turn my thoughts toward Him, toward Christ. Then I had found that by following any such reading with a passage from the New Testament every day I was gradually filling my unconscious life with God's message. And as I was revealing myself to Him in confession, He was revealing His character and purposes to me through the reading again of the way Christ reacted throughout the story of His life, death, and resurrection and of His spirit in the formation and development of the early Church.

—Keith Miller, *The Taste of New Wine,* pp. 64–65.

2. Life Together in a New Family—Unity of Fellowship

How does the New Testament define koinonia?

Koinonia is a word frequently employed by the apostles to describe the essential character of the Church. The English translation, "fellowship," is quite inadequate to carry the full meaning of the word. The New Testament employs it in several ways that give varying shades of meaning to the pattern of experience the early church meant by *koinonia*. The different translations given in the Revised Standard Version are an illustration of how the context necessitated several usages.

There are those passages that seem to use the word to describe the close spiritual relationship between the believers and God, either through the person of Christ or the Holy Spirit. . . .

And then there are those places where the writer uses the word to indicate the common life of the community of believers only. . . .

Sometimes this is used even more specifically to relate to mutual interdependence and responsibility for the weaker members of the group. . . .

Koinonia in the New Testament seems to be a comprehensive description of the unique life of the community of believers. It is a community that is closely and personally interdependent, but deriving its life from the amazing power of God that is the Holy Spirit. . . .

The Church defined as *koinonia* seems close to being a psychological description. This does not mean that it was unreal, or something completely the subjective experience of the people who were gathered together. In fact, it means almost the opposite. *Koinonia* was a recognizable togetherness that people felt in their whole being, their mind and body. This togetherness was there only because they felt the reality of God impinging upon their minds and physical beings. The translation "participation" is well used, because it avoids the chicken-and-egg argument about which precedes which, human association or awareness of the divine. It is true that the sense of commonality was based upon finding themselves companions on the same road upon which they had been set by Christ. But also there is little sense of surprise in the New Testament that Christ should have revealed God to others in the same way. An integral part of the wonder of *koinonia* with God, was that he should have come to dwell in the midst of all humanity, of which they were just a small part. It was the furthest possible distance away from "My God and I, we walk the fields together."

Furthermore, after the initial sense of the gift of grace, the continuing presence of God is expected to manifest itself within the community of the faithful. Nelson says that "the Holy Spirit is henceforth a corporate, not an individual possession. The Spirit dwells in the body. Apart from this corporate community, there is no gift of the Holy Spirit." The church as *koinonia* is a sphere of faith, experience, social intercourse, and loyalty that has unquestioning primacy in the lives of those who are a part of it. This primacy does not arise from a sense of duty or responsibility, but rather from the experience of the reality of God's presence in the midst of the congregation.

—Robert W. Spike, *In But Not Of The World*, pp. 4–7.

Solidarity with all sorts of folks.

Koinonia with Christ, moreover, produces in the church a new solidarity with all other communities, the nations, races, tongues, and peoples which constitute the world. In every encounter with Christ the church meets a Lord "whose only concern is for others." His love is the point where the church sees God's omnipotence, omniscience, and omnipresence—the point where these divine attributes are redefined by the weakness, ignorance, and limitations of incarnation and death. His love is the measure both of God's distance and of his nearness. There were no limits to the love of him who was hung between two thieves. He established a solidarity with mankind at its lowest denominator: sin, flesh, futility, death. He was raised as the first fruits of God's harvest which will include all creation. The only line between his community and all others is drawn by a love which is so exclusive only because it is so inclusive. He welds into his community a genuine solidarity with all men, not last with the last, nor least with the least. He sets it in the world to bear the sin of the world and thus to serve as trustee of the world's reconciliation. Therefore, the sanctuary rightly stands not on the fringe of the city, but at its center, even though this means being destroyed in the holocaust of hydrogen bombs.

—P. S. Minear, *Horizons of Christian Community*, p. 125.

Koinonia transcends denominations and creates Christian unity.

The contemporary form of the ecclesiastical *koinonia* is far more complex than the collection of money which St. Paul gathered for the saints of Jerusalem. It involves the immense problem of reducing our separation as denominations or self-sufficient communions. The New Testament certainly knew nothing of denominations in the modern sense of them; and if it had, there is strong reason to think that such ecclesiastical anomalies would have been categorically condemned. For they perpetuate the divisions of the one Church in a manner wholly incompatible with the concept of the Church which the New Testament, and especially Paul, plainly taught. The apostle's collection of money was one device for holding together the Church in its unity. Today we have an astonishing and exciting array of effective devices for the same purpose. Inter-church co-operation in cities and larger regions is an accepted pattern, although its potentialities have by no means been realized as yet because of the tendency of divided churches still to hold back from full participation with each other. Church councils are certainly here to stay, and within them the member churches or denominations are discovering what it means to 'grow together in unity'. (It is worth noting that the World Council of Churches is designated by the Greek Orthodox Church, using modern Greek, the *Koinonia* of Churches.) And throughout the world in country after country the denominations which have lived in mutual estrangement for generations are coming together in church unions, in numbers and at a rate unprecedented in the whole of church history.

—J. R. Nelson, *Criterion for the Church*, pp. 66–67.

The company of those who have passed from death to life.

The membership of the church is, foremost, that company of those who have passed from darkness into light, from death into life. What tie is deeper than the common experience of knowing the same Lord as Redeemer? Only in so far as men gathered together recognize that the same God has spoken to them all is there Christian brotherhood. Then they discover with delight that he speaks to them together. If there is no experience of the leadership of God in this brotherhood, then *koinonia* is absent.

—Robert W. Spike, *In But Not Of The World*, p. 13.

Where can difficult questions be discussed?

To deal directly and in depth with these controversial and difficult issues is one of the fundamental tasks of the church. If the church is truly a *koinonia*, if there is genuine concern to know the will of God, then it is within this type of fellowship where these difficult questions can best be discussed. If they cannot be faced within this fellowship of love and concern, where can they be discussed? Not to be able to consider difficult, even explosive, issues within the church is tacit admission that Christ is not *the answer*.

—Findley B. Edge, *A Quest for Vitality in Religion*, pp. 121–22.

Which relationships to discover and nurture.

Briefly, we seek at least the following relationships to be discovered and to grow in our life together.

Unity in Christ: The Meaning of "Koinonia." The Church is a community of love where the personal presence of Jesus Christ is known and where his love masters the community and builds it into a genuine unity. In our world of many human fellowships it is almost impossible to capture with any impact the biblical word *koinonia* which is translated by "fellowship." . . .

Openness to All Men. The first major battle of the early church had to do with the admission to membership of non-Jews. Did a person have to become a Jew first; that is to say, to enter into a religious, racial, and national community as a first step in commitment to Christ? The answer was an emphatic "no." . . .

Bearing One Another's Burdens. A missionary congregation depends upon the mutual ministries of all members of the family. . . .

Speaking the Truth in Love. In a family brothers speak the truth in love. This necessary family relationship is relevant also for a missionary congregation. . . . Without this gift, the congregation remains a collection of individuals, determined to avoid conflict and maintain pleasant but largely innocuous relationships.

—George W. Webber, *The Congregation in Mission*, pp. 122–25.

In family relationships there is no growth without some pain.

In the Church of the Saviour we live in community, and you cannot live in community and hide your problems. In fact, community will bring into light problems which, though they are yours, are often hidden even from you. Relationships in depth will always do that. Christian community probably comes the closest of any community to the family of our childhood, and all the unassimilated hurts and unresolved problems of that family come to light again in the context of the new "family of faith." Sometimes apparently well-adjusted persons come into the life of the church, people of action, ready to get on with the mission of the church, and then a few months or a year later things do not appear to be as well with them. They are actually much better off, because a lot of their activity had been motivated by anxiety of one kind or another, or simply the need to belong. Others are afraid of relationships in depth and discover that, while they yearn for community, they back away when people get too close. Still others find stirring in them yearnings that had been quieted and are now raised to life by the life around. The reasons are different for each person, but the experience is always pain. No real growth takes place without pain. Nothing is born into the consciousness without suffering.

—Elizabeth O'Connor, *Journey Inward, Journey Outward*, pp. 53–54.

Secure enough to be honest.

I am NOT suggesting the starting of some sort of "honesty cult." Such groups are often harmful and almost invariably wind up being *un*Christian. The object of honesty in adventure teaching is not to reveal immoral and lascivious incidents. The object is rather to begin to acknowledge to God and to each other the true nature of the personal struggles of living in the world today, so that we can begin to find freedom, healing, and forgiveness—and provide a place where others can experience these things. One does not rip off his mask (or anyone else's). Rather he becomes willing for God to remove the unnecessary part of his facade gradually by providing the security he needs to be more honest. Also a ground rule in this type of group is never to share something in such a way that it may make *another* person vulnerable. The highest value in the Christian life is not honesty— but *love* (I Corinthians 13). This is a very important basic difference between Christian joint-adventuring and some (humanistic) psychologically oriented groups.

—Keith Miller, *A Second Touch*, p. 142.

3. Training for Vocation in the World

Pastor, be a teacher.

A variant on this theme is that in which a pastor, willing to share what he has learned in the theological seminary, will enter into individual learning ventures with particular members or seekers. Many who hope to grow in the faith will surely welcome this kind of personal instruction, which produces as a by-product, a valued relationship between teacher and student. It is a little surprising to learn how many people ask eagerly for reading lists. They mean business, but they do not know where to start. There is undoubtedly a right order in study, and the person who cares about the intellectual aspect of his faith naturally wants to know what this order is.

—Elton Trueblood, *The Incendiary Fellowship*, p. 69.

Make each congregation a lay academy.

We must now take the next step, already suggested in Chapter 2, and make each local congregation into a Lay Academy, with the pastor as the chief instructor. Because the logic of renewal requires preparation, if the miracle is to occur, we must plan such instruction with care, and this ought to be the major function of each pastor. The book table and the study group become two parts of one whole, and they will always be provided if we really understand that theology is a relevant discipline, not merely for experts, but for everyone who seeks to be Christ's representative in the world.

—Elton Trueblood, *The Incendiary Fellowship*, p. 68.

The spark of interest.

Too often the lukewarmness of the Christian—not to mention his dullness—
is due to an uninformed mind. There is no dearth of good, provocative books
for every stage of growth. Often laymen and sometimes ministers tell us that
within their churches they find no Christian fellowship; but there is no one
who is denied the fellowship of Christian authors, communion with the saints
of today and yesterday, through the written word. The exciting people in
any field are those who have live and questing minds. It would seem to us
that an important task of the minister is to put into the hands of his people
vital books of the faith. This means to come to know a people well enough
to guess what might spark interest here and interest there—to know what will
help the housewife with her task and the scientist with his.

—Elizabeth O'Connor, *Call to Commitment*, p. 96.

Training for the adventure of living.

When we talk of the matter of "Christian education in the local church,"
I think we are talking about *training for the adventure of living this life* by
the bringing together of fellow adventurers. Each adventurer brings the
needs and witness of his own pilgrimage. Each one already wants to find out
all he can about God and about Christ and His character and purposes, not
so he can impress other people, but so he can find out how to cope with the
problems of living out this adventure on which he has embarked in the real
world. He is, in fact, tremendously eager and thus teachable—*if* the content
is presented in relation to the life.

—Keith Miller, *A Second Touch*, p. 139.

Where is the ordinary Christian to be trained?

The revolt of the laymen will be abortive and inconsequential unless we
can produce a far better training than most laymen now enjoy. It is important
to get laymen ready to speak to laymen, because they often have marked
advantages in this vocation, but there will be no short cut to success in the
enterprise. One of the most surprising facts about the Christian cause today
is the fact that so little thought has gone into the problem of how and where
the ordinary Christian is to be trained, if we are to take seriously the idea of
every Christian as one engaged in the ministry. It is obvious that the task
is an enormous one, but, up to now, we have done little about it.

—Elton Trueblood, *Your Other Vocation*, p. 108.

For want of a message.

The first part of the fallacy, then, is to think that the whole church is ready
to be sent out into the world, out into the secular society, out into the public

sector of government, and business, the professions, and the arts, without any means for the nurturing of their own faith.

Cut away the congregations from the life of this pie-shaped wedge of the church's mission into the central city, and where and how would the people's faith be born or be nurtured and nourished, built up and strengthened? Would all Christians suddenly sign up for courses at the Cathedral Church? Would they all even go to services in the Cathedral? Would each one be even more diligent in his duty to pore over the Scriptures daily, to read the classics of devotion, and to fall to his knees in prayer?

He should. Indeed, he should! But if we know our humankind at all, we know very well that they would not. The plain fact is that the church was given, among many things, for the nurturing and encouraging and challenging of the lives of men. And without this spur to their faith there is grave doubt that there would ever have been a church or a faith to last all these two thousand years. The Lord has given us the church—and particularly here, the local, gathered church, where men live, and move, and worship, and work—to keep the faith of Christians alive, to encourage them in their faith and discipline, to inspire and challenge them and keep them free, and alive, and growing.

And this is the element that has been found wanting in contemporary, ecumenically minded Christianity, by the evangelicals, the "conservatives." They have looked at the rising tide of criticism of the church and the growing movement for reform and renewal of the church, and they say, "But where is the faith? Where is the very motivating power with which you hope to do all these things? What are you going to say to the world when you get there? What will your message be when you sit in the boardroom of the corporation, or when you face the artist at his easel, or the housewife in her kitchen? Will you have a message for them? Will you have a real Christ who died and lives again for man? Will you offer them a real salvation, an honest change in sinful life—a change great enough in their life so that they, in Christ's name, can change the world's life?"

—Arthur A. Rouner, *The Free Church Today: New Life for the Whole Church,*
                                                                    pp. 107–8.

Adult education, special groups, and new members.

There are a number of areas in which serious study could be done.

1. An "adult" education program in the church is a starting place. One of the things which has made the Sunday School and other church organizations as successful as they have been, is that they are basically lay-led. In the worship service, the staff handles practically everything, but in the Sunday School and various organizations, laymen assume the major responsibilities. If adult Christian education is to be encouraged, the content and the perspective of most of the curriculum material needs to be up-dated to the level of thoughtful adults of the Twentieth Century. Denominations try to

find a common denominator in their preparation of materials about the Bible and the Christian life. Unfortunately this common denominator too often is at the level of the disinterested and the irregular.

2. There is the possibility of a number of study groups with special groups within the church. Sometimes the pastor who seeks renewal within the church, or would like to see a more responsible understanding of the Biblical faith, is discouraged because he cannot bring it about by one sermon or one resolution passed in the business meeting. It may be better to begin in a small group.

In a strategic church in Texas the pastor met with his deacons and discovered they had very little to do except to go over the treasurer's report and share tidbits of information about maintenance that needed to be done around the building. The pastor decided men of this leadership ability in the church could probably use this time more wisely. He secured copies of several books and passed them among the deacons with the suggestion that they would read a portion at every meeting.

Included in the book list were Dietrich Bonhoeffer's *Cost of Discipleship* (New York: The Macmillan Company, 1948), Elton Trueblood's *Company of the Committed* (New York: Harper and Row, 1961), and Robert Raines' *New Life in the Church* (New York: Harper and Row, 1961) and *Reshaping the Christian Life* (New York: Harper and Row, 1964). Each time they met they would discuss how the portion of the books they had read related to their church and to their town.

The result of this was two-fold: First, the deacons reorganized themselves in areas of ministry which needed to be performed in the church and in the community. Second, they became the spearhead in interesting the church as a whole in the question they had been discussing, "What Does It Mean To Be A Christian in a Church in a Day Like This?"

What this church experienced by way of renewal as it gave serious thought to its theology and its relatedness could be duplicated by thousands of churches.

3. The church could eventually raise the whole level of Biblical understanding by giving help to its new members at the time they come into the church.

Dr. C. A. Roberts came to Altus, Oklahoma, in his first pastorate out of the seminary. As new members were added to the church he formed a "New Members" class. However, it was not a class where church leaders were introduced, church programs explained, and church loyalty urged. It was a thoughtful, practical class taught by the pastor in lay theology. Everything from the nature of the Bible to world religions and their relationship to Christianity was discussed in an open meeting. The pastor had one problem with the class. The new members were getting so much help in their understanding of the Christian faith that many of the "old timers" expressed a desire to enroll. Some threatened jokingly to move away and come back so they could get in this class.

—Kenneth Chafin, *Help! I'm a Layman*, pp. 20–22.

The Christian life is a pilgrimage, not a program.

What then is the solution? In coming back into the problems of being identified with the Church, I have found that the thing which has helped me most is that during these past few years I have begun to become *conscious* of what I think it actually does mean to live and grow as a Christian. I have begun to believe that the Christian life is a *pilgrimage*, not a *program*; a pilgrimage with people who want to be willing to love, live, and possibly die for Christ, each other, and the world. I have begun to experience what it is like to take the risk of revealing *my* true needs, and to love other Christians enough to let them *help me* when I really hurt—as well as trying to help them. And built into this life is a yearning to share with others the freedom and healing one is finding. To know these things is giving a possible unity and direction to my whole life and to all the programs of the church in which I am involved. And when there are choices to be made about program, these criteria help me to evaluate where I should invest my time.

I'm beginning to believe that before we can formulate programs in the church which will affect anyone's real life situation, we will have to be educated in such an atmosphere that our inherited *perceptions* can change about the whole Christian enterprise. I feel that we need to look at Christian Education in the Church with new eyes.

—Keith Miller, *A Second Touch*, pp. 125–26.

One must teach others out of his own personal adventure of faith.

Am I suggesting that Christian educators give up their vocations and that lecturers and evangelists stop traveling? Of course *not!* But I am suggesting that anyone who hopes to have the people he is teaching make a transition from *passive listening to active loving, must teach and witness primarily out of his own personal adventure of faith.* I am *not* suggesting subjective *content.* I am saying that as you are teaching any course, say a course in "the prophets of the Old Testament" or "social issues of the 1960's," that along with the content, you tell the people what the study and the involvement with the material *means to you* in your life now—how this study has excited your mind or changed your relationships. And if the subject has not helped *you* to more adequacy in your own pilgrimage as a person, or captured *your* imagination, then I would question whether or not this should be taught *by you* in the parish Christian education program. Let someone teach that to whom it has relevant existential meaning. There is a real place for academic learning for scholarship's sake, but I do *not think that place is in the Christian education program of the average local congregation.* Time is *very limited* for the contact between teacher and lay students in the church's educational opportunities, and a very real choice must be made about this issue.

—Keith Miller, *A Second Touch*, pp. 131–32.

D. Koinonia Groups, A Dynamic Nucleus

The definition of koinonia: shareholding in a common life.

Perhaps the Greek word *koinonia* suggests an adequate answer. The usual translation is fellowship, but this rendering is altogether too subjective, too sentimental, too weak. C. H. Dodd prefers the idea of shareholding. *"Koinonoi* are persons who hold property in common" as joint owners. The solidarity is as objective and tangible as that. But *koinonia* goes much deeper than financial partnership, since Christians have been made partners with Christ and in him. They are joint heirs of a common life bestowed by him through the Spirit. This solidarity is so complete that what belongs to the whole community belongs to each member, and vice versa. . . . Sharing in this life changes the status of each partner and decisively redefines his existence.

—P. S. Minear, *Horizons of Christian Community*, pp. 122–23.

What happens in a prayer cell? Join and find out.

The most difficult question to answer which is ever put to us concerning our prayer cells is this: "What happens at your meetings?" The meetings are always basically the same, and yet each one is different and each one is always totally unpredictable. The form is so simple as to be almost dull in description, yet is so vital as to be exciting in real life. The content is devotional but it includes whatever is of concern to those who share the group life. Each person lays his soul bare in such a manner that we know one another in an intimacy not to be equaled anywhere else, and yet no one pries and everyone respects the unrevealed intimacy of his fellows. Each group develops a corporate personality which is thoroughly recognizable but no group has developed a spirit of exclusiveness or cliquishness. In light of all this, how are we to answer the stranger at our gates when he asks, "What happens at your meetings?" He must experience life within the cell before he can understand what we are saying.

—John L. Casteel, *Spiritual Renewal through Personal Groups*, pp. 53–54.

Renewal has always started with a person or a small group.

Several years ago I spent some time going back through the Church's history to try to see what did happen in the renewal movements which seemed to have lasting integrity. But instead of looking at the methods and activities of each movement when it was *at its crest*, I tried to peel back the layers and see how these renewals *began* in each case. Because, for most of us, the problem is not how to sustain a renewal in the church, but how to *begin one*. As the evidence began to stack up, I came to a revealing conclusion. In most of the great vital movements in the Church's life a simple almost identical pattern unfolded. One person in a local situation—who was usually not very important at the time—decided to give himself wholly to God with no strings attached. Then a few others gathered around this person, because total conscious commitment by a sensitive individual evidentially makes people somehow "hungry" or "homesick," for God. And as these few lives bcome deeply committed to the living Christ, a common vision came through the small groups' life together which gave them the particular shape their obedience would take in the world. Up to this point in each group's development the institution usually had no idea who these people were. I began to realize that the beginnings of genuine renewal were *invisible to the Church at large*. But once the group members had committed themselves to the Lord and to each other and had experienced the common adventure of beginning to try to live wholly for Christ, *then* what the Church calls renewal began in all sorts of different ways, *depending on the needs the group saw in the world of its time* (from its new perspective). Great numbers of people were then drawn to commit themselves to God and the purposes of the group. And great teaching, preaching, and movements to change social abuses poured new life into the Church.

—Keith Miller, *A Second Touch*, pp. 149–50.

Congeniality is a false basis for koinonia groups.

Both the narrow exclusiveness and the superficial fellowship of many congregations are due to the commonly held idea that Christian community is built upon the mutual congeniality of its selected members. The greater the degree of independence and autonomy of the congregation, the more its members adhere to this belief. Now one ought not to disparage friendliness and congeniality within the household of God. Dismal is the church where they are lacking. But they are an utterly false basis for *koinonia*. The true basis of community is Jesus Christ and faith in him, as attested and sealed by Baptism and expressed through devotion to the Gospel and performance of Christ-like works of love.

—J. R. Nelson, *Criterion for the Church*, pp. 59–60.

Koinonia groups are not gimmicks, but channels of God's communication.

The development of small groups in the life of the church is not a gimmick. It is not a technique to add more programs to churches which, for the most part, are already overburdened with programs. The only purpose is to provide God with an effective channel of communication, whereby he can reveal himself to his people; and the gospel can become a living reality. Small groups, if they are to have a place in the life of our church, must be redemptive fellowships of love in which the living Christ can be known. God alone can give birth to such a community.

—John L. Casteel, *Spiritual Renewal through Personal Groups*, p. 78.

A koinonia group can minister to its own members.

Every member of a small group should strive to be involved in a specific project of mission, witness, or service. But a group must not be considered a failure if this is not the case. An important part of the mission of the church is its ministry to its own members, especially those who have special needs. I recall a girl whom I shall call Juanita. She had slashed her wrists in attempted suicide. After several months in a prayer group she became a healthy, well-integrated person. I also remember a couple with marital problems. The husband, who was not a church member, came very reluctantly to my office for counseling. Charlene (not her real name) came for counseling also. She responded best, though, to spiritual growth in the prayer group. Later when I visited her still unchurched husband in the hospital, he said warmly, "I want to thank you for what a difference the church has made with my wife. She is not the same person. She is a better wife and mother— she's just not the same person." *This is the Church on mission just as surely as involvement is social change or political action.*
—Russell Bow, *The Integrity of Church Membership*, p. 121.

Koinonia groups supplement preaching and teaching.

A new pattern began to work itself out in my mind. Something more than good preaching and teaching was needed. In our culture men live for the most part outside the framework of God for six days a week and therefore find it difficult to accept a message from the pulpit. So they sit in our pews with tongue in cheek or shift into mental neutrality as the word is preached, for they have never really known to what they have committed themselves. Teaching and preaching were indispensable but they needed to be implemented. Modern man needs to find a vocabulary by which he can communicate religious ideas and feelings to another. He must have an experience of God as well as possess knowledge about God. In every other science modern man has a vocabulary whereby he can express himself. Not so in religion. Old words and symbols have lost their meaning. New content needs to be grown. The Protestant Church should be a laboratory where religious principles could be discovered, understood, and practiced. If laymen would come to a clear understanding of what they believed, they would be more eager to live these spiritual truths. Perhaps it could be done through small fellowship groups where a religious vocabulary and a religious meaning could be hammered out as a basis of faith.
—Thomas M. Steen, "Renewal in the Church," *Spiritual Renewal through Personal Groups*, ed. John L. Casteel, pp. 31:32.

Face-to-face support and criticism.

It is difficult in today's world for a Christian to confront the dilemmas of daily living. It is even more difficult to make responsible Christian choices if there is no place within the local church for an intimate sharing of the burdens, the joys, and the consequences of Christian behavior. Worship can provide that moment of sharing and personal confrontation in the presence of God, but what the Christian needs most is the face-to-face support and criticism of his fellow Christians. This is best provided in small groups developed for this purpose.

—Thomas R. Bennett, II, "Project Laity: Groups and Social Actions," *The Creative Role of Interpersonal Groups in the Church Today*, ed. John L. Casteel,
p. 68.

When a person is known by his first name.

Part of the power of small groups lies in the fact that they can be a source of mutual support for the group members. When a person is known by his first name, known as a distinct individual, his personal dignity, his faith in himself and his sense of personhood are all enhanced. . . .

A recent meeting of a Bible study group in the Bronx illustrated this rather clearly. The meeting was held in an apartment. A lady attending for the first time had an opportunity to talk about her anxieties as a new member of the community. (Incidentally, this topic came up as a digression from the discussion of the Bible passage of the evening.) She explained her feelings of not knowing anyone in the huge apartment building in which she lived, and she expressed gladness that she had found a Bible study group to join. Her sense of lostness and isolation were communicated vividly as she told of her experience in trying to get a neighbor to go bowling with her. In the very act of expressing these feelings and having them accepted and understood by the others, the loneliness and lostness abated. She was asked some questions about herself and in answer poured out some of her anxiety. In this act of sharing, the group gave her genuine support—an almost tangible expression of Christian love, although they would not have called it that. The support she found gave her strength and she left eager to know when and where the group would meet again. It was perhaps significant that she had not been to the church which sponsored the group and even expressed some fear about attending where she "didn't know anybody."

—Clyde H. Reid, "Small Groups Are Here To Stay,"
Union Seminary Quarterly Review 18:395–96.

A koinonia group is of personal value to the clergy.

These groups keep me from being in spiritual isolation. They enable me to share in the new creation. In times of dryness or despair or just plain weariness, when I would rather go home, I go to one of these meetings. Someone in the time of quiet offers a prayer, and I am ministered to. Someone shares an insight or an experience; I watch the light of dawning faith break forth on someone's face; I look at these couples who have hired baby-sitters in order to come and seek God together—and I am lifted up. I watch the Holy Spirit working in their lives, and I am warmed and encouraged. I have a box seat for the constantly new and exciting drama of changed and changing lives. There is nothing more joyful than beholding people who are being transformed. To be at the growing edge of another's conversion is to share the joy in heaven over one sinner who repents.

I have discovered I am now dependent on this *koinonia*, this holy fellowship. If I were to go to another church, the first thing I would do is try to create such a group, for my own selfish need. These groups keep me closer to the people. They serve to sharpen and in some instances modify my own judgments and interpretations. I have learned more from the people in these groups than from many books about the new life in Christ. Often I have gone, like John Wesley, "unwillingly" to a *koinonia* group meeting and have come away with my own heart-warming experience in which God refreshed and powered me to go on.

—Robert A. Raines, *New Life in the Church*, p. 102.

Koinonia groups reach lapsed members.

The small fellowship group does not only draw into itself those who are active members; it is also effective in reaching lapsed members. In a number of instances it is found that persons who have dropped out of the public worship of the Church and are loath to return to it when invited to do so, are perfectly willing to join a group in some private house. Once having been reached again by a situation of transparent reality, these persons may later be drawn into the total life of the Church. However valuable public worship is, there are some sensitive people who find it cold and impersonal. Such persons must be reached in other ways, after which the public worship may be more meaningful to them.

—Elton Trueblood, *The Incendiary Fellowship*, p. 71.

Koinonia groups have no set patterns, but they must have leadership.

There is perhaps no set pattern the little congregation must follow. In two such cell groups in which I have shared with my students, we employed a very simple and variable pattern consisting mainly of prayer. Meeting before classes one day a week, we ordinarily began with a prayer of dedication. This was followed by an opportunity to reflect on our failings and to offer a prayer of confession. Then, we spent some time considering persons or matters of particular concern and offered a prayer for them. We concluded with a prayer of thanksgiving. We used the Bible and Christian devotional classics as springboards and guides. They have particular value for integrating theology and Christian life.

The small Sunday School class, of course, could be led in this direction. In any small group, two problems must be faced—purpose and leadership. Members must agree on purpose, and they must have leaders who can direct interest and effort toward it.

—E. Glenn Hinson, *The Church: Design for Survival*, pp. 79–80.

Small, disciplined, structured—three crucial principles.

Three guiding principles seem crucial. First, the group must be small enough for personal interaction—or, in other words, it must be a face-to-face group. Twelve may be a maximally productive number, though a group may be smaller and, I believe, as large as twenty or slightly more. Indeed certain qualities of good group life may come into being when there are twenty-five or thirty; and it is our hope that to some extent an entire congregation may realize its potential as a community. Six to eighteen is probably the range of maximum productivity, however, and some would insist on a maximum of seven or eight.

Second, the group must be sufficiently disciplined for order to be maintained. It cannot wander at will, whether it be a planning group or a study group. Maves' distinction between "task centered" and "need centered" groups is a legitimate one, and he is no doubt right when he insists that the Church ought to have more groups which seek specifically to answer men's needs, not engage them in a particular task. But even a group which is quite free to deal with immediate needs must be ordered so as to deal with those needs, and further, a task to which people give themselves may actually become the cohesive element which forms a group and makes it capable of dealing with needs.

Third, the group must be sufficiently structured so as to accomplish its purpose. Some leadership, except in the most informal situation, is necessary, even though it may shift from time to time, even within the same session.

—Howard Grimes, *The Rebirth of the Laity*, pp. 141–42.

The possibilities of koinonia groups—five principles.

We gather up these comments upon the possibilities and the promises of personal groups in a few brief principles:

1. Personal groups are first of all *creative* and *unique:* the means, methods, purposes, possibilities, for one group are never quite the same as those of another.

2. In terms of the Christian faith, personal groups are the *work of the Holy Spirit:* they come to life through the leading of the Spirit; they grow, struggle, and triumph as the Spirit gives them light and power; they are bound together by a common life lived *in the Spirit.*

3. Life in a personal group has its cost: the work of study, praying, meeting, serving; the cost of giving up old centers of interest and gratification;

the cost of learning to accept, then to forgive, then to love, other members of the group, and other people, in every circumstance; most of all, the cost of moving the center of life from self to God.

4. The group does not exist by and for itself; its true life is to be found *in the church*. Although at the beginning, a group may have little connection with the church, and although it may find that keeping itself centered in the life of the church is beset by many problems, still the church is its goal, haven, and home, and it moves toward that larger frame of worship and service as steadily as it can.

5. Personal groups do not depend upon exceptional abilities or strong personalities either to get started, or to continue and grow. They depend upon *committed men and women*. The answer to every complaint that what is needed is the right person to get things started, or to keep the group moving, is, "Be that person yourself."

—John L. Casteel, *Spiritual Renewal through Personal Groups*, pp. 212–13.

The disciplines of an enduring faith, study, and prayer fellowship group for women.

We begin by working on ourselves first. We want to learn to relate God in all affairs—to contact the power of God and see it visible in us. Spiritual growth takes time. We have to be patient with ourselves. We find we go farther, faster with a definite program. There are three items included in the daily disciplines of our group members:

1. A quiet time in the morning. It may be necessary to get up at least 30 minutes earlier than we are accustomed to, but reading the Bible, meditating on what we have read, praying and listening to God *must* become part of our lives each day.
2. Prayer twice a day for those in the circle.
3. Prayer once a day for the names on our prayer list.

Other disciplines which this group keep are:

a. Prompt and regular attendance at the meetings.
b. Careful preparation of lesson in the Bible and in the book we are studying.
c. Making a sincere effort to keep the Seven Disciplines as set out by St. Stephen's Church.

Our meetings are held in a home each Monday night. They begin promptly at 7:00 P.M. and close promptly at 8:00 P.M. The leadership rotates each week, as does the giving of the meditation. One of the responsibilities of the leader is to guide the meetings so that the members do not indulge in irrelevant conversation. Each member sits in the same place each meeting. This makes it easier in praying for the group and enables us to have a prayer chain for emergency prayers. Each member calls the one on her right in the circle in case of an emergency.

The meetings follow the procedure set out below:
1. Meditation (given by one member)
2. Quotations from the Bible (each person says a Bible verse around the circle)
3. Reading aloud together the Seven Disciplines
4. Witnessing to the love and power of God in our lives during the past week (each person shares in turn around the circle)
5. Reading aloud in the group one chapter in the Bible
6. Discussion of current spiritual book we are reading
7. Spontaneous intercessory prayers (around the circle)
8. Lord's Prayer and Mizpah Benediction.
    —Claxton Monro and William S. Taegel, *Witnessing Laymen Make Living Churches*, pp. 79–80.

A testimony from the ranks of pro-football.

When I joined the Cleveland Browns in 1962, I shared with others the wonderful privilege of showing three different players on the team what it meant to be a Christian. Jim Ray Smith, a teammate of theirs, had lived the Christian life before them and they had become vitally interested. It was important that these three young Christians have a proper foundation in the Christian life. We started with a Bible study fellowship group and met every Friday night in a different home. There were six couples that met together— the Shofners, the Smiths, Mavis and I, and the three couples who had just become Christians; and we continued this fellowship group all through the playing season. After supper together we would begin our discussion group. We started with prayer. I was the group leader, but I tried not to talk any more than anyone else. Each member of the group discussed a passage of Scripture. For example, we worked through Ephesians, taking one chapter each night. We rewrote the chapter in our own words, averaging eight words per verse. If there were ten verses in a chapter, we had an eighty word total in our summary. When we rewrote the passage in our own words, we were surprised at how well we came to know the passage. The Apostle Paul has some introductions to his letters. In our attempts to rewrite his introduction in the most contemporary English, we'd just say "Hi!" We felt that this was what he was trying to get across in our modern day language. The summaries were all very interesting, and we all received some wonderful help from our work on the Scripture. It was also amazing how much these new Christians grew in Christian understanding after rewriting these passages in their own words. We would start by letting each person read his passage summary and by having a discussion of each summary after it was read. Then we would go back around the group having each person tell what he thought was the key verse, and have a discussion of that. We'd go back around the group for the third time asking each person to tell how this passage blessed him personally. We would conclude the evening by having each person in the group pray a brief prayer. There was probably more genuine Christian growth in this little group than would have ever been possible with another method.

—Bill Glass, *Get in the Game!*, pp. 47–48.

One woman's testimony: "God speaks to me through the group."

God often speaks to me through the members of the group with whom I'm meeting. Quite often, it seems, I do not want to hear what He would say to me through other Christians because it hits too close to my pride. For example, during the time we were meeting with our first group I had to face the concept of the Scriptures in regard to the relationship of husband and wife. Paul is pretty pointed about who he thinks should be the head of the household (Ephesians 5:22), and, as an emancipated woman, I resented what this implied. Our group discussed this passage of Scripture and my friends would not leave me alone about my attitude until I had resolved my problem of pride. Fortunately, I have several close Christian friends who are tuned into my wave-length because they can usually put their finger on my sore spot—the thing I am protecting in a self-centered way. This constructive criticism can only operate effectively in the context of love and concern, for honesty and hostility can be a devastating combination.

Since that first experience, Bob and I have participated in many different groups. The members have varied widely in background, denomination, and understanding, but the "magic" is always there. The requirements for a group like this are simple—openness to God's Holy Spirit; willingness to be honest about oneself; a feeling of concern for the welfare of other members of the group; a commitment to do the work involved in study. This kind of group has special meaning to me because it was in one of them that I learned how to be a real person, to respond to others in a natural way. I had been ingrown for so long that my response was slow and painful, but I learned to be open and to dare to be myself. The Book of Common Prayer of the Episcopal Church contains a beautiful phrase, "the company of all faithful people." This seems descriptive of the great host of Christians who find together in the presence of God and each other a depth and richness of human relationship that could never be theirs except on the terms of the Holy Spirit.

—Nancy Peerman, *The Real and Only Life*, pp. 48–49.

Would people accept me if they really knew me?

I was so afraid that people wouldn't accept me if they really knew me. For me, to reveal my true feelings to a group of strangers has always been a little terrifying; but I've come to realize that the group will be no more open and honest than the leader. I think this is why a lot of groups structured by religious professionals have failed—because the professional ideal is that the leader must be the strong one. We are subtly trained this way in our leader-ship training on almost all levels—to believe that we, "the leaders," must be the strongest in the faith. But Paul keeps saying: "I'm the chief of sinners. I'm the worst failure of all." And it sounds almost phony at first. But when one begins to realize at a deep level how terribly inadequate he is with regard to the perfection of Christ, then he can afford to say: "I've failed." And when a leader talks about his real inability sometimes to get along with God and the other people around him, he creates a "floor of vulnerability" down to which it is safe for anyone in the group to go without being rejected.

You have to be real with this. You can't just use it as a technique, or it becomes phony. And this is a real battle. Some people are almost professional at being honest, and I have fallen into this trap before. Further I definitely do not think that this should just be a confession session.

I think it's best to start out very slowly. You begin with just being honest about the problems you've had that week. This might include sharing resent-ment that you feel because of the pressures of your family, or pride, or per-haps something in your business has hurt your pride. How does a man handle these things under God? You just have to play it by ear and see what the group comes up with.

And this kind of natural openness and requesting prayers for each other brings real love and power into the group. But the leader must show the way and this is a form of dying to one's self. But I have had to realize that when a man dies to himself other people can be born to freedom. Two people have written to me and say: "Mr. Miller, in your books you are very negative." This hurts me terribly because I feel that this is such a positive faith—my freedom to tell you I have problems is paradoxically a real joy. I don't have to bottle them up or be afraid you'll discover I'm not great. I have the security in Christ that sometimes allows me to let you see the real me. To me that's good news. But some people will say: "Look how inadequate he is." And people do say that. And when they do, it is a threat to me, it hurts my feel-ings; but I have come to realize that other people can be unlocked by this approach and on my best days I am more interested in seeing other people freed than I am in people's opinions—even of me.

There is a richness that comes from real sharing. If I share with my wife the fact I am really mad and don't fake it, then we can really go through this experience and understand how we hurt each other. And afterward we can laugh about it; then somehow we are closer than we ever were because we have seen the worst of each other and we've accepted it. I think that this is the kind of thing that happens in these small groups—this going through trials, seeing ourselves and each other better, and then sharing the joy of new wholeness and discovery.

If you can laugh in the face of your own frailty and tragedy, that's the greatest freedom there is. In a group I've heard a man in a prayer tell us that he and his wife have found each other after months of separation and everyone was touched to the point of tears. And the next minute he said:

"You know, I'm a real so-and-so, and I just let my wife have it this morning."
He had forgotten that he prayed that they are now together. We all roar with
laughter then, because we know that the new togetherness is big enough to
include the fusses. This is creative freedom. The freedom to laugh and to cry
means that you are emotionally flexible and that you can flow in or out of
the circumstances so that you bring real creativity rather than stereotype
responses.

—Keith Miller, "The Freedom of a Positive Faith," *Home Missions,*
April 1968, p. 10.

The "Spirit" permeates the congregation through "small groups."

I have in mind the conviction that there can be no general renewal in the
local church unless and until the Spirit creates *ecclesiolae*—little churches—
within the congregation. Before they come into being, the most we can hope
for is a scattering of "star performers" throughout the parish. These are
people who have been given valid insights regarding the Gospel and the life
in Christ, but who live in virtual spiritual isolation—even though they are
members of the institutional church—because they have not also been given
a vital relationship with other persons who have received similar insights.
Renewal will occur in the church when these isolated persons find themselves
in dynamic association with persons of comparable experience in the Christ
life.

This is a way of speaking about the phenomenon variously called "cell
groups," "personal groups," or "prayer groups." In the proper context they
may even be known as "study groups." Because of the spontaneous and
dynamic character of these groups, no two of them fit the same pattern or
are capable of adequate description in the same words. I consider a group
to qualify for inclusion in this general category if it possesses the following
characteristics: it must exist within the parish life of a local church; it must
come into being in response to the felt need of its members for some such
experience as a discipline of prayer and study, a wiser and more significant
use of the Scriptures, a keener understanding of the social implications of
Christianity, a companionship in intercession, or a permissive fellowship
within which to discuss personal queries concerning the Christian life; it
must be small, consisting of no more than twelve or fifteen; it must meet
regularly, preferably once a week; it must order its meetings so that they
are started and stopped reasonably on schedule and so that they normally
include periods of silence, study, and audible prayer; it must resist all tempta-
tions to organize itself and all attempts to be organized into the institutional
structure; and it must be open-ended in its membership.

Put negatively, such groups cannot: free-wheel without reference to the
church; be formed artificially as part of a program; be unwieldly in size;
be free of self-imposed discipline and order; be one-sided in content or concern; be "used" by the institution; or be private clubs.

The only experience of renewal in the church with which I am existentially familiar would be utterly unimaginable apart from the work of the Spirit manifested in the creation of such personal groups. I have witnessed one man as he was led to an awareness of his need for companionship with persons in a like stage of development in the Christian life; I have seen him led to persons whom he had scarcely known previously but who were aware of a similar need; I have been present when they met as a group for the first time, and I remember how they haltingly admitted to one another that they did not know what the group was "to do" (shades of our institutionalism) but that they all yearned for an opportunity to discuss with sympathetic persons the implications of the Christian life; I have shared the life of that group over a period of years as it seriously studied some of the classics in Christian devotional literature; and I have watched every member of that group as he has grown perceptibly in understanding the dimensions of Christian discipleship.

With the creation of that group—which I can only credit to the work of the Spirit—genuine renewal began in the local church. Its presence encouraged other persons to admit their longing for an intimate personal relationship which would stimulate them in their growth in the Christian life. Within the space of a decade, no less than fifty such groups have come into being. At least a third of them still exist, and some of them have a ten-year history.

—John W. Meister, "Requirements for Renewal,"
Union Seminary Quarterly Review 16:259–60.

The crucial role of the group leader.

It is the task of the group leader in most instances to free the group from emotional dependence upon him, allowing it to emerge into a style of life in which each member shares responsibility for the life of the group.

—Clyde Reid, *Groups Alive—Church Alive*, p. 30.

Tests for koinonia groups to keep them from becoming "ingrown."

Small groups, like any other structure, however, do not guarantee renewal or vitality. They may afford a new possibility of faithfulness, but they easily become ends in themselves or fall into other dangers. There are several tests against which the life of the group may be judged.

1. Issues of fundamental importance in life in dispersion are discussed. This means real issues, not smoking and drinking, but the issues people want to evade—for doctors, medical care for the aged; for teachers, unionization.

2. As free as possible from ideology so that issues can be faced honestly and without more distortion than is inevitable. Professional groups, for example, need to be challenged by material other than from their own organizations.

3. The group seeks to act together or at least to arrive at a consensus.

4. The group backs up the person who does act in accordance with the claims of obedience. That is, the group takes seriously its solidarity.

All four of these tests underlie the fact that small groups are for mission and not primarily for purposes of personal religious growth.

—George W. Webber, *The Congregation in Mission*, p. 131.

The dangers in a koinonia group do not invalidate it.

There is, of course, a need for withdrawal and retreat—for the alternation between work and worship, witness and prayer, action and study, life lived in the world and life lived apart from the world. The dangers inherent in the fellowship group do not invalidate such a group. It is necessary, however, that retreat be directed toward the life of the world; that the self-conscious group be made aware of the life beyond; that the common meal be seen as equipping one for the common life.

—Howard Grimes, *The Rebirth of the Laity*, p. 89.

The temptation to move away from engagement in koinonia groups is very strong.

As we will be severely tempted away from an engagement with God and an engagement with self, so will we be tempted away from an engagement with others. The temptation to withdraw will be at the crisis points in our relationships—at times of real confrontation, and at times when we see nothing happening. And, of course, it will come always at the point of a Rachmilevitch. We will rationalize that it is unprofitable to stick with this particular grouping when there are more congenial people and more congenial circumstances in other places—"people who think the way I think and feel like I feel"—all of which, when you reflect on it, is rather dull, and in the second place probably a fiction, since a sure fact about the next group one joins is that one person there is certain to be the same—saying the same things, doing the same things, and evoking the same kind of response. But of course, we can always move on again when we have settled in enough for the rough edges of another person to rub against our own rough edges. We might even be able to withdraw and maintain the illusion that we still belong to Christ and to his mystical Body, but it will remain an unconfirmed opinion. The New Testament does not know very much about this mystical Body. It is concerned with twelve who have a life together. It talks always about the church at Corinth or the church at Rome. The answer that is often made to this is that the Church is wherever two or three gather in His Name. But this does not only mean the choosing of a few kindred friends with whom to pray. We gather in that Name when with other faltering, estranged persons we agree to live a life in depth, which means learning something about forgiveness and what it means to be forgiven. It means staying locked in a concrete, given web of relationships until we come to know ourselves as belonging to one another and belonging to the Body of Jesus Christ.

—Elizabeth O'Connor, *Journey Inward, Journey Outward*, pp. 26–27.

E. THE RENEWAL OF THE CLERGY

The pastor and the problem of his image.

More and more the problem is that of image. The professional ministers, especially when they are persons of outstanding integrity, as many are, simply cannot accept the mold into which they are supposed to be cast. The best mind hates to be looked upon as the official pray-er at all ceremonial occasions.

—Elton Trueblood, *The Incendiary Fellowship*, p. 37.

Is a professional clergy even necessary today?

The minister, insecure in his vocational identity, often attempts conforming to traditional clergy roles in establishing his place in society. Such attempts are sure to fail.

For example, Sunday worship was once a "high point" of the week for those who might expect to hear the prophetic word. Today the authentic role of clergyman as *prophet* has degenerated. The prophet must be aware of God's activity in the world and then speak of this activity to the religious community. An urbanized world requires full-time attention if there is to be prophetic discernment. Institutional demands of the parish church compel the minister to stand aloof from the market place, observe its activities through the mirrors of religiosity and then pretend to be spokesman for God. The clergyman seeking true prophetic involvement in today's society will threaten his ordained status through neglect of his clerical duties.

Ministerial efforts to be *shepherd of the flock* are also doomed. There is no valid basis upon which the flock is gathered today. We cannot expect men to be called out of the world in which they live and group themselves on a spiritual basis. The foundation of the residential congregation was that members lived closely together from economic and social necessity. The local congregation was once a functional unit of a primary community. Now citizens of the metropolis find such basic community in vocational, professional, political and economic spheres beyond the community of residence. Yet the clergyman still addresses a ministry to "his parish," vainly trying to call the sheep together. There is nothing more pathetic than a shepherd treading well-worn paths to call sheep that are not there. . . .

Another symbolic role of the professional clergy is demolished as the average cleric attempts to be a *burden bearer* for his people. He may try to lift the weights from bent shoulders, but finds that, although he can occasionally patch the raw skin, he cannot shoulder the burdens. He is cut off from the source of the problems that are piled on the backs of men and women today. There was a time when such burdens were primarily spiritual and when the confessional function of the ordained priest was a necessity. But as man has come of age seeking wholeness of life, he has been unable to separate the religious from the political, social and economic. His burdens are one. There is no place for a man with the special task of bearing spiritual burdens. . . .

Consider finally the ancient role of clergyman as *father*. Each time I have donned the clerical collar to officially represent the church in today's society, I have been addressed by many as "father." But I cannot ignore the smirk of some who hear me called father. They realize any organic relationship I may have had to society as a family is gone. And thus any authority as a father in the family has been destroyed. In the new world that is coming to be, the clergyman can no longer expect to be the authority father figure. . . .

In the face of such disturbing evaluation of the ministry today, what alternatives are open for the future? There seem to be only two. Men can continue to dedicate themselves to the ordained clergy and to exist in the illusory world of the religious institution, convincing themselves that we can return to the Christendom of the Middle Ages. . . . But for those who reject such false satisfaction, there can only be faith that today's laymen and clergymen will face the plain fact that there is no need for an ordained professional ministry.

—Stephen C. Rose, *Who's Killing the Church?*, pp. 14–17.

The practical starting point for renewal.

The more we ponder this practical question the more clear it is that the practical starting point is the ministry, though this does not mean that the ministry is everything. The whole conception of the ministry is perplexing, partly because the term "ministry," as used in the modern world, is highly ambiguous. There is a deep ineptitude in equating the terms "clergy" and "churchman," not wholly different from the ineptitude of equating "the religious" with those who have adopted the discipline and garb of a separate order. In the ideal sense, all Christians are ministers, but for practical purposes this is not true. Those who think of themselves as ministers, whether lay or professional, are people who may be assumed to have a degree of dedication which makes the beginning of renewal possible. Ministers are important, because both potentially and actually, they are multipliers. If we can reach these people with a new vision of the Church, we can consequently reach others through them. The ministry is the point at which to begin because ministers are usually placed where they can make a difference.

—Elton Trueblood, *The Incendiary Fellowship*, pp. 34–35.

Clergy must live a life of renewal before leading others.

I am convinced that many renewal attempts have been ruined by being wooed to a premature numerical success. This is what I mean: If we are thinking that renewal will spring from a relationship with God which touches and potentially transforms *all* of one's ordinary human relationships, then the leaders of a renewal with this emphasis had better try this life themselves *together,* personally and privately, so they will know the pain and joy of actually living every part of it. We had better learn how to be open with each other and God and have experienced the struggles this involves *firsthand.* Because if we haven't lived it awhile before large numbers of people come flooding in, we may find that our roles as leaders can make it very difficult to have enough real emotional privacy so that we can learn to *live* the life at all—rather than *publicly performing it*—the life we are telling other laymen to risk all in which to participate. I know some sad ministers with considerable ability who have "gone for the renewal bit" and have gotten lots of people excited, only to find that they, themselves, really did not know how to lead their people to be open in small groups, for instance. They did not know, because they had never invested the time and energy to live in a small group as a *vulnerable, uncertain member.* I am becoming convinced that it is not just the great renewal movements of the past, but *any lasting* renewal, local or individual, which takes place in this way. And I believe this learning first to live the life together without a program is essential for another reason—because of the way authentic ventures for Christ seem to develop from this perspective.

—Keith Miller, A Second Touch, pp. 152–53.

Clergy must initiate renewal in the congregation.

We can begin by asking how the process of renewal might begin, assuming that the local congregation, in its present form, was maintained as the basic institution of Protestantism. First, one must consider the resources that are available.

Despite a needed emphasis on the importance of the laity, the crucial factor in the *initiation* of renewal is the minister of the congregation. If he lacks vision, if he is wedded to traditional views, if he counts his success in terms of shiny new buildings and the ability to run a cozy social club, then the chances for renewal are irreparably damaged. It would be better if the congregation had no minister at all. For the first prerequisite of renewal is a minister who can lead the laity to see the need for a more relevant Church. The first, most positive step a congregation can take is to call the right minister.

It is rare to find a clergyman with all the qualifications a renewal-minded congregation has in mind. The congregation that wishes the minister to combine four or five specific skills, in addition to being outgoing and having an attractive but not too aggressive wife, is probably more interested in having a showpiece than a man who can point the way to the mission that lies beyond the sanctuary walls. Thus the local church would be best advised to choose a specific mission and seek out a minister who is able to devote his skills to a fairly specific area. The choice of mission is largely dependent on the nature and location of the particular congregation.

—Stephen C. Rose, *The Grass Roots Church*, pp. 67–68.

Clergymen do for the Church what laymen do for the world.

Originally the laity of God meant all Christian people, including clergymen. It is this whole laity which is Christ's embassy and the world's priesthood. But to refer to baptism as ordination and to speak of a variety of ministering gifts raises the question of the role of the ordained clergy, the set-apart ministry within the total royal priesthood.

Clergymen are and do for the church herself what laymen are and do for the world. The distinction is important, but it is a difference of function and emphasis only. Within the total priesthood some exercise their gifts and spend their time and energies largely among fellow Christians. Others (the non-clergy Christians) exercise gifts and spend themselves primarily in relation to the rest of the world. Clergymen, then, are those who first of all minister to laymen ministers.

—Frederick K. Wentz, *The Layman's Role Today*, p. 28.

The clergy specializes in making the lay ministry real.

Any person who cares about the Christian cause is bound to be deeply concerned about the ministry. Those on the front lines in the major spiritual and moral struggles of our time are undoubtedly the lay people, but the lay people are not likely to make an effective witness unless they are guided, instructed, and inspired by those engaged in a vital ministry. Whenever we discover something new and exciting in the church we always find that, in the midst of it, there is a *man*. It is men who make the difference and some of the men who are most effective in our total civilization are those whose lives are dedicated to the public or professional ministry. The Christian ideal is that of the universal or lay ministry, but this ideal cannot be realized unless there are men who specialize in making it real.

—D. Elton Trueblood, "Introduction," *The Renewal of the Ministry*,
Thomas J. Mullen, p. 7.

Renewed laymen are often rejected by the clergy.

This growing body of new Christian disciples is constantly amazed at certain ministers' (often in their own denominations) rejection of them. This question must be faced if the new life being experienced by God's people is to be channeled through the existing structures of the institutional church.

—Keith Miller, *The Taste of New Wine*, p. 106.

Clergy may fear the lay renewal groups.

Some ministers and church people have seen the restless stirring among laymen and the clamor for "change" and "honesty." But because of their past experience with cliques of gossips and malcontents these ministers may *perceive* unsponsored lay activities as irresponsible and almost go into a spasm at the perceived danger.

—Keith Miller, *A Second Touch*, p. 123.

His job is to get them to play the game.

As the Protestant pastor seeks to stir up a ministry among his people, his role is analogous to a man trying to direct and help others participate in a program of recreation. His job is not to put on an exhibition which people watch and possibly even cheer. Nor is it to get them out in the middle of the floor in order to feed him the ball while he scores. His job is to get them to play the game. When they throw the ball to him, he must fire it right back to them or to another teammate. He may score in some ways, but not always will he be the star. He may have to help some of the players learn how to play the game and develop their skills, but once they learn, he should let them alone to develop further on their own.

—Thomas J. Mullen, *The Renewal of the Ministry*, p. 90.

The chaplain to the laity on mission to the world.

Rather, a missionary congregation will develop an image of the clergyman not as the chief executive of a flourishing organization, but as a chaplain to the laity in their mission to the world, as one who assists the laity in the work of God in making and keeping men truly human. In this light, the role of the clergy will assume its proper place within the gathered life of the church, not as superior or more important, but simply as a vital and necessary part of the total missionary purpose of the congregation.

—George W. Webber, *The Congregation in Mission*, p. 168.

The pulpit becomes the prompter's box.

A layman—a *laikos*—is a representative of God's mission people *(laos tou theou)*. He constitutes the vanguard and the first thrust of the apostolate. I would venture the thesis that the minister has become unsuited for the apostolate by virtue of his ordained status. His task is a different one. He must try to equip the laity for their service (Eph. 4:12). We can see it around us: a clergyman can share in the apostolate again and do something essential in it, once he represents himself and behaves as a layman (priest-laborer). I certainly would want to reverse very decisively the usual order which has come to be accepted in our churches as the normal order: the layman is not the aid or an extension of the minister, a clergyman in miniature or (if he really tries that) in caricature, but rather, the minister is the servant of the laity. His work will have to be directed at this: that God's mission people behave as such. He himself does not appear on the stage of the world: there the layman performs. The clergyman cannot join in that—professionally he has become unsuited for it; he can do a little directing, but further especially serve as a prompter. The pulpit becomes the prompter's box. It is only too bad that the prompter can remain hidden, whereas the man in the pulpit remains so dismally visible and sometimes annoyingly present.

—J. C. Hoekendijk, *The Church Inside Out*, pp. 86–87.

"Coach" is the best term for the pastor.

What then shall the equipper be called, if not the minister? Here we have real difficulty since all of the familiar terms have unacceptable overtones. "Elder" won't do for it sounds stuffy, and is as ridiculous when applied to a young man as is "Father" when applied to a bachelor. "Preacher," which was once conventional on the frontier, won't do for it refers to only one aspect, though an important one, of a complex function. In many ways "pastor" is best, partly because it is dignified by New Testament usage, but even more because it places emphasis upon the relationship to those who are being led. The Lutheran tradition has made zealous use of this term, with many good results, one of which is the avoidance of the temptation to make an indiscriminate and illicit use of the honorific "Doctor." In spite of these advantages, the word pastor implies much that we do not mean and ought not to mean. Sheep are not particularly productive, except in providing wool and mutton. Futhermore, sheep are notorious for their placidity while they are being led, but this is no part of the ideal of Christian men and women in the common ministry of common life. A man who supposes that his relationship to the members of a congregation is in any sense identical to the relationship between a shepherd and a flock is in for some big surprises. Another serious difficulty with pastoral terminology is that modern men have very little knowledge of the ways of sheep, some city dwellers never having seen a sheep in their whole lives. Here is a vivid example of how language can become almost meaningless because of a radical change in manner of living.

Some are now coming to believe that the least inadequate or distorting term for a spiritual leader in a congregation is "coach." This word has over-tones which modern man comprehends very well, indeed. Furthermore, the image of the coach is one which can be universally honored by young and old alike. Everyone knows that, in the development of a football or a baseball team, the quality of the coaching staff often makes a crucial difference. With no essential change in the personnel of the players, the effectiveness of the team is sometimes changed radically when a new coach begins to operate. He sees that Smith can profitably be shifted from guard to halfback and that the fullback, having never been used in defense, may have in him the possi-bility of becoming a successful line-backer.

The glory of the coach is that of being the discoverer, the developer, and the trainer of the powers of other men. But this is exactly what we mean when we use the Biblical terminology about the equipping ministry. A Christian society is made up of men and women whose powers in the ministry are largely unused because they are unsuspected. The Christian coach will be one who is more concerned, therefore, in developing others than in enhancing his own prestige. Ideally, he will not do anything himself, if another can be enabled to grow by being encouraged to do it. If the sermon can be given effectively by an ordinary member, the pastor, in so far as he is truly a coach, may keep silent while the other speaks, even though the training of the other person may cost him far more in time and toil than his own preparation for speaking would have cost.

—Elton Trueblood, *The Incendiary Fellowship*, pp. 42–43.

The "soldier-teacher" of the congregation.

As long as we hold out the office of the minister as a position of superior prestige and diginity in the community, the young men of the world are going to turn us down. They know better! Those days are gone. All we can become—indeed should become—are foot washers of the congregation, as-sistants to the true professionals and ministers who are the church within the world. We need an image of the clergyman as the "soldier-teacher" who scouts the terrain and cares for his men in the midst of battle.

—W. A. Holmes, *Tomorrow's Church: A Cosmopolitan Community*, pp. 65–66.

Active in the Church, active in the world.

It seems to me that there are real dangers of lay arrogance in an attitude which seems to say to the clergy: 'We do the real fighting: you prepare us for it.' An attitude which regards the parson as the domestic chaplain to the faithful is quite as erroneous as one which regards the laity as the 'backers-up' of the clergy. Many of the great missionaries and pioneer evangelists have been clergy, so have the founders and heads of schools in this country and abroad. Clergy have had their part in the intellectual debates and encounters with the Church's attackers, they have written some of the best books on the Church and the social order. . . .

The whole people of God has a ministry in and to the world. That means that the parson, like Chaucer's 'parson of the towne,' has his role in the world as well as in the gathered congregation. It is part of the duty of lay people to encourage and enable him to fulfil it. It means also that the layman should be concerned, along with the clergy, to think about the future role of the congregation, of Sunday and what happens on Sunday, in the total life of the Church which is the presence of God's people in the world.

For this to happen there has to be a mutuality of regard for the lay and the clerical life within the people of God. *Lay people* must not be led to think that daily work is important only because, or in so far as, it offers opportunities for evangelism. Earning a living, working to produce goods or services, playing one's part in making the working community as far as possible a true community of persons—these are all activities of response to God's creation of the world through Christ. *Clergy* are, in a world which has so largely rejected God, the visible reminders of this rejection. That is one of the reasons why they suffer ridicule and attack. Yet they are constantly meeting men and women at the points in their lives where many of them still want to remember, want to keep open by a narrow chink a door back to active faith. All Christians are called to minister to the world, but clergy are entrusted on behalf of us all with the exceptional means of confirming forgiveness, of holding out to us the means of illumination and grace in scripture and sacraments and of maintaining the Church in the fullness of the truth of the faith.

—Kathleen Bliss, *We the People*, pp. 123–25.

The Church's most important professional.

The local clergyman may well prove to be the most important professional the church possesses. Dan Wakefield has characterized the minister as "one of the last remaining members of our society who can't afford specialization." The minister of a local congregation is a generalist who must concern himself with anything and everything that affects the life of his flock. In the life of metropolis, he is a professional who is "amphibious." As a trained worker with professional standing, he has access to all the other professions. At the same time, he is supposed to maintain a close tie to the people of his congregation and the community in which he serves. He thus can look at the problems of urban renewal both through the eyes of those who must draw the plans and carry them out, and through the eyes of those affected by the plans. By virtue of his dual ties, the local clergyman can be highly influential in securing the kind of dialogue and communication most needed to temper the work of planners and redevelopers.

—George D. Younger, *The Church and Urban Renewal*, p. 175.

F. The Ministry of the Laity—The Priesthood of Believers

The lay renaissance.

Now the Lay Renaissance has its own forms of radical search, but self-understanding is less an object of search than the base for exploration. With a new self-understanding as the *laos* ("the people" of God), Christians are rediscovering that *they* are the church, clergy and laity together—not a building, or a hierarchy, or an organization, but "the company of all faithful people." And with this self-understanding has come a new sense of mission and responsibility. Feeling called by God to *be* the church wherever they are in the world, lay men and women are probing deeply the Christian message and its relevance to all the forms and issues of modern life. Real pioneering is taking place. At some centers of lay training the search for meaning is as persistent as anything to be found in the context of the "second revival." However, the result is not moral chaos but moral recovery, as may be seen in the acceptance of personal discipline and in the sense of Christian vocation in the ordinary occupations of everyday life.

If we ask where this movement came from, we shall find that its sources are various and world wide, with the chief impetus coming from creative lay centers, orders, and institutes in western Europe—experiments that have multiplied since World War II in the effort to supplement traditional patterns of congregational life.

Since the nineteenth century American Christianity has been the most active Christianity in the world in terms of lay participation; yet the new awakening in this country is new in kind. Whereas the older lay movements were chiefly auxiliaries of the institutional church, the new movement is the church itself moving out of its institutional walls to live for Christ wherever Christian people work and live. Although no date can be given to any breath of God's Spirit blowing over a continent, we can say that only in the last few years has this breath approached the mighty wind of Pentecost. Its history lies chiefly in tomorrow. Then perhaps we shall see it as a *third* religious revival—the real one, able to redeem the other two.

—Julia A. Lacy, "The Lay Renaissance," *Religion in Life* 31:19.

1. Opening Up the Ministry

The frustrated feelings of laymen.

Two experiences have made me realize how much both pastor and people need to re-examine their relationship to each other and to the mission of the church. First, at a convention where I was a messenger I voted on a particular issue, and the two pastors sitting next to me voted differently. They won. But they were not satisfied in merely winning, they had to know why I had not agreed with them on the vote. One asked me, "What church are you from?" When I named the church, he asked, "Are you the pastor?" When I told him that I was "only a member" he remarked, "Well, you wouldn't know what this is all about anyway." The rather obvious impression was that only a minister would understand the business of the church.

A second experience told me something about the frustrated feelings of the laymen. At a lay meeting I expressed my joy at being with them, and how on occasions I envied the freedom of the lay members of the church. I jokingly suggested that if they had a service of rededication in which people came and gave up certain things that I might come forward and give up ordination. The entire group began to applaud. I had the feeling that there was a great deal more involved here than just a response to a joke. There was a sense of surprise at a minister's identification with them as laymen.

—Kenneth Chafin, *Help! I'm a Layman*, pp. 2–3.

Laymen need not wait for church renewal to begin their ministry.

What has been accepted for more than six hundred years will not be lightly changed, certainly not by writing letters—or even books! The church urgently needs renewal. Too often, the need is seen and discussed simply in terms of organizations and programs. A layman begins to see the possibilities of a real ministry of the laity and decides to consult the parson and other men in his home church with a view to developing a plan that will soon produce such a ministry. A woman decides she will get the women's guild of which she is a member to make "The Ministry of the Laity" the study program for the next year. The clergyman who begins to see the possibilities just groans, for he realizes that what is required is no mere tinkering with the church's program, but a revolution in the church's life. Those who have worked for renewal know something of the cost it will demand.

Fortunately, the laity do not have to wait for the renewal of the church before they can begin a real ministry. It is not a question of *either* the renewal of the church *or* going on a journey of one's own. The renewal of the church will take place in and through the development of a ministry of the laity. . . .

The first step in the renewal of the church is to encourage as many laymen as possible to see themselves as ministers. The gap between talk and action will continue until a vivid demonstration of a true ministry is given. If laymen delay until their whole congregation begins to move, nothing will happen. Some will find help and support from the clergy, some from other laymen, some from both. Others will have to rely for help and fellowship on those who are doing the Lord's work in the world without knowing it.

—Francis O. Ayres, *The Ministry of the Laity*, pp. 19–20.

What does the New Testament say about laity?

So it is sometimes argued that we ought to develop the use of the term "laity" by stressing its reference to Christians as the called people. This proposal is highly questionable for several reasons. Basically, the historical usage of "laity," "lay," and "layman" within the church is quite unrelated to the Biblical concept of God's *laos*. The predominant influence in this ecclesiastical terminology came from the Graeco-Roman political environment of the church. The government was divided between the *klēros*, or "magistrates," and the *laos*, or "people." The former were those who possessed wisdom, were trained, and had power to act. The latter were ignorant, uneducated, and so were to submit passively to direction. Likewise, in Western culture, including the church, the term "lay" came to indicate the mass of the uninformed (in any field) who are incapable of making responsible judgments or of acting with authority.

Nothing could be further from the Biblical idea of God's chosen *laos*. His people have been called into being out of the mass of humanity, and the people as a whole are distinguished by their knowledge of God and their power to do his will. When this collection of men cease to know God and to do his will, they cease to be his people. And they failed precisely when they came to think that being God's people was something natural, inherent, and guaranteed, because then they abdicated their right to knowledge in preference for professional prophets; they forfeited their own worship to the mechanics of priestly ritual; they yielded their responsibility to act to the sovereign power of a king.

It is little wonder, therefore, that the New Testament does not typically refer to the Christian community as a people. The Hebrews' emphasis on their being a people and a nation chosen by God had blinded them to the purpose of their calling: to be a light to the Gentiles. They conceived of their call as one to a place of privilege, rather than to a life of service. So there is only one passage in the New Testament (I Peter 2:9) that directly characterizes the Christian community as a nation and people, and that is written by Peter, the apostle "to the circumcised" (Gal. 2:7–8). Elsewhere, the disciples of Jesus are called an *ekklēsia*, a congregation of men held together by the call of Christ and by the fellowship *(koinōnia)* of the Holy Spirit. And the major thing that is said about this community is that it is called to be God's servant (minister, agent) of reconciliation. And the very nature of this ministry of reconciliation, as will be explored in the next chapter, should prevent Christians from thinking of themselves as an elite people of privilege.

Thus we see that the historical concept of the laity is totally foreign to the New Testament understanding of the church.

—Arnold B. Come, Agents of Reconciliation, pp. 88–89.

What is a layman?

Ask a doctor what he means by the word "layman," and he will say, "Somebody who hasn't been trained to understand medicine." And that is one normal meaning of "layman" today—someone who is an amateur, who doesn't understand, who isn't an expert. In that sense of the word, this book wants to abolish the Christian "layman"; we want to make Christian experts instead.

—Mark Gibbs and T. Ralph Morton, God's Frozen People, p. 11.

The word "layman" is now returning to its original significance.

We are witnessing in the twentieth century the recapture of this conception of Christian community. The recapture often appears in the form of a new doctrine of the laity. Along with other Christian words, this term has suffered drastic erosion in meaning, but its original force is slowly returning. The root of the original meaning is in the Greek phrase, the people *(laos)* of God. "The ministry of the laity" refers to the privilege and responsibility of this whole people to share in Christ's ministry to the world. Every member of the laity *(laos)* receives this privilege and this responsibility. In the church he represents his world. In the world he represents Christ's work.

—P. S. Minear, *Horizons of Christian Community*, p. 115.

How to jump from one to five hundred ministers.

So far as the Christian faith is concerned the practical handle in our time is lay religion. If in the average church we should suddenly take seriously the notion that every lay member, man or woman, is really a minister of Christ, we could have something like a revolution in a very short time; it would constitute both the big dose and the required novelty. Suddenly the number of ministers in the average church would jump from *one* to *five hundred*. This is the way to employ valuable but largely wasted human resources. The change that could come in the visitation of new families, in the spoken and written word, and in public witness might be incalculably great. In a few communities, where the idea has been seriously tried, the change has already been encouragingly great.

—Elton Trueblood, *Your Other Vocation*, pp. 29–30.

A theology of the 99.5%.

The conclusion we are reaching is that there is no such thing as a theology of the laity alone, but that there is the possibility of a real shift of emphasis in the doctrine of the Church. Supposing it could be that the word 'laity', instead of calling at once to mind the 99.5% of church members who are not ordained, made one think of the essential people-like character of the Church of God? As one uses 'unity', not to mean anything organizational or structural but to express the existing unity of the Church in its one undivided Lord and the earnest and prayerful search for its visible expression, so one ought to see in the use of such a phrase as 'the laity of the Church' a reminder of the people-character of the whole Church. 'A theology of laity' ought not therefore to mean 'a theological interpretation or justification of the existence and functions of the 99.5% of the Church's membership who are not clergy, monks, paid workers of the Church, etc.' It should mean 'a theology of the whole Church as the people of God'. It should define and describe in understandable theological terms (for a theology *of* the people of God must be *for* the people of God) what it means to see the Church in this aspect, and therefore what God is calling his people to be and do.

—Kathleen Bliss, *We the People*, pp. 76–77.

Ordination is a false standard of total commitment.

Ordination, therefore, in the eyes of the average layman has become a religious status symbol of total commitment. And some are afraid to make a serious commitment, since they know they are not cut out to be ordained ministers.

I remember that I went to seminary because I wanted to serve God in the fullest way possible—even though I honestly *did not* want to become a parish minister, nor did I feel called to be. But unknowingly the church has sometimes implied that if you are *really serious* about wanting to serve God totally, this decision is tantamount to a call to the ordained ministry. But I do *not* believe this is true—nor scriptural. In the earliest New Testament accounts, committed Christians within the fellowship were set aside or ordained for certain special tasks or *functions*. The first deacons were appointed and set apart by the laying on of hands to wait tables (Acts 6:1–6). These men were ordained not because they had reached a certain level of commitment which other Christians had not reached; but they were ordained because someone trustworthy was needed to *wait on the tables.*

I believe this is still true in the Christian community—that men are ordained to preach (for example) not because they are the most committed, but because they have been given certain specialized gifts to be used to help equip God's (equally committed) people for work in His service "to the building up of the body of Christ," the whole Church (See Ephesians 4:11f). But as long as an ordained pastor feels (even unconsciously) that his decision to become ordained and his subsequently acquired theological education are signs of a will *more* given to God than that of a committed lawyer or housewife, then that pastor will think of his language as the true language of commitment. He will try to educate his people to become as he is, a trained theologian—instead of helping them to become the *creative business men and parents and housewives* they were born to be.

—Keith Miller, *The Taste of New Wine*, p. 110.

A bold new image of the missionary.

We need a bold new image of the missionary. No longer can he be seen as a professional clergyman with a Bible in one hand, a machete in the other, marching to some uncivilized and distant land. The new missionary is a layman disembarking from a plane or riding on the freeway. He is a father talking to his son about a life style, an engineer talking to a scientist about responsibility in a nuclear world, a housewife conversing with her neighbor about a phony program of censorship at the PTA, two diplomats at a conference table in exhaustive dialogue over a peace treaty, management and labor bargaining for equity and fair employment, a student maintaining his inquisitiveness and critical perception as he listens to his teacher explain some new philosophy or concept. Our image of the missionary, like our image

of the mission field, must be rethought, resurrected, and renewed; and perhaps, above all else, it will involve a keen insight into what it means to be
found living as a corporate man.

—W. A. Holmes, *Tomorrow's Church: A Cosmopolitan Community*, pp. 60–61.

Laymen who "attend faithfully" are not necessarily committed.

What has apparently happened is that those of us who have been in policy
making positions in local churches have made some very faulty assumptions
about laymen and the Church. We have assumed that a man's presence at
vestry or deacons' meetings indicates a deep personal commitment to God
and His purposes. We have assumed that these men have a freedom from
self-centeredness and fear of other people's opinions. We have *acted as if we*
believed that they are ready to go out and openly share the freedom and
understanding of their faith (which they are presumed to have), if only we
could come up with the right vehicle for them, the right program. *But it is
not so!* At least for me and for dozens of men whom I have asked in moments
of honest sharing, these assumptions simply *are not true.* Most of us had not
been elected to vestries for qualities of dynamic personal and loving Christian
involvement with people. Some were elected because of financial success.
Others, the minister had asked to run. Some were elected to keep the "spiritual
element" (or even the minister) from going off half cocked. Many of these
elected saw the vestry's function as a sort of financial advisory board to
which the minister was to provide the spiritual direction (when there was
time). For, other vestrymen membership was an honor, like other civic
honors.

Most of us did not have any clear conscious picture of what it might mean
for us to *really be* committed Christians in our world. And yet the ministers
assumed that we were the spiritual center of the church. But the truth was
that most of us did not even know what the central human problems of
alienation are—to which the Gospel might speak in the world.

—Keith Miller, *A Second Touch*, pp. 121–22.

The Protestant Reformation of the twentieth century.

We must shatter the image of the uninformed, illiterate, impotent layman.
Otherwise, the church will be incapable of fulfilling its mission in the world
today. But the reverse is just as true. If every member is a minister in the
church, then we must cease referring to one group of members as ministers,
or as comprising *the* ministry of the church. Indeed, they are ministers but
just as all other members also are ministers. They are not qualitatively or
personally different or unique; they are only *functionally* unique. But every
other member is also functionally unique in that he shares in one or more
forms of ministry that are not shared in by all other members. Not everyone
shares equally in every ministry, no one shares in every ministry, everyone
shares more intensively in one or several ministries than in others. . . .

The church, therefore, must shatter the traditional image of the pastoral minister as *the* minister. He no more has a peculiar and indelible stamp placed upon his soul or person than any other Christian. He is a sinner before God just as every other member of the church. There is no other or higher standard of Christian behavior for him than that which obtains for every Christian. His life is no more "full time" for God and his Kingdom than that of any other one who has been called as a disciple of Christ. . . . We must now see that the *whole life* of the congregation and denomination is the means through which Christ imparts his truth and life to his body, the church. Every member's ministry is a ministry of Christ's grace. And holiness does not inhere more in one ministry than in another. It is a simple fact that the holiness of the Spirit of God often dwells more richly in a member who performs some obscure, inarticulate ministry than in the one who ministers as pastor and preacher. In the end, we must see that no individual possesses true holiness as his own in his own person. We only share in the holiness of God as we are in the relation of servant and friend to him. And every sincere servant is as sacred and precious to God as every other. This view of the means of grace does not in the least mitigate the necessity and importance of the ministry of Word, sacrament, and worship in the life of the church. But this ministry must take its place along with all the others so that the church will make bodily growth by every joint and member with which it is supplied.

—Arnold B. Come, *Agents of Reconciliation*, pp. 117–20.

Training schools for laymen.

The third vehicle for renewal is the education of the dynamic nucleus at a level commensurate with the demands of the day. Seminary-level training would be highly desirable. Seminaries could arrange special summer or vacation curricula for interested laymen. The purpose would be giving laymen tools comparable to those now offered to ordained clergy. However, since seminary training will not be within the reach of all who would like to have it, the churches must utilize all resources immediately available to give quality theological education to the committed company. Denominational colleges could help in this inasmuch as most of them have theological departments. Area schools sponsored by local churches, both denominational and interdenominational, could also assemble competent faculties from the seminaries or colleges during the summer or between semesters. Such schools could take the place of many purely promotional meetings which are attended by the committed nucleus but which do little to prepare them for their tasks.

—E. Glenn Hinson, *The Church: Design for Survival*, p. 81.

Develop your pastoral gifts.

Many laymen have pastoral gifts and should be given every encouragement and opportunity to develop them. A man or woman may be in a position with many people under him. He may be a member of an office staff, a worker in a factory, a parent. Always he is a neighbor. He will have opportunities for patient and sensitive listening, for standing with others in joy and sorrow, for helping in some concrete way, for giving advice in all humility and in answer to real questions. There are some who by the very nature of their work have to act as pastors. Shop stewards, personnel officers, parents, clergy, doctors, lawyers, and corrections officers are some of them. They should be frank to recognize their gifts. If their gifts lie elsewhere, as teachers or administrators, for instance, they should be honest enough to seek the help of those with the pastoral gifts needed in a particular situation.

There has to be an authority in any body, and each member has to submit to that authority in discerning, developing, and using his gifts, for they were given for the common good and the common task. Until such an authority is developed and until the whole church becomes concerned, the present haphazard arrangement will continue, with men and women using their gifts as best they can and without the source of the gifts being made known. The church cannot be the church except in so far as all its members are seen as having received gifts from the Holy Spirit and are encouraged to use them as housewives, students, doctors, professors, union officials, factory workers, politicians, parents, neighbors, friends. What area of life today does not need wisdom, knowledge, faith, healing, and "the power to do great deeds"? (I Cor. 12:10, Phillips' translation. RSV: "the working of miracles.") You have been given gifts by the Holy Spirit. With whatever help you can get, discern, develop, and use them, wherever you find yourself.

—Francis O. Ayres, *The Ministry of the Laity*, pp. 65–66.

In pursuit of the new layman—some warnings.

In the pursuit of a new layman, I think there are some dead-end streets. They do exist but they are not a part of renewal for the laity of the church.

1. *The power struggle.* If the only thing at stake between the pastor and the laity is who is going to run the church, then all we really have is a power struggle. And a power struggle, whether it is in the church or in the democratic party, is still a power struggle and not a terribly spiritual thing.

2. *Anti-Church or Anti-Clergy.* Much has been said about the institutional church, usually used to denote the church organized and functioning for itself and not for outside purposes. Nearly all that has been said was needed, but we need to look at the shortcomings of the institutional church as cause for renewal and not for rejection.

It is also true that many pastors and laymen live together in a very frustrating relationship. Pressure builds up and sometimes explodes. For all of my desire to see both the role of the pastor and the people of God interpreted in more Biblical terms, I do not see any future for an approach that is basically anti-clergy. It may be emotionally satisfying to attack the church or the clergy but little good comes of it. A self-defeating lovelessness is usually the product.

3. *Little Preachers.* This is the approach where a layman simply becomes a part-time, untrained, unpaid, volunteer preacher. Amateur preaching wins by its freshness, but very often, if continued, apes the very ministry it replaces. A great deal more is involved in discovering what it means to be a layman in the church in this day.

4. *Testimony Religion.* There is some danger that at the moment the layman begins to think seriously about his religion, he turns inward, basing nearly everything on his own testimony or the sharing of his testimony with others. Unchecked subjectivism can make a serious layman an ineffectual spiritual neurotic. God never intended for us to grow to our fullest maturity alone, and He did not intend for us to find most of our solutions inside ourselves.

—Kenneth Chafin, *Help! I'm a Layman,* pp. 9–10.

The form of the woman's ministry in the Church.

If we can approach this new possibility for women humbly and experimentally, we may learn not only what *their* vocation in the ordained ministry may be but gain a deeper insight into the *whole* ministry to which God calls all his people, including men in the ordained ministry.

—Alden D. Kelley, *The People of God,* p. 112.

"Gee! Women in the ministry!"

I suspect that a woman can have more freedom in changing patterns of doing things than a man minister might.

I suspect that a woman can get away with a different type of presentation of truth better than a man can. A man is expected to present a "good sermon." I feel free to *explain* the Way of the Lord.

A woman who chooses the subjection that is in the Lord will find a response from people that is healthy and has no relationship to an Oedipus complex. The maturity that comes with added years is an asset here.

It especially behooves a woman in the ministry to follow the scriptural admonitions to simplicity and modesty. The Apostle Paul would add another doctrine today: the doctrine of the covered knee! A woman has no right in a pulpit unless she is there with a message. It is the *message that provides the credentials.*

—Anna B. Mow, "Gee! Women in the Ministry,"
Brethren Life and Thought 12:60.

The suburban parish is an ideal place for the lay ministry.

The suburban parish is a place where the ministry of the laity could most quickly reach its fullness. The accumulated ability, education, and resources

available to the average member of a suburban congregation represent opportunities for real lay leadership. Suburban members can read, they can
think, and they can act. They have been trained to do all of these. Many of
them are eager to read, think, and act as members of Christ's body but have
often grown weary under a situation which calls for none of these. Suburban
men especially are in places of significance if not importance in business,
politics, and society. The suburban parish can potentially reach these places.

—Roy Blumhorst, "In the Suburbs," *Death and Birth of the Parish*,
ed. Martin E. Marty, p. 104.

2. Daily Work

I never relate my faith to my job.

Said one active churchman in North Carolina: "I never try to apply what
I learn and affirm on Sunday to my job during the rest of the week." This
was an unusually bold declaration, but it is not uncommon for modern Christians to deny by their acts and attitudes that Christ is Lord in their workaday
world. Many a businessman is convinced that he'd go bankrupt in six months
if he applied Christianity to his business. Recently, some Americans who
claimed they considered religion something "very important" were asked,
"Would you say your religious beliefs have any effect on your ideas of politics
and business?" Fifty-four per cent answered "no."

It may be that there are church people who are not bothered by the fact
that they think and act one way on Sunday and another way during the other
six days. They may not care much about integrity. They may even refuse to
notice that they believe one thing when they are being religious and believe
quite the opposite when they are working or playing. It may not seem important that they can on occasion fervently claim, for example, that all men
are their brothers and yet in the daily routine regularly reject or ignore or
sneer at certain individuals or ethnic groups.

Surely, however, most churchmen need a sense of integrity, some unity
and wholeness as persons. These people regularly live under a tension between
their commitments in the church and their commitments in the world. This
has always been true for the Christian; but in America today that tension
is so great—because the gap between church and world is so vast—that few
can bear it in a constructive manner. Most lay people, men and women, fall
into a crippling compromise.

—Frederick K. Wentz, *The Layman's Role Today*, pp. 5–6.

The Church feels like a stranger in the factory.

Protestant Christianity is taking more and more seriously the responsibility
to work and become knowledgeable in the "other worlds" man inhabits. This
work takes place on the basis of the following assumptions: that God is at work

in the world; that it is the responsibility of the Church to point to those places where God is at work and to join Him in His work; that the Church is ill prepared at the present time, given its almost exclusive residential base, to know where God may be at work in the world.

These assumptions have led the new ministries in structures to stress "presence" in the nonresidential world. Until recently, preachers and theologians spoke of the brokenness, the anonymity, and the turmoil of the metropolis to the exclusion of almost any other insights into urban culture. Today, in a new spirit of humility, the Church is beginning to confess that it has much to learn from the world of strip cities, suburbs, cybernetics, and satellites that is positive and good. The Church is moving out, tenuously, into the structures man has built, in which it is recognizing with fresh insight that God is at work. It is standing alongside the production worker and the manager, the public official and the educator, the scientist and the artist. To be sure, the Church feels strange in these surroundings: naked, shorn of the glib responses in which it has clothed itself. But it stands, and in its stance the Church encounters the God of men and events.

—Richard E. Moore and Duane L. Day, *Urban Church Breakthrough*, pp. 107–8.

A place to start.

1. We must witness in the world where we live. When I resigned the pastorate to teach I became a "lay" member of a church in the Seminary community and was put on the evangelism committee. In connection with one of the church's meetings my committee was to be in charge of inviting people who were not already Christians to attend a banquet. The purpose of the dinner meeting was to allow them to get acquainted in a more relaxed atmosphere than a worship service. The problem we faced was that we did not have anyone to invite. Although the committee was quite large there were only two members on it who had any meaningful relationship with an individual whom they could invite. This upset me and I did what so many men do when they are upset. I fussed about it to my wife. After I had finished berating the other men for having withdrawn from the world my wife had this to say, "Don't be too hard on them. Maybe they're like us. Maybe they have been so busy going to church that they haven't had time to get acquainted with the people all around them." This struck me because, in spite of the fact that I was teaching evangelism in the Seminary and was on the evangelism committee of my church, I did not really know my neighbors as I ought.

2. We must witness in the world where we work. There is a sense in which we witness by the way we do our job. A poor employee and a good witness never go together. We witness by the way we treat people. A person cannot live his Sundays listening to sermons on love and live his weekdays operating by the law of the jungle and be a witness. A person can be a witness by his interest in the persons with whom he works. We miss a lot if we only see the

surface of those who spend most of their lives around us. They have families, fears, ambitions, frustrations, and a desire for meaning in their lives. Sometimes they wonder if anyone cares who they are or what they are or even *that* they are. A person can witness by how he relates to the typical at-work discussions. The world of work is a world in which sex, government, football, kids, taxes and almost everything else gets discussed. A Christian who identifies with people cannot stand nervously by waiting for a lull in the conversation when he can give a commercial for the church. What he feels about what is going on in the world is a part of his witness.

—Kenneth Chafin, *Help! I'm a Layman*, pp. 125–26.

Witness on the job may be more important than work in the Church.

We are making a serious mistake, however, if, in stressing this volunteer work, we seem to suggest that work is not Christian work unless it is work for the churches. Actually the witness made in regular employment may be far more significant and productive than any service rendered in free time. It is a gross error to suppose that the Christian cause goes forward solely or chiefly on week ends. What happens on the regular weekdays may be far more important, so far as the Christian faith is concerned, than what happens on Sundays. A minority ought to leave their secular employment in order to engage in full-time work, for the promotion of the gospel, but this is not true of most. Most men ought to stay where they are and to make their Christian witness *in* ordinary work rather than beyond it. A deeply concerned banker may be sorely tempted to leave his bank in order to give his full time to some volunteer service, but deeper reflection may show him that this would be a mistake. The investment of funds, especially for great charities, may be a task which it would be wrong for such a man to escape.

—Elton Trueblood, *Your Other Vocation*, pp. 57–58.

How to be obedient to Christ on the job.

1. The willingness of the Christian to accept his work, no longer as a curse, but as the locus of his obedience. This is not to cross out all the questions of jobs a Christian cannot rightly enter into or the possibility of changing jobs. These are important, and in freedom men must make decisions in these areas. Here we only affirm that in earning their daily bread men are called to perform their task with faithfulness.

2. His willingness to live by grace; that is, not driven in any situation to try to excel others nor to be more moral or more honest, but as best one can, seeking only to do God's will through the power of the Holy Spirit. The Christian recognizes fully the ethical dilemmas, the gray shades of decision, and faces with honesty the difficulty of decision making and yet takes the risk involved in responsible life. This is to live in the recognition that the work of the world is carried on in imperfect terms. Faith in God's redeeming

love can resolve the impossible tension between high ethical idealism and the practical necessity of life in community.

3. Willingness to take the job seriously on its own terms, good or bad, as the locus for loving service to others, in the common struggle with neighbor for justice and the assertion of humanity in the midst of degradation. This is not to be sentimental.

—George W. Webber, *The Congregation in Mission*, p. 146–47.

Needed: a guild of Christian writers.

The ministry of books requires readers and dedicated salesmen, but, first of all, it requires writers. If the concern for an adequate theology is to be implemented, we must have more writers who learn to think rigorously on the most important questions and who discipline their minds to write in such a way that the rank and file can understand. Far from there being any necessary incompatibility between profundity and clarity, both are required. We have, it is true, a plethora of current books, but we do not have enough good ones. Who, we may reasonably ask, will take the place of the late C. S. Lewis or the late John Baillie? It is practically certain that there are undeveloped literary powers, which are undeveloped chiefly because the possessors of these powers have never thought of themselves as producers. Perhaps the recognition of the minority status of committed Christians may make some of these persons realize that their gifts are needed and that they must, accordingly, be developed. Young Christian writers can help one another to a surprising extent by the sympathetic yet critical reading of one another's manuscripts.

—Elton Trueblood, *The Incendiary Fellowship*, p. 67.

Needed: a guild of Christian politicians.

Just as we have a Guild of Christian Writers who assist one another, regardless of their fields of interest, we need a Guild of Christian Politicians. Such a guild might be composed of young men who know something of where power for good resides in the modern world and who propose to do something about it by helping one another—both to get ready and to operate when they *are* ready. Each man is almost helpless alone, but together they might do wonders. They would stand at the opposite pole from those sincere but misguided Christian groups who suppose that a Christian cannot even vote, much less hold office. The fault in their understandable position is that they automatically create a power vacuum which others—perhaps less qualified or less conscientious—are sure to fill. The young men in the ideal Guild of Christian Politicians will not meet exclusively for prayer, though they may pray; they will meet to raise one another's sights, to stimulate, to advise, to learn. We must remember that while thought may be *developed* in privacy it is seldom *engendered* in that way. We are creatures who need one another, especially in all intellectual endeavors. That is the essential reason for the artificial societies called colleges.

—Elton Trueblood, *The Company of the Committed*, p. 82.

Needed: a guild of Christian professors.

In the long run the best solution of the problem of a fragmented and secularized education is the development of a Guild of Christian Professors who are equally skilled in some secular field of learning and in the unapologetic support of the Christian view of reality. Such people, who may teach geology or psychology or physics or anything else in the entire academic curriculum, can, if they will, become the spearhead of the Christian movement in even the most secularized of universities. It also seems, to our sorrow and shame, they are now needed equally in some of the institutions founded and supported by Christian conviction.

One of our urgent needs is to find men who can go to colleges and universities for what is called religious emphasis week. This work is so grueling and requires powers so unusual that the only hope lies in training persons specifically for the task. They must be prepared to lecture, to lead symposiums, to meet individual seekers at all hours, to listen to ancient objections with respectful attention, and to present the truth of Christ persuasively. The persons who can learn to do all this will not be under any delusion that skeptics can be argued into the kingdom, but they will know that there are thousands kept *out* of the kingdom by some little barrier or misgiving that can be handled with comparative ease, providing the missioner is ready. A good example of the beneficent elimination of such a barrier concerns the idea of God as truly personal. A girl says she cannot think of God as personal, though Christ obviously did, because God seems to her a great cosmic "force." Part of her motivation is that she is very eager not to have her idea of God too small or, as she would say, anthropomorphic. The member of the academic task force, if he understands his business, can show the girl that in her effort to avoid limiting God she has done exactly what she has sought to avoid. If *she* can know her friend and God *cannot* know him, this means that God is incapable of something of undoubted worth. The upshot is that she is really imposing a limit on God. The odd consequence is that the creature is recognized as greater, at one point, than the Creator. Suddenly the girl may see this with clarity and, as a result, gain a grateful sense of intellectual relief. The point is that she cannot do it alone; she needs help; and it is the work of the Christian professor, whatever subject he may teach, to provide that help.

—Elton Trueblood, *The Company of the Committed*, pp. 84–86.

3. The Home

Christianity shows up best in the home.

We may truly say, then, that just the lay ministry finds a fuller expression in ordinary daily work than it does in church, so it finds a fuller
expression in the family than in employment, and perhaps more in the family
than anywhere else in our world. If our religion does not lift the level of our
family life it is not likely to be sincere or really effective at any other point.
What occurs at the altar is insignificant unless what occurs there is supported
by what occurs in the kitchen. The sermons by which Christian men and
women may be rightly judged are the silent sermons of co-operative affection.

—Elton Trueblood, *Your Other Vocation*, p. 82.

Worship at the family table is an example.

As a very modest illustration of what starting from life rather than liturgy
might mean, I would tentatively mention some exploration we have been
doing at our own family table.

Despite the fact that our children have been at Parish Communion almost
every Sunday of their lives from the carry-cot onwards, it was becoming
increasingly clear that most of it simply passed them by, because the service
in church corresponded with nothing concrete in their everyday experience
and relationships. A dissatisfaction with family prayers, with Communion
preparation, with grace before meals—together with the fact that I was so
frequently out when the children were home—combined to make us resolve
to set aside one meal in the week (at present supper on Saturday), to which
we would all give a priority and which we would make a sort of family
celebration. It is not a Eucharist, but a rather special meal, to which we all
look forward, which includes a bottle of wine. The procedure is extremely
flexible, but at the moment we normally begin (in winter) by lighting the
table candles and singing the very early Christian hymn, "Hail, gladdening
Light." Then in prayer we share freely whatever is concerning us, our doings
and our relations, bringing in also those with whom we shall be meeting at
the Lord's Table the next morning. At the close of this we say together an
adapted verse of a eucharistic hymn:

> Come, risen Lord, and deign to be our guest;
> Nay, let us be thy guests; the feast is thine;
> Thyself at thine own board make manifest,
> In this our fellowship of bread and wine.

I then cut a slice from the loaf and pour out a glass of wine, both of which
we pass round, ending with a salutation, or the grace, and a joining of hands.

After the meal we do some Bible study based on the Epistle or the Gospel for the next day, and end the evening by playing a family game.

—John A. T. Robinson, *The New Reformation*, pp. 84–85.

The Church at our house.

We insist on the participation of at least one parent in the life of the church because we believe the child cannot enter into a faith that is being denied by the people who are most significant to him. Children pick up more from the home atmosphere than from anything they might be told on a Sunday morning at a church school. It is at home that it is made difficult or easy for them to rest back in the grace of God, to believe or disbelieve in love. The home is the outpost of the Christian Church in the world and it is here that the church succeeds or fails, according to the faithfulness of those involved.

—Elizabeth O'Connor, *Call to Commitment*, p. 72.

A service of dedication for the home.

One of the specific ways the church helps the home in its mission is through a service of dedication. The parents, sometimes together with the children, decide on the kind of service, which may take many forms. The Bryans wrote theirs and then mailed a copy to each of the members so that the others would be aware of the pledges they had made during a dedication which ended with their own prayer.

—Elizabeth O'Connor, *Call to Committment*, p. 74.

4. And Thy Neighbor As Thyself

Lay piety today takes the form of a good Samaritan.

Traditional lay piety was wholly derived from that of the clerics. The call to the Church to be a lay community of Samaritans, not of priests and levites, has only now become impelling.

—Hans Jurgen Schultz, *Conversion to the World*, p. 97.

Christianity in the neighborhood.

1. The Christian enters into community organizations. . . . 2. The Christian will enter into politics. The obvious vehicle in most situations for community participation is party politics. . . . 3. The center of concern is real need. Part of the wisdom of faith is discerning both immediate need and ultimate need in one's brother. . . . 4. Loving service is its own justification. . . . There is no ulterior motive, for the Lord of the church is not served by gaining

"rice Christians." . . . 5. The setting of Christian service is suffering, amid the brokenness of life and the frustrations of depersonalization.

—George W. Webber, *The Congregation in Mission*, pp. 151, 153, 154, 156, 157.

Laymen, scatter and permeate.

The church's task of scattering and permeating belongs fundamentally to the ministry of laymen. They are the priests for the secular world. If the light image makes laymen ambassadors who bring something from beyond to bear upon this secular world, then the salt image makes laymen priests who are real parts of this secular world. They belong integrally to all facets of the transient, relative life of mankind and can fully represent it before its creator and redeemer. The church is dispersed salt in the persons of its laymen during their weekday activity.

—Frederick K. Wentz, *The Laymen's Role Today*, pp. 122–23.

How does the Church make contact with the world?

The need to restore the broken connection between the Church and life as it is actually lived demands a radically new understanding of the place and function of the lay members of the Church. There is a great deal of talk in church circles at the present time about the importance of the laity. But the question is approached almost invariably from the wrong end. What is usually meant is that more laymen should come in and give their support to the Church as it is. That is just what a large number of the best lay people at present standing on the fringe will not do. The much more important question to which the Church needs to address its mind is its own need of the experience which these people have of life to widen its outlook and deepen its understanding, so that it may become a more effective force in society. If Christianity is not something existing apart from life but is the transfiguration of life itself—and that means in the end the transfiguration of the whole of life—it is those who are in the front line of the battle and are exposed to the severest tests who can best teach us what Christianity means as a living faith. It is through its lay members that the Church makes contact with the life of the world.

—J. H. Oldham, *Life Is Committment*, pp. 97–98.

Metropolis is evoking the servanthood of the laity.

If the Church as responsible laity is the only Church that can minister to a technological society, then the clericalized church of the active pastor and passive laity may give all the outward signs of being a church but it is not participant in the world and, in this respect, is not God's people in the world. Metropolis, as a complex process of planned interdependence of life, is evoking a new form of the Church—the servanthood of the laity.

—Gibson Winter, *The New Creation As Metropolis*, pp. 10–11.

Disperse or the work of Christ will not be done.

Thus in this emphasis on the laity in dispersion we are not dealing with lofty idealism; rather we are concerned with a realistic necessity: either the laity must respond more fully, or the work of Christ will not be done in our time.

—Howard Grimes, *The Rebirth of the Laity*, p. 94.

When laymen speak on controversial issues, the world listens.

Churchmen are on public record about altogether too many petty issues— pet ones, at that, which are identified in the public mind as being inherent in the church lobby. Just as the veterans' lobby has an interest in relief to veterans, and the real estate lobby is opposed to public housing, so the Protestant church lobby has a vested interest in being against gambling (particularly Bingo), alcohol, and for separation of church and state. No one is surprised or very much influenced when bishops testify on these matters. But when Protestant churchmen speak out in controversial areas like political candidacy, housing, and civil rights, people do listen. A sense of outrage marks the church's awareness of the Kingdom that is yet to come.

—Robert W. Spike, *In But Not Of The World*, pp. 106–7.

To show the solidarity of Jesus Christ with the world.

The layman does not represent the Church, he is the Church. It is not just that he has a personal interest in salvation. He is the instrument of salvation. He is called to fulfil the Church's mission to the world. He must be proof that the Church and its theology is directed worldwards. Among laymen a dialogue takes place without which the Church fails to become Church, theology fails to become theology and the world fails to become world. It is in the layman's breast that both the world and the holy scripture confront each other and strive to be understood.

    . . . The laity, the people of God, include the clergy and embrace the whole Church. The lay movement does not aim at an elimination of the different functions and talents now in existence but at the long overdue removal of false distinctions between the ordained and the unordained. The solidarity of Christ with humanity establishes a completely new relationship between God and the world, one in which the contradiction between the sacred and the profane is eliminated. It is the function of the laity to exemplify Christ's solidarity with the world. To demand this type of involvement from the laity is simply to expect the Church to be the Church.

—Hans Jurgen Schultz, *Conversion to the World*, pp. 95–97.

5. Laymen Point to Christ

Witnessing is primarily a lay ministry.

Christian witnessing is primarily a lay ministry. The non-Christian cannot readily identify with an ordained minister who is, in his opinion, a professional trained and paid to talk about God's glory. In his eyes, the ordained minister is someone set apart. But when he hears about this glory coming into the life of a layman like himself he is encouraged to seek the same hope for himself through pursuing a living relationship with God in Christ. When he does this he has begun to be a believer and he turns to the Church for instruction and discipline, for worship and the opportunity to minister to others. So, God is calling the clergy to minister to believers in such a way that they can in turn minister effectively to the world of unbelievers. This requires a revolution in the ministry in the local congregation, for the witnessing community has again become the focal point of power in the life of the Church.

—Claxton Monro and William S. Taegel, *Witnessing Laymen Make Living Churches*, p. 17.

Future church power will pass to witnessing laymen.

In the Reformation the Protestants shared the priestly functions of pastor and teacher with the whole congregation. But the apostolic and prophetic functions were still reserved for the institution and its ordained ministers. Then the priestly witness of voluntary sacrificial living was shared with the congregation, but the prophetic witness of proclamation was still reserved for the ordained ministry.

Now, in this new age, the congregation will be involved in both the prophetic witness and the priestly witness. The prophets in the Reformation were preaching clergy, but in this era they will be witnessing laymen. In this era the institutional Church and clergy will return again in their function to that of the apostle.

His role in the congregation is so to lead and to teach that the body of Christ, the witnessing community, is faithful in its life together (its priestly witness) and effective in its prophetic witness to the world. He is basically a teacher, a preacher, a rabbi, a coach.

In this era the Church will no longer be thought of as primarily a place we go to worship God (medieval) or to hear the Gospel preached (Protestant). Now the Church will come to be regarded as the people of God with whom we live, the peculiar community of the faithful to whom we belong in a pagan world which finds us unacceptable. The witness in this era will be concerned less with theological positions and more with a quality of living inspired by sacrificial love and obedience to the leading of the Holy Spirit.

So the focal point of power will pass again to the *koinonia,* the witnessing community. It will temporarily be taken away from the institutional Church which has been the center of power in the West since Constantine, about 300 A.D. We will still have ordained clergy—apostolic orders—but the glory will now be seen in the *koinonia* rather than the *ecclesia.*

—Claxton Monro and William S. Taegel, *Witnessing Laymen Make Living Churches,* pp. 22–23.

The human embodiment of good news.

In a class in our School of Christian Living, Gordon Cosby was speaking on the subject of Christian vocation. He said in summarizing that the primary task and primary mission of the Christian is to call forth the gifts of others. "We are not sent into the world in order to make people good. We are not sent to encourage them to do their duty. The reason people have resisted the Gospel is that we have gone out to make people good, to help them do their duty, to impose new burdens on them, rather than calling forth the gift which is the essence of the person himself." He then said that we are to let others know that God is for them and that they can "be." "They can be what in their deepest hearts they know that they were intended to be, they can do what they were meant to do. As Christians, we are heralds of these good tidings."

How do we do this? "We begin," Gordon said, "by exercising our own gifts. The person who is having the time of his life doing what he is doing has a way of calling forth the deeps of another. Such a person is Good News. He is not *saying* the good news. He *is* the good news. He is the embodiment of the freedom of the new humanity. The person who exercises his own gift in freedom can allow the Holy Spirit to do in others what He wants to do."

—Elizabeth O'Connor, *Journey Inward, Journey Outward,* pp. 36–37.

To show how the world looks when flooded with light.

Since Christ is the light of the whole world, the layman's ministry is primarily to show how the world looks when flooded by that light. His task in the world is not centrally to point to his own bright personal experience, nor even to point to the light from which his experience came. It is rather *to point to the world as it is newly revealed in the light,* seen from this radiant perspective, enlightened by these fresh insights. The Christian moves into the world bearing a gift with which he can make more out of that gloomy and narrow place. It is as when the shade is raised in a previously darkened room or like the sun breaking through the clouds suddenly to brighten the whole setting.

He does not so much meet the nonbeliever by declaring a distant, exalted Savior, a mighty but invisible lighthouse or sun. Nor does he brashly set forth what Christ means in his own life. Rather, in his meeting with the other person, he, unconsciously perhaps, holds out promising possibilities for the tender psychic territory between them. He brings the light of Christ into the human relationship here being forged, weaving golden thread into the otherwise drab fabric of personal ties.

—Frederick K. Wentz, *The Layman's Role Today*, p. 88.

The chief witness of Christians is now made during the week.

Though the institution of the Sabbath has been one of the most beneficent social inventions in the history of mankind, encouraging a wholesome rhythm in the week, and even making the week a meaningful idea, there are ways now in which concentration upon the one day of worship may be harmful. It is harmful whenever such concentration involves the relegation of all of the rest of the week to pagan standards of success. In an earlier agricultural economy the concentration of religious interests into one day each week was naturally the best that could be done, but, in a highly urbanized economy, it is possible that the chief witness of many must be made on the weekdays.

—Elton Trueblood, *Your Other Vocation*, p. 60.

Deed plus word, word plus deed.

The spoken word is never really effective unless it is backed up by a life, but it is also true that the living deed is never adequate without the support which the spoken word can provide. This is because no life is ever good enough. The person who says naively, "I don't need to preach; I just let my life speak," is insufferably self-righteous. What one among us is so good that he can let his life speak and leave it at that? We should make our lives as good as we possibly can, but at the end of the day we are still imperfect and unworthy. If our expressed faith were not better than our practice, we should make practically no progress at all. Anyone can end hypocrisy simply by lowering his principles to accord with his practice, but it is easy to see that the result would be loss rather than gain.

—Elton Trueblood, *The Company of the Committed*, p. 53.

Witness must be done by laity on a person-to-person basis.

Most of the work of witness must be on a person-to-person basis, and the number of clergy in relation to the laity is too small for much to happen. If the Church is to make an impact on the world, it must do so through those whose life and work are carried on in the world—and these are the Church's laity.

—Howard Grimes, *The Rebirth of the Laity*, p. 93.

A secular age will accept the authority of personal testimony.

I BELIEVE THAT THE ANSWER IS THIS: A witnessing fellowship of need, a fellowship of really converted Christians, acknowledging at least in small groups that their lives hang on Christ—and what this means in terms of how they eat breakfast, how they go to the office, how they treat a spouse in marriage, how they deal with their secretary or boss, what they do with their spare time, and what they do with their friendships. The very basic actions and reactions of daily living are all involved in what Christ means to me. Each moment takes its meaning that Christ has for me. And it is this that the fellowship shares together, each with the other. None claim to have found the final answer, but each individual can know the reality of Christ at work in the heart. We bear witness to each other of how Christ deals with us as individuals. What has become real to us, we share in this fellowship.

The humanistic, scientific, and pragmatic spirit of this age will accept the authority of experiential personal encounter with the living God.
—Claxton Monro and William S. Taegel, *Witnessing Laymen Make Living Churches*, p. 39.

The potential of personal testimony in witnessing.

It would be difficult to over-estimate the potential of the personal testimony in witnessing. There are reasons. (1) The personal testimony is interesting. People like biographies better than essays and a testimony better than a devotional. (2) The personal testimony is authoritative. All of us who attempt to witness will be asked questions for which we do not have answers. We will be aware of Scripture for which we do not know the interpretation. But, when it comes to our own personal experience, we are the authority. (3) People can identify with a testimony. When a person who lives in this town says God has changed his life it is easier to identify with his experience than with Paul's experience on the road to Damascus. (4) Every Christian has a testimony. Our experiences are not the same and we do not express them in the same words but every follower of Christ has something to say.

—Kenneth Chafin, *Help! I'm a Layman*, pp. 128–29.

Spiritual principles that guide the layman in his witnessing and healing ministry.

1. God is our quest; not what He can do for us; but God, Himself, above everything and everyone else; God adored, God worshiped, God loved, God served.
2. God's will is our highest good. God is perfect wisdom, perfect love. His will for each one of us, can we discover it, is the blueprint of the best possible life.
3. Jesus said God's will for us is:
   Bread—the supply of our physical needs;

Peace—"My peace I give unto you," the fruit of the Spirit is love, joy, peace;

Healing and Health—So far as we know Jesus never refused to heal anybody.

4. When, therefore, we pray for material needs, for peace, for health, we are praying that God's will may be done. This is not a "cult of success" but a cultivation of the knowledge of the will of God for those who live in obedience and devotion to Him.

5. Our emphasis is upon wholeness of life, mental integrity, moral purity, spiritual insight, as well as, and even more than, physical well-being.

6. There is no encouragement to those who are seeking an "easy road" through life. We believe that only through constant and heroic self-discipline can one find true Christian discipleship. We summon men and women to accept Jesus Christ as their Lord and Saviour. We teach that He saves us, provides for us, heals us and guides us to make us more useful and fruitful in doing His will. We are not seeking to use God but rather to become the kind of persons whom God can use most effectively in the work of His Kingdom.

7. "Otherness" is exalted. Prayer for others is encouraged. Letting our lives (our attitudes, our words, and our deeds) be a witness for Christ is explicitly taught as the privilege and the duty of a Christian.

—Claxton Monro and William S. Taegel, *Witnessing Laymen Make Living Churches*, pp. 92–93.

Personal evangelism—what it is not.

First, personal evangelism has to be broader than a church membership drive. The change from witnessing because people need to hear, to witnessing because the church needs more members is gradual, subtle, and deadly.

Second, personal evangelism must once again find meaning for the average church member. As the institutional church has developed, the emphasis has been on a paid staff and a promoted program. The layman has seen his role as supportive. The work of evangelism has been identified almost completely with the pastor and staff. This attitude so pervades the church that when an individual initiates a discussion of religion it is assumed that he is a preacher or some religious fanatic. . . .

Third, personal evangelism must be divorced from a special activity or a set technique. The excuse of "I don't have time" suggests that witnessing is an activity separate from life. The command of Christ in the great commission is more accurately translated "going" instead of "go." Witnessing is not so much going somewhere else to do something but is rather doing it in the every-day context of life. The excuse "I never could sell anything" suggests that witnessing has something to do with a selling technique. . . .

Fourth, we need to be more realistic about where people are religiously.

The average discussion on evangelism leaves the impression that the people we meet have never heard the gospel and have had no contact with the church. Most of the people to whom a witness needs to be given already have information about the church, and in many cases have some relationship to the church.

Recently on a one-day trip which took me to several states I decided that I would try to find out the religious background of those people with whom I came in contact when it was possible. Beginning with the taxi driver who took me to the airport, I was able to have extended conversations with eight different persons of different ages and occupations and who lived in different parts of the country. Not one of the eight had a vital faith but all of them had been members of some church for years.

—Kenneth Chafin, *Help! I'm a Layman,* pp. 118–19.

G. Building Up the Body through Worship

1. Patterns of Worship

The Church contributes to its growth by worship.

The question here is: How does the church contribute to its own growth and development? In the broadest sense, the answer is quite simple—it worships! Since the church does not create its own life but receives it from the risen Christ, it strives continually to experience his life within it, whether it be gathered for worship or dispersed for service. Moreover, to be vigorous, the church must make the experience of Christ real to every one of its members. In all of its activities, it must serve as the means of transmission for Christ's life. All of its institutions must be so designed and used that they will help and not hinder the transmission.

—E. Glenn Hinson, *The Church: Design for Survival,* p. 65.

The Church will die without it.

In the life of the Christian church nothing is more important, in any age or at any time, than the life of its people at worship. If the church is irrelevant and meaningless here, it will be irrelevant and meaningless in the world. If it is exciting and victorious here, it will be exciting and victorious in the world. Charge the church to be active and influential in social causes, yes. Spur it on to activity in every area of life, by all means. But neglect its mission and its ministry here, and it will die. It will be a dead institution with nothing to say anywhere to anyone.

—Arthur A. Rouner, Jr., *The Free Church Today: New Life for the Whole Church*,
p. 82.

Not just ritual, but a mode of action.

It is not just ritual but rather a mode of action in which celebrant and people together offer themselves corporately before God in thanksgiving, praise, confession, receptivity, and commitment.

—Howard Grimes, *The Rebirth of the Laity*, pp. 167–68.

Tolerable only when directly relevant to life.

In prayer and worship, one sees that the question of direction is primary. Such questions as, Is this useful? and Will I be successful? take their proper place. Sometimes they are valid questions, but they are not nearly so important as modern culture insists. In prayer and worship, one learns that God can use all that one does for his purposes: the frustrations, mistakes, failures —even outright rebelliousness—when they are offered to him. Through prayer and worship all life becomes meaningful and purposeful. Man is seen for the greatness that is in him, as sharing in the glory and purpose of God.

Prayer and worship, like other parts of a discipline, do not come naturally to most men any more than do skill at games or ability to study. Indeed, they become tolerable only when seen as directly relevant to life. The trouble with many devotional books is that they deal with the "inner life" as though it existed independently of life in the world. Nothing could be farther from reality as revealed in Jesus Christ. For him, prayer was always intimately connected with the work he had been given to do and the life to which he had been called. He prayed about the decisions he had to make, the people with whom he lived and worked, the problems he had to meet the next day or the next minute. He wept over Jerusalem, he asked God to forgive those who nailed him to the cross, he prayed that God would be with those who were to carry on his work after him. There was such a wholeness to Christ's life that "inner" and "outer" become practically indistinguishable. Whatever a man's work, whatever his relationships, whatever his responsibilities, being conformed to Jesus Christ means that his prayer and worship are an integral part of his whole life.

—Francis O. Ayres, *The Ministry of the Laity*, pp. 121–22.

The straight-jacket of a set time.

There is probably no place where Protestant churches have straight-jacketed themselves so much as in reference to time. With perhaps one exception in a thousand, to cite one example, Southern Baptist churches meet at 11:00 on

Sunday morning and 7:30 on Sunday night. They hold prayer meetings at 7:30 p.m. on Wednesdays. I once sat through a forty-five minute debate over whether a certain congregation should set the time for revival services at 7:00 or 7:30 in the evening. One person vehemently opposed 7:00 o'clock because "we always meet at 7:30."

—E. Glenn Hinson, *The Church: Design for Survival*, p. 75.

Would the New Testament Christians feel at home in our worship services?

We do not know as well as we should like to know what the meetings of the first Christians were like in detail, but we have in the New Testament some extremely helpful indications. In any case we know enough to realize that these meetings were not at all what we think of as characteristic Christian gatherings in our own day. The probability is that there was no human audience at all and not the slightest thought of a pattern in which one man is expected to be inspired to speak fifty-two times a year, while the rest are never so inspired. A clear indication of procedure is provided by Colossians 3:16 where we read "as you teach and admonish one another in all wisdom." The most reasonable picture which these words suggest is that of a group of modest Christians sitting in a circle in some simple room, sharing with one another their hopes, their failures, and their prayers. The key words are "one another." There are no mere observers or auditors; *all are involved*. Each is in the ministry; each needs the advice of the others; and each has something to say to the others. The picture of mutual admonition seems strange to modern man, but the strangeness is only a measure of *our* essential decline from something of amazing power. The contemporary Communists have taken over the essentials of this pattern for their own dissimilar purposes, but we must remember that they did not invent it. They took it over after Christians had largely abandoned it. Their doing so may constitute a justified rebuke to those who take their Christianity so lightly that they never see themselves as members of a task force.

—Elton Trueblood, *The Company of the Committed*, pp. 31–32.

Persistence but no uniformity.

If a church can realize its true nature and calling only as it devotes itself to prayer, are there certain irreducible dimensions of worship which must not be neglected? The question implies an affirmative answer. But this affirmation does not in any sense mean that there must be uniformity of prayer and worship in the many churches. The apostolic criterion signifies primarily the persistence in Christian prayers. It does not imply that all must pray alike. Far from it! One of the most widespread and tenaciously held misconceptions about the present movement towards church unity is precisely the fear that all congregations in a united church would be forced to worship according to one form only. It needs to be said again and again that this need not be so. Not only is a wide range of liturgical variation permissible in the united church; it is desirable and valuable to maintain it, simply because Christian people, like other human beings, are not uniform in mentality and sensibility. The familiar debate over the question of whether prayers should be "set" or "free" is usually a sterile one. It calls forth the defensive attitude and dogmatism of Christians whose experience is narrow and prejudice fixed. Obviously there are some virtues in both forms, and these are complementary. The same may be said of other contrasting forms of liturgical expression: hymns, postures, actions, words. The plain fact that diversities exist within present denominations without breaking their unity ought to lay to rest the fear of uniformity.

—J. R. Nelson, *Criterion for the Church*, pp. 125–26.

All join together on the second verse.

The good effects of a trained sense of reverence in church members will be to no avail, however, if there is inadequate provision made for the personal, faithful and intelligent participation of the whole congregation in acts of worship. Whatever the liturgical crudities or emotional excesses of many so-called "sects" of the land, with their whooping and shouting and reverberating "Amens," they at least do not suffer from the kind of congregational apathy and aphasia which are now too familiar in some churches. And even while the churches of the Pentecostal and Holiness types are taking some cautious measures to introduce form and dignity in their worship, their opposite in the Catholic tradition are endeavouring to bring the people into real participation again. The familiar slogan of the Catholic liturgical revival is "Pray the Mass"—meaning that Catholics should cease being either atoms at prayer in the pew or bored spectators of the drama enacted by the priest and his servers at the altar. Already there is a notable resurgence of Roman Catholic congregational life as a result of this integration of priest and people in the liturgy. How much more vitality might be expected in the churches of the Protestant tradition if the members accept not only their share in the active programme of the church but in the regular corporate prayer life as well!

—J. R. Nelson, *Criterion for the Church*, pp. 127–28.

An anthem is no substitute for the hymn.

One of the stubborn obstacles to vital worship in many churches is the unspoken assumption that a worship service is a program or a performance to be observed. People come without any specific understanding of their role except that they are hopeful that something will be said or done that will move them or interest them.

There is need to recapture that sense of movement, of drama, in which the congregation has an important function of response and participation in order to make the whole service an offering to God. To this end, the restoration of congregational singing as one of the major ways in which the congregation responds to the Word, and offers up its praise, is long overdue. An anthem by the choir, no matter how skilled, can never substitute for the hymn.

—Robert W. Spike, *In But Not Of The World*, p. 56.

Prayer for others.

In addition to a concern that reaches out to the problems and involvements of the physical community, the church must pray for others. This is an area we have taken all too lightly. We have never neglected the omnibus references to all 'sorts and conditions' of men, but this was as much the reminding of God that we were not really so selfish, as anything else. Intercessory prayer is one of the most important parts of the worship life of the church. Intercessory prayer means earnest waiting upon the Lord for specific needs. Here the multitude of human relationships that reach out from the church like a network of sensitive wires, are brought together and held up to God for empowering wisdom.

People should be prayed for by name in the church. Problems should be mentioned specifically. The dying of the old prayer meeting happened when people began to think that intercessory prayer was not valid, and also when it became a time for the display of public piety. There is great need for the re-establishment of special times of intercessory prayer in the life of the church. This, of course, should be a part of the corporate Sunday service, but also at other stated times.

Intercessory prayer for healing, mental and physical healing, must be restored to the church. If God is the redeemer of all of a man's life, then we know through the example of Christ that he is concerned for the body of a man too. Psychosomatic medicine has shamed us into recovering what the ancient church knew to be true—it is impossible to separate sin and mortality, the physical and the eternal.

—Robert W. Spike, *In But Not Of The World*, pp. 86–87.

An orderly progression of thoughts in prayer.

Some have attempted to demonstrate that there is a given pattern of worship and prayer which is authentically Christian. It may be a coincidence only that the pattern they describe bears very close resemblance to that of the denomination they happen to represent. So far as all sorts of Christians and churches are concerned, it is most doubtful whether anyone can prescribe a *lex orandi,* if this means a rigid order or prayer which alone will please God.

The very nature of the Christian's knowledge of God in Jesus Christ suggests, nevertheless, a certain orderly progression of thoughts in prayer. The order is not immutable, but the elements within it are indispensable. The incalculable weight of experience in prayer over the centuries has fortified the claims of essentiality for the following types of prayer: adoration and thanksgiving, confession of sins, supplication for others and ourselves, and personal commitment through faith.

—J. R. Nelson, *Criterion for the Church,* p. 132.

Freedom for liturgical developments.

Although there are advances, real advances, in the liturgical field, one feels that a genuinely renewed church would be much freer in its liturgical development. In the past the church's year has revolved around Sunday, for sociological as well as for biblical reasons; but the development of the long week-end makes it questionable that this old pattern should persist without some change. It is no use trying to impose on society a pattern derived from ecclesiastical usage. The church must develop forms and structures which make sense of life as it is lived, rather than attempt to put the clock back to life as it used to be lived. At the same time one may question whether some attempts to gain participation in worship are not overdone. It is possible to make laymen so busy in church in the interests of liturgiology that they have not a moment in which to worship with reverence and quiet. It is possible to emphasize the converting power of liturgy to such an extent that we forget that liturgy can only convert those who participate in worship, whereas the great mass of population do not so participate. These dangers are real; nevertheless signs of genuine renewal can be seen in what is beginning to happen liturgically. New churches are even being built to suit liturgical needs, instead of liturgy having to conform to a given conventional structure. Again the house church movement has brought alive for some the truth that the church does not need church buildings in which to worship. There are times when a special ecclesiastical structure may impede rather than assist liturgical devotion. What matters is the asssembly of the church not the church building. If liturgy is to be relevant to life, it must sanctify life as it is lived; and this can often be understood best if the sanctification of life takes place where it is lived, and not in a building removed from ordinary life.

—Hugh Montefiore, "The Renewal of the Church," *Encounter* 27:109–10.

The pattern of worship—an example.

At this moment our basic pattern of worship is as follows:
1. Recital of our church covenant
2. Presentation of our concerns and prayers
3. Proclamation of the Word

4. Confession of sin

5. Presentation of resources

Our worship begins with the reading of the church covenant. Essentially this is a declaration of our purpose as the church of Jesus Christ.

The next act is the presentation of the concerns of the church for the world. This is a time when we bring to the attention of the rest of the church the problems or opportunities about which we are concerned in our personal lives, our immediate neighborhood, our city, our nation, or our world. We write our concerns on small index cards placed in the pew racks. The ushers collect them and bring them to the communion table where the pastor reads them aloud and then structures the morning intercessory prayer around them.

At first very few of us used the cards. In fact, one Sunday no one submitted any concerns at all. That time, instead of a prayer of intercession, we joined in a confession of sin. Soon, however, we began to get used to the idea that so-called "worldly concerns" have a very real place in worship. We began to mention our concerns for sick friends and relatives, our concerns for the city, for good elections, for good legislation, and so forth. Some of our concerns were so important to us that we even began to discuss them with one another in this section of our worship. We discussed the Civil Rights Bills of 1964 and 1965. We made decisions to send letters to our representatives, to send members to demonstrations in Washington and Selma. We heard reports from the members during this part of worship when they returned from their involvements.

We discussed the New York state bill against capital punishment, and we decided to urge our assemblyman to support it. We later made a trip to Albany to familiarize ourselves with the site of the legislative process.

At times we invited local civic leaders to speak to us on local neighborhood problems during this section of worship. As the result of one speaker and the ensuing discussion, we became somewhat involved in local housing issues.

Our third act of worship is the proclamation of the Word. Here our pastor reads and preaches on the scripture passage which we have read and studied at the neighborhood meeting the week before.

The fourth act is a unison and then silent prayer of confession which is followed by words of assurance and the Lord's Prayer.

Our final act of worship might be called the presentation of our resources. In this section the offering is collected and brought to the communion table where one of our ushers gives the prayer of dedication. The service is concluded at this point with a responsive benediction.

—Paul C. Carter, Jr., "The Changing Face of a Church," *The Church Creative*,
M. Edward Clark et. al., eds., pp. 47–48.

Artless art.

We learned to our sorrow that it is unwise to attempt to communicate with an entire congregation via unfamiliar art media without considerable advance interpretation.

—Robert A. Raines, *The Secular Congregation*, p. 2.

2. The Lord's Supper

Prepared to enact a drama together.

It is never a supper that we go to as attenders. The requirement is that we be participants, prepared to enact a drama together. This means that we will come prepared to extend the "kiss of peace," or—said in another way—we will come prepared to be open to one another, to take the initiative of love with the stranger. In the early community, if the celebrant could not pass the peace, he could not stay for the Communion service. As we ourselves live in community, the reason for this becomes clear. We see how easy it is to say week after week the words that appear in church bulletins and never relate them to one's life. Of course, it is not only the church that has holy words. Social reformers and community organizers with plans for changing the city and no plans to change themselves, wear their piety in secular dress. The truly authentic person in or out of the church reflects in his outward stance the work of his inward parts. There is no cleavage between the outward and the inward.

—Elizabeth O'Connor, *Journey Inward, Journey Outward*, pp. 89–90.

Communion finds its clearest expression in the Lord's Supper.

Our communion, or koinonia, with the Lord and with our brethren finds both its impetus and its clearest expression in the Lord's Supper.

. . . It is the supper of the sinful saints. The holy people of God, called to be saints in His service, are yet the community of forgiven sinners. So at the Communion we sense both the depth of our unworthiness and the joy of being joined in fellowship with the holy God. Here the communion of saints becomes an experienced reality. As the forgiven ones we can worship in company with the whole Church in heaven and on earth.

It is because of this awareness of being members of the worshipping community that all merely individualistic feelings are a threat to the integrity of the Communion service. Indeed the kind of individualistic piety which is actually encouraged in many churches is a deplorable distortion of the purpose of the sacrament. Already the common chalice has been surrendered in the interests of social hygiene.

—J. R. Nelson, *Criterion for the Church*, p. 114.

To make an offering at the communion table.

The second requirement was that we come to the Communion supper prepared to make an offering out of our day. It could be a symbolic offering of our work—an eraser or a slide rule. It could be a report of what was happening in our own individual life, or in the life of our mission group. It could be God's World as it came in an event of the day, or a reminder to our community of the covenant under which we live. It could be a happening somewhere in the world, on behalf of which we gathered. It might be simply our silence offered up upon the Communion table. To make this kind of preparation was to grasp the possibility of living through the day in a different kind of way. The fact that it could be offered up at the Communion meal was to perceive it—to be present to it and therefore a celebrant in it, to understand that there was some relationship between the world and the Communion table, the secular and the sacred.

—Elizabeth O'Connor, *Journey Inward, Journey Outward*, p. 90.

3. Baptism

The difficulty of interpreting baptism today.

We are well aware of the difficulties which confront us when we try to interpret the conventional rites of Baptism in accord with such sense of personal identification and participation with Christ as the New Testament teaches. But this much ought to be obvious: even as the Baptism of Jesus was not limited in time to that moment or so when He went with John into the Jordan, so in the case of Christians the effect of Baptism is not confined to the time and action of the rite itself. Baptism means being brought into a continuing life, becoming part of an onward process of salvation, during which one is ever threatened and dragged backward by sin, and yet in which one who retains his faith is sustained by the grace of God. Can that be believed today by the millions of men and women who have been baptized in the name of the Triune God?

—J. R. Nelson, *Criterion for the Church*, p. 72.

The meaning of baptism.

A minimized theology of Baptism may be due to a partial blindness of some Christians to the objective, saving work of God in Jesus Christ which the apostolic witness sets forth as the basic faith of the Church. It is encouraging and instructive to note that precisely those local churches and denominations which have been making earnest effort to provide satisfying education in the faith and training in faithful discipleship have come to a new level of appreciation for Baptism. . . . The radically ethical content of the Christian faith, for example, with its requirement of vicarious love and self-giving, is enhanced by the baptismal insight into the dying and rising of the Christian with Jesus Christ. The teaching on the atoning effect of Jesus' life and death, the grace of God, and the present power of the Holy Spirit is likewise given force and focus by the better understanding of Baptism.

Finally the oneness of Baptism as an expression of the reconciling, unifying work of Jesus Christ challenges the churches to re-examine not only their diverse view of Baptism but, much more, their actual reasons for permitting the perpetuation of church divisions. . . . Baptism testifies to the faithfulness and love of God for the salvation of us creatures through our identification with the one Christ. Baptism presupposes the possible existence of only one Church, and of the common life of Christians under the one Spirit. The one Baptism precedes the one Eucharist, or Lord's Supper; and the wide recognition of valid Baptism across the lines of divided churches calls into sharp judgement the practice of those same churches excluding one another's members from the Table of the Lord. Baptism is, finally, an indispensable element in the reconciling mission of God to all nations and all generations, and thus it judges all temporal and transient obstacles to the manifesting of the Church's unity in the fulfilling of its mission.

—J. R. Nelson, *Criterion for the Church*, pp. 80–81.

What did Christ mean by baptism?

Christ's own statement about His central purpose is remarkable for its double emphasis upon both mood and scope. His single expression is so vividly clear that it makes us understand that the work of Christ's Church, whatever else it may be, must be both flaming in spirit and total in application. It is the "earth," not just the religious element, that requires ignition. It is obvious that this purpose is somehow connected with the experience of baptism. One indication of this is that the author of the Third Gospel follows the fire passage with the words, "I have a baptism to be baptized with" (Luke 12:50).

What did Christ mean by baptism? Evidently He was projecting this experience into the future and therefore was not referring back to His own ceremonial baptism by water in the Jordan. The people who say that all Christians must be immersed, because they are called to be like Christ, and He was immersed, are making a fundamental mistake, the essence of their mistake being the failure to take seriously Christ's metaphorical use of the baptismal experience.

—Elton Trueblood, *The Incendiary Fellowship*, pp. 103–4.

Baptism and the outsider.

In the mission to non-Christians the churches must face the question of their conviction concerning the indispensability of Baptism for admission to the life in Christ. Especially in the various cultures of Africa and Asia, which are dominantly non-Christian in tradition and character, it is being asked whether converts to Christ should incur the painful rejection by family and society which is often consequent upon their being baptized. . . . What counsel should they be given by church members? It is easy enough to say that Baptism is just a formality, that salvation does not depend upon it, that one can be a good Christian without it. But does the New Testament, or the example of the apostolic church, give us any warrant for such a facile circumvention of the problem? Surely it does not. There is no firm ground in faith for prudentially avoiding suffering for the cause of Christ, since in the long run the vitality of the person's faith, or of a church's fidelity, may depend upon the person's willingness to suffer. Moreover, it should not be overlooked that Baptism as a public act in a pagan culture can be a powerful means of evangelical witness.

In countries which are traditionally Christian, however they may fail really to qualify for that name today, the churches which practice Infant Baptism must become bolder and more rigorous in making decisions concerning the acceptance and rejection of little children for Baptism. . . . One can never be sure of the consequences of a gentle rebuff. But the risk is worth taking, lest the grace of God, membership in the Church, and faith in Christ be made to seem even cheaper than they now appear to be.

And what about those baptized members of the Church who are clearly inclined to fall away from the faith? Obviously the rite of Baptism cannot guarantee sustained faithfulness and persistence in the Christian life. Since numerous Christians neglect the grace of God and resist the Holy Spirit by ignoring or violating their baptismal vows, the churches are constrained to exercise a wise, merciful but supple discipline. Churches today can afford neither arrogance nor carelessness in their pastoral care for the nominal members. Their purpose is always to call back the negligent and support the weak. The difficulties of administering a discipline which displays both the tenderness and the virility of Jesus Christ are manifest, but they are not a valid excuse for avoiding it.

—J. R. Nelson, *Criterion for the Church*, pp. 75–77.

4. The Pulpit

The significance of preaching for new life.

New life in any parish comes by the Holy Spirit through the living Word confronting persons through persons. This essential confrontation employs many different human activities. Preaching is one of the most significant.

—Wallace E. Fisher, *Preaching and Parish Renewal*, p. 8.

The preacher must receive before he can give.

The churches of the Reformation claim to be the churches of the Word. Are they? Is it God's Word that comes down from the pulpit, "cutting the heart" of those who listen, or is it human words dictated by human wisdom? . . . The preacher's task is a hard one, because he must hold the two-edged sword which cuts the hand of him who handles it. Always he must first receive what he is going to give out. It is the function of a praying church to bear up the servant in charge of the proclamation, and to hear what God wills to say through him as a word from God and not from man. In a living church there is a secret and deep relation, a constant give-and-take, between the preacher and the community.

—Suzanne DeDietrich, *The Witnessing Community*, p. 149.

Involve laymen in sermon preparation.

The dialogue of preaching and its vitality can be encouraged in many ways. One method is to involve laymen in the sermon preparation itself. In the East Harlem Protestant Parish the minister responsible for the Sunday sermon goes through this process. On Monday he studies the passage with his colleagues at a staff Bible study, seeking to acquire, with the help of all critical tools, the necessary professional preparation concerning the passage. On Wednesday at a noon staff lunch he outlines his sermon as he then sees it, accepting suggestions and picking up ideas and usually criticism. This provides for his colleagues, who will be in lay Bible study groups scattered through the parish that evening, some basis for focusing the group discussions. Often one or another of the groups will discuss what they think should be included in the sermon or what topics dealt with. On Thursday morning after eight-thirty worship, the preacher receives the reports of these groups and on the basis of them writes the final draft of his sermon. This process is not as complicated as it sounds and does bring a vitality to preaching that often engenders true dialogue between God and his people.

—George W. Webber, *The Congregation in Mission*, p. 83.

The insufficiency of sermon hearing.

The insufficiency of sermon hearing as a religious exercise is well demonstrated in the life of James Boswell, whose newly published *London Journal* reveals that his frequent practice of listening to sermons did not prevent him from planning, at the same time, his outrageous escapades. We need to understand that the Christian witness lies not in some passive attendance, but rather in sharing the missionary effort at some point in human contact. In this case, at least, it is more blessed to give than to receive and men learn more of Christian truth by what they share than by what they hear.

—Elton Trueblood, *Your Other Vocation*, p. 49.

Is preaching a substitute for dialogue and involvement?

The emphasis on preaching is another indication of the unconscious avoidance of religious depth. Religious leaders are well aware that genuine communication demands dialogue and personal encounter, yet they continue to rely primarily upon one-way communication to convey the important message of the gospel. Preaching is safer, more comfortable, more easily avoided, and therefore more acceptable to both minister and laymen. It allows the minister to *talk about* the faith and to avoid the implications of acting upon that faith, because the minute he finishes the sermon he must busy himself preparing the next one. Rarely, if ever, does the minister attempt to involve his people in actually struggling with ways of carrying out the implications of the sermon; indeed, he may be frightened if they try.

—Clyde Reid, *The God-Evaders*, p. 59.

The pulpit is no longer the center of evangelism.

Our sacraments are not primarily evangelistic—they are not created to bring souls to Christ but rather to feed spiritual life that already exists in Christ. Most unfortunately, today, the pulpit alone is trying to fill the desperate need of this hour to win people to Christ. And one thing I can tell you right now that is so clear to me as to be unmistakable: No longer will the pulpit be the center of evangelism in the Church, if this insight God has granted me is correct. Preachers will go on preaching but sermons will not be the main means by which people are evangelically brought to Christ.

—Claxton Monro and William S. Taegel, *Witnessing Laymen Make Living Churches*, p. 38.

"Talk-back" after the Sunday evening sermon.

One of the strongest opportunities for nurture in many churches is through the use of a technique which we call "Talk-back." In the Sunday night service the pastor steps out of the pulpit and stands on the same level with the congregation. After a twenty minute sermon, he tells the congregation that now it is their opportunity to talk back to the preacher. He asks their opinion of the ideas presented in the sermon. Do they disagree? Many pastors, myself included, may experience great difficulty in a service of this sort. We make ourselves quite vulnerable when we open up for questions from the pew. As preachers, many of us have assumed that we must always close the door on, or finalize, or have the last word on the issues we present. What a shock to realize that an intelligent and committed layman may be better informed than we are, and may even disagree.

—Russell Bow, *The Integrity of Church Membership*, pp. 84–85.

Prophetic preaching—its meaning for today.

For several centuries the prophets were the channel of God's revelation to his People. When the Fulfiller came, prophecy, in the Old Testament meaning of the word, ended. Yet there is a prophetic function of the church: it must proclaim God's Word and interpret it to every generation. The problem of the preacher is whether he will listen to that Word until it takes possession of him so that he too will be, not a man "dreaming dreams" or speaking out of his own wisdom, but the "mouth of God"—the channel through which the Spirit does his witnessing work. Then, and then only, will he be a true watchman in church and city.

To stand under God means to see all things in his light. The Word, earnestly listened to, makes *free men*, able to look at themselves and at the world in all fairness and independence of mind. This is the great lesson that we all have constantly to relearn. And this freedom under God should not be the attribute of the preacher only, but of all church members. There must be a corporate as well as a personal "standing under God's word" if we are to interpret his will for our own time. It is a task that requires ever-renewed searching of heart. The contemporary world, so full of slogans and catchwords, needs nothing so much as to hear the voice of such free men. Their insights are needed in all walks of life, in education as well as in industry and politics. If the church does not provide them, who will?

We have seen all through this chapter that one of the prophets' main attacks is directed against the divorce of religion from everyday life. Religion is not a kind of life insurance for the future, nor a soothing panacea amidst the troubles of this world. What the God of Israel requires is total commitment of the whole life. "You shall have no other gods before me"! The prophets are relentless destroyers of idols, and idols are not only Asherah or Tammuz —they include the Temple, the state, power, money, and success: Man deified.

We have also seen how seriously the prophets take professional responsibility. The place where we live and work is the real place where our obedience toward God must find its most concrete expression.

And finally, all through, there is a tremendous concern for justice. In the prophetic writings as in the law of Israel, God is the defender of the defenseless. God stands with the underdog! Is not this one of the points where the church has failed? How weak during the nineteenth century was the church's defense of the exploited workers! In Europe, as a consequence, it has lost the world of labor. Is not the rise of communism God's judgment on the compliance of the church with the wealthy and powerful of this world? Has not the church all too long tolerated the current policies in matters of race and of subject peoples? Has it not often been more vigorous in its defense of the rights of property than in the protection of human lives?

Today, of course, the church awakens to these problems; but so does the secular world! Shall we always deal with yesterday's problems rather than tomorrow's?

—Suzanne DeDietrich, *The Witnessing Community*, pp. 99–100.

Preaching and critical social issues—an example.

On a score of occasions pointed observations had been made concerning that virus in the body politic. Suddenly in 1954 this no longer seemed to be adequate. Senator Joseph McCarthy was scheduled to appear in Lancaster to address the Lancaster Manufacturers' Association. Some weeks prior to his coming a series of three sermons was announced on first the philosophical-practical nature of communism, then how the "guilt by association" concept obscured "due process of law" and human freedom, and finally the need for a voluntary revolution in the life of the saints.

Promptly two vestrymen whose friendship and counsel had especially supported Trinity's new ministry sought to alter this announced series. They argued that so controversial an issue should not be taken into Trinity's pulpit, particularly with the senator coming to the city. Their logic was sobering: "The day will come when you can speak on controversial issues. We shall welcome that day, but it has not arrived. If you preach on the issue presently, you will disrupt—possibly split—the congregation." Because these vestrymen were honestly concerned for the congregation's welfare, devoted much time to its work, and also abhorred McCarthyism, I consented to reconsider. Would the proposed series really embroil the congregation in bitter controversy? Would it split the congregation? The situation *was* potentially explosive. That was fat, affluent, complacent 1954—a bad year for prophets! On the other hand, should fear muffle the church's judgment on guilt by association tactics? Was God's clear Word to be denied because some feared that the institutional church could not stand the strain? The preacher's conscience fell captive to the Word of God; he was constrained to preach as announced.

On that particular Sunday in 1954 when McCarthyism was exposed to God's Word, the church was filled, the only time in those days other than Palm Sunday and Easter. Perhaps a hundred business and professional people from other churches, several responsible political leaders, and three hundred or so members who rarely had heard any sermons in Trinity except the meditations at the Communion services were present among the regular worshipers that day. The sermon, delivered in a highly charged emotional atmosphere, was pointed, but carefully documented.

Some visitors were incensed. They said so at the door quite unkindly. The majority of Trinity's congregation, however, departed without comment. Over a hundred letters and phone calls during the next week were evenly divided. The anonymous attacks were harsh, occasionally vicious: "meddling preacher," "Roosevelt lover," "enemy of America." Four times the preacher was identified as "the anti-Christ"! Many signed letters and self-identified callers expressed appreciation and support. The two vestrymen who had sought to dissuade their pastor from preaching on the issue advised him that same morning that a Christian witness had been made and that they would support that witness. Another vestryman, having endorsed the series from the outset, called it into print and distributed it widely. Harsh criticism came from one segment of the parish, but scores of laymen shared that sermon throughout the community. The decision to bring God's Word to bear on McCarthyism in those frenzied days was one of the more significant specific decisions at Trinity in demonstrating the prophetic utility inherent in gospel preaching.

Thereafter, laymen as well as clergy exploited that dramatic breakthrough. God's Word was proclaimed formally and informally to social man on many fronts by many members. Lancaster's ghettoed Negroes, fair employment practices, open housing, urban renewal, the "organization man," American-Russian relations, nuclear testing, mental health, teen-age sex education, marriage and family, the super-patriots, the 1960 and 1964 presidential elections, civil rights, the acceptance of the Russian Orthodox Church by the World Council of Churches were a few of the political, social, and ecumenical issues hailed before the tribunal of biblical evidence. Trinity Church began to accept its Christian responsibility to examine man and society in the light of God's Word. Learning first that Christianity does not provide pat answers for pressing political problems, or solutions for complex social issues, the parish discovered that Christianity does provide the most relevant frame of reference and the best resources for tackling those problems and issues constructively.

—Wallace E. Fisher, *From Tradition to Mission*, pp. 61–63.

H. But the Sabbath Was Made for Man—The New Understanding about Structures

Drastic alterations are required.

This is to say that to take seriously the new insights into the role and function of the laity is not simply to abandon older formulations, to discuss a new theology of the church, to better discern God's creative and redemptive activity in a world that he has not abandoned, but also to realize that drastic alterations are required in the traditional and conventional forms of church life and in the structure of the church as now organized.

—Alden D. Kelley, *The People of God*, p. 46.

The structures exist to serve the Church.

We learned again and in another way that we did not exist to serve the structures, but they existed to serve us. We had set in the public eye a coffee house and for some of us it came above all other things—and we had good spiritual reasons, for we had said it belonged to God and named it the

Potter's House, and dedicated our nights there to Him. We had articulated for one another the Law of the Potter's House, the Rule by which we would live; a holy rule it was, for it would enable us to channel the life of the church to the world. But all laws are schoolmasters to draw us closer to Christ. It is difficult to get that forever straight. Time and again the sleeping Pharisee, the standardbearer in each one, rose up to flay us with harsh words and make us judges over our brothers. It all seemed right because Christ's work was at stake, the witness of His Church. Then out of the community came a voice to say again that the structures were not important. It was the same voice that was forever telling us how important they were. We understand nonetheless, and had anew the discovery that we were not made for the sabbath, but the sabbath for us.

The conversation on structures more than any other helped some of us to free others to do the impossible, and to free them to bear their own burdens. We often have the temptation of the professional to want to rush in and to somehow hold everything together. It is easy to see why we have kept going in our churches those things which should have been allowed to die natural or unnatural deaths. We keep propping up that which should be recognized for the disaster it is so that it can either receive transfusions of new life, or be allowed to expire, in which case we can face our sin and know that we are forgiven and face our inadequacy and know that we are acceptable.

For the church is God's church and He watches over it, and there is a sense in which we who love that church need never be anxious for it. This is hard to grasp because there is another sense in which it is dependent upon us, and our response is the only all-important thing.

In our little fellowship it is our response which has sometimes made us fearful for the structures which hold and nurture our life together. On the way to building them, we have often stopped to discuss with one another who was the greatest, in the subtle and not-so-subtle ways that knowledgeable people do. We know why Christ said so many times, "Whoever would be great among you must be your servant, and whoever would be first among you must be slave of all." We forever find ourselves seeking the highest place at the table. There is a glorious sense in which we are bound to one another under the lordship of Christ, and a terrible sense in which we have known under this lordship all the problems of the Twelve together.

—Elizabeth O'Connor, *Call to Commitment*, pp. 179–80.

The Church breaks through old boundaries.

This new ecclesiology, we have said, will direct us to new *places* of obedience and new *forms* of obedience; leading to identification with particular people and groups struggling for historical air. It will also lead us into the struggle for *new community* life in which the church seeks to be the sign of the society of God that transcends old tribalisms and breaks through the limitations of our national communities.

—Colin W. Williams, *The Church*, pp. 45–46.

The organization man is ill-served by present structures.

The traditional men's fellowships centered in the churches have a difficult time meeting the needs of organization man. Usually they can relate in only a superficial way to the traveling members of the congregation, because they have little relevance to the interests and connections the men have outside the church.

The most meaningful men's fellowships are generally in those churches most of whose members are locally employed. Thus churches whose rolls are drawn principally from the lower middle income group frequently have stronger and deeper associations. Where the members have performed actual physical labor together on a church building, there is a sense of involvement. . . . It is probably foolish to think that the local parish church can come to terms with the total complex life of the organization man.

—Robert W. Spike, *Safe in Bondage*, pp. 42–43.

Hardheaded intellectually, warmhearted emotionally.

Fortunately we are seeing the beginning of a change. There is emerging among us a new style of Christian living, in which the adolescent fear of emotion is being overcome. The men who are beginning to give the most potent contemporary Christian leadership are *rational evangelicals,* who recognize no difficulty whatever in being both hardheaded on intellectual problems and warmhearted in their love of Christ. Far from being fearful of passion, these men are well aware that nothing of importance is ever created without it. Certainly we could have no great poetry without passion. Intense caring, far from hindering intellectual integrity, supports and encourages it. Accordingly, while we need many kinds of courage, our supreme need is of the courage to care.

One interesting evidence of the new mood, which indicates some outgrowing of the fear of religious emotion, is found in the new hymnals, particularly *The Methodist Hymnal,* just published. This, which is probably more widely distributed than is any other, now restores to the Number One position Charles Wesley's "O For a Thousand Tongues to Sing."

—Elton Trueblood, *The Incendiary Fellowship*, p. 117.

Transformed to meet the needs of a post-Christian culture.

We can no longer assume that the culture in which we live is Christian, even though it retains many of its Christian qualities. If this is the case, then it means that again, as in the early Christian church, men of faith must live in two worlds. Most of the life of the layman is spent in a sub-Christian, or in Communist countries an anti-Christian, culture. The Church must be *in* but not *of* the world, and so must the individual Christian. The interior life of the Church must make of it a "colony of heaven," but its purpose as a colony is to be an agent of reconciliation to the world. Old patterns of church life are inadequate in preparing the laity for their work both in Church and world. If the social observers are right, then the structures of church life still need to be transformed in order to meet the new needs of our post-Christian culture.

—Howard Grimes, *The Rebirth of the Laity*, pp. 110–11.

Working through nonchurch structures in the world.

For the church to go into the world means, increasingly in our day, that it must find ways of making its witness in the areas of public policy formation and public responsibility. It means being present not only among the victims of collective injustice, but also at the centers of freedom and power where human life is affected for good or evil. In a pluralistic society, for the church to be in the world means being present primarily in nonecclesiastical forms and in the midst of an essentially secular, or nonreligious, community. It means working through nonchurch structures and discovering new patterns of ministry.

—E. Clinton Gardner, *The Church As a Prophetic Community*, p. 226.

The nonchurch.

It may well be that we are in for a period when there will be no clearly-defined pattern of the Church at all. In some places it may be that *ad hoc* groups, chosen from local personnel (in a factory or a school, for instance) will meet occasionally to discuss how love can be expressed in their situation (though they will probably not speak of it in those terms). *And for these people this will be the Church.* Elsewhere groups may gather for informal times of discussion or worship in the homes of those who give the lead. For them this will be the Church. Others again will wish to meet occasionally for a celebration of the Eucharist—though not in Anglican Cranmerian or Free Church hymn-sandwich style. But these may well be a minority of the whole.

I foresee the breaking down of central structures, and the springing into life of local expressions of the Christian community, with different communities varying considerably from one another. The dangers of wrong beliefs and practices creeping into such a situation are offset by the inevitable freedom from the dead hand of conformity which must accrue. It may be that with such a pattern the Church will once again begin to stand for something which is real in men's lives, instead of standing as the guardian of a tradition which is generally rejected because its essential worth is hidden behind ecclesiastical jargon, imposing edifices and clerical collars.

The Church is dead. Long live the non-church!

—Ray Billington, "Church versus Non-Church," *The Princeton Seminary Bulletin* 60:44.

The Church must provide a variety of worship services to meet the needs of metropolis.

Metropolitan living has revealed how rural the Churches' schedule of activities and services still are. Churches still expect a large numerical response at Sunday evening and mid-week services and infer growing god-lessness or apostasy on the part of those who do not come. They expect that youth should be in large attendance at both the Sunday church school and the Sunday-evening meetings scheduled for them. And which church among the Churches would question the adequacy of the eleven o'clock service of worship on Sunday morning!

Are Churches justified in planning and scheduling their services and activities in such a way that all members are expected to meet at the same time to share in the same service of worship or activity? And when all those who are expected do not come, are the Churches justified in concluding that they are becoming increasingly secular or that the Churches' leaders no longer have the support of their memberships?

It would seem that the new conditions created by Metropolis are telling us that Churches must become as diversified in the time and place and content of their program and services as is Metropolis itself. Obviously the people of Metropolis are different in taste, interests, and religious experience. Not every worshiper attending the eleven o'clock worship service on Sunday morning will find the sermon preached adequate to his need for that particular day. He will have to content himself with the expectation that the personal word of the gospel will come to him at another time or in some other way.

Not every member of the church will find the mid-week service suitable or meaningful to him. He may not like the form it takes. He may wish it to have more or less content than it has or a different kind of content altogether. While some may find special grace in coming to the church building for this service, others may find it impossible to do so because of distance, physical handicap, family difficulties, work, or other responsibilities. Still others may prefer private to public prayer and thus turn away from the mid-week service. Do not the differences recognizable in church memberships suggest a diversification of time, place, and content of program—and worship?

In addition to the long-established church ways which are evidently still means of grace for the many church people who cherish them, the servant Church will have to provide a variety of experiences of worship and services which may be shared at various times during the day and/or the evening throughout the week. Services of worship and study in homes for small groups must also be arranged and encouraged.

Why should the Churches expect to do their whole job of equipping the saints through the Sunday church school, the Sunday morning service of worship, and the mid-week service, however well-conceived and performed these ministries are? Can it be that there are other times and places in which the efficacy of the redemptive activity of God in Christ may be experienced, in which the people of God may find real meaning and vitality in the Christian faith and yet maintain a sense of the unity of the congregation?

—Jesse McNeil, *Mission in Metropolis*, pp. 53–54.

The image of the pastor will have to become "unchurchly."

The attitude toward the church receives a concrete form in the relationship toward the clergymen, who are looked upon as "professional church people." Whether he likes it or not, the clergyman is, in the eyes of the unchurched, the church incarnate (he often behaves himself as if he *wants* it that way). In the world he is treated as an outsider and stranger, viz., one's association with him is formalized through stereotypes. There is still a place for him as "traveling salesman in solemnities" (Germany) or, if need be, as "the helper of the gravedigger" (France), but he can hardly be a common friend anymore. If he wants to become that, then he will have to be dismantled and begin to "act normally."

It seems to me that *two practical conclusions* are quite obvious in this situation. First: *the professional churchman can in general no longer be the best-suited organ for the apostolate.* His very appearance mobilizes all the post-ecclesiastical feelings and sensitivities that are present. I believe that this first conclusion is now accepted in wide circles. On this basis a drastic curtailing (among other things) of the number of full-time ministers was recently advocated.

With the second conclusion, which, in my judgment, is just as obvious, we will probably face stronger opposition. *The organs of the apostolate will have to distanciate themselves as far as possible from everything that looks "churchly."* We have something else in mind than just a tactical gesture with which to meet objecting outsiders. We will have to learn to act soberly, from the realization that everything that bears a distinct "churchly" label *for that reason* already is misunderstood. Even before a word has been said, "propaganda" is suspected to be behind it, some sort of clever gimmick to gain new members for a "party," which people believe has become antiquated long ago.

We can't just *talk* away this misunderstanding; it will have to be *outlived.* Wherever in our apostolate we seek *a convincing demonstration of Christ's solidarity with the world, we* will clearly have to be present *in* this world with solidarity, not just now and then in a sortie from the ecclesiastical enclave only to return thereafter with great, great speed, but *permanently,* because we know that as Christians we have our *Sitz im Leben* (life situation) *in the world*, not in the church. In the world one must live as a "child of the Kingdom, that has been planted on the acreage of the world."

— J. C. Hoekendijk, *The Church Inside Out*, pp. 53–54.

A training class for prospective members.

Dr. Arie D. Bestebreurtje, who was a lawyer and a ruling elder before entering the ministry, was determined to develop a vital fellowship like that of the early Christian church. He feels that the secret is to develop a fellowship so vital that instead of soliciting members and attracting them by superficial methods, they will ask, "How do I join?"

Dr. Bestebreurtje's approach is briefly as follows: The purpose of his first visit to an interested person is to get acquainted. On the second visit he mentions that the person has been regular in attendance and explains what he must do to join the church. Reactions to these demanding requirements vary. When persons are told that they must attend a training class, some are furious. "Why, I have been a Presbyterian all my life!" the prospective member may exclaim. "Those who object make the poorest members," states the pastor. On the other hand others welcome the idea. "I have always wanted to ask some questions about religion," or, "I have always wondered what the Apostles' Creed meant where it says, 'He descended into hell,'" are typical reactions.

If the prospect responds affirmatively on the second visit, he receives a letter of invitation to five sessions of a training class. The final session is held in the presence of the elders, where four aspects of membership are stressed. They are:

(1) Participation in the worship and study program of the church on a regular basis. The pastor explains that the church will not accept excuses such as "company coming on Sunday." "Tell your excuses to God," he says.

(2) Service to the local church and community. An extensive list of service projects and opportunities (both church related and non-church related) is given to the new member to indicate the areas of Christian life and work in which he will participate.

(3) Financial support of the church. The Chairman of the Finance Committee explains the total financial program of the church and the prospective member then makes his financial commitment to the church.

(4) Living the Christian faith in a secular context. Now the pastor explains that the most important thing to remember is that we are Christians twenty-four hours a day and our Christian witness extends to all areas of life.

Critics suggest that membership in this church is a status symbol, but after studying its program, I am convinced that it is not exclusive except at the point of commitment. The status of which its members are justly proud is that of belonging to a dynamic Christian fellowship. Although it is located in an upper-class residential area, business executives and janitors serve together on an equal basis on the same church committees.

—Russell Bow, *The Integrity of Church Membership*, pp. 60–61.

Retreats—a chance to look inside.

The retreat, a practice with a noble heritage in Christian history, should offer a place of withdrawal from the hum and din and clatter of modern man's demanding existence. It should give him an opportunity to "find himself." Increasingly, as the pace of life speeds up, he needs to pause to get his bearings; he cannot afford to drift without this.

But thus far, Protestant centers for retreat have not been overly successful at doing what retreats should. Too often, "retreat" means doing with greater vigor what we do several times a week—sing, hear sermons, listen to lectures, participate in organized games, make plans for keeping the organization humming, and so on. Our "retreat" facilities are astounding in size and design. We assume that spiritual success means visible activity *en masse* and leave little place for looking inside to see whether something really is there. We seem afraid to be still.

—E. Glenn Hinson, *The Church: Design for Survival*, p. 80.

One church that broke the traditional patterns.

South Main Baptist Church of Houston, Texas, is another example of an urban congregation breaking out of traditional patterns of ministry to meet the needs of the surrounding community. The ministry has taken on the name of SMILE (South Main's Informal Learning Experiences) and is the result of many months of researching, planning, training, and contacting. The ministry consists of seven group learning opportunities.

Beginning with infants through five-year-olds, there is the Learning Lads 'n Lassies. Children participate in a planned curriculum of music, games, creative activities, and relevant Bible stories.

Next comes the Peanut Butter Bunch including grades one through three. Here the curriculum includes unit studies such as "God's Wonderful World," music, creative games, and story time.

The Kids Klub is for grades four through six. Discussion groups, supervised recreation in the gym, Bible study, crafts, and field trips to points of interest hold this group together. Tutoring in any area of school work is available on request.

Tuff Time (Teens United for Fun) is for junior highs. They meet each Thursday evening for discussion groups centered around topics of their interest, such as personal grooming, vocational and moral decisions. They have Bible study groups and field trips for cultural enrichment.

There are two women's clubs for those over eighteen or married. One embraces a large segment of the international women who reside in the immediate neighborhood. Most of these are wives of interns and residents at the nearby Houston Medical Center, and graduate students at both Rice University and the University of Houston. The International Women's Club includes English lessons, crafts, ceramics, field trips, sewing, and special guest speakers from the Houston community.

The oldest group, the Triple L (Live Long and Like It) Club, is one of the most active within the entire ministry. They take field trips, have book reviews and films, share table games, and hear speakers on topics such as medicare and personal health care.

Not every local congregation or group of Christians can reproduce the ministry and experimentation of the three groups here described. Yet, each congregation can, and I believe must, duplicate the spirit of freedom and creativity that these groups exemplify if the church of Jesus Christ is to play a significant role in shaping the future of the world. Whether or not we do depends largely upon what we decide about our response to the call of Christ to be his disciple in the twentieth century.

—James F. Bailey, "An Exploding World: What Kind of Church?" *Baptist Student*, February 1968, pp. 32–33.

The program of "Ten Brave Christians"—a plan that worked.

It was a simple exercise which was designed to help the individual put God first in his daily life. The invitation was extended in the Sunday school class as well as in the whole church:

"Wanted: Ten Brave Christians for the month of March 1965.

1. Who will meet once each week to pray together.
2. Who will give two hours time each week to God.
3. Who will give God one-tenth of earnings during this month.
4. Who will spend 5:30 to 6:00 each morning in prayer-meditation.
5. Who will witness for God their experience to others."

The word "brave" was not intended in any way to suggest superiority. It was simply assumed that it would take a *brave* Christian to undertake such a discipline for thirty days. The number "ten" was used because it was thought that if *ten* people could be found who would accept such a discipline, a spiritual revolution could be expected in the church. Each person who was interested in trying the program was asked to study these five disciplines carefully so that there could be no misunderstanding as to what was involved in expressing a new commitment in these specific ways. Anyone who wanted to enroll in the group was required to request, take with him, sign at home, and then mail to the church a written commitment to these disciplines. When all the cards had been returned they counted the names of twenty-two people who seriously wanted to take part in this experiment.

The weekly hour-and-a-half meeting was divided between prayer, sharing of experiences, and study or discussion of books which members of the group had read during the week. Each person who volunteered for the experiment was furnished a mimeographed list of church-related needs from which he could select his "two hours work for God." It was amazing what a difference this made in the life of the church.

Tithing may have kept many people from volunteering for the experiment, but we now know that when this requirement has been weakened in any way, the results have not been comparable. The secret seems to be that this is a minimum level of commitent necessary for honesty. If one does not want his life changed enough to be willing to make this kind of commitment not much is likely to happen.

The morning study and prayer time is probably the most important discipline of all. This is the time when a person opens his life to God in such a way that he can be transformed. Most persons who are unaccustomed to spending thirty minutes in prayer need some guidance. The suggested schedule for morning prayer was as follows:

5:30-5:40 Read Scripture for the day. Pray and meditate on this Scripture. Write out in less than 50 words how this passage of Scripture applies to your life.

5:40-5:50 Write out one totally unselfish and unexpected act of kindness or generosity that you will do today. Name the person—then act, during the day, vigorously and with love and compassion. Keep a written record of the (1) reaction of the person toward whom the kindness is extended and (2) the effect of this act upon you personally.

5:50-6:00 Write out carefully how you would like to build and develop your life. Go into great detail if you desire. Take your time—be thoughtful and prayerful. One well prayed out and thought out sentence per day would be excellent progress.

Each participant was furnished a carefully selected list of Scripture passages for each day for the first month.

Many people hesitated to enter the experiment because they felt they would be unable to witness their experiences to other people. But an amazing thing happened. As God began to change their lives, they responded eagerly to opportunities to tell others about the new life they had found.

—Russell Bow, *The Integrity of Church Membership*, pp. 17–19.

The local parish must be supplemented with other forms.

It is generally recognized that the parish type of congregation may still have significance in our day for the "preserving" pastorate, but that, generally speaking, it is not well suited for the "outreach" and the apostolate and that it will in any case have to be supplemented with other forms of parish life. A church that wants indeed to be pro-existent—to be there for the other—can therefore never be organized exclusively in local parishes. In its place, or at least parallel with it, all sorts of other forms of church life must be developed. If the church does not do that, she will come to stand outside of her own time, and will no longer be able to serve the people who have become our contemporaries. . . .

. . . The parish system was designed for village relationships. In the system of the city it cannot function, unless the city too is molded by a village mentality. There are, furthermore, so many memories of a past era, even though we just hold on to them. On Sunday morning we go to church about ten or eleven o'clock, because this time fell in between two feedings of the cattle. But just try to change it outside of the rural milieu!

In our whole ecclesiastical life, there is very little that would indicate that we have moved into an industrial society. Where, for instance, in our hymn-books does one find a single reference to the factory, wages, and social justice? When do we sing about leisure time? When do all those questions come into view which occupy us so intensely from Monday through Friday? And these are only a few outward manifestations (although they speak volumes!) of the absence of the church in our time. Behind this and beneath this is by and large a strong desire to preserve all that has been. We think that we "honor our fathers and our mothers" by exact imitation.

Always again restoration is the order of the day. In the meantime we know—it can be demonstrated with the clear evidence of various investigations—that when the church in her life just orientates herself to the past, when she aims her life at "the people who are still around" (just notice how often this is said: "the people who are *still* around"), it can be predicted with certainty that her style of life will become ever more old-fashioned, more archaic, so that she becomes increasingly a foreign element in our time and finally will maintain herself only as a religious ghetto.

—J. C. Hoekendijk, *The Church Inside Out*, pp. 73–75.

The Underground Church.

"The Church" will be seen less and less as a building, on a corner to be visited to confess masturbation and adultery and to indulge in a period of "magic." Smaller Christian communities will replace larger ones; clergy will be employed in "the world," and the lay-clerical dichotomy will be relaxed— so there will be clerical functions with only distant memories of a priestly mystique; cult will continue, but God alone knows precisely how; "prayer," as we have known it, will be unheard-of, for the other figure in prayer is God, who is, absurdly and actually, being redefined; the patently ridiculous, assumed contradiction between mysticism and pragmatism will vanish; morality will not be seen as a neat category; Newman Clubs, Canterbury Clubs, Wesley Foundations, Westminster centers, and other denominational campus ghettos will have slipped beneath a convenient bay; Vatican XVIII will be urgently awaited; some will be tentatively suggesting clerical celibacy as a unique idea for institutional purification; the Buddhist-Christian dialogue will be the subject of a major piece in the Sunday *Times;* a black Pope will take the unprecedented step of naming a white Cardinal (an ex-Anglican, at that); and there will be furious, underground rumblings concerning the need for an absolute revolution in the Church in order to avoid its demise within a decade.

Meanwhile, however, the arena in which we find ourselves is *now.* Our basic task is neither to study history nor predict the future, but to live responsibly so that there may be a history to chronicle and a future in which other men and women may have the opportunity to live. For many, the Underground Church is seen as a present and necessary way of experiencing Jesus Christ in community and, therefore, is the basis of social possibilities for human servanthood. Increasingly, Underground Churches, like catacombs, will be found as communities. It is understood that these do not comprise a "new" Church but a locus for community, worship, and service. Action of Church unity will continue to be matched by radical (not liberal) participation in social concerns. *Imitatio Christi* will come to mean, more and more, the development of a Christian secular, rather than a "religious," style of life.

—Malcolm Boyd, *The Underground Church,* pp. 245–46.

Will the Church go underground?

A reporter for a national magazine called recently to ask me what I thought about the "underground church." The notion of an underground church is being batted around by a number of Christians who feel that current church organizations are obsolete. The phrase—"underground church"—is used sometimes to refer to persons from denomination to denomination, Protestants and Catholics, who feel that unity has already taken place, who are themselves unified in struggling for justice and in worshiping a God who has no patience with any Christian organization that profanes its name by rejecting the will of Christ, insofar as that will seems clear.

In this sense, there may be an underground church today—the people from place to place, from congregation to congregation, who really *are* the salt of the earth. It is underground in the sense that its existence is obscured by the relative apathy of the church as a whole.

But in the sense of a true "underground"—a movement so "dangerous" that its operations must be secret, a movement which is opposed to the status quo and trying to gain power—the notion of an underground church is as false today as the notion that a few militants are responsible for the rioting in our cities.

That is to say, there is no organized underground strategy to redirect the energies of the church. There are no clandestine meetings in progress among the clergy who have been frustrated by the unwillingness of denominations to fund experimental ministries or take courageous stands.

The most recent example of an underground church in modern history was the Confessing Church that emerged in Germany to oppose the established church's capitulation to Adolf Hitler. Dietrich Bonhoeffer, a young leader of the Confessing Church, took active part in the German resistance when World Ward II was in progress. Finally, he was executed for his part in a plot to assassinate Hitler. The circumstance which produced the Confessing Church was the utter moral bankruptcy of the mass of German Christians during the 1930s.

To be perfectly honest, there is a growing number of American Christians today who feel that our country is in the midst of a period parallel to that of Germany in the 1930s. Such Christians see in Vietnam an involvement not unlike German participation in the Spanish Civil War. The relative failure of American society to deal with its domestic crises is also cited. Also important is that the most affluent nation in the history of man seems to have little conscience about the incredible poverty facing Asia, Africa, and Latin America.

Such parallels are dangerous. They smack of paranoia and a conspiratorial view of things. But it does seem at times that America is immobilized, that it is moving toward a new McCarthyism, and that it has no real commitment to racial and social justice. . . .

One thing is sure. There may well be a real underground church in the future. If so, there will be no publicity because the true underground works in secret. Such a church would emerge if Christ called us to resist American policies in the name of Christian obedience. It would emerge if the steepled churches of today, that are above ground, failed to find their own souls soon enough.

—Stephen C. Rose, "Underground Church?" *Renewal*, October 1967, p. 23.

Centers of renewal in the United States.

The winds of renewal have also reached the United States. The centers here are so numerous and so diverse that little more can be done than to give a brief description of a few that may be considered typical. The Faith at Work Movement under the impetus of Samuel Shoemaker was one of the earliest that caught the modern spirit of renewal and has continued to be one of the strongest. This movement places an emphasis both on personal relationship to Jesus Christ and on concern for the social situation in which one lives. It carries out its work primarily in two ways, through conferences held in various parts of the country and through a printed publication, *Faith at Work*.

The Yokefellow Movement was founded by Elton Trueblood, who through this movement and through his numerous writings has become one of the most influential men in church renewal, either in the United States or in the entire world. The purpose of Yokefellow is to seek commitment in depth for the renewal of the church. Self-discovery and commitment are sought through small fellowship groups. Central in its approach are the five disciplines: Daily prayer, Daily scripture, Regular worship, Money and Time, and Witness. Week-end retreats in various centers and conferences along with small groups are the primary means used in seeking a deeper life in Christ.

Laity Lodge, seventy miles west of San Antonio, Texas, is sponsored by the H. E. Butt Foundation. It is interdenominational in approach. Until recently Keith Miller, an Episcopalian, was the director. The emphasis here is almost completely on personal spiritual renewal. Conferences are held each week-end throughout the summer and on numerous week-ends during the winter. Recently Paul Tournier was a resource leader for a week-end.

The Laymen's Movement was founded in 1921 and in 1951 established Wainwright House in Rye, New York, as its headquarters. The major thrust of this movement is to seek to relate the Gospel to an individual's business life. This is done through seminars, retreats, and personal groups. A very fine course of study was published under the title, *Living My Religion on My Job.* This movement was also instrumental in initiating the interdenominational observance of Laymen's Sunday, establishing the Meditation Room at the United Nations, and the Prayer Room in the Capital Building in Washington.

Pendle Hill, a center for study and contemplation sponsored by Quakers, is unique in that its emphasis is on education and the new life. The courses deal with the faith and practice of the Society of Friends, the Bible, theology, and devotion. Strangely no examinations are given and no degrees are awarded. The primary purpose is to give guidance and to live with the person during his own personal spiritual quest.

Packard Manse is "an ecumenical center working for the renewal of the Church and the visible unity of all men in the one Lord." On the staff is a Baptist minister, an Episcopal priest, and a Catholic. This makes Packard Manse probably the only ecumenical center in the United States with a religiously integrated Protestant-Catholic staff. In addition to conferences and seminars the Manse provides facilities for groups, families, and individuals who wish to pursue their own study or reflection.

—Findley B. Edge, "Renewal Movements in Contemporary Protestantism," *Review and Expositor* 64:192–93.

A catalog of new forms.

From the theological premise that the burning point of God's work is the secular present, it is a short step to a new ecclesiological posture. . . .

One cannot blueprint or forecast with precision what these new forms will be, for their birth is situational; they emerge when faithful men participate in the secular flow, relating faith and facts in a specific context. At best, one can suggest some "parables" or "paradigmatic clues" as to the direction we must go.

1. Some parables cited (and proposals for redirection rising from them) suggest that the heritage and resources of the church be grafted onto those

places and people in the world which show evidence of power and promise, on the one hand, or anguish and need, on the other. The growth of "chaplaincies," "missions," "little congregations," and "vocational groups" in business, shopping centers, education, government, and the leisure and entertainment world are clues to the former. The hospital chaplain, the lay "lifeline" team, and the chaplain to the city's "night people" are examples of the latter. . . .

2. Another parable of relevance is the community of ordered withdrawal. Within sight of the secular stream by way of the concerns uppermost to its constituents, such a community as this is a life together of reflection and healing. In this spectrum we find the European and American evangelical academies. . . .

3. The ad hoc group or task force brought into being around an issue that cries out for Christian ministration is ranked high by new formers. Of limited life-span, tailored to contextual immediacies and capable of traveling with light institutional baggage, it fits in especially well with the flexibility and relevance prized by the critic of older forms.

4. Very recent thought on the restructuring of the church has moved from the specifics of chaplaincies, academies, and task forces to a consideration of total strategy. Taking as a new fundamental unit of human community in an urban world, the "zone humaine" or metropolitan area, reformers are striving to spell out the shape of mission commensurate with it. . . .

5. For one breed of renewer, the foregoing proposals still smack too heavily of "churchiness." To "bring" the church to the world by way of chaplain or academy or over-all planning with the concomitant Bibles, prayers, and religious words represents the "Constantinian turn of mind" bent upon re-ecclesiasticizing the secular arena.

There are two schools of thought on alternative approaches. One declares that the first step in restructuring the church is the act of participation in the places and among the people of ferment and anguish. . . .

A second school of thought finds even this counsel tainted with hidden churchy designs. The logic of a secular God leads rather to an unabashedly religionless Christianity and hence a totally secular conception of mission unencumbered by the grand descent of a "deus ex machina." What this means ecclesiologically is that the secular shapes that God has brought into being for his secular tasks *are* the church. To participate in a movement or event that is in the current of rehumanization is to "join" the church. . . .

6. Implicit in the five preceding designs for restructuring is an emphasis enjoying strong support in recent years throughout the church: the rediscovery of the laity. Set in the midst of the world, the laity become the logical candidate for the cutting edge of secular mission. The critic may, in fact, describe the laity *as* the new form of the church. . . .

7. There is one other ecclesiological posture allied to the criticism of the local church which is, strictly speaking, not a "new form" but yet is part of the total spectrum of redirection. It, too, is a re-formation of the church in

terms of its secular mission. Yet it may look like the local church in that it may gather in residential community, include families, and even have a conventional church building. What marks it as part of the critical spectrum is the limitation of its membership to those who have clear secular accreditation. It is a congregation but is "stripped down to fighting weight," having "cut the fat out," and restored "integrity of membership." It is a "company of the committed," including in its ranks only those who are willing to accept the strenuous demands of a common discipline and the vigor of deep participation in secular mission.

—Gabriel Fackre, "The Crisis of the Congregation: A Debate," *Voluntary Associations: A Study of Groups in Free Societies*, ed. D. B. Robertson, pp. 283–86.

V

The External
Renewal of the Church

Some Emerging Strategies
of the Journey Outward

A. INTERNAL RENEWAL MEANS EXTERNAL MISSION

Private prayer leads to public action.

Just as we are committed to being on an inward journey for all of time, so are we committed to being on an outward journey, so that the inner and the outer become related to one another and one has meaning for the other and helps to make the other possible. If this does not happen, then those who are critical of the contemplative man are rightly so. If engagement with ourselves does not push back horizons so that we see neighbors we did not see before, then we need to examine the appointment kept with self. If prayer does not drive us out into some concrete involvement at a point of the world's need, then we must question prayer. If the community of our Christian brothers does not deliver us from false securities and safe opinions and known ways, then we must cry out against that community, for it betrays.

—Elizabeth O'Connor, *Journey Inward, Journey Outward*, p. 28.

1. The Unresolved Debate: What Is God Doing in the World?

Look at what God is doing in the world.

Here we seem to be at the heart of the theological problem of the forms of the missionary presence of the church in the world. What are the marks of

God's presence in the world? How can we read 'the signs of the times'?
How can we undertake the perilous task of judging what God is doing in the
events of our time? How can we determine the ways in which the church is
called to be present with Christ in what he is doing in the critical events of
the day? How can we be given sufficient freedom from the relativities of
history to witness to Christ's purpose for history?

—Colin Williams, *What in the World?*, p. xx.

God moves in mysterious ways among the unbelievers.

There is, however, an authentic secularism, singularly unpopular in religious America these days. It is critical of the church not so much because
of what the church professes as because of its retreat from the struggle for
freedom and justice, its fear of the truth whenever the truth does not correspond to its creed, its loss of the sense of the beauty and the terror of
natural life. There are secularists who speak disparagingly of the church
because they know very well what the Lordship of Christ means, but find
themselves unable to accept the relationship between this Christ and the
bland, middle-class Christianity which the church represents to them. Usually
unawares, although sometimes quite consciously, they propagate the gospel
and demonstrate its relevance in the idiom of the arts, the sciences, in the
field of politics and human relations. They often misunderstand and distort
the meaning of the faith, but despite themselves, some of these people are
caught up in and used by the action of God for reconciliation.

—Gayraud S. Wilmore, *The Secular Relevance of the Church*, pp. 25–26.

Signs of Christ are in the secular.

In Latin America the churches to-day are facing a major crisis brought on
by a major transformation that is occurring in the attitude of the masses.
After centuries of mass despair in which the vast majority assumed that
there was for them no hope of meaningful participation in the benefits of
life in this world, there is now taking place what can only be described as a
'secular conversion'—a turning from secular despair to secular hope; from
resignation under injustice to a determination to build a society where all
men will have a new dignity and a freer participation in a more truly human
community. For the churches the question is: how is this 'secular conversion'
to be treated? Is this a sign of Christ's presence, calling the churches into the
struggle for this new hope? During the period of mass despair the Protestant
churches have said to the people—and properly—'In the world there is for
you despair and exclusion; but in the community of the church you will
receive the acceptance the world refuses you, the dignity the world denies
you, and the spiritual guidance and community that will be for you a fore-
taste of that life in the kingdom of God for which you were created.' But
now, in the emerging new situation of secular hope, what are the churches

to say? Is this now a call from Christ to the church to turn its life out into the mainstream of the world's struggle? Is this a call which says 'In the years of your despair, I called you out from the world to fashion for myself a people who know my grace and are formed by love; but now the hour has struck for you to see the signs of new hope that I am giving to my people in the world; and to join me in the midst of the struggle, interpreting that hope, struggling to keep it free, and helping the people to know me as their Lord and Saviour in the midst of the events of their daily life'?

—Colin Williams, *Faith in a Secular Age*, pp. 110–11.

2. Engagement with Culture—The Secular Setting of Mission

Corporate worship is rehearsal.

Our assembled, corporate worship is, so to speak, rehearsal. Here on Sunday at eleven we worship God in practice session *among ourselves* in order that we may more skillfully worship him the rest of the week scattered among other people. Liturgy has been called the family activity of the church. Here we adore God and intercede for the world before him encouraged and guided and inspired by our fellow Christians. The rest of the week it is our ministry, as the people of God, to adore him and intercede for the world *in the midst of the world.*

—Frederick K. Wentz, *The Layman's Role Today*, p. 36.

Two changes are necessary for a redemptive approach.

Any redemptive approach by the church in the community in transition will involve at least two changes: (1) The church must decide that it wants to be more than a reflection of a community where everyone is the same. (2) The church needs to decide that it is willing to make whatever changes are necessary in its structure to reach the people and help them to develop. These are not easy questions. At the heart of the question is the role of the laity in the church. Until all of the people of God are willing to become aware of the nature of the problem and to discuss prayerfully what the will of God is for the church at this particular time and place, there can be no solution.

—Kenneth Chafin, *Help! I'm a Layman*, p. 93.

Climbing Jacob's ladder.

If God is on the second floor and mankind as a whole is on the first floor, the church should be running the stairs between (to use a homely illustration). Actually, too many Christians and much too much of the church's organized life remain on the staircase landing—out of touch, knowing God only as footsteps above and knowing human need only as so much sweat and outcry below. What is badly needed is that Christians shall constantly be moving up to God, thrusting themselves more profoundly into their Christian resources of Bible study, prayer, sacraments, spiritual retreat, and discipline. *And at the same time* they should be hurrying down with healing for all the open sores to be found along man's daily concourse and for all the hidden abscesses in human hearts and minds.

The church's life is a rhythm or dialectic. Its members go up and come down, move in and then out, retreat and attack, withdraw only to penetrate the world once more. One's picture of the church should draw it as stretched thin between God's Word and the world, showing it as people moving in alternation between the cross and human need.

—Frederick K. Wentz, *The Layman's Role Today*, p. 33.

Not should we be involved, but how should we be involved.

The question today is not *whether or not* the Churches should be involved in the life and ways of an urban world whose paradoxes and problems, complexities and imbalances are brought to focus in the modern phenomenon called Metropolis. The question is *how* they should be involved. If by some strange power today Churches could change their nature or obliterate the historic fact of their call to mission so that they could be indifferent to the world, they would still find themselves being involved by the world in the very processes they would like to avoid, because they are institutional in character. For in times of revolutionary change, indifference and neutrality, indecision and inaction on the part of an individual or institution are impracticable. Sides must be taken and plans of action followed. But what side to take and what plan of action to follow becomes the critical question for the responsible individual as well as for responsible Churches.

—Jesse McNeil, *Mission in Metropolis*, p. 10.

3. The Strategy of Penetration

Evangelism and social action are the same.

How does a church organize its life for outreach into the community? The first step is a negative one; that is, to resist the temptation of keeping so much activity going inside the walls that there is no time to look outward. The second step is the development of an awareness of parish responsibility— a continuing sense of identification with the common life of the geographical community in which it is set. At this point, evangelism and social action become the same process. There is no more potent evangelistic witness in a community than the church's concern and action on behalf of justice or in the meeting of some critical human need. We must remember that we prate a good deal about love and compassion and justice. Therefore, when the opportunity to exercise these virtues in a community crisis is ignored, the silent witness is deafening. What has been wrong with much of our social action projects in the church is the same that has characterized our evangelism efforts. The projects have been short term and often highly hortatory about somebody else's sins. A community is not fooled by highly publicized efforts to be the Good Samaritan on the corner. If the people of a congregation are not regularly identified with school problems, community planning, recreation, discrimination in housing, and identified as completely concerned about the people who suffer because of these problems, then no one is impressed by high-sounding calls to citizenship from the pulpit one Sunday before election.

—Robert W. Spike, *In But Not Of The World*, pp. 79–80.

Disperse—penetrate—identify.

"You are the salt of the earth," Christ tells his disciples. Obviously the Christian's saltness comes from Christ. But salt serves its purpose as it loses itself in the soup or permeates the meat. Here is the emphasis upon dispersion. Laymen must scatter themselves and enter thoroughly into all parts of the world to which they minister. They will want to identify themselves with the world's causes and preoccupations, expending themselves as they enter into the struggles and serve the needs of their many neighbors, immersed in all kinds of secular stew—politics and civic affairs and business enterprises and mass entertainment and vacation projects and youth activities and the rest of it. Ultimately our home is in heaven, but our role on this earth carries us into eager participation in this world and close association with secular-minded people. When salt is put on meat it disappears—or else it isn't working! Better than light, this figure of salt represents the quality of penetration and identification with the world.

—Frederick K. Wentz, *The Layman's Role Today*, p. 113.

A catapult to hurl Christians into the world.

Our definition of the church ought to describe it as a fellowship of believers who assemble and then disperse, moving out from preaching and sacraments to carry the Word to the world. The church must be a catapult that hurls Christ-bearers into every distant corner of human society.

The Reformation raised as one of its great battle cries this phrase: the priesthood of all believers. This meant that each Christian is his own priest, standing directly before God without an intermediary. And it also meant that the church is a mutal ministry—each Christian caring for his fellow churchmen. Today we must add that this priesthood is the whole church as one royal priesthood functioning in behalf of the whole human race.

—Frederick K. Wentz, *The Layman's Role Today*, p. 39.

With Christ outside the church building.

There is something about the building and the structure of the meeting we conduct which intimidates the lost man. Therefore, if the people do not go to the church, the church should go to the people.

There is some fear on the part of church members that the gospel might not make it without a certain number of religious props. I spoke to a Saturday night youth rally which met in a gymnasium. There were two parts to the program. First, a folk music group from one of the churches was to entertain by singing folk songs. Then I was to speak to them on the theme, "Christ and the Teenager." The leader was a little embarrassed with the arrangement and suggested that to help make the transition between the folk music and my talk, a few choruses could be sung. However, I requested that he introduce the folk singers and me at the beginning of the program in order that I could follow them without interruption.

In this service I realized that many people do not think the Christian religion applies to people who pat their feet, clap their hands or yell. They think that before the Christian religion can be presented they have to be worked into a certain mood. I think when Paul said, "I am not ashamed of the gospel: it is the power of God for salvation to everyone who has faith" (Romans 1:16 RSV), he was not suggesting that the gospel has power only when we create a certain psychological condition. The gospel which we preach speaks realistically to people wherever they are.

As a part of this effort to give a corporate witness to the non-church community, the church should find a neutral place. A school gym where basketball is played, or a stadium where football is played, sometimes becomes a good place for the preaching of the gospel. Even if there were a sanctuary large enough to seat all the people, it would probably still be wise for Billy Graham to conduct his services in public places.

Often if a sermon does not have to be followed by a hymn or benediction, but can be followed by questions from the group, an atmosphere of openness and freedom results with which to examine the claims of the Christian religion. Strangely, the good news proclamation of God through Jesus Christ has come to be a religious talk, given to some religious people in a church house. The last thought in our mind is that someone might get interested enough to stand up and ask a question. The parlor of a fraternity house or a college dormitory is a good place for the church to give a witness.

—Kenneth Chafin, *Help! I'm a Layman*, pp. 107–8.

We meet to disperse.

The point here is that the church exists always in *two phases*. Its constant rhythm is one of *Assembly* and *Dispersion*, just as Christ alternatingly urged his followers, "Come unto me" and "go into all the world" (Matt. 28:19, John 17:18). Only a filmstrip could adequately show the church as assembling and dispersing and assembling again unceasingly. We assemble in order to worship, study the Bible, pray, and have intense Christian fellowship. We disperse into our many places in the world in order to serve, to do our work, and to fellowship with these other people.

—Frederick K. Wentz, *The Layman's Role Today*, p. 34.

B. ORGANIZING FOR RENEWAL—
REACHING OUT FROM THE RESIDENTIAL BASE

A Christian style of life in the world.

This distinction between "instituted" and "prudential" means of grace would seem to be useful to guide us in our attempt to evaluate the experiments which today are trying to discover the forms of church life that will express the Church's mission. The stress on "instituted" means is a warning against any restructuring which threatens to jettison those means of grace given to the Church by Christ as permanent and essential characteristics of her life. This we have already discussed in connection with the "marks of the Church." Now the stress on "prudential" means takes us a step further by reminding us that the Church must always develop forms of life which will provide the ways by which these "means of grace" may produce a Christian style of life as the believers participate in the particular structures of the life of their own age. The "prudential means of grace" are changeable, because they must be related to the changing needs of the time; *but they are not optional.* A living Church must be seeking for the forms of life which will provide for the presence of Christ with his people at the particular places where the life of their time calls forth a particular form of Christian obedience.

—Colin Williams, *Where in the World?*, pp. 62–63.

The local Church is a creative center for mission.

The problem, of course, is that many denominational leaders have tended to give up on the local church as a front-line mission. They have ambivalent feelings about it. They use it. They manipulate it. It is the object of all their promotion and programs. But rarely have they trusted it. Rarely have they said to the local church: "Obviously you know the needs of your community better than we. You know what is most needing to be done. You go ahead with the mission as you see it. We trust you. We know the Holy Spirit will guide you. We leave you to him. God bless you! If we can help you with our resources, let us know!"

Quite a different thing from the concept of congregations as merely "outlets" for a vast organization, or as the lowest level in a chain of command. And yet, when they are put on their honor to do it, some of the most creative thinking in the whole church's life comes out of local congregations. That is, when officials and ministers alike make it plain that they want such creative contribution and participation.

—Arthur A. Rouner, Jr., *The Free Church Today: New Life for the Whole Church*, p. 116.

A word to the wise from the building committee.

In our church building a shift ought to take place *from "the church at the center" to an addition to the new housing developments of our society.* In our buildings too it must become clear that the church has "no permanent city" here. She is passing through and lives as a stranger in the world. She is a *paroikia* (from which our word "parish" has been derived), a settlement outside the homeland, therefore only "added." Her house can be nothing but an addition, an annex. Perhaps one large room in a big new apartment building?

—J. C. Hoekendijk, *The Church Inside Out*, pp. 82–84.

What is a good location for a city church?

There is a fairly standard question that churchmen invariably ask me: "So you're a city planner. Well, tell me, what *is* a good location for a church from your vantage point?"

This question is asked for two reasons. First, a great many people in regional and national denominational offices are very much caught up in the demands of selecting sites for new churches and for financing the early stages of their operations. The second reason is that church people, like most other citizens, have a limited perspective on city planning and tend to see it strictly in its role of helping to determine the locations of things.

Usually I can parry this question, especially when it is posed as a general one.

"There are so many variables that it's hard to make any useful generalizations."

—Perry L. Norton, *Church and Metropolis*, p. 87.

Give us more smaller churches, not larger congregations.

A denomination will achieve a deeper penetration into the total population with many smaller churches than with a few larger congregations.

Larger churches tend to be more selective in their appeal and tend (there are many exceptions!) to draw lightly from over a large area while small congregations tend to reach more people in a specific area. Furthermore, the larger number of churches provides a larger number and a greater variety of points of contact with the unchurched.

A good illustration of this is to contrast the slow growth of urban Methodism, which tends toward large congregations, and the rapid growth of the Wesleyan and Free Methodist churches and the Church of the Nazarene (all three, like Methodism, developed out of the Wesleyan tradition), which tend toward small congregations.

Thus if growth is the goal churchmen should plan for many small congregations; if a broad and varied program is the goal they should plan for fewer but larger congregations.

—Lyle E. Schaller, *Planning for Protestantism in Urban America*, p. 142.

Basic guidelines for church structures.

1. The structure needs to be described so that there is *openness to change*—a fundamental characteristic of modern life which the church as institution must share with the institutions of the world. In discussing church structure, however, it is essential to affirm that the church is not simply responsive to the changing shapes of the world. The church's structure must express not only servant presence in the structures of the world but also the converting and renewing claims of Christ. So, for example, the church should not simply follow national boundaries, but is called to express the mission of the community of Christ to break through such limitations.

2. The structure needs to have places where decisions are made concerning the strategy of mission. The description of order in a document for a united church should not spell out in detail the variety of structures for missionary presence, for these will be subject to constant change. But it does need to spell out the way in which decisions will be made in the church through representative bodies that carry responsibility for the structural life of the church. A pattern of accountability is essential so that it is clear who is accountable to whom.

3. The structure needs to take into account the fact that the churches' forms are in process of change from a basically single-form system of the rural past to the multiple-form pattern of the present, and the representation systems that are devised must reflect the realities of what now is as well as the form of what is coming to be.

—Colin W. Williams, *The Church*, p. 161.

A pluralistic society calls for a pluralistic Church structure.

Although it is clear that an infinite variety is possible in the structuring of witnessing communities, it is still possible to suggest several basic *types* of structure that correspond to the types of functions which they serve. One type is that of the *family structure*. This structure is basically residential in character and sees as its function the service of a particular segment of God's world in which it is located. Such a structure needs to be small enough so that solidarity in the service of the larger community is possible among those who feel called into a family of mutual trust and service. Another type is that of the *structure of permanent availability*. This structure is basically oriented around long-term tasks and seeks to make services available to people whenever and however they need them without necessarily trying to involve them in the life of that community. A third type is that of the *task force structure*. This structure is formed around a particular need or function and goes out of existence when that need has been accomplished.

—Letty M. Russell, *Christian Education in Mission*, pp. 40–41.

Helping people in need is a form of witnessing.

In a seminary class a respected professor asked the students why they thought Jesus healed the sick and fed the hungry. The entire class replied, "To prove He was the Messiah." The teacher sadly commented, "Do you suppose that because He loved people and was moved by their need and had within Himself the capacity to meet those needs, that He did it because He was God?" For me this was a broadening of my understanding of the compassion of God for His creation. It planted the seed for a broadened understanding of my role as a Christian and my church's role as an institution in a ministry to the needs of people.

The church, and especially the church in a community of transition, lives in the midst of needs. And yet, sometimes it is completely oblivious to these needs. The lay person's frustration at the church's self-centeredness is expressed in the question one man asked, "Besides getting new members, what is the church for?" This was a Christian who was the principal of a junior high in an impoverished community. Because he was moved by the needs he saw there, he wondered why his church could not focus some of its attention upon those needs.

In most communities there is illiteracy, delinquency, unemployment, the breakdown of family life, one parent families, alcoholism, addiction—all sorts of human ills. Many churches are now giving serious thought to using their building, their financial resources, and the talents of their lay people to reach out in love to meet some of these needs.

—Kenneth Chafin, *Help! I'm a Layman*, pp. 109–10.

A demonstration of concern—how one Church responds.

Each Sunday morning following the sermon we had a brief period called the "concerns of the church" in which the minister presented to the congregation (and invited them to announce) those public issues and social problems where our energies and time could be expended. In the summer of 1963 when the National Council of Churches helped to organize teams of young people to assist with voter registration in Mississippi, I urged the congregation one Sunday morning to bring canned goods and food packages to be sent to the Mississippi project. In the week that followed they brought half a truckload of food to the church. During the Selma, Alabama, crisis in March of 1965 we took a special offering on Sunday morning to underwrite the expenses of representatives from our own congregation and students from Perkins School of Theology who went from Dallas to join with others in the Selma march to Montgomery. That same Sunday I invited the congregation to meet me on the church parking lot at one-thirty, whence we went downtown to join with several thousand other white and Negro citizens who that afternoon marched peacefully through the main streets of the city. It was a demonstration of our concern for and our support of those who stood in for us in Alabama. About forty members of the congregation were in the Dallas march and four represented us in Selma.

Let me hasten to acknowledge that these attempts at Northaven were only fragmentary breakthroughs in the revolutionary style of servanthood that must be required of institutional churches. The public forums and concerns of the church were probably so infrequent and marginal in impact that they could hardly have justified the budget, building, staff, and superstructure needed to maintain them.

—W. A. Holmes, *Tomorrow's Church: A Cosmopolitan Community*, pp. 155–56.

C. STRATEGIES OF MISSIONARY OBEDIENCE: SELECTED EXAMPLES

1. The Strange New Shapes of Mission

Shaped to fit the world's needs.

Out of this context, this viewpoint insists that the present structures of the church are so dominated by the church's surrender to its own worldly security, and that the church is so imprisoned within the expensive facades of buildings that relate to men only in a very limited portion of their life, that she can find renewal only as she surrenders these securities and pours herself out upon the world, careless of her own safety or reputation or wealth, allowing *the forms* of her renewed life to grow around all *the shapes of worldly need*. The signs of such renewal are seen by this viewpoint at points of discontinuity with the structures of our present congregational life. The signs of the new shape are seen forming

> around a Yale theological student who goes out to gather together white and NEGRO volunteers to give their summers in a concerted attempt to work amongst those NEGRO students whose hope has died and whose despair is revealed in their academic failure, their drop out from school, and their unemployed status;

around those who struggle amidst hatred, fear and persecution to find new forms of integrated life across the terrible barrier of race conflict;

around worker priests, unsupported by and even thrust out by the church authorities;

around a dialogue situation with the world in coffee shops; around small Christian groups involved in renewal action in the tragic areas of urban life—with narcotics, or in political action or urban renewal;

around small "koinonia" groups gathered together to wrestle with the problems of their vocational life and their *being* the church in their work of the world;

around a lay training center seeking for forms of witness in the areas of modern culture lost to the church.

Such new forms of life have only tenuous connections with the present congregational structure; and to some critics it even seems that we cannot hope for a direct transition from our present congregational pattern to the new shapes the church's life must take.

—Colin Williams, *Where in the World?*, pp. 59–60.

Great discoveries of a ministering church.

Many churches in transitional areas have decided that their only alternative is to minister to the community. Once this decision has been made they have given themselves to finding ways to ministering which are more effective. In these churches several wonderful discoveries have been made.

(1) *There are more people than the pastor.* The traditional approach to the ministry of the church has viewed the pastor as the one who performs the ministry and the people as those who support the work. The discovery of the laity as the church's greatest resource for ministry is the greatest discovery of this day. These churches which have decided that they really want to do something for God and for the people have discovered talent, interest, and a commitment far beyond their expectation. *The hope of the ministering church is the informed, inspired, committed layman. . . .*

(2) *There are more days than Sunday.* The church is being strangled to death by its preoccupation with one day of the week. So much of its interest and activity has been limited to one building and one day that the impression is left that this is the only place and time God is at work. Many congregations have discovered that by moving into the week-days with activities, better use can be made of buildings and leadership, and more people can be reached in an effective ministry.

(3) *Sometimes a witness begins by meeting some need.* This is not new to Christianity. Jesus fed the hungry and healed the sick and His compassion shown in the deed became a witness for the Father. The community in transition has many people with many needs. There are students who are having a hard time staying in school. There are families with serious problems. There are children with no place to play but in the streets. There are

mothers who bear the whole responsibility for the rearing of a family of children. There are unemployed and unemployable. There are juveniles who are in trouble and need help.

Sometimes these problems are so intense that it is impossible for an individual really to believe that the church cares for him if it is not interested in his problem. Many churches have established an effective ministry with groups they had been unable to reach by first meeting some obvious need in the life of the person.

—Kenneth Chafin, *Help! I'm a Layman*, pp. 97–98.

2. Coffeehouse Ministry

What's the difference in a Christian coffeehouse?

In the first place, the motivation is different. In a Church-sponsored coffeehouse the goal is not to make money or even to meet expenses. Virtually all these operations are heavily subsidized; most have financial problems in maintaining a sufficiently sound financial base to continue in business. The motive is to reach out to people on behalf of the Church, to help people relate to one another in a fellowship deeper than the glad hand, and to provide a context within which honest confrontation, discussion, and acceptance can take place. The conditions of urban life make it difficult for these experiences to happen by chance, and the Church, through its involvement in dialogue ministry, acts as an enabler.

Second, a Christian coffeehouse is different from a commercial venture because it involves a committed group of people who, beyond manning the coffeepots, are trained to initiate discussions, draw people out of their self-conscious in-dwelling, and express their own faith in the conversations which ensue. One coffeehouse with which the writers are familiar calls its waiter-participants "servants." For several months prior to the opening of this particular ministry, the servants studied books together, exposed to one another the deeply personal dimensions of their own faith, splashed paint on walls, and built tables and benches for the store they had rented for their venture. When the coffeehouse opened each agreed to serve for a given period of hours each week. This particular servant group continues to meet together for two hours a week. They study the Bible and books of theology; they share their experiences in the coffeehouse, they discuss problems that have arisen and develop policy for the ministry.

A third difference between the commercial and the Christian coffeehouse is this: in the house committed to ministry, decisions regarding procedure are made by a board consisting of the waiter-participants and those who are part of the life of the establishment. In practice this has usually meant that Christian ministry has been the presupposition on which policy decisions are made. Pressures such as meeting expenses or weeding out "undesirables," which might become the basis for decisions in a program for profit, are measured against the concern for witness and service.

—Richard E. Moore and Duane L. Day, *Urban Church Breakthrough*, pp. 113–14.

Lessons learned around a coffee cup.

There is now sufficient experience in dialogue ministry to permit a measure of generalization: First, the "teaching" ministry that takes place within the context of dialogue is essentially undogmatic in nature. Doctrinal statements are not offered as answers to those who ask questions. Explicit statements of faith are usually preceded by a nonargumentative, "This is what I believe." And yet it is obvious to all who serve and who come that the motivation of the coffeehouse is grounded in the Christian faith, and that the waiter-participants are engaged in a servant discipline related to this Christian faith. . . .

Second, the quality of commitment of the waiter-participants—the servant group—is crucial in developing a significant ministry. In virtually all the dialogue ministries, including other than coffeehouse ministries, there is a supportive lay group that works with the clergyman. In some ministries no ordained clergyman is even present. The entire program is directed by the laity of the Church. Servants must develop a group identity, must understand the purposes of the ministry, and must be so informed and secure regarding their own faith that they can express it with confidence even in face of attack. A period of training, an explicit discipline, and a continuing group life are necessary if the servants are to minister effectively.

Third, in a majority of the dialogue ministries there is a concern for art and the artist. The Church has seldom known how to relate to the artist, even when it has tried. Sometimes it has ignored him, sometimes censured him; sometimes it has tried to use him—and only too often has alienated him. In the person-centered ministry as exemplified in the coffeehouse, the Church has had moderate success in establishing common cause with poets, painters, and those who make music. . . .

Finally, and most important, it is clear that genuine community and commitment can develop through dialogue ministry. People do care about others they have come to know through discussion and argument; people with whom they have shared artistic and aesthetic pleasures. In the dialogue ministry reconciliation across racial lines, between age groups, and among economic and social levels has occurred. There are moments akin to worship as the group celebrates the sacrament of life. One young adult finds absolution and acceptance through informal confession at the coffee table; another individual struggles through doubt to a faith that works. Because dialogue ministries in the world of leisure create the climate in which experiences like these can happen, the ministry is amply justified.

—Richard E. Moore and Duane L. Day, *Urban Church Breakthrough*, pp. 117–18.

Coffeehouse Church—"hippie" style.

"Go see Bruce, man. He can help you." This is the whispered advice a confused group of Atlanta residents give to one another when they are in trouble. Who are they? They are the thousands of young hippies or would-be hippies living in a 165-block area of the city, and Bruce Donnelly, 27, is the pastor of Atlanta's only coffeehouse-church—the Twelfth Gate, located in a sprawling green house with a red door.

"Basically," Donnelly said, "we are trying to minister to the 18 to 25-year-old group in our neighborhood. There are about 25,000 in this area." Probably less than 3,000 would be considered hippies, teenagers who have virtually alienated themselves from "straight society" and who are characterized generally by drugs and poor health.

The Twelfth Gate, a three-story frame house with peeling paint, houses a church. But Donnelly doesn't like to call it that. "The kids," he said, "are down on church."

There are no crosses or pictures or other symbols of religion. Instead, there are cigarette machines on the dingy front porch, incense burners in corners, televisions in small rooms at the top of narrow, splintered stairs. Entertainers sit on wooden stools under colored lights on the first floor, while young customers relax there or in the psychedelic shop and crafts room upstairs.

Donnelly's approach is as unorthodox as his church.

"You don't ever preach to them about the right or wrong of what they're doing. You go to the root of their problem," Donnelly said, folding his slender fingers together.

"A lot of them have illusions about life," he said. "They want to take drugs to find out who they are. The question isn't who you are, but what you are going to do with yourself.

"My aim," Donnelly said, "is to bring them to that point, where they make that decision."

The Twelfth Gate's ministry is geared to giving confused young people the chance to decide what they will do with themselves. Open every night except Monday, the Twelfth Gate offers a variety of programs seldom, if ever, found in other churches.

"We have a craft shop where people who make things can sell them. We have classes going here—the parables of Jesus just ended, and we have a Zen workshop just started—and they're all taught by volunteers," Donnelly said.

"Then," he continued, "I talked to a fellow today, and we're going to be setting up a radio station just in our area, basically as an information thing."

On Friday and Saturday nights, "tourist nights," the Twelfth Gate offers folk music entertainment and coffeehouse food. Sunday, there is a worship service between 12:30 and 2:00 p.m.

"We start them at 12:30 because nobody gets up any earlier," Donnelly explained. "Then, at 5 we have what we call a 'Sunday Strategy Session.' We talk about what our problems are and see how we can solve them."

As a result of one session, the Twelfth Gate, in cooperation with the Fulton County Medical Society, set up a medical clinic for the hippies. Begun May 1, the clinic is open two nights a week and is staffed by volunteer physicians. Regular Twelfth Gate customers take care of the paper work and screen the patients.

They also decided to set up an employment agency.

"Some of them have trouble getting jobs," Donnelly said, "because they have long hair. And some of them just have trouble."

The Twelfth Gate first opened near Grace Methodist Church in November, 1966. Donnelly, an ordained Methodist minister, was youth director for Grace Church. "Cecil Myers, the pastor, came to me and said, 'Bruce, why don't you do something for these kids? Why don't you open a coffeehouse?'

"At first I said, 'Nah. A coffeehouse? It'll never work.'

"You see," he explained, "in '59, while I was in school, three coffeehouses folded in Atlanta. There never has been a successful, independent coffeehouse in this city.

"But I got a book, and found out there are over 1,000 church-sponsored coffeehouses in the United States. I didn't have anything else to do, so I opened the Twelfth Gate."

Donnelly and some of his 'kids' swept out an old, church-owned home and put in pool tables, ping-pong tables, juke boxes and television sets.

"It was a great setup; everything was free. People used to wander in, put their own pizzas in the oven, and everything. We had kids running all over the house," he said.

"By April and May, after opening in November, we had 200 to 300 young people a night, and we were only open on Thursday and Friday nights. We were all over the place, flowing out the doors and over the front porch."
—Pat Thigpen, "12th Gate in Atlanta: Hippies, Southern Style," *Home Missions*, August 1968, pp. 21–22.

3. The World of Art

Christ and the fine arts.

During a year of study in New York I went several times to watch the single production *An Evening's Frost*. A narrator and three actors presented the life and philosophy of Robert Frost through his poetry. They did it magnificently. With no background except the occasional notes of a flute, these four carried the audience to the heights and depths of the experiences of this great American poet. There was laughter and there was crying. There was gaiety and there was seriousness. No one exposed to those three hours will ever get away from Robert Frost.

As I sat in the theater I was saddened by the fact that while we have in our churches tremendous dramatic talent and significant insights to present, we have done so little to use drama to present Jesus Christ in all His power and attractiveness.

Church drama seems to bounce back and forth between two extremes. On the one hand there is the "Biblical Drama" in which a group of people parade around dressed in bathrobes with their heads wrapped in turban towels speaking Old English. On the other hand there is the church drama group which presents a Christmas play so far out that when the local drama critic reviews it he comes to the conclusion that the point of the play was that "Jesus made a mistake in coming in the first place." Somewhere between these two there is a place for the church to call upon the talent of its people, not only in drama, but in journalism, in music, and every area of the arts, to say something to this world about the meaning that comes in life through Jesus Christ.

A small struggling church in mid-town New York City had a splendid choir which did a presentation of the opera, "The Prodigal Son." The place was packed, for here was a Bible story communicated through a medium in which many of these New Yorkers had an interest.

—Kenneth Chafin, *Help! I'm a Layman*, pp. 113–14.

Making the scene at Greenwich Village.

Probably one of the best examples of letting the world write the agenda for the church is that of Judson Memorial Church, located adjacent to the famous Artists' and Writers' Center in Greenwich Village. The church has tried to learn what it means to be a congregation, obedient and faithful, in the midtwentieth century in a highly urbanized setting. Their ministry to the surrounding community has included a study group on Kierkegaard in a Greenwich Village coffeehouse, standing up with teen-age delinquents in court, art exhibits of great impressionistic artists in its own art gallery, discussion of contemporary writers such as Dostoevski and Camus in the Village art studios, publication of its own literary quarterly, *Exodus*, and sponsorship of a center for narcotic addicts at a time when very little was being done by any local agency.

Today the church continues its narcotic program, and the operation of a coffeehouse for teen-agers. It also operates an off-Broadway theater that is held in high regard; fifteen plays are produced each year. It continues to operate its own publishing house, giving many creative young people of the Village an outlet for expression. It operates a dormitory for transient students, both American and international. One of its most effective ministries is the Hall of Issues where artists and writers can express and exhibit their protests while at the same time being called upon to defend their stance. Here the church listens to the world, and from it the world realizes that the church

cares. Many within the Village have become committed worshipers and what the villagers call "card-carrying Christians."
—James F. Bailey, "An Exploding World: What Kind of Church?", *The Baptist Student*, February 1968, pp. 30–31.

4. Ministry in High-Rise Apartments

Guidelines for an apartment-house ministry.

Out of this experiment we see emerging three basic guidelines for an apartment house ministry.

First, the church must take the apartment house dweller seriously. Because of his need for privacy, his mobility, his rootlessness, his distrust of institutional busywork, the apartment dweller often does not find the traditional program of the church very meaningful. It does not meet his needs. Therefore, the church must shape its ministry to the dweller at his point of interest and concern rather than to try to involve him in a pre-planned structure or program.

Second, the church as an agent of reconciliation must be willing to go where people are living—go where people are, for they cannot be expected to come to the church. One reason for the effectiveness of the groups in Kips Bay is that they met where people lived and not in the church recreation hall. The church must leave the institutional walls so that the apartment dweller begins to see the church not as the building on the corner but as the people who meet on Monday evenings in apartment 1-A. For this task laity must be trained to serve as catalytic agents of reconciliation in order to develop groups within the apartment buildings.

Third, the church must meet people around a common need or interest. Our booming population presents certain challenges. It is creating people without roots—people living in constant transition. Therefore, there is real need for small group involvement in which people can meet to share life together. Such involvement might take the form of (1) groups that center in the concerns of work, (2) groups that meet to discuss common issues of the world—poverty, housing, racial differences, (3) groups that meet around community problems, housing, or school issues, or (4) groups that discuss the meaning of life in relationship to film and drama and the arts.
—David C. Rich, "Ministry in High-Rise Apartments," *The Church Creative*, M. Edward Clark et. al., eds., pp. 176–77.

5. Students

Christ and the campus crowd.

The student assumes an increasingly significant role in the life of the nation.

First, the student is grappling with more central issues than ever before. . . .

Second, the student will now commit himself to something. . . .

Third, he is asking the key question. . . .

In the churches we have had basically two attitudes toward the student, neither of which has helped us. First, we have had an idea of containment. We try to baptize the offspring of our own members and hold onto them and mold them as teenagers. We don't hold on to many.

Second, we tend to be afraid of the student who is not already in the church. This is because he has an inquiring mind and is not as sure of everything as his adult friends think they are. He asks embarrassing questions. He voices his doubts aloud. Unfortunately, some of the adults he confronts have a faith that is about as immature as his, and so they are intimidated. The immature student deserves a mature witness about Jesus Christ.

In spite of all of the turmoil going on in the life of the student he is capable of profound religious experience. He is asking the religious question to which the gospel addresses itself. A generation ago students were asking a more academic question, "Can you prove rationally the existence of God?" This is not the question being asked by students anymore. The question now asked is, "Is there any evidence of purpose in life?" God who revealed Himself in Jesus Christ speaks to man's need for a purpose for existence.

In spite of our awareness that the academic community represents a vital aspect in today's America, it is usually the last place where a denomination begins work. It puts less money and less personnel into its effort to get a hearing with the student than any other segment of society. The church that does not speak to the student mind will not speak to tomorrow.

—Kenneth Chafin, *Help! I'm a Layman*, pp. 105–6.

6. Mass Media

The creative use of mass communication.

A very fine church was left a large sum of money with instruction that the money was to be used in some ministry outside the church. In addition to supporting various missionary efforts, the church sponsored a thirty-minute television program. They had an excellent pastor, and he did a splendid job with the program. They decided to conduct a survey concerning the listening audience and found that the program was being listened to by the "already convinced." This is true of the majority of the church efforts with mass media.

The pastor and church members involved in the production of this program were very discouraged and sought various solutions. One prominent individual in communications made the following suggestion, "Pastor, up to now you have been the program. Why don't you *let someone else be the program and you be the sponsor?"* This is what American advertisers do. They choose a program with a desirable audience, and they use that program as a medium by which they introduce their idea for their product.

The group went to work preparing not thirty-minute religious programs, but sixty-second "religious commercials." Instead of using one station, they used all the stations. Instead of running them on Sunday they set them in spots which were considered "prime time." This represents one good creative effort on the part of one church What this one church has done could be multiplied many times by other congregations. . . .

We need to be less preoccupied with what the other churches might think and more occupied with getting a hearing for the gospel. The church is too preoccupied with its own reputation to realize what is at stake in trying to communicate. The church has not been at all reluctant to use the testimony of splendid lay preachers, who are also professional football players. The layman should express his interest in speaking to the world about Christ through the mass media. He should support it with his talent and his money. Otherwise the church will be chained to its traditional and quite often ineffective means.

—Kenneth Chafin, *Help! I'm a Layman*, pp. 110–12.

7. Race

What can Christians do in this critically important area?

Learn the facts about race and racism. Study the nature of prejudice. Through the church, secure recommendations of a few good books on the subject and then buy those books and read them for the topic is far too important not to be informed about. Get acquainted with individuals of other races and classes, making a continuing effort as a Christian to understand each one as a person and to love each one individually as you do yourself. Avoid the paternalism which treats another as a thing and not really as an individual. In conversation shun those categorical stereotypes which subtly downgrade those of other races or nationalities. Follow the wise counsel of James to let your speech be without offense in conveying prejudice, fomenting strife, expressing hate, or encouraging hostility. Bear positive Christian witness concerning the worth of every man before God, remembering that the basic Bible truth concerning the worth of the individual will never be generally applied to the victim of prejudice unless the doctrine is spelled out in concrete and minute detail. Oppose those unprincipled and unscrupulous people in public life who seek to exploit the racial situation for their own political purposes. Support legislators who are faithful to Bible teachings and Christian insights concerning race relations. Encourage your church to preach and practice the truly reconciling gospel of Jesus Christ bearing in mind that there is no other ultimately satisfactory solution to the racial ills that beset mankind. Lend your influence, contribute your money, and give your time for the solution of specific racial problems that arise in the community. Recognize the deep economic and social roots from which racial problems grow and work somehow daily against the survival of those poisonous roots. Take the initiative against the race problem, not against people, remembering that the goal is not increased bitterness but expanding Christian brotherhood.

—Foy Valentine, *The Cross in the Marketplace*, pp. 91–93.

The church of the open door policy.

Many factors must be weighed before a church with an announced policy and practice of open membership, racially, can conclude that Negroes do not want to "integrate." Negroes themselves are widely different in training and affluence, interests and inclinations, and equality must not be equated with sameness among them. Some have matured beyond the constant need of some kind of therapy to offset the more destructive effects of racial discrimination and exclusion. But others still need the emotional support and the opportunity for individual expressions, hence significance, which derives from close identity with their own racial group. These differences in social and emotional need among Negroes are also reflective of a difference in their religious needs and inclinations. This is a fact which the younger clergyman who condemned all racial and ethnic churches as unChristian did not see and appreciate. It needs to be understood and appreciated that, where churches are maintained to protect those persons who need the support of racial or ethnic solidarity from a complete loss of identity and significance, they would seem to be serving a worthy purpose. Especially does this seem to be true today when city people generally are threatened by the fragmentation, disorganization and normlessness so characteristic of life in our urbanized and technological society. But when the social order is brought into conformity with the will of God, these needs, too, will disappear.

—Jesse McNeil, *Mission in Metropolis*, pp. 68–69.

8. Poverty and Welfare

The poor you have with you always.

Judged by standards that really matter, by the health and vigor, the hopefulness in the lives of those who are in need, their freedom of choice, their ability to exercise normal human rights and undertake normal responsibility, our system has not been given the chance to show what it can do. Its dignity has been slowly whittled away, by making relief rolls less confidential, by "suitable home" provisions, by demands that there be control of how a family spends its money, and above all, by continuing wholly insufficient grants, which are below the health and decency level. A man cannot be self-respecting if we take respect from him, nor responsible if we deny him responsibility. He cannot be vigorous if we underfeed him, nor secure enough to assert his independence if we keep him insecure. Throughout the centuries we have tried to force man into self-reliance by punishing him or treating him like a child. It has not worked. It cannot work. Punishment does not touch the root of the problem, even with the few who are inclined to dishonesty. It is not by shaming people or making their decisions for them that men were, are, and will be redeemed. It is by an immense valuation of even the poorest and sorriest of them. Our system has been too Christian to be accepted. More has also been expected of it than any system could deliver. The system has been expected to cure all social ills—illegitimacy, family breakdown, lack of education and skill. It is blamed because there are still, in an economy of plenty, many people who are in need. Yet the belief that he can abolish poverty is one of man's fondest illusions. God almost seems to take a delight in showing him that he cannot do so. Every new "advance" in social conditions creates a new category of need, as improvements in medicine have in our days created need among the aged and replaced a few "orphans" with a greater number of children whose parents are alive but sick. Undoubtedly there are many families today who will be permanently in need and whose children may be the same, although it may surprise some people to know, for instance, that a greater proportion of the population of supposedly self-reliant colonial Virginia received public relief than do in the same state today.

—Alan Keith-Lucas, *The Church and Social Welfare*, pp. 39–40.

If the gospel means anything, it cannot be indifferent to the poor.

The church knows that it cannot be indifferent to the poor if the Gospel means anything. It knows as well that it cannot be indifferent to the form that society will take, as the church also lives in and with society. It knows further that it cannot be indifferent to the disintegration of meaning and the massive superficiality that confronts this society on all levels.

It is not the function of the church to solve the details of this problem, but it *is* a function of the church to bear witness to the principles of love and justice which must inform every detail of solution and to plead for that form of mind, that openness, that can responsibly hear what all sides are saying and attempt a solution that sees clearly the commonweal and the interdependence of all sectors of society.

—Perry L. Norton, *Church and Metropolis*, pp. 70–71.

Soup is no substitute for social legislation.

The Salvation Army does the work of the good Samaritan in the urban areas while the other denominations ride by on the new expressways in their station wagons. But soup, crackers, and a dormitory bed if you will listen to an evangelistic sermon is no substitute for social legislation and direct pressure on city authorities to do something about the problem of homeless men.

—Gayraud S. Wilmore, *The Secular Relevance of the Church*, p. 10.

The preaching of the gospel does not depend on social change.

In any event, the preaching and service of the Gospel do not depend upon any special social change, ideationally or in any other way. The Gospel does not even depend upon the American way of life, either in its integrity or its breach.

I am as much in favor of social change in the urban ghettos as the next man, perhaps more (though I am by no means persuaded that the standard of social improvement should be that of the great American bourgeoisie), but the message and mission of the Church in the world *never* depend upon the specific physical, political, cultural, social, economic, or even psychological situations in which the Church, or the people of the Church as missionaries, find themselves. If the Gospel is so contingent as that, it is no universal Gospel. If the Gospel is so fragile that it may not be welcomed by a man who, say, is hungry, unless he first be fed, then this is no Gospel with any saving power, this is no Word of God which has authority over the power of death. The Gospel, if it represents the power of God unto salvation, is a Word which is exactly addressed to men in this world in their destitution and hunger and sickness and travail and captivity and perishing, in a way which may be heard and embraced by men in any of these, or in any other, afflictions. That is, by the way, the original portrait and report of Christian witness in the world, in the days of the Acts of the Apostles.

—William Stringfellow, *My People Is the Enemy*, pp. 87–88.

D. The Secular City—God's Gift to the Church

Metropolis is the new chance God is giving the Church.

Metropolis is the new chance God through His Son Jesus Christ is offering the Churches to preserve and to demonstrate their integrity as the Church of the Living God through whose Son they are called to a reconciling ministry in the world. He offers the Churches in our contemporary and rapidly changing society the chance to fit their faith and deeds to the revolutionary changes of the times that they may communicate intelligibly and meaningfully to a society that is not only urbanized and industrialized but also highly secularized. For it will be His glory and the salvation of Metropolis that the

Churches in their redemptive activity in the world today are alert and informed, concerned and competent, relevant and true, creative, adventuresome,
and effectual.

—Jesse McNeil, *Mission in Metropolis*, pp. 31–32.

Reasons for celebrating God's gift, the city.

The city is going to confront the church and force her to state in unmistakable terms what her mission is in the world. While not giving official
sanction to the dance, the church has developed one step which would do
credit to Fred Astaire—the "sidestep." When confronted with a major
question or issue the church has tended to sidestep it and involve itself in
lesser discussions. The city faces the church—in a way not true before—with
the necessity of laying aside all that is peripheral and laying hold to that
which is central to her mission in the world.

The city can be the occasion of revival and renewal within the church. Not
all share this optimism. Some feel that the church is dead and that their job
is to embalm her. Some feel that her disease is terminal and their task is to
mourn her passing. Others feel that the church is under formidable attack
and their responsibility is to defend her. The church is neither dead nor
dying, nor was she ever intended to be on the defensive. The church whose
calling in life is to minister to herself will not make it. But the cleansed,
repenting church, which takes the initiative in the world can have a vital
ministry in the secular city. When Christ founded the church and promised
that "the gates of hell shall not prevail against it" (Matthew 16:18), He
intended that it should seek to penetrate the world with its presence and its
message. Rather than the city becoming the graveyard of the church, it could
well become the place of its new birth.

—Kenneth Chafin, *Help! I'm a Layman*, pp. 87–88.

1. Metropolis: The New Setting for Mission

The cloverleaf is a symbol of our times.

What is the context of the church's witness in urban America today? What
is the environment into which we go, the conditions we may expect to encounter? What are some of the signs of the times in which we live?

Urbanization: The majority of people now prefer to congregate in urban
areas. In the lifetime of many of us we have seen this mass migration of human life to the economic, cultural, political and social centers of our nation—
and of the world. No longer can America be described as a rural, agricultural
or small-town nation. This century has witnessed a complete reversal of urban-
rural population. As late as 1900, two-thirds of the population lived in small
towns and in the countryside. Now more than two-thirds live in vast and

rapidly growing metropolitan regions. Some are saying that by the year 2000 a majority of the 300 million population will live within two gigantic urban areas—one, a megalopolis stretching in an unbroken mass from the Chicago region, around the Great Lakes, to the Boston area and down the Eastern Seaboard past Norfolk; the other a megalopolis reaching from the Mexican border, up the West Coast, past San Francisco. Herman Kahn and Anthony Wiener, in their book *The Year 2000*, have broken down these two regions into three, and given them names: "Chipitts" (extending from the Great Lakes area around Chicago all the way to Pittsburgh, home of 13 per-cent of the nation's people); "Boswash" (the area that snakes down the Eastern Seaboard from Boston to Washington, in which 25 percent of the population will live); and "Sansan" (the 475-mile stretch from San Diego to San Francisco, housing 6 percent of the population).

This panoramic view, however, photographed by a satellite called DODGE (Department of Defense Gravity Experiment), 21,000 miles out in space, shows little of the pulsing activity or kind of life within these densely popu-lated regions. Nothing is seen of the beauty or "whiteness" of the spreading suburbs; the squalor of "blackness" of the inner city; the polluted air or contaminated streams; the crawling lines of endless traffic; the luxury of multi-storied buildings; the smog of sprawling industrial complexes; the misery of the dispossessed, the lonely, the aged; the predominance of young people under 26; the crowded airports; the ghettos of races and cultures, both in the central city and in the suburbs; the centers of power—political, economic, military; the church buildings with uplifted spires and locked doors. These demand a closer and more sympathetic look. It is in this matrix of urban life and environment that the Christian witness is set, where the decisions and discoveries and dramas of existence and the future are found. Here, in this context of mass population and a secular society are seen the concentration of the handicapped, the hurt, the desperate, the aged, the sick in body, mind, heart, the illiterates, the delinquents, the minority groups of race, culture and religion, the lost, strayed, stolen. Here it is that the church is to minister in the name of Christ. Here, to the powerful and the powerless, it is to speak and act in a redemptive way.

—J. N. Evans, Jr., "The Context of Witness," *Home Missions*, October 1968, pp. 17–18.

The local community and the vanishing American.

The parish as a geographic area inhabited by people more or less integrated by a common set of values, including a common faith, and considered by a local church to be its area of responsibility and service, continues to be a part of the imaginative life of the Churches, although the facts of the situation argue to the contrary. It is no more true today for the Churches than for the elementary school that the local community can serve as the basic unit of social organization and its boundaries as those of the parish. It is a sociological

fact that the local community as we tend to think of it—as a limited area
characterized by neighborliness, a sense of belonging, and common values—
has all but disappeared in modern American life.

—Jesse McNeil, *Mission in Metropolis*, p. 62.

City churches are in a do-or-die battle.

To the extent that the Churches study Metropolis merely for the purpose of
finding ways to save themselves and to preserve their present structures and
forms, they are not on mission for their Lord but in a struggle for survival
in our urbanized technological society. And whether they can emerge from
this encounter viable and strong will depend upon how successfully they can
shift ground and purposes for mission instead of for combat. Whether they
can emerge with prestige and power will depend upon how willing they are
to understand and listen to Metropolis, to understand themselves in the light
of metropolitan needs and demands; how willing they are to allow the Holy
Spirit to transform them in a creative response to the rapid social changes of
the times; and to take the initiative through positive acts in the everyday
affairs of men to bring them under the influence of the redemptive activity
of God in Christ.

But let it be known that the renewal, re-education, and re-tooling of the
Churches for mission in Metropolis must be undertaken prophetically,
courageously, and fully, lest their inadequacies turn their mission into a
mere but costly encounter, lest they survive this encounter with only a
Cadmean victory.

—Jesse McNeil, *Mission in Metropolis*, pp. 33–34.

What can the Church do in metropolis?

To provide guidance toward metropolitan community the Church can: (1)
affirm community by forming a ministry to the whole metropolis; (2) offer
a vision and experience of metropolitan community by exemplifying a community; (3) inform the metropolitan struggle for community with its own
prophetic concern for the common good of the metropolitan area. The de-
formation of Protestantism came about by the severing of its ministry from
participation in the whole of metropolitan life; the reformation of Protestantism will come about through the participation of its ministry in the whole
and the representation of the whole community in the communities of
Protestant faith.

—Gibson Winter, *The Suburban Captivity of the Churches*, p. 170.

The new urban image of congregation, laity, and faith.

First, in order to proclaim the gospel, we need an urban image of the
congregation, one that includes all sorts and conditions of men. Metropolis

will shatter traditional ghettos located in the core of the city. Now all men—
the rich and the poor, the educated and the uneducated, the black and the
white—will be in close proximity to one another. This is not to say that
through metropolis men will be brothers. It is to say that through the metropolis the bringing of all men together will be a real possibility. Hence on any
given Sunday morning the church can truly reflect the body of Christ in
totality. Moreover, the local church on the corner can fulfill this possibility.

No longer will any church be able to hide behind the old cliche that "We do
not have any Negroes, or any hillbillies, or any Spanish-speaking, therefore,
our church just reflects the parish." Truly, metropolis will force the whole
church to be "in mission" in a more complete sense than merely through
benevolent giving. The day of the affluent church and the traditional "mission" church is rapidly disappearing. . . .

Secondly, in order to proclaim the gospel, we need an urban image of
the laity. Basically, the traditional image of the laymen in the church has
been a pew-squatter, an usher, or a rubber stamp. While this is obviously a
caricature, it nevertheless contains enough truth to enable us to contrast this
image with an urban image of the laity.

If we are truly concerned about the proclamation of the gospel in the
metropolis, this is the only possible urban image of the laity. The complexity
of modern urban life will demand more and more specialization. The day of
intellectual "jacks-of-all-trades" is no longer a real possibility. The day of
the parson's being "the person" in the community, because of his education,
culture, and intellect, has long since passed. The clergy simply cannot expect
to proclaim the gospel alone.

Thirdly, in order to minister in the metropolis, we need an urban image of
the faith. Traditionally the faith that has been handed down from generation
to generation is a rural-oriented one. Our symbols and our use of language
deal with fig trees, sheep, shepherds, fields, and seeds. There is little in the
faith to suggest that God is on the assembly line, or concerned about urban
renewal or the freeway. The church is desperately in need of a faith that is
urban. This is not to suggest that the faith once given is not adequate; but
it is to plead for a faith that can interpret this crowded, highly impersonal,
bureaucratic structure we call urban into the symbols and language of faith.

The time has come to stop saying our biblical knowledge is rural and to
begin to speak in urban biblical terms. For example, the contemporary story
of prostitution has all the biblical symbols of the story of the Good Samaritan.
There are the prostitutes left in the ditch to die when they are old and ugly.
There are those who see this modern road to Jericho as a place for all kinds
of lawlessness and immorality. And there are those passing by on their way
to the church bazaar and the PTA, the Moose, the Elks, and the Rotary who
couldn't care less. In modern twentieth-century urban language, we need to
define the Good Samaritan not on the road to Jericho, but on the Main and

Market Streets of our great cities. And until we see Main Street as the road to Jericho, the Bible will never be understood by urban man.

—Robert Lee, ed., *The Church and the Exploding Metropolis*, pp. 110–11, 112, 114.

The new role of the Church is an inglorious one.

If Metropolis has certain expectations that the Churches must meet in order to command its attention and response, the Churches must remember that they have a commitment, a mission, and standards to which they must remain faithful if they would be good servants of Christ on mission in Metropolis. . . . And in the immediacy of the conflict the servant Churches must expect to play an inglorious role. They are sometimes tempted in such situations, however, to save themselves and come down from the cross. And so they do—sometimes.

—Jesse McNeil, *Mission in Metropolis*, p. 44.

Three signs of God's hand in metropolis.

Perhaps the greatest witness the church in metropolis can make is to be the spokesman for the poor. What is desperately needed in metropolis is for the poor to have someone to articulate their plight. Furthermore, the church dares not witness to the idea, "Well, the affluent also have a right." To do so is a complete denial of the God revealed in Scriptures, who without exception places his weight and compassion on the side of the poor. . . .

The witness that the church makes for justice in metropolis will be indicated to a large degree by its treatment of the minority person. As a Christian church, long devoted to and worshiping a just God, our witness in metropolis must be concerned with the minority! This is what God is concerned about. Let us not confuse our witness to the minority as a method for institutional survival. Our witness should be thought of in terms of ministry. To paraphrase Martin Luther King, the tragedy of the metropolis will not be the noise of the bad people, but the silence of the Christian church in respect to its ministry to minorities. . . .

The metropolis does not need to be reminded of the resurrection by referring to nature. To urban man, if God is only the God of nature, then he cannot be too powerful, for man does a pretty good job of overcoming the elements himself. What urban man needs to feel in his very bones is "if a city die, shall it live again?" Can we as Christians point to the resurrection of buildings, stones, mortar and brick? God is the God of the resurrection and not just the God of Easter festivities. The resurrection is his eternal act. Can we make this witness a witness to God's resurrection even among urban men? If we can't, then the very stones and bricks and mortar and concrete will. For, "I tell you," says Jesus, "if these were silent, the very stones would cry out."

—William R. Grace, "Proclamation and Witness in the Metropolis," *The Church and the Exploding Metropolis*, ed. Robert Lee, pp. 117–19.

The Church confronts urban renewal.

The most important role for the church to play in the process of urban renewal is not the adaptation of its own life and program to deal with the results of urban renewal policies. Rather, it is to raise questions about the policies themselves while they are still in the making. The crucial task for the church is to raise the question of values. In connection with every plan and every decision, questions like these need to be asked: Toward what ends is this plan working? Whom does it intend to benefit, and will they truly benefit? Whose interests does it hurt, and can they stand to be hurt? What effects will there be on the rest of metropolis if this plan is carried out? What kind of city will we have when this plan—and the other associated with it—takes shape? And what kind of city will we have in the meantime?

In the past some churchmen—and occasionally churches or denominations, have raised such questions about the operation of urban renewal in their city. However, they have usually done so either because their church building or some members in their congregation were to be included in the urban renewal area, or on the basis of a concern for people. Yet, the Christian church has a deeper reason for questioning the policies of urban renewal and the values on which they are based. To be sure, it is to be concerned for its own life; to be sure, it is to be concerned for people as people; but its primary concern is for people and the material world as valued by God.

—George D. Younger, *The Church and Urban Renewal*, pp. 157–58.

Four stumbling blocks to the ministry of reconciliation.

Christians who are concerned to see this all-inclusive Church come about must dare to leave their gifts on the altar and involve themselves in a reconciling ministry in the everyday affairs of the world. They must recognize the four great obstacles to a reconciling ministry in America: (1) the denial of human dignity and individual worth, (2) the limitations in education and employment among large segments of the population, (3) residential segregation, and (4) socio-economic stratification. These obstacles must be overcome with a positive program of justice and freedom for all Americans and a deeper, more courageous commitment to the reconciling ministry of God through Christ Jesus. This is their responsibility as the Churches in Metropolis to all people. This is their mission received from their Lord.

—Jesse McNeil, *Mission in Metropolis*, pp. 69–70.

In the arena of public decision.

A wide variety of roles is open to the church as it seeks to define the part it is called on to play in the politics of urban renewal. First and foremost, the Christian fellowship must eschew any attempt to substitute its own structures and decision-making processes for the wider circle in which public policy is decided. Rather than bringing public issues into the life of the church on the assumption that they will receive clarification there, the church is under obligation to take its understanding of God's will into the arena of public decision to be clarified and made effective. Instead of having its grasp on God's purposes diluted or corrupted by this exposure, the church actually requires such involvement to discover the particularities of God's concern for the life of men in metropolis.

—George D. Younger, *The Church and Urban Renewal*, pp. 160–61.

2. Saints in the Suburbs

Suburbia as a Christian symbol.

Who is foolish enough to suggest suburbia as a symbol bearing Christian meaning? Does not everyone know that God made the country and the devil devised the city? Who, then, made suburbia? Perhaps, like Topsy, it "just growed." Regardless of its genesis, here is the place where evil and good currently are locked in mortal combat. Which will prevail is not yet known. God and man, however, newly teamed together in living relationship can accomplish amazing things. To the victor belongs the suburbs.

—Frederick A. Shippey, *Protestantism in Suburban Life*, p. 36.

How to count the cost of servanthood in suburbia.

There must be a willingness to face creatively the inner city as well as the world far removed. That there has been the ability to wax warmly eloquent about the hardships of foreign missionaries while ignoring the trials of courageous ministers in the concrete jungles close to home testifies to the escapist mentality of suburban Christianity.

Suburban churches must affirm and cultivate their peculiar resources of free men, available money and potential for political power. Miracles in men and society could be wrought overnight by a Christian power bloc committed to a war against social injustice and inequity.

There must be orientation and training in concepts of servanthood by the churches. Unfortunately, suburbanites are functionally illiterate in the language of service to persons unlike themselves. Consistent, firm, understanding effort at education for service is a priority item before every suburban church. Among its hardest lessons will be that of learning a sense of mutuality with less affluent congregations in the inner city. The lesson must be learned, however, lest the sin of paternalism be perpetuated in Christian mission. . . .

Cooperative ministry must play a large role in grappling with urban crises. Cooperation across denominational lines will involve humility, inasmuch as one local church or denomination will not get all of the credit. . . .

Youth should receive the emphasis in any urban ministry. They are the generation of hope for servanthood in the suburbs because their prejudices, fears and defensive characteristics have not yet hardened into permanent handicaps. . . .

Suburban churches must not cease to minister to the suburbs. The current glamour of ministry in the central city does not mean that the blighted areas contain the only persons of value. . . .

Courageous leaders in the churches of suburbia are essential to the realization of servanthood. The necessary unity of laymen and the ordained was never more obvious. Controversy is bound to be the order of the day for years to come. Unless unpurchasable men of commitment stand together, the churches will expend their energies in internal conflict. If they stand together, this will be Christianity's finest hour.

—Joe Wortman, "Servanthood: Missing in Suburbia," *Home Missions*, November 1968, pp. 19–20.

3. The Downtown Church

The inner city is a testing ground for the church.

Experimental ministries in depressed areas of the inner city provide clues to the residential mission of the Church, since they are maintained under the most difficult conditions. The residential mission of the Church will be successful only if it can cultivate and sustain a broad, rich and total mission to the inner city. Such a mission must emerge as an integral part of the daily life of the churches—not as an extra or special missionary "endeavor." To be the Church is to be involved in mission. To be the Church in the metropolis is to be rooted in the missionary task to inner city and suburb as an interdependent process. For our purposes, therefore, the Church in the metropolis requires forms in which inner city ministry is integral, not because the inner city is the most important part of the metropolis but because it is the test of an inclusive church. The inner city is a valuable testing ground, moreover, since the blight and demolition of this type of area spreads in ever-widening circles each decade.

—Gibson Winter, *The Suburban Captivity of the Churches*, p. 139.

The mass exodus of the denominations.

The breakdown of social homogeneity in inner city areas and the spread of inner city blight account for the decline of central city churches. Central cities reveal two adverse features for the major denominations: (1) central cities tend to be areas of residence for lower social classes; (2) central cities tend to be more heterogeneous in social composition. The central city areas, in other words, exhibit the two characteristics which violate the life principle of congregations of the major denominations: they have too few middle-class people; they mix middle-class people with lower-class residents. Central city areas have become progressively poorer locales for the major denominations since the exodus of middle-class people from most central cities. With few exceptions, the major denominations are rapidly losing their hold on the central city.

—Gibson Winter, *The Suburban Captivity of the Churches*, p. 70.

Inner city ministries are difficult, demanding, and dangerous.

Ministries to the inner city are difficult and costly in every sense. Long-standing members of congregations are often hurt by the priority of this claim of the surrounding community over their own investments in the congregational life. Clergy and laity become involved in difficult and even dangerous situations; furthermore, concern with a neighborhood means involvement in social, political, and economic interests which conflict with the pietistic strain in American Protestantism. The leaders in these ventures would be the first to minimize the sacrifices involved in being *present* in the inner city. Nevertheless, it is a fact that sacrifices which cannot possibly be anticipated are implicit in such situations. This is true, however, of every human encounter. The response to another person is the recognition that his very presence lays claims upon one's own existence. The task of being present in the inner city, therefore, dramatizes and intensifies the dangers implicit in every human encounter.

—Gibson Winter, *The Suburban Captivity of the Churches*, p. 142.

The "area of access" approach.

The obvious problems of inner city ministries, and, before long, of ministries to the central city areas, are finance and personnel. How can ministries be sustained in blighted areas without outside help or ministers who earn a living in other ways? Furthermore, how do you get competent men into those ministries and give them the moral support to stay there? One obvious way is to stake out an area of Christian responsibility from the outer edge of the city to the heart of the inner city along a major line of access or freeway. This area, then, becomes the sphere of responsibility for a ministry—from blight to suburb, Negro to White, blue collar to white collar, down-and-out to privilege. Finances, buildings, lay and ordained ministries, time, and other matters would be allocated over this whole area by decisions of councils of representatives from the area. Such an area—call it an area of access or of organic interdependence—would constitute the basic unit of ministry and the minimal unit of the Church. It would extend its ministry outside the residential sphere but its minimal space would embrace a whole sector of metropolitan life along a major freeway. The specific way of bounding such a unit would, of course, vary with the character of the metropolis. The key to this conception is that the minimal unit of ministry will be a *sector* (or a *cross-section*) of the metropolis.

—Gibson Winter, *The Suburban Captivity of the Churches*, pp. 144–45.

The in-city church can't go it alone.

1. The in-city church can't go it alone. It needs the guidance and support of the denomination of which it is member.

2. Guidance and support should be given by the denomination before it is too late. To be effective, support should bolster inherent strength rather than compensate for inherent weakness.

3. If a denomination expects to begin new churches it must be willing to discontinue others where the ministry is not needed, or where the situation is beyond repair. The existence of a building or a loyal remnant is insufficient justification for the continuation of a congregation. Most denominations are not willing to admit this, and therefore temporize and postpone until desperation forces their hand to action.

4. The primary issue in aiding a church in the "middle" of the city is not the survival of a particular institution, but responsibility for ministry in a particular situation.

5. Main-line denominations can serve changing or difficult neighborhoods when the motivation is witness and service rather than the perpetuation of a dying institution.

6. Money doled out by a denomination to a weak, ineffective, and poorly planned ministry is wasted. Money adequate to provide competent staff and full program can be dramatically effective.

7. Proper ministerial leadership is crucial in effectively ministering in the city. An encouraging sign is the number of young men coming out of seminary who see the inner city as a frontier of service. The church in the inner city does not have to be a dumping ground for incompetents.

8. The in-city church must not run a conventional building- and membership-centered program. Ministerial leadership and laity must identify with neighborhood needs and aspirations, participating in the organizational life of the community and offering building and staff resources to the community. In its situation the church must be a "reality-shaped parish."

9. Denominationally based urban specialists with special responsibility for liaison between the denominational unit and the inner-city church in the areas of staff, budget, and program can play an important part in effective ministry.

10. Above all, the mission in and through the local church must be understood by the local congregation involved as a partnership in mission with the denomination.

—Richard E. Moore and Duane L. Day, *Urban Church Breakthrough*, pp. 43–44.

The three handles available to cosmopolitan Christians.

How does a community of faith go about its prophetic mission in a particular location?

There are three handles that a cosmopolitan Christian can hold to have a part in the history-making of his own community. First, there are the handles of social agencies and community services which are genuinely involved in caring for the indigent and underprivileged. We have already discussed Northaven's use of the public forums and concerns of the church as communication centers for the distribution of worldly information and personnel enlistment in these structures.

Second, there is the influence that can be brought to bear on the power structure of any community which seeks to deal with civic problems. Persons in influential positions are not insensitive to public opinion, letters to the editors in local newspapers, and other barometers of community concern. Members of Northaven were encouraged to exercise their franchise of free speech and conversation with other people about the issues of the day. A number of our businessmen in banks, law firms, and corporations were in daily contact with power centers in the city, and had many opportunities to be a leaven in the shaping of community affairs.

The third handle available to a cosmopolitan Christian who wants to have a part in the shaping of his community is through the number of action organizations in every city which are organized to get things done and bring certain programs into being. These organizations range from groups banded together for the election of members to the school board and the city council, to groups that are involved in the championing of civil rights, to Republican and Democrat organizations. These groups bring a creative agitation to the city's life, and without them any community would be considerably impoverished.

—W. A. Holmes, *Tomorrow's Church: A Cosmopolitan Community*, pp. 159–60.

E. ECUMENICAL EXPLORATIONS IN METROPOLIS

What makes the word "ecumenical" so valuable?

What makes the word "ecumenical" so valuable today is that it holds together things that must not be separated. It refers at once to the *whole* Church and to the *whole* world. "An introverted ecclesiastical ecumenism," says Dr. Visser't Hooft, "is therefore self-contradictory." It contains all that is meant by "Catholic" or would, if Catholic had more overt reference to the presence and mission of the Church *in the world*. "Ecumenical" means more than "universal," and far more than "international" on the one hand or "interdenominational" on the other.

The recovery to the word of its full meaning has been piecemeal over the past 150 years. Today the phrase "ecumenical movement" is not a synonym for the World Council of Churches or any other organization. Nor does it describe what is already achieved. It is a movement seeking after the unity of Christ's Church and the fulfilment of its purpose in the whole world.

—Kathleen Bliss, *We the People*, pp. 37–38.

Unity is a footprint of God in the sands of time.

We appear, therefore, to have reached a point in the Church's history where we have come across one of the footprints of God in the sands of time showing us which way we should go. And the direction that these footprints show and the signs indicated seem to agree with what the New Testament also says. It is towards the reconciliation of Christians and the reunion of the Churches. It is significant that so many have read the same signs, and that so many lines seem to converge on the same conviction that we must accept our unity in Christ. For this reason an immense store of goodwill and mutual trust is being built up within the Churches towards one another, and already on the personal level the atmosphere has completely changed. It is a time of rapprochement and mutual acceptance as well as of hope that the time cannot be as long as we had feared before many of the great divisions of the Church will be healed. And it is important that we should go on encouraging this goodwill and that we should not allow the suspicions of the past to affect our relations with one another.

When the right attitude of goodwill and trust has been created, and a purposeful charity is at work, the task of reunion is well on the way. For no techniques will succeed where charity and wisdom are absent, but even when they are present, it is necessary to be aware of the pitfalls and opportunities as well as of the most fruitful methods used in other places.

—B. N. Y. Vaughan, *Structures for Renewal*, pp. 137–38.

Can a servant church "go it alone"?

Southern Baptist churches must abandon their "go-it-alone" attitude before they can accomplish much in the inner-city, a special committee studying the ministry of urban churches has declared. . . .

In recommending more cooperation with non-Baptist groups, the study group on "the church's ministry in an inner-city, multi-problem area" said that neither theology nor principles need to be sacrificed.

It pointed out that the problems of the inner-city are so staggering that only the combined resources of all interested parties can hope to cope with them. . . .

It was suggested that church educational programs be enlarged to include literacy programs for adults and immigrants who need help with the English language; opportunities for deprived adults to get birth control information and to learn domestic skills; and courses in Negro history, weekday study halls and field trips for ghetto children.

In addition, the study group said churches should get involved in programs that provide employment information, day care for ghetto children, housing assistance for low income persons and more recreation facilities.

Citing the special needs for ghetto children who are starving for a little "elbow room," the report said that churches could help meet this need "by taking the padlocks off the church parking lots" and turning them into weekday playgrounds.

"Our churches must further refuse to allow their buildings to be large vacant barns from Monday morning until Sunday morning," the researchers said.

Churches were urged to undertake a sweeping campaign to inform ghetto residents about services already available through government and private agencies. It was suggested that local ghetto residents be used in this program, and that local persons be given a vote in what new projects will have priority. . . .

In a summary report on guidelines for elements of strategy in urban ministries, the seminar participants agreed on the need for some kind of clearinghouse in metropolitan areas to maintain communication with various organizations both private and public, and to assist churches with information and help in implementing programs. . . .

Members of the seminar affirmed their belief that evangelism is the "core purpose" of urban ministry. Evangelism must continue to be directed toward individuals, the report said, "but social structures and substructures must also be addressed through word and action toward the end of redemption through Jesus Christ."

—"Can a Servant 'Go it Alone'?", *Home Missions*, September 1968, p. 32.

Who can mount God's mission in metropolis?

In the metropolis there is no Methodist version of racial justice; no Baptist answer to unemployment; no exclusively Episcopal position as to what God is up to in the city. No single denomination, however effectively it can organize and administer local congregations, has either power or mandate to speak and act with authority for the Protestant community. Only a council of churches organized as an extension of the denominations for mission can really mount God's mission in the all-pervasive metropolis. The capacity to create such an instrument has been demonstrated; the mandate to do so throughout the metropolitan areas of our nation is before the Church.

—Richard E. Moore and Duane L. Day, *Urban Church Breakthrough*, p. 131.

The time is ripe for a council of renewal and unity.

The time is now ripe for such a council.

1. The renewal ferment now recognizes no denominational boundaries. The concerns welling up across the churches should be seen as the work of the Spirit calling us to recognize the task of renewal not only as a common calling but as a task which we are being called to face together so that God may renew us together as he calls us out of past isolation into the unity of our common mission.

2. So far there has been an incredible surge of mutual discovery across the historic confessional barriers on the Biblical and theological levels. The logic of this is that we must now follow this path of mutual discovery into the institutional channels where the day-to-day missionary tasks of the church are carried out.

3. The time has come for such an encounter. The work of the World Council of Churches in studies such as "The Missionary Structure of the Congregation" and the many experiments that are under way to discover the forms of contemporary mission together are but part of the agenda material that has in fact prepared the way for such a council. The task of the preparatory commissions would be to take such material and order it into a working agenda for the council so that the churches could begin to make the institutional responses that are now required.

4. We face now a time of institutional crisis. The ferment has reached the point where the level of recognition of the need for re-formation (renewal) is now becoming focused in a question: Can the renewal that God is bringing to his church come about through a planned restructuring of the churches toward the missionary obedience that is now required, or is the inertia and resistance of present structures such that renewal can come only from outside?

5. The very existence of a church union development such as COCU, and the direction it has taken toward affirming that radical renewal is the prerequisite to a true unity-for-mission, has given to many a hope that renewal can also come from within.

What this proposal suggests is that a council for renewal and unity can now seek to correlate the movements for renewal from below with the movement to renewal-in-unity from above.

A council, of course, would not be a cure-all. It would be long and costly. It would create severe tensions and open up deep conflicts. But it is only as we are prepared to pay that cost together that we will be reborn for the mission we are being called to fulfill together.

—Colin W. Williams, *The Church*, pp. 167–68.

Essential elements in a council of churches structured for renewal.

There are several essential elements in a council of churches structured for servanthood in the world rather than service to the churches.

1. The denominations through their executives and appointed representa-

tives must be responsible for the program and the financing of the council.

2. Program units must have freedom to act within certain boundaries, and to take positions with which all of organized Protestantism may not agree.

3. Staff members must relate primarily to the denominational representatives who sit on their commissions. Because each denominational representative sits on only one commission, he has the time necessary to develop sufficient background to act responsibly.

4. Denominational representatives on administrative boards, departments, and commissions must report regularly to, seek advice from, and involve the judicatory of the denomination they represent. The council must be in every sense an instrument of the denominations for mission, rather than an instrument apart.

—Richard E. Moore and Duane L. Day, *Urban Church Breakthrough*, pp. 130–31.

Proposals for Christian unity.

1. That there be an agreed acceptance that the local church, when true to Jesus' injunction, constitutes equal authority in the church with other parts of the church. That it is fully the church, even though it is not the whole of the church. This would mean an acceptance of the congregation as the basic unit and means of life of the whole church.

2. That there be an acceptance of mutual orders of the ministry. That the apostolic succession of faith and spirit and the laying on of hands of all God's people (through deacons and brother ministers) be accepted as valid for service in the sanctuary for administering the two basic sacraments, and for the preaching of the Word, and the leading of the people.

3. That baptism be formally agreed upon as a universal sacrament and that the Lord's Supper be likewise accepted as a common sacrament binding all Christians together and therefore to be recognized as valid in every church as long as instituted by the words of Jesus and carried out by congregation and minister faithfully in his Spirit.

4. That it be agreed that denominations as such remain intact, but conceive it their task to serve and support the local churches of their tradition. That denominations—in mission—especially—seek to engage in ministries together. . . .

5. That agreement on a simple covenant be reached and denominations and local churches enter into covenant agreements with each other "to walk together in the ways of the Lord" in every area of life that they now can, and that they will be able in future to do. . . .

6. That the ministers in local towns or cities come together at regular intervals for common spiritual discipline and study, leading to a renewal of the ministers' lives as well as the congregations'.

7. That each denomination agree to send a pastoral letter to all its churches suggesting such local plans of action.

8. And that to begin the new covenant relationship between local churches a "Scripture service" of praise be held by all the participating churches in a central auditorium on a Sunday evening, looking forward to their work and worship together. That common communion services between Protestant churches be held as soon as such are possible.

—Arthur A. Rouner, Jr., *The Free Church Today: New Life for the Whole Church,* pp. 157–59.

F. The Church in the Next Decade

Change, change, change.

The only certainty today is change. Even death and taxes seem uncertain.
—Allan R. Brockway, *The Secular Saint,* p. 15.

The final days of the Church?

We are witnessing the last years of the church. . . . The final days of the church as we have known it during our lifetime.
—David Poling, *The Last Years of the Church,* p. vii.

The nature of the church will be altered.

The central thesis of this volume is that Protestant churches are involved in a deep and entangling crisis which in the years ahead may seriously disrupt or alter the very nature of the church.
—Jeffrey K. Hadden, *The Gathering Storm in the Churches,* p. 5.

How will the clergy of tomorrow differ from today?

Several trends already are apparent which suggest that the clergyman of tomorrow will differ from his counterpart of today and, more particularly, from the clergyman of yesterday. Foremost among these trends is the increasing emphasis on specialized training. The general practitioner is fast disappearing from the ranks of doctors, lawyers, engineers, teachers, physicists, chemists, and other professions. The age of specialization also is affecting preparation for the ministry. Most of the mainline Protestant denominations now require a college degree and seminary graduation for final ordination. In addition, many of the newer sects which until recently ridiculed the need for formal theological education are now developing their own colleges and seminaries.

—Lyle E. Schaller, *Planning for Protestantism in Urban America,* pp. 199–200.

Prediction: the clergy will minister to those who serve.

Prediction based on present trends! The chaplain of the future will be increasingly involved in a ministry to those who man the structures of captive communities. In the area of health and welfare, even now the Church cannot carry out a ministry to individuals with special needs through its ordained clergy, whether these happen to be related to congregations or to service institutions. But Church laymen now man the staffs of private and public institutions at all levels, and are in daily contact with individuals who seek help from these agencies. If the Church has a ministry in the areas of health, welfare, and—of course—education, should it not be related to what its members are already doing in their vocational structures? This approach will use the ordained clergy of the Church for ministering to those who serve, rather than for directly serving patients, inmates, clients, or students to the exclusion of staff.

—Richard E. Moore and Duane L. Day, *Urban Church Breakthrough*, p. 149.

The Church of the future—incognito.

The future Church will not be a closed institution, sheltered and secure, but one that is open, designed to address itself to all men. With its past position of social security eroded, it will need to fall back in the most literal sense on its "interest" in the whole world—its being *among men*. It will be challenged to abandon its ineffective official stance and to enter upon its true task of being effectively present *incognito*. Its life will be full of surprises, dispersed, unadministrable, endangered, full of risks; it will need to be mobile, never taking itself for granted and yet filled with greater responsibility and greater enthusiasm than ever before. There is no better way of describing it than as the salt of the earth. The food we eat is improved by salt. The salt is lost in that food. It is never restored to its original condition. It becomes part of other substances. It is scattered and dispersed beyond recognition. And yet it is essential.

The Church will go its way unknown, a stranger. Its hallmark may well be to go unrecognized in the world.

—Hans Jurgen Schultz, *Conversion to the World*, pp. 122–23.

Not old cloth, but new garments.

When we therefore view the role and shape of the church in the world of tomorrow, we must not foreshorten our question to one that seeks simply to know how the church might reshape itself in modern form to carry on traditional tasks—as if it really remains the same and only a few bits of hardware have been changed. We are dealing with fundamental shifts in our mental world, our social world, our scientific world, our world of art, and our world of religion. Without this awareness we continue to ask the wrong questions. We ask how to patch the old cloth when there is need for a new garment.

—David S. Schuller, *Emerging Shapes of the Church*, pp. 2–3.

The parish with its back to the world.

What we are suggesting is quite simple. The sharp edge of the Christian engagement with the modern world is not likely to be in the parish.

—Peter L. Berger, *The Noise of Solemn Assemblies*, p. 167.

Tomorrow's tensions.

First, the church must face people's inability to employ leisure time creatively. Within a decade or two, millions of people will be working a three- or four-day week. Many, having three or four full days on their hands, will be devastated; they are at a loss now to employ one day creatively! The problem is staggering in a culture where so many people already pursue pleasure without purpose and employ leisure without zest.

Second, radical changes in the patterns of employment are occurring as automation surges into all areas of production, management, distribution, and communication. What positive word will the church offer in the rising controversy over a guaranteed annual wage? How will it deal with persons who find no significance in their work? How will it address those people whom electronic technology is reshaping?

Third, can the church—which missed a place of leadership in the racial revolution of the 1960's—mature so rapidly that it will be able to lead creatively in the new revolution which is shaping up between the technically skilled and the unskilled throughout the world? Will the church speak relevantly to this emerging new class in America—the "meritocracy" (those who possess the know-how)?

Fourth, will the church fashion effective ways to evangelize persons in those cultures which are thoroughly informed by paganism, Communism, Mohammedanism, Hinduism, and Buddhism?

Fifth, can the church speak healingly to persons in an American society where family stability is shattered by one divorce in every four marriages and harsh human relationships maim persons in one of every two homes? Can it speak to those who separate sex not only from marriage but also from love?

Sixth, the pressures and problems posed by an old-age culture and a youth culture have engulfed an unprepared church. Can it offer more than institutional programs for the former and occasional retreats and moral platitudes for the latter?

Today is intimidating. Tomorrow threatens to be overwhelming. Whatever the church's tactics might be (critical cooperation with secularists), its strategy must be fixed: confidence in the living Word and a disciplined willingness to let Christ confront persons through persons. Every member in any congregation anywhere is free to do that. The results are in the hands of God. He requires only that his stewards be found faithful. But Christian faith —critical, flexible, daring—exists only *in* the world.

—Wallace E. Fisher, *Preface to Parish Renewal*, pp. 139–40.

The Church of 1975—priorities.

The Church must identify itself much more radically with the interests of the poor, the "losers," the outcasts, and the alienated. While one of the American Church's great strengths is its direct channel to the power structure of the nation through its most influential members, it will be disastrous if the Church pulls back from the course tentatively begun (e.g., civil rights activism and involvement in community action programs in the cities) in order to preserve undiminished this influence on the power structure. The mark of the presence of the awaited Messiah is still related to the poor having the gospel preached to them and the captives being released. The American Church would be foolish to ignore suburbia and the concerns of influential members, but its life will depend on involving many of these members in the social revolution that will continue to develop in the cities of this nation.

In addition to the parish congregations that still remain the essential form and substance, the Church must further develop specialized ministries in the cities, colleges and universities, and in labor unions and industries. So far most of the "pilot projects" have not led the way to program patterns that are repeatable. When the charismatic leader is called away, too many specialized ministries promptly fold up or are domesticated by buildings and budgets.

I do not agree with those who have given up on the parish congregation. But I am sure that to the extent that twentieth-century city life is our concern, the Church dare not center all its life and money inside the great stone piles that still dot the urban scene. The people, especially the poor and the powerful, are just not there. New patterns of involvement in mission and service at both ends of the social spectrum must be developed.

The denominations must further develop unity in mission and service. In 1946 I addressed the plenary meeting of the Federal Council of Churches in Seattle on the subject "The Evangelization of America." I do not remember much of what I said, except that I made the point that unless the denominations radically changed their expenditures from separate sectarian programs toward united ecumenical programs, no one could take seriously their claim to be interested in the evangelization of America. Twenty years later I stand by that statement.

I would add, however, one additional conviction that arises out of the last fifteen years of national ecumenical involvement. Although budget appropriation still gives a useful index to the seriousness of the denominations' ecumenical concern, I am more impressed today than I was in 1946 by the need for the national denominational leadership to give their time to developing united programs. The most excellent interdenominational staff that can be recruited cannot do the job without the major involvement of the churches' leadership in planning programs and implementing them.

And to any who have given up on councils of churches because of their frustrations with them, I would say that the only alternative is to proceed at once toward church union. Sectarian mission is not a viable alternative in 1966.

Increasing involvement of lay men and women must be a prime objective of the Church. Such involvement means a revolution in the thinking of most ministers and lay people. Presently few ministers are able to speak effectively to their members or to hear their members speaking to them. The theological insight of most ministers is entirely inadequate, and that of most lay people is nonexistent.

The best channel for the world to speak to the Church is through the lay members engrossed in that world. The best channel for the gospel to reach the world is from theologians through ministers through lay members. The channel presently seems blocked both ways.

Finally, the Church must get on with her theological work. Although I began this article with the observation that the ecumenical theology that has most affected our churches and all of us for the last half-century is under increasing criticism, I confess that I do not see anything better on the horizon. Perhaps Dietrich Bonhoeffer could have provided it had he not been martyred. Maybe William Temple would have had even more to contribute if he had lived ten years longer.

Whatever the reason, no strong theological voice is yet heard to redirect the Church on its pilgrim way for this next decade. We must pray for such a new and persuasive voice. For always it is more important that theological assumptions be examined and corrected than that conclusions or programs be disputed.

—Eugene Carson Blake, *The Church in the Next Decade*, pp. 147–52.

What will the Church of the 21st century be like?

Let us suppose that the church continues basically along the lines of its current situation in America. I think the church in America will look something like this.

Organized religion, as a social institution, will have become big business. . . .

The accent will be on efficiency, with effectiveness coming in a poor second. . . .

There will commonly occur instances of a sizable segment of a congregation getting overly interested in a particular social activity of the church. . . .

Attendance at corporate worship will decline, especially in proportion to the size of the congregation. . . .

People will join churches in increasing numbers because it will be the socially respectable thing to do. . . .

The church will become a place where you are baptized, married, and buried. These rites will mark the critical points in the life membership of the individual. Other participation will be over-and-above involvement. . . .

Trying to draw a crowd will occupy much of the time of the pastor and leaders of the congregation. . . .

Pastoral care will be highly organized and institutionalized. In many respects it will come to be very much like outpatient care in a modern metropolitan hospital. . . .

Mass media will be significant in the projected church of the 21st century. They will provide a reasonably convenient way of approaching and appealing to the masses. . . .

Mass media will heighten the competitive relationship among congregations in a given community. . . .

The clergy will be strongly committed to the corporate structure of the church and to the socially supporting society. . . .

Within the supporting society the minister will be very well accepted but not taken too seriously. . . .

In general the clergy will be luxury items in an increasingly affluent society. . . .

Recruitment for the ministry will become even more a problem. . . .

On the denominational level there will be amalgamations for the sake of efficiency. . . .

Denominationally the great emphasis will be on maintaining the appearance of size, particularly in comparison with the Roman Catholic group.

At the same time the number of new offbeat religious groups will increase. . . .

Will the church die out in America? I doubt it, although the answer depends on what you mean by "church." But I do believe that the church is headed toward a subtle but complete evolution that will make it one of the most socially significant but impotent institutions of the 21st century.

The alternative is a reawakening of a sense of the church. This involves recognizing that although the church is represented among us as a social institution, it is first and foremost that unique, eternal institution brought into being by the sacrifice of Christ.

Membership within this church, this body of Christ, is the result of the power of the Holy Spirit working through the Gospel. Those who make up the church, as Paul put it, are no longer strangers and aliens living in a way that is foreign to God but persons who have in Christ become fellow citizens with God's people in all time and are indeed God's holy family. There is a uniqueness about all such persons. They are still, as Paul also said, social persons living within the temporal bounds of this world, but in their received way of life they are not of this world and the things of this world. . . .

The "alternate" church of the 21st century will be preoccupied with proclaiming the Gospel through word and deed. . . .

The church will not try to be a judge or divider among men. . . .

On the local level the church member of the 21st century will regard the congregation only as a resource. . . .

In the church of the 21st century there will be more congregations and fewer buildings. . . .

Within the church of the 21st century the clergy will be busier than a generation earlier but with a different kind of busyness. . . .

The minister will be one of the most astute persons in the community on the sociological facts of life. . . .

In the church of the 21st century there will be less denominational organization. . . .

Within the church as a whole there will be an elimination of most of the social activities that threatened to dominate the church about the middle of the 20th century. . . .

Will the church of the 21st century really be like either the first or the second alternative? There is every probability that the first alternative will develop if the church among us continues along its present lines. As for the second alternative, much as I would like to see it occur, I think it will take more than the few years remaining before the 21st century to accomplish so radical a shift in the orientation of the institutional church. Repeated practice sinks a deep furrow, and we have been treading deeper and deeper in the same furrow for so long that it will take a tremendous effort, plus the full blessing of God, to effect a shift. In matters of this kind a generation is a very short time.

What the church of the 21st century becomes will indeed depend on the Lord of the church and on the Holy Spirit. God has never let His people down, though they have often slipped miserably because of themselves. God, who neither slumbers nor sleeps, is more than ready to do His part. The big question mark is you and I. We can wiggle and twist and rationalize all we want, but ultimately we cannot avoid our responsibility and accountability to the Lord of the church.

—Richard Sommerfeld, *The Church of the 21st Century: Prospects and Proposals*, pp. 95–103.

Who can foresee the future?

Few are able to write in detail concerning the precise forms for the Church in the future.

—Martin E. Marty, *The Search for a Usable Future*, p. 145.

BIBLIOGRAPHY

Books

Ayres, Francis O. *The Ministry of the Laity*. Philadelphia: Westminster Press, 1962.

Baker, Wesley C. *The Split-Level Fellowship*. Philadelphia: Westminster Press, 1965.

Berger, Peter L. *The Noise of Solemn Assemblies*. Garden City, N.Y.: Doubleday & Co., 1961.

Berton, Pierre. *The Comfortable Pew*. Philadelphia: Lippincott Co., 1965.

Blake, Eugene Carson. *The Church in the Next Decade*. New York: Macmillan Co., London: Collier-Macmillan, 1966.

Bliss, Kathleen. *We the People*. Philadelphia: Fortress Press, 1964.

Bloesch, Donald G. *Centers of Christian Renewal*. Philadelphia: United Church Press, 1964.

Bloy, Myron B. *The Crisis of Cultural Change*. New York: Seabury Press, 1965.

Bow, Russell. *The Integrity of Church Membership*. Waco, Tex.: Word Books, 1968.

Boyd, Malcolm. *The Underground Church*. New York: Sheed and Ward, 1968.

Brockway, Allan R. *The Secular Saint*. New York: Doubleday & Co., 1968.

Brunner, Emil. *The Misunderstanding of the Church*. Philadelphia: Westminster Press, 1953.

Casteel, John L. *The Creative Role of Interpersonal Groups in the Church Today*. New York: Association Press, 1968.

Casteel, John L., ed. *Spiritual Renewal through Personal Groups*. New York: Association Press, 1957.

Chafin, Kenneth. *Help! I'm a Layman*. Waco, Tex.: Word Books, 1966.

Clark, M. Edward; Malcomson, William L.; and Molton, Warren Lane, eds. *The Church Creative*. Nashville: Abingdon Press, 1967.

Come, Arnold B. *Agents of Reconciliation*. Philadelphia: Westminster Press, 1960.

Dewolf, L. Harold. *A Hard Rain and a Cross*. Nashville: Abingdon Press, 1966.

DeDietrich, Suzanne. *The Witnessing Community*. Philadelphia: Westminster Press, 1968.

Edge, Findley B. *A Quest for Vitality in Religion*. Nashville: Broadman Press, 1963.

Fisher, Wallace E. *From Tradition to Mission*. Nashville: Abingdon Press, 1965.

——————. *Preaching and Parish Renewal*. Nashville: Abingdon Press, 1968.

——————. *Preface to Parish Renewal*. Nashville: Abingdon Press, 1968.

Gardner, E. Clinton. *The Church As a Prophetic Community.* Philadelphia: Westminster Press, 1967.

Gibbs, Mark, and Morton, T. Ralph. *God's Frozen People.* Philadelphia: Westminster Press, 1964.

Gilkey, Landon. *How the Church Can Minister to the World Without Losing Itself.* New York: Harper & Row, 1964.

Glass, Bill. *Get in the Game.* Waco, Tex.: Word Books, 1965.

Grimes, Howard. *The Rebirth of the Laity.* Nashville: Abingdon Press, 1962.

Hadden, Jeffrey K. *The Gathering Storm in the Churches.* New York: Doubleday & Co., 1969.

Halverson, Richard C. *Relevance.* Waco, Tex.: Word Books, 1968.

Herzog, Arthur. *The Church Trap.* New York: Macmillan Co., 1968.

Hinson, E. Glenn. *The Church: Design for Survival.* Nashville: Broadman Press, 1967.

Hoekendijk, J. C. *The Church Inside Out.* Philadelphia: Westminster Press, 1964.

Holmes, William A. *Tomorrow's Church: A Cosmopolitan Community.* Nashville: Abingdon Press, 1968.

Hooft, W. A. Visser't. *The Renewal of the Church.* Philadelphia: Westminster Press, 1956.

Howard, Walden. *Nine Roads to Renewal.* Waco, Tex.: Word Books, 1967.

Keith-Lucas, Alan. *The Church and Social Welfare.* Philadelphia: Westminster Press, 1962.

Kelley, Alden D. *The People of God.* New York: Seabury Press, 1962.

Lee, Robert. *The Church and the Exploding Metropolis.* Richmond, Virginia: John Knox Press, 1965.

Lee, Robert, and Marty, Martin E., eds. *Religion and Social Conflict.* New York: Oxford University Press, 1964.

Lloyd, Roger. *The Ferment in the Church.* New York: Morehouse-Barlow Co., 1964.

McCord, James I., and Parker, T. H. L., eds. *Service in Christ.* Grand Rapids: Eerdmans, 1966.

McNeil, Jesse Jai. *Mission in Metropolis.* Grand Rapids: Eerdmans, 1965.

Marty, Martin E., ed. *Death and Birth of the Parish.* St. Louis: Concordia, 1964.

Marty, Martin E. *The Search for a Usable Future.* New York: Harper & Row, 1969.

Metz, Donald L. *New Congregations.* Philadelphia: Westminster Press, 1967.

Miller, Keith. *The Taste of New Wine.* Waco, Tex.: Word Books, 1965.

————————. *A Second Touch.* Waco, Tex.: Word Books, 1967.

Moore, Richard E., and Day, Duane L. *Urban Church Breakthrough.* New York: Harper & Row, 1966.

Minear, Paul S. *Horizons of Christian Community.* St. Louis: Bethany Press, 1959.

Monro, Claxton, and Taegel, William S. *Witnessing Laymen Make Living Churches.* Waco, Tex.: Word Books, 1968.

Morton, A. Q., and McLeman, James. *Christianity in the Computer Age.* New York: Harper & Row, 1964.

Mullen, Thomas J. *The Renewal of the Ministry.* Nashville: Abingdon Press, 1963.

Nelson, J. Robert. *Criterion for the Church.* Nashville: Abingdon Press, 1962.

Norton, Perry L. *Church and Metropolis.* New York: Seabury Press, 1964.

O'Connor, Elizabeth. *Call to Commitment.* New York: Harper & Row, 1963.

——————. *Journey Inward, Journey Outward.* New York: Harper & Row, 1968.

Oldham, J. H. *Life Is Commitment.* New York: Association Press, 1959.

Peerman, Nancy. *The Real and Only Life.* Waco, Tex.: Word Books, 1968.

Poling, David. *The Last Years of the Church.* New York: Doubleday & Co., 1969.

Raines, Robert A. *New Life in the Church.* New York: Harper & Row, 1961.

——————. *Reshaping the Christian Life.* New York: Harper & Row, 1964.

——————. *The Secular Congregation.* New York: Harper & Row, 1968.

Reid, Clyde. *The God-Evaders.* New York: Harper & Row, 1966.

——————. *Groups Alive—Church Alive.* New York: Harper & Row, 1969.

Robertson, D. B., ed. *Voluntary Associations, A Study of Groups in Free Societies.* Richmond, Virginia: John Knox Press, 1966.

Robinson, John A. T. *The New Reformation.* Philadelphia: Westminster Press, 1965.

Rose, Stephen C. *The Grass Roots Church, A Manifesto for Protestant Renewal.* New York: Holt, Rinehart & Winston, 1966.

Rose, Stephen C., ed. *Who's Killing the Church?* Chicago: Renewal Magazine and Association Press, 1966.

Rouner, Arthur A., Jr. *The Free Church Today: New Life for the Whole Church.* New York: Association Press, 1968.

Russell, Letty M. *Christian Education in Mission.* Philadelphia: Westminster Press, 1967.

Schaller, Lyle E. *Planning for Protestantism in Urban America.* Nashville: Abingdon Press, 1965.

Schuller, David S. *Emerging Shapes of the Church.* St. Louis: Concordia, 1967.

Segler, Franklin M. *A Theology of Church and Ministry.* Nashville: Broadman Press, 1960.

Shippey, Frederick A. *Protestantism in Suburban Life.* Nashville: Abingdon Press, 1964.

Schultz, Hans Jurgen. *Conversion to the World.* New York: Charles Scribner's Sons, 1967.

Sommerfeld, Richard. *The Church of the 21st Century.* St. Louis: Concordia, 1965.

Spike, Robert W. *Safe in Bondage.* New York: Friendship Press, 1960.

——————. *The Freedom Revolution and the Churches.* New York: Association Press, 1965.

——————. *In But Not Of The World.* New York: Association Press, 1957.

Stammler, Eberhard. *Churchless Protestants.* Philadelphia: Westminster Press, 1964.

Stringfellow, William. *My People Is the Enemy.* New York: Holt, Rinehart & Winston, 1964.

Trueblood, Elton. *The Company of the Committed.* New York: Harper & Row, 1961.

——————. *The Incendiary Fellowship.* New York: Harper & Row, 1967.

——————————. *Your Other Vocation*. New York: Harper & Brothers, 1952.
Valentine, Foy. *The Cross in the Marketplace*. Waco, Tex.: Word Books, 1966.
Vaughan, B. N. Y. *Structures for Renewal*. London: A. R. Mowbray & Co., 1967.
Webber, George W. *The Congregation in Mission*. Nashville: Abingdon Press, 1964.
——————————. *God's Colony in Man's World*. Nashville: Abingdon Press, 1960.
Wentz, Frederick K. *The Layman's Role Today*. Garden City, N.Y.: Doubleday & Co., 1963.
Wieser, Thomas. *Planning for Mission*. New York: The U.S. Conference for the World Council of Churches, 1966.
Williams, Colin W. *Faith in a Secular Age*. New York: Harper & Row, 1966.
——————————. *The Church*. Philadelphia: Westminster Press, 1968.
——————————. *Where in the World?* New York: Office of Publication and Distribution National Council of the Churches of Christ in the U.S.A., 1963.
——————————. *What in the World?* New York: Department of Publication Services National Council of the Churches of Christ in the U.S.A., 1964.
Wilmore, Gayraud S. *The Secular Relevance of the Church*. Philadelphia: Westminster Press, 1962.
Winter, Gibson. *The New Creation As Metropolis*. New York: Macmillan Co., 1963.
——————————. *The Suburban Captivity of the Churches*. Garden City, N.Y.: Doubleday & Co., 1961.
Younger, George D. *The Church and Urban Power Structure*. Philadalphia: Westminster Press, 1963.
——————————. *The Church and Urban Renewal*. Philadelphia: Lippincott Co., 1965.

Periodicals

Bailey, James F. "An Exploding World: What Kind of Church?" *Baptist Student*, February 1968, pp. 30–33.
Billington, Ray. "Church versus Non-Church." *The Princeton Seminary Bulletin* 60:44.
Brooks, Sue Miles. "Depth Through Discipline." *Home Missions*, April 1968, pp. 1–13.
Cosby, N. Gordon. "Outside the Structure? Church Renewal: Outside . . . Or Inside?" *The Christian Advocate*, 12 September 1963, p. 7.
Edge, Findley B. "Renewal Movements in Contemporary Protestantism." *Review and Expositor* 64:192–93.
Evans, J. N., Jr., "The Context of Witness." *Home Missions*, October 1968, pp. 17–18.
Fray, Harold R., Jr., "The Search for New 'Wine Skins.'" *Union Seminary Quarterly Review* 16:318–19.

Garrett, James Leo. "Seeking a Regenerate Church Membership." *Southwestern Journal of Theology*, April 1961, pp. 35–36.

Lacy, Julian A. "The Lay Renaissance." *Religion in Life* 31:9.

Meister, John W. "Requirements for Renewal." *Union Seminary Quarterly Review* 16:259–61.

Montefiore, Hugh. "The Renewal of the Church." *Encounter* 27:109–10.

Mow, Anna B. "Gee! Women in the Ministry." *Brethren Life and Thought* 12:60.

Miller, Keith. "The Freedom of a Positive Faith." *Home Missions*, April 1968, p. 10.

Reid, Clyde H. "Small Groups Are Here To Stay." *Union Seminary Quarterly Review* 18:395–96.

Rose, Stephen C. "Underground Church?" *Renewal*, October 1967, p. 23.

Staff. "Can a Servant 'Go It Alone'?" *Home Missions*, September 1968, p. 32.

Thigpen, Pat. "12th Gate in Atlanta: Hippies, Southern Style." *Home Missions*, August 1968, pp. 21–22.

Trueblood, D. Elton. "Post-Denominational Christianity." *Christianity Today*, 24 November 1967, pp. 171–72.

Wortman, Joe. "Servanthood: Missing in Suburbia." *Home Missions*, November 1968, pp. 19–20.